Toyota Production System

Toyota
Production
System

An Integrated Approach to Just-In-Time

Second Edition

Yasuhiro Monden

Industrial Engineering and Management Press
Institute of Industrial Engineers
Norcross, Georgia

© 1993 Yasuhiro Monden. All rights reserved
Published in 1993 by the Institute of Industrial Engineers
Printed in the United States of America
First edition published in English in 1983 by the Institute of Industrial Engineers. Second edition originally published in Japanese as *The New Toyota System* in 1991 by Kodansha, Ltd., Tokyo

ISBN 0-89806-129-6

99 98 97 96   7 6 5 4 3

Additional copies may be obtained by contacting:
Institute of Industrial Engineers
Customer Service
25 Technology Park/Atlanta
Norcross, Georgia 30092 USA
(404) 449-0460 phone
(404) 263-8532 fax
Quantity discounts available.

Senior Editor: Maura Reeves
Production Editor: Susan Call
Editorial Assistant: Sonja Lee
Cover Design: Susan McBride

Monden, Yasuhiro, 1940-
    [Shin Toyota shisutemu. English]
    Toyota production system : an integrated approach to just-in-
    time / Yasuhiro Monden. -- 2nd ed.
        p.   cm.
    Translation of: Shin Toyota shisutemu.
    Includes bibliographical references and index.
    ISBN 0-89806-129-6
    1. Production management--Japan. 2. Automobile industry and trade--Japan--Production
control. 3. Toyota automobile. I. Title.
    TS155.M66713 1991   92-27711
    658.5--dc20   CIP

Contents

Toyota Production System Japanese Terms .... *xi*
Foreword to the First Edition .... *xiii*
Preface .... *xv*
Acknowledgments .... *xvii*

PART I TOTAL SYSTEM

1. Total Framework of the Toyota Production System 1
Primary Purpose *1*
Kanban System *6*
Production Smoothing *8*
Shortening Setup Time *9*
Process Layout for Shortened Lead Times *10*
Standardization of Operations *11*
Autonomation *12*
Improvement Activities *13*
Summary *13*

PART II SUBSYSTEMS

2. Adaptable Kanban System Maintains Just-In-Time Production 15
Pulling System for JIT Production *15*
What Is a Kanban? *16*
Kanban Rules *24*
Other Types of Kanbans *29*

3. **Supplier Kanban and the Sequence Schedule
    Used by Suppliers** **37**
    Monthly Information and Daily Information *38*
    Later Replenishment System by Kanban *39*
    Sequenced Withdrawal System by the Sequence Schedule Table *42*
    *Problems and Countermeasures in Applying the Kanban System to
    Subcontractors* *46*
    *Guidance by the Fair Trade Commission Based on the Subcontractors Law
    and the Anti-Monopoly Law* *48*
    Supplier Kanban Circulation in the Paternal Manufacturer *53*
    Structure of the Supplier Kanban Sorting Office *56*

4. **Smoothed Production Helps Toyota Adapt to Demand
    Changes and Reduce Inventory** **63**
    Smoothing of the Total Production Quantity *63*
    Smoothing Each Model's Production Quantity *67*
    Comparison of the Kanban System with MRP *71*

5. **The Information System Between Toyota, Its Dealers, and
    Parts Manufacturers** **75**
    The Order Entry Information System *75*
    The Information System Between Toyota and Parts Manufacturers *79*
    Production Planning System in Nissan *84*

6. **Computer Control System in an Automobile Factory** **89**
    Centralized Control System and Decentralized Control System *89*
    Structure of a Hierarchical Decentralized Control System *90*
    New ALC System at Toyota *99*

7. **How Toyota Shortened Production Lead Time** **105**
    Four Advantages of Shortening Lead Time *105*
    Components of Production Lead Time in a Narrow Sense *106*
    Shortening Processing Time through Single Production and Conveyance ..*107*
    Shortening Waiting Time and Conveyance Time *114*
    Broad Approach to Reducing Production Lead Time *116*

8. **Reduction of Setup Time—Concepts and Techniques** **121**
    Setup Concepts *122*

9. **Practical Procedure for Reducing Setup Time** 131
   Analyzing Setup Actions *131*
   Procedure for Setup Improvements *132*
   Informing Operators of Improvements *139*
   Organization Structure for Promoting Setup Time Reduction *142*

10. **Standard Operations Can Attain Balanced Production**
    with Minimum Labor **145**
    Determining the Components of Standard Operations *145*
    Proper Training and Follow-Up: The Key to Implementing a Successful
    System *158*

11. **Machine Layout, Multi-Function Workers,**
    and Job Rotation Help Realize Flexible Workshops **159**
    Shojinka: Meeting Demand through Flexibility *159*
    Layout Design: The U-Turn Layout *161*
    Attaining Shojinka through Multi-Function Workers *166*

12. **Improvement Activities Help Reduce the Work Force and**
    Increase Worker Morale **177**
    Improvements in Manual Operations *177*
    Reduction of the Work Force *179*
    Improvements in Machinery *183*
    Job Improvements and Respect for Humanity *185*
    The Suggestion System *186*
    Kanban and Improvement Activities *190*
    QC Circles *193*

13. **5S—Foundation for Improvements** **199**
    Visual Control *202*
    Practical Rules for Seiton *207*
    Seiso, Seiketsu, Shitsuke *214*
    Promotion of 5S System *217*

14. **"Autonomous Defects Control" Assures Product Quality** ...**221**
    Statistical Quality Control *222*
    Autonomation *224*
    Autonomation and the Toyota Production System *227*
    Robotics *236*
    Company-Wide Quality Control *237*

15. Functional Management to Promote Company-Wide Quality Control and Cost Management 239
Quality Assurance *240*
Cost Management *240*
Organization of the Functional Management System *245*

PART III QUANTITATIVE TECHNIQUES

16. Sequencing Method for the Mixed-Model Assembly Line to Realize Smoothed Production 253
Goals of Controlling the Assembly Line *253*

17. New Sequence Scheduling Method for Smoothing 265
Basic Logic of Sequence Scheduling *265*
Sequence Scheduling Using Artificial Intelligence *270*
Diminishing Differences Between the Product Lead Times *275*

18. Determining the Number of Kanban Pertinent to the Alternative Withdrawal Systems 279
Constant Quantity, Nonconstant Cycle Withdrawal System *280*
Constant Cycle, Nonconstant Quantity Withdrawal System *283*
Changing the Cycle Time of Standard Operations Routine Instead of the Number of Kanban *285*
The Influence of the Supervisor on the Total Number of Kanban *286*
Constant Withdrawal Cycle System for the Supplier Kanban *287*

19. Computer System for Kanban System Support 291
Technology Data Base Subsystem *291*
Kanban Master Planning Subsystem *293*
Actual Performance Collection and Transition Subsystems *300*

20. Numerical Analysis for Productivity Improvement 303
Analysis Method for Work Place Improvements *303*
Performance Analysis of Facility and Worker *307*
Evaluation of Overall Production Performance after Improvement *311*

PART IV IMPLEMENTATION

21. Review of Kanban System Principles 313
Functions of a Kanban *313*
Controlling Production–Ordering Kanbans *318*
Control of Tools and Jigs through the Kanban System *322*
Sequenced Withdrawal and the Later-Replenishment System Withdrawal .. *323*

22. Prerequisites to Implementing the
Toyota Production System 327
Introductory Steps to the Toyota Production System *327*
Introduction of JIT at Toyo Aluminum—A Case Study *330*

23. Applying the Toyota Production System Overseas 335
Conditions for Internationalizing the Japanese Production System *335*
Advantages of the Japanese Maker-Supplier Relationship *337*
Reorganization of External Parts Makers in the United States *339*
Solution of Geographical Problems Involving External Transactions *340*
External Transactions of NUMMI *342*
Industrial Relations Innovations *343*
Conclusion *348*

Appendix 1: JIT Delivery System Can Ease Traffic Congestion
and the Labor Shortage 349
JIT Will Contribute to Rationalization of Physical Distribution *349*
Genuine JIT System Has Prerequisite Conditions *350*
External Environment for Physical Distribution Should Be Rationalized *351*

Appendix 2: Goals Coordination Method 353
Experiment Outline *353*
Conclusion *364*

Appendix 3: Quantitative Analysis of Stocks in a JIT
Multistage Production System Using the Constant Order
Cycle Withdrawal Method 367
Introduction *367*
Hypothetical Production System *367*
Analysis of the Hypothetical System Using the Simulation Approach *376*

Appendix 4: Quantitative Analysis of Lot Size in a JIT Production System Using Constant Order Quantity Withdrawal Method **381**

Introduction *381*
Hypothetical Production System *381*
Modeling the Hypothetical JIT System *382*

Epilogue *401*
Bibliography and References *407*
Index *419*

Toyota Production System
Japanese Terms

Andon – a lighted sign giving information about work being done; for example, progress

Ato-Hoju – later replenishment system

Bakayoke – see Pokayoke

Five S – Seiri, Seiton, Seison, Seiketsu, Shitsuke

Heijunka – smoothing

Ikko-Nagashi – single-unit production and conveyance

Jidoka – autonomation; autonomous defect control

Junjo-Biki – sequenced withdrawal

Kaizen – improvement

Kanban – tag-like card that communicates product information

Kinohbetsu Kanri – functional management

Mizusumashi – whirligig

Muda – slack or waste of resources

Ninben-no-aru Jidoka – see Jidoka

Pokayoke – foolproof

Ringi – circulation among top executives

Seiketsu – maintaining Seiri, Seiton, and Seison

Seiri – identifying & separating necessary items from unnecessary items

Seiso – maintaining a clean workplace

Seiton – neat placement and identification of needed work items

Shitsuke – instilling Seiri, Seiton, Seison, and Seiketsu in workers

Shojinka – flexible work force

Shoninka – reduction in the work force

Shoryokuka – reduction in work hours required to produce a unit

So-ikufu – creative thinking or inventive ideas

Te-i-in-se-i – quorum system

Yo-i-don – ready, set, go

Foreword to the First Edition

The technique we call the Toyota production system was born through our various efforts to catch up with the automotive industries of western advanced nations after the end of World War II, without the benefit of funds or splendid facilities.

Above all, one of our most important purposes was increased productivity and reduced costs. To achieve this purpose, we put our emphasis on the notion of eliminating all kinds of unnecessary functions in the factories. Our approach has been to investigate one by one the causes of various "unnecessaries" in manufacturing operations and to devise methods for their solution, often by trial and error.

The technique of Kanban as a means of Just-in-time production, the idea and method of production smoothing, and Autonomation (Jidoka), etc., have all been created from such trial-and-error processes in the manufacturing sites.

Thus, since the Toyota production system has been created from actual practices in the factories of Toyota, it has a strong feature of emphasizing practical effects, and actual practice and implementation over theoretical analysis. As a result, it was our observation that even in Japan it was difficult for the people of outside companies to understand our system; still less was it possible for the foreign people to understand it.

This time, however, Professor Monden wrote this book by making good use of his research and teaching experiences in the United States. Therefore, we are very interested in how Professor Monden has "theorized" our practice from his academic standpoint and how he has explained it to the foreign people. At the same time, we wish to read and study this book for our own future progress.

At no other time in history has the problem of productivity received so much discussion. No longer is it solely an economic problem; now it presents a serious political problem in a form of trade frictions. At such a time it would be our great pleasure if the Toyota production system we invented could be of service to the problem of American productivity.

Although we have a slight doubt whether our Just-in-time system could be applied to the foreign countries where the business climates, industrial relations, and many other social systems are different from ours, we firmly believe there is no significant difference among the final purposes of the firms and people working in them.

Therefore, we hope and expect that another effective American production system will be created utilizing this book for reference.

TAIICHO OHNO
FORMER VICE PRESIDENT,
TOYOTA MOTOR CORPORATION

FORMER PRESIDENT,
JAPAN INDUSTRIAL MANAGEMENT ASSOCIATION

FORMER CHAIRMAN,
TOYODA SPINNING AND WEAVING CO., LTD.

Preface

The Just-in-time (JIT) manufacturing system is an internal system in use by its founder, Toyota Motor Corporation, but it has taken on a new look.

Toyota Production System, Second Edition systematically describes the changes that have occurred to the most efficient production system in use today. Since the publication of the first edition of this book in 1983, Toyota has integrated JIT with computer integrated manufacturing technology and a strategic information system.

The JIT goal of producing the necessary items in the necessary quantity at the necessary time is an internal driver of production and operations management. The addition of computer integrated technology (including expert systems by artificial intelligence) and information systems technology serve to further reduce costs, increase quality, and improve lead time. The new Toyota production system considers how to adapt production schedules to the demand changes in the marketplace while satisfying the goals of low cost, high quality, and timely delivery.

The first edition of this book, *Toyota Production System,* published in 1983, is the basis for this book. It was translated into many languages including Spanish, Russian, Italian, Japanese, etc., and has played a definite role in inspiring production management systems throughout the world.

In parallel with the distribution of the first edition of this book, the Toyota production system (also known as Just-in-time) has been applied throughout the world. This is evidence that the JIT concept within the Toyota production system is applicable to any country regardless of location, economic, and civil development. Additionally, this production system can be utilized in any size company in any industry.

Although this book is based on my previous work, *Toyota Production System,* it was written as an entirely new book. Nine chapters have been added, and chapters from the first edition have been revised or enlarged. Written for practitioners and researchers alike, this new book will provide a balanced and broad approach to the Japanese production system.

The major differences between the Toyota production system of a decade ago and the current system are twofold: (1) computer integrated manufacturing and strategic information systems have been integrated into the JIT approach to facilitate flexibility in responding to customer demand; and (2) continuous improvement activities ("kaizen") have been incorporated to maintain the integrity of the overall process and to increase worker morale.

Strategic Information System and CIM

Linkage of marketing, production (manufacturing), and suppliers through an information network (Toyota Network System) allows each component of the company to make timely decisions concerning volume and variety of end products. Changes in consumer preferences and sales trends for certain product types can be swiftly conveyed to the people in product development, sales, production, and parts manufacturing, who can quickly respond to the data. The end result is a more responsive company.

Within the Toyota Network System is a subsystem for in-house production information called the Assembly Line Control System (ALC). The ALC includes information used in computer-aided manufacturing and computer-aided planning systems.

In the development of this strategic information system, Toyota used the basic premises found in the JIT production system. The ALC works as a pull system in which each line and process in each plant requests, receives, and uses only the information it needs at the moment.

This book will show in detail how the above approaches are harmoniously integrated into JIT and how Toyota's new approach can be useful in many ways to a variety of industries.

Yasuhiro Monden
Professor, Ph.D.
Institute of Socio-Economic Planning
University of Tsukuba
Tsukuba, Japan

Acknowledgments

This book is the fruit of much guidance and cooperation of many people to whom I am very grateful. Above all, I am grateful to the original founder of the Toyota production system, the late Mr. Taiichi Ohno (former vice president of Toyota). Mr. Ohno shared generously his concept for the system and he authored the foreword to the first edition of this book. He was also my co-editor for a Japanese-language book titled *New Development of Toyota Production System.*

Mr. Joji Arai, executive director of International Productivity Service (former director of U.S. office of Japan Productivity Center) kindly arranged the publication and authored the introduction to the first edition of this book. The generosity of these two men will never be forgotten.

Further, I am indebted to the kind guidance of many manufacturing managers within and outside of Japan. It was these people that provided me with the most important information for this book. They allowed me opportunities to observe their manufacturing plants and to consult with many others.

From my research office at Tsukuba University in Japan, Ms. Waka Katagiri contributed to data collection and Ms. Masako Yoshinari contributed greatly to the preparation of the English draft.

Thanks also go to Dr. Mohammad Aghdassi, my graduate student at the University of Tsukuba, who collaborated on the quantitative analysis to evaluate the usefulness of the JIT system described in Appendices 3 and 4.

The English language version of this book was prepared while I was serving as a visiting professor of the School of Management and Economics, California State University, Los Angeles, during my sabbatical year from September 1991 to August 1992. I am indebted to Dr. John Y. Lee for arranging that opportunity.

Also, I wish to thank the Institute of Industrial Engineers. The contribution of Ms. Maura Reeves is greatly appreciated.

Through the network of communication and collaboration among all of these people, this book was born. I feel that the greatest pleasure in life lies in this kind of collaboration.

Finally, I would like to dedicate this book to my wife Kimiko whose daily support is the basis for my work in both Japan and in the United States.

PART I
TOTAL SYSTEM

1
Total Framework of the Toyota Production System

The Toyota production system was developed and promoted by Toyota Motor Corporation and is being adopted by many Japanese companies in the aftermath of the 1973 oil shock. The main purpose of the system is to eliminate through improvement activities various kinds of waste lying concealed within a company.

Even during periods of slow growth, Toyota could make a profit by decreasing costs through a production system that completely eliminated excessive inventory and work force. It would probably not be overstating the case to say that this is another revolutionary production management system. It follows the Taylor system (scientific management) and the Ford system (mass-assembly line).

This chapter examines the basic idea behind this production system, how it makes products, and especially the areas where Japanese innovation can be seen. Furthermore, the framework of this production system is examined by presenting its basic ideas and goals with the various tools and methods used for achieving them.

PRIMARY PURPOSE

Profit Through Cost Reduction
The Toyota production system is a viable method for making products because it is an effective tool for producing the ultimate goal—profit. To achieve this purpose, the primary goal of the Toyota production system is cost reduction, or improvement of productivity. Cost reduction and productivity improvement are attained through the elimination of various wastes such as excessive inventory and excessive work force.

The concept of costs in this context is very broad. It is essentially cash outlay to make a profit in the past, present, and future to be deducted from sales. Therefore, costs in the Toyota production system include not only manufacturing costs, but also sales costs, administrative costs, and even capital costs.

1

Elimination of Overproduction
The principal consideration of the Toyota production system is to reduce costs by
completely eliminating waste. Four kinds of waste can be found in manufacturing
production operations:

1. excessive production resources
2. overproduction
3. excessive inventory
4. unnecessary capital investment

First, waste in manufacturing workplaces is primarily the existence of
excessive production resources, which are *excessive work force, excessive facilities,* and *excessive inventory.* When these elements exist in amounts more than
necessary,whether they are people, equipment, materials, or products, they only
increase costs and add no value. For instance, having an excessive work force
leads to superfluous personnel costs, having excessive facilities leads to superfluous depreciation costs, and having excessive inventory leads to superfluous
interest.

Moreover, excessive production resources create the secondary waste—
overproduction, which was regarded as the worst type of waste at Toyota.
Overproduction is to continue working when essential operations should be
stopped. Overproduction causes the third type of waste found in manufacturing
plants—*excessive inventories.* Extra inventory creates the need for more manpower, equipment, and floor space to transport and stock the inventory. These
extra jobs will further make overproduction invisible.

Given the existence of excessive resources, overproduction, and excessive
inventory over time, demand for the fourth type of waste would develop. This
fourth type, *unnecessary capital investment,* includes:

1. building a warehouse to store extra inventory
2. hiring extra workers to transport the inventory to the new warehouse
3. purchasing a fork lift for each transporter
4. hiring an inventory control clerk to work in the new warehouse
5. hiring an operator to repair damaged inventory
6. establishing processes to manage conditions and quantities of different types of
   inventory
7. hiring a person to do computerized inventory control

All four sources of waste also raise administrative costs, direct-material
costs, direct or indirect labor costs, and overhead costs such as depreciation, etc.

Since excessive work force is the first waste to occur in the cycle and seems
to give way to subsequent wastes, it is very important to first reduce or eliminate
that waste. (Figure 1.1 shows the process for eliminating waste and achieving cost
reduction.)

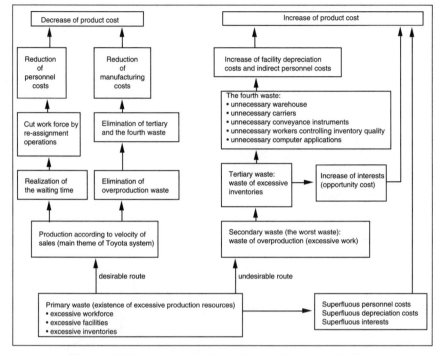

Figure 1.1. Process of waste elimination for cost reduction.

By clarifying that an excessive work force creates idle time (waiting time), worker operations can be re-allocated to decrease the number of workers. This results in reduced labor costs. Furthermore, additional costs caused by the second, third, and fourth wastes mentioned earlier can be reduced.

As seen above, it is the principal subject of the Toyota production system to control overproduction—to ensure that all processes make products according to the sales velocity of the market. This ability to control overproduction is the structure of the Toyota production system.

Quantity Control, Quality Assurance, Respect for Humanity
Although cost-reduction is the system's most important goal, it must first meet three other subgoals. They are:

1. Quantity control, which enables the system to adapt to daily and monthly fluctuations in demand of quantity and variety.
2. Quality assurance, which assures that each process will supply only good units to subsequent processes.
3. Respect for humanity, which must be cultivated while the system utilizes human resources to attain its cost objectives.

It should be emphasized here that these three goals cannot exist independently or be achieved independently without influencing each other or the primary goal of cost reduction. It is a special feature of the Toyota production system that the primary goal cannot be achieved without realization of the subgoals and vice versa. All goals are outputs of the same system; with productivity as the ultimate purpose and guiding concept, the Toyota production system strives to realize each of the goals for which it has been designed.

Before discussing the concepts of the Toyota production system in detail, an overview of this system is in order. The outputs (results)—costs, quantity, quality, and respect for humanity—as well as the inputs of the Toyota production system are depicted in Figure 1.2.

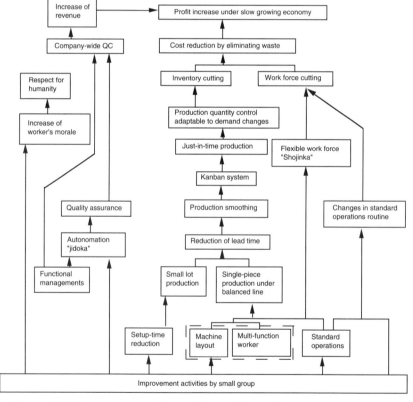

Figure 1.2. How costs, quantity, quality, and humanity are improved by the Toyota production system.

Just-in-time and Autonomation
A continuous flow of production, or adaptation to demand changes in quantities and variety, is created by achieving two key concepts: *Just-in-time* and *Autonomation*. These two concepts are the pillars of the Toyota production system.

Just-in-time (JIT) basically means to produce the necessary units in the necessary quantities at the necessary time. Autonomation (in Japanese, "Ninben-no-aru Jidoka," which often is abbreviated to "Jidoka") may be loosely interpreted as autonomous defects control. It supports JIT by never allowing defective units from a preceding process to flow into and disrupt a subsequent process (see Figure 1.2).

Flexible Work Force and Originality and Ingenuity
Two concepts also key to the Toyota production system include *flexible work force* ("Shojinka" in Japanese) which means varying the number of workers to demand changes, and *creative thinking or inventive ideas* ("Soikufu"), which means capitalizing on worker suggestions.

To realize these four concepts, Toyota has established the following systems and methods:

- "Kanban system" to maintain JIT production (Chapters 2, 3, 18, 19, 21).
- "Production smoothing method" to adapt to demand changes (Chapters 4, 16, 17, Appendix 2).
- "Shortening of the setup time" for reducing the production lead time (Chapters 8, 9).
- "Standardization of operations" to attain line balancing (Chapter 10).
- "Machine layout" and "multi-function workers" for the flexible work force concept (Chapter 11).
- "Improvement activities by small groups and suggestion system" to reduce the work force and increase worker morale (Chapters 12, 13, 20).
- "Visual control system" to achieve the Autonomation concept (Chapter 14).
- "Functional management system" to promote company-wide quality control, etc. (Chapter 15).

JIT Production
An example of JIT in the car part assembly process is for the necessary types of subassemblies from the preceding processes to arrive at the product line at the time needed and in the necessary quantities. If JIT is realized in the entire firm, then unnecessary inventories in the factory will be completely eliminated making stores or warehouses unnecessary. The inventory carrying costs will be diminished and the ratio of capital turnover will be increased. However, it is very difficult to realize JIT in all processes for a product like an automobile if the central planning approach (*push system*) which determines and disseminates production schedules to all processes simultaneously is used.

Therefore, in the Toyota system it is necessary to look at the production flow conversely; in other words, the people of a certain process go to the preceding process to withdraw the necessary units in the necessary quantities at the necessary time. The preceding process produces only enough units to replace those that have been withdrawn. This method is called the *pull system.*

KANBAN SYSTEM

In this system, the type and quantity of units needed are written on a tag-like card called a "Kanban," which is sent from workers of one process to workers of the preceding process. As a result, many processes in a plant are connected to each other. This connecting of processes in a factory allows for better control of quantities needed for various products.

In the Toyota production system, the Kanban system is supported by the following:

• smoothing of production
• standardization of jobs
• reduction of setup time
• improvement activities
• design of machine layout
• autonomation

Maintaining JIT by the Kanban System

Many people incorrectly call the Toyota production system a Kanban system. The Toyota production system makes products; the Kanban system manages the JIT production method. In short, the Kanban system is an information system which harmoniously controls the production quantities in every process. Unless the various prerequisites of this system are implemented perfectly (i.e., design of processes, standardization of operations, and smoothing of production, etc.), then JIT will be difficult to realize, even though the Kanban system is introduced.

A Kanban is a card which is usually placed in a rectangular vinyl envelope. Two kinds are mainly used: the *withdrawal Kanban* and the *production-ordering Kanban.* A withdrawal Kanban details the quantity which the subsequent process should withdraw, while a production-ordering Kanban shows the quantity which the preceding process must produce.

Information via Kanban

These cards circulate within Toyota factories, between Toyota and its many cooperative companies, within the factories of cooperative companies. In this manner, the Kanbans can convey information on withdrawal and production quantities in order to achieve JIT production.

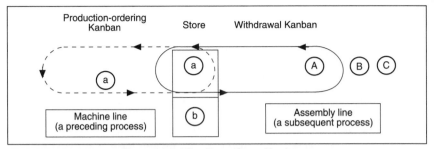

Figure 1.3. The flow of two Kanbans.

Suppose we are making products A, B, and C in an assembly line (see Figure 1.3). The parts necessary to produce these products are *a* and *b* which are produced by the preceding machining line. Parts *a* and *b* are stored behind this line and the production-ordering Kanbans of the line are attached to them.

The carrier from the assembly line making product A will go to the machining line to withdraw the necessary part *a* with a withdrawal Kanban. Then, at store *a*, he picks up as many boxes of this part as the number of withdrawal Kanbans he has and detaches production-ordering Kanbans from these boxes. He then brings these boxes back to his assembly line, again with withdrawal Kanbans.

At this time, the production-ordering Kanbans are left at store *a* of the machining line showing the number of units withdrawn. These Kanbans will be the dispatching information to the machining line. Part *a* is then produced in the quantities directed by the number of Kanbans. The same process is utilized even when a machining line produces more than one type of part.

Adapting to Changing Production Quantities
Let's consider the fine-tuning of production by using a Kanban. Assume that an engine manufacturing process must produce 100 engines per day. The subsequent process requests five engines per one-time lot be the withdrawal Kanban. These lots are then picked up 20 times per day, which amounts to exactly 100 engines produced daily.

Under such a production plan, if the need occurs to decrease all production processes by 10 percent as a fine-tuning procedure, the final process in this example has to withdraw engines 18 times per day. Then, since the engine process produces only 90 units in a day, the remaining hours for 10 units of production will be saved by stopping this process. On the other hand, if there is a need to increase production quantities by 10 percent, the final process must withdraw the engines 22 times per day with the Kanban. Then the preceding process has to produce 110 units, and the additional 10 units would be covered by overtime.

Although the Toyota production system has the production management philosophy that units could be produced without any slack or unnecessary stock, the risk of variations in production needs still exists. This risk is handled by the use of overtime and improvement activities at each process.

PRODUCTION SMOOTHING

Production in Accordance with Market Demand

The smoothing of production is the most important condition for production by Kanban and for minimizing idle time in regard to manpower, equipment, and work-in-process. Production smoothing is the cornerstone of the Toyota production system.

As described previously, each process goes to its preceding process to withdraw the necessary goods at the necessary time in the necessary quantities. Under such a production rule, if the subsequent process withdraws parts in a fluctuating manner in regard to time or quantity, then the preceding processes should prepare as much inventory, equipment, and manpower as needed to adapt to the peak in the variance of quantities demanded.

Therefore, the assembly line of finished cars, as the final process in the Toyota factory, will produce and convey each type of automobile according to its own time interval within which one unit of the car can be sold on average. (This time span is called *cycle time.*) The line will also receive the necessary parts, in similar manner from the preceding processes.

In short, a final assembly line produces equally each kind of product in accordance with its own daily cycle time. The variation in the withdrawn quantity of each part produced at each subassembly line is minimized, thereby allowing the subassemblies to produce each part at a constant speed or at a fixed quantity per hour. Such a smoothing of production can be illustrated by the following example.

Determining the Daily Production Sequence

Suppose there is a production line which is required to produce 10,000 type A cars in 20 eight-hour operating days in a month. The 10,000 type A cars consist of 5,000 sedans, 2,500 hardtops, and 2,500 wagons. Dividing these numbers by 20 operating days results in 250 sedans, 125 hardtops and 125 wagons per day. This is the smoothing of production in terms of the *average daily number* of each kind of car produced.

During an eight-hour shift of operation (480 minutes), all 500 units must be produced. Therefore, the *unit cycle time,* or the average time required to produce one vehicle of any type, is .96 minutes (480/500) or approximately 57.5 seconds.

The proper mix or *production sequence* can be determined by comparing the actual cycle time to produce a specific model of the type A car. For example, the maximum time to produce one type A sedan is determined by dividing shift time (480 minutes) by the number of sedans to be produced in the shift (250); in this sense, the maximum time is 1 minute, 55 seconds. This means that the cycle time for a sedan is 1 minute, 55 seconds.

Comparing this time interval with the average cycle time of 57.5 seconds, it is obvious that another car of any type could be produced between the time one sedan is completed and the time when another sedan must be produced. So, the basic production sequence is sedan, other, sedan, other, etc.

The maximum time to produce a wagon or a hardtop is 3 minutes, 50 seconds (480/125). Comparing this figure with the cycle time of 57.7 seconds, it is obvious that three cars of any type can be produced between each wagon or hardtop. If a wagon follows the first sedan in production, then the production sequence would be sedan, wagon, sedan, hardtop, sedan, wagon, sedan, hardtop, etc. This is an example of the smoothing of production in terms of the cycle time of each kind.

Adapting to Product Variety by General-Purpose Machines

Considering the actual manufacturing machines or equipment, a conflict arises between product variety and production smoothing. If a great variety of products is not produced, having specific equipment for mass production will usually be a powerful weapon for cost reduction. At Toyota, however, there are various kinds of cars differentiated in various combinations by types, tires, options, colors, etc. For example, three or four thousand kinds of Coronas are actually produced. To promote smoothed production in such a variety of products, it is necessary to have *general purpose* or *flexible machines.* By putting certain instruments and tools on these machines, Toyota has specified production processes to accommodate their general usefulness.

The concept of smoothed production as a response to product variety has several advantages. First of all, it enables the production operation to adapt promptly to fluctuations in daily demand by evenly producing various kinds of products every day in a small amount. Secondly, smoothed production allows for response to the variations in daily customers' orders without relying on product inventories. Thirdly, if all processes achieve a production according to the cycle time, balancing between processes will improve and inventories of work-in-process will be eliminated.

Realization of the smoothed production requires reducing production lead time (the time span from the issue of a production order by Kanban, etc., through processing, to warehousing) to promptly and timely produce various kinds of products. Reducing lead time then requires shortening the setup time for minimizing the lot size. The ultimate goal of reducing the lot size is a *one-piece* production which will be discussed later.

SHORTENING SETUP TIME

The most difficult point in promoting smoothed production is the setup problem. In a pressing process, for example, common sense dictates that cost reduction can be obtained through continuously using one type of die, thereby allowing for the biggest lot size and reducing setup costs. However, under the situation where the final process has averaged its production and reduced the stocks between the punch-process and its subsequent body line, the pressing department as a preceding process must make frequent and speedy setups. This means altering the types of dies for the press corresponding to a great variety of products, which are withdrawn frequently by the subsequent process.

During the period of 1945 to 1954 at Toyota, the setup time of the pressing department had been about two or three hours. It was reduced to a quarter-hour in the years 1955-1964, and after 1970, it dropped to only three minutes.

To shorten the setup time, it is important to neatly prepare *in advance* the necessary jigs, tools, the next die and materials, and to remove the detached die and jigs *after* the new die is settled and the machine begins to operate. This phase of setup is called the *external* setup. Also, the worker should concentrate on changing over the dies, jig, tools, and materials according to the specs of the next order *while the machine is stopping*. This phase of setup actions is called the *internal* setup. The most important point is to convert as much as possible of the internal setup to the external setup.

PROCESS LAYOUT FOR SHORTENED LEAD TIMES

Consider the design or layout of processes in a plant. Previously in this factory, each of five stands of lathes, milling machines, and drilling machines were laid out side by side, and one machine was handled by one worker, e.g., a turner handled only a lathe. According to the Toyota production system, the layout of machines would be rearranged to smooth the production flow. Therefore, each worker would handle three types of machines. For example, a worker would handle a lathe, a milling machine, and a drilling machine at the same time. This system is called *multi-process holding*. In other words, the single-function worker, a concept which previously prevailed in Toyota factories, has become a *multi-function worker*.

In a multi-process holding line, a worker handles several machines of various processes one by one, and work at each process will proceed only when the worker completes his given jobs within a specified cycle time. As a result, the introduction of each unit to the line is balanced by the completion of another unit of finished product, as ordered by the operations of a cycle time. Such production is called *one-piece* production and conveyance and may lead to the following benefits:

- As products are created one by one, it is possible to shorten the specified product's production lead time.
- Unnecessary inventory between each process can be eliminated.
- The multi-process worker concept can decrease the number of workers needed, and thereby increase productivity.
- As workers become multi-functional workers, they can participate in the total system of a factory and thereby feel better about their jobs.
- By becoming a multi-functional worker, each worker attains the knowledge to engage in teamwork and help each other.

Such a multi-process worker or multi-functional worker concept is a very Japanese-like method. American and European plants have excess job divisions and many craft unions. As a result union laborers are paid on the basis of their job class. Because of these agreements, a turner, for example, handles only a lathe and will not usually work on any other kind of machine. Whereas in Japan, the seniority-ordered wage system and one enterprise-union to each company is the dominant influence, which makes the mobility of laborers and the multi-process holding very easy. Obviously, this difference must be overcome by American and European companies that might wish to adopt the Toyota production system.

STANDARDIZATION OF OPERATIONS

The standard operation at Toyota mainly shows the sequential routine of various operations taken by a worker who handles multiple kinds of machines as a multi-functional worker.

Two kinds of sheets show standard operations: *the standard operations routine sheet* which looks like a man-machine chart, and the *standard operation sheet* which is posted in the factory for all workers to see. This latter sheet specifies the cycle time, standard operations routine, and standard quantity of the work in process.

A cycle time, or tact time, is the standard specified number of minutes and seconds that each line must produce one product or one part. The necessary output per month is predetermined from market demand. This time is computed by the following two formulas:

$$\frac{\text{necessary output}}{\text{per day}} = \frac{\text{necessary output per month}}{\text{operating days per month}}$$

$$\text{cycle time} = \frac{\text{operating hours per day}}{\text{necessary outputs per day}}$$

Late each month the central planning office conveys to all production departments the required quantity per day and the cycle time for the following month. This process is characteristic of the *push system*. In turn, the manager of each process will determine how many workers are necessary for his process to produce one unit of output in a cycle time. The workers of the entire factory then must be repositioned so that each process will be operated by a minimum number of workers.

The standard operations routine indicates the sequence of operations that should be taken by a worker in multiple processes of the department. This is the order for a worker to pick up the materials, put them on his machine, and detach them after processing by the machine. This order of operations continues for each machine that he handles. Line balancing can be achieved among workers in this department since each worker will finish all of his operations within the cycle time.

The standard quantity of work-in-process is the minimum quantity of work-in-process within a production line, which includes the work attached to machines. Without this quantity of work, the predetermined sequence of various machines in this whole line cannot operate simultaneously. Theoretically, however, if the *invisible conveyor belt* is realized in this line, there is no need to have any inventory among the successive process. The *invisible conveyor belt* allows work pieces to flow one-by-one between successive processes even though the conveyor does not exist.

AUTONOMATION

Autonomous Defects Control System

As noted previously, the two pillars which support the Toyota production system are JIT and Autonomation. To realize perfect JIT, 100 percent of defect free units must flow to the subsequent process, and this flow must be rhythmic without interruption. Therefore, quality control must coexist with the JIT operation throughout the Kanban system. Autonomation means to build in a mechanism to prevent mass-production of defective work in machines or product lines. The word *Autonomation* is not *automation,* but the autonomous check of the abnormal in a process.

The autonomous machine is a machine to which an automatic stopping device is attached. In Toyota factories, almost all machines are autonomous so that mass-production of defects can be prevented and machine breakdowns are automatically checked. One such mechanism to prevent defective work by putting various checking devices on the implements and instruments is called *foolproof* ("Bakayoke" or "Pokayoke").

Toyota expands Autonomation to the manual production line in a different way from the so called "Automation with feedback mechanism." If something abnormal happens in the production line, the worker stops the line by pushing his stop button, thereby stopping the whole line.

Visible Control System

Toyota's *visible control system* is an electric light board called *Andon,* which is hung high in a factory so that it can easily be seen by everyone. When a worker calls for help and delays a job, he turns on the yellow light on the Andon. If he stopped the line to adjust the machines, the red light would be activated.

IMPROVEMENT ACTIVITIES

The Toyota production system integrates and attains different goals (i.e., quantity control, quality assurance, and respect for humanity) while pursuing its ultimate goal of cost reduction. Improvement activities are a fundamental element of the Toyota production system and they are what makes the Toyota production system really tick. Each worker has the chance to make suggestions and propose improvements via a small group called a *Quality Control (QC) circle.* Such a suggestion-making process allows for improvements in quantity control by adapting the standard operations routine to changes in cycle time, in quality assurance by preventing recurrence of defective works and machines, and in respect for humanity by allowing each worker to participate in the production process.

SUMMARY

The basic purpose of the Toyota production system is to increase profits by reducing costs through completely eliminating waste such as excessive stocks or work force. To achieve cost reduction, production must promptly and flexibly adapt to changes in market demand without having wasteful slack time. Such an ideal is accomplished by the concept of JIT: producing the necessary items in the necessary quantities at the necessary time.

At Toyota, the Kanban system has been developed as a means of dispatching production during a month and managing JIT. Production smoothing to level the quantities and varieties in the withdrawals of parts by the final assembly line is needed for implementing the Kanban system. Such smoothing will require the reduction of the production lead time, since various parts must be produced promptly each day. This can be attained by small lot size production or one-piece production and conveyance. The small lot production can be achieved by shortening the setup time, and the one-piece production will be realized by the multi-process worker who works in a multi-process holding line. A standard operations routine will assure the completion of all jobs to process one unit of a product in a cycle time. The support of JIT production by 100 percent "good" products will be assured by Autonomation (autonomous defects control systems). Finally, improvement activities will contribute to the overall process by modifying standard operations, remedying certain defects, and finally, by increasing worker morale.

Where have these basic ideas come from? What need evoked them? They are believed to have come from the market constraints which characterized the Japanese automobile industry in post-war days—great variety within small quantities of production. Toyota thought consistently, from about 1950, that it would be dangerous to blindly imitate the Ford system (which minimized the average unit cost by producing in large quantities). American techniques of mass production have been good enough in the age of high-grade growth, which lasted until 1973. In the age of low-level growth after the oil shock, however, the Toyota production system was given more attention and adopted by many industries in Japan in order to increase profit by decreasing costs or cutting waste.

The Toyota production system is unique and revolutionary; therefore, when applying this production system outside Japan, special attention and consideration of management-labor relationships and transactions with external companies will be required. See Chapter 23 for an in-depth discussion of applying the Toyota production system outside of Japan.

PART II
SUBSYSTEMS

2
Adaptable Kanban System
Maintains Just-In-Time Production

The *Kanban* system is an information system that harmoniously controls the production of the necessary products in the necessary quantities at the necessary time in every process of a factory and also among companies. This is known as *Just-in-time* (JIT) production. At Toyota, the Kanban system is regarded as a subsystem of the whole Toyota production system. In other words, the Kanban system is not equivalent to the Toyota production system, although many people erroneously call the latter the Kanban system. In this chapter, the various types of Kanbans, their usages, and rules are described. How Kanbans are connected with many supporting routines in production lines is also discussed.

PULLING SYSTEM FOR JIT PRODUCTION

Toyota's JIT production is a method of adapting to changes due to troubles and demand changes by having all processes produce the necessary goods at the necessary time in the necessary quantities. The first requirement for JIT production is to enable all processes to know accurate timing and required quantity.

In the ordinary production control system, this requirement is met by issuing various production schedules to all of the processes: parts-making processes as well as the final assembly line. These parts processes produce the parts in accordance with their schedules, employing the method of the preceding process supplying the parts to its following process, or, the *push system*. However, this method will make it difficult to promptly adapt to changes caused by trouble at some process or by demand fluctuations. For adapting to these changes during a month under the ordinary system, the company must change each production schedule for each process simultaneously, and this approach makes it difficult to change the schedules frequently. As a result, the company must hold inventory among all processes in order to absorb troubles and demand changes. Thus, such a system often creates an imbalance of stock between processes, which often leads to dead stock, excessive equipment, and surplus workers when model changes take place.

By contrast, the Toyota system is revolutional in a sense that the subsequent process will withdraw the parts from the preceding process, a method known as the *pull system*. Since only the final assembly line can accurately know the necessary timing and quantity of parts required, the final assembly line goes to the preceding process to obtain the necessary parts in the necessary quantity at the necessary time for vehicle assembly. The preceding process then produces the parts withdrawn by the subsequent process. Further, each part-producing process withdraws the necessary parts or materials from preceding processes further down the line.

Thus, it is not required during a month to issue simultaneous production schedules to all the processes. Instead, only the final assembly line can be informed of its changed production schedule when assembling each vehicle one by one. In order to inform all processes about necessary timing and quantity of parts production, Toyota uses the Kanban.

WHAT IS A KANBAN?

A *Kanban* is a tool to achieve JIT production. It is a card which is usually put in a rectangular vinyl envelope. Two kinds of Kanbans are mainly used: a withdrawal Kanban and a production-ordering Kanban. A *withdrawal* Kanban specifies the kind and quantity of product which the subsequent process should withdraw from the preceding process, while a *production-ordering* Kanban specifies the kind and quantity of product which the preceding process must produce (Figures 2.1 and 2.2). The production ordering Kanban is often called an in-process Kanban or simply a production Kanban.

The Kanban in Figure 2.1 shows that the preceding process which makes this part is forging, and the carrier of the subsequent process must go to position B-2

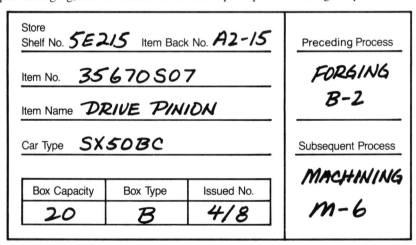

Figure 2.1. Withdrawal Kanban.

Store Shelf No. **F26-18** Item Back No. **A5-34** Item No. **56790-321** Item Name **CRANK SHAFT** Car Type **SX50BC-150**	Process **MACHINING** **SB-8**

Figure 2.2. Production-ordering Kanban.

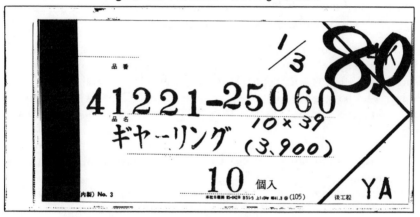

Figure 2.3. Actual withdrawal Kanban (actual size 4"x8").

of the forging department to withdraw drive pinions. The subsequent process is machining. Each box contains 20 units and the shape of the box is B. This Kanban is the fourth of eight sheets issued. The item back number is an abbreviation of the item. The Kanban in Figure 2.2 shows that the machining process SB-8 must produce the crank shaft for the car type SX50BC-150. The crank shaft produced should be placed at store F26-18. See Figure 2.3 for a photograph of a withdrawal Kanban.

Several other kinds of Kanbans exist. For making withdrawals from a vendor (a part or materials supplier, also called a subcontractor), a *supplier* Kanban (also called a subcontractor Kanban) is used. The supplier Kanban contains instructions which request the subcontracted supplier to deliver the parts. In the case of Toyota, in principle, the company withdraws parts from the subcontracted factories. However, since the shipping costs are included in the unit price of the part based on the contract, the supplier generally delivers the parts to Toyota. If Toyota actually withdraws the parts, the shipping cost must be deducted from the part price. Therefore, the supplier Kanban is, in its real sense, another type of withdrawal Kanban.

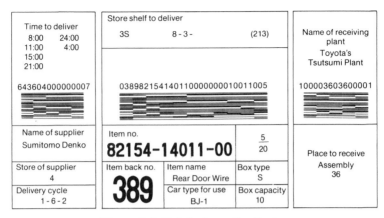

Figure 2.4. Detail of supplier Kanban.

The Kanban in Figure 2.4 is used for delivery from Sumitomo Denko (a supplier) to Toyota's Tsutsumi plant. Although Kanbans used within the Toyota plant are not bar coded, all supplier Kanbans of Toyota are bar coded. The number 36 refers to the receiving station at the plant. The rear-door wire delivered to station 36 will be conveyed to store 3S (8-3-213). The back number of this part is 389.

Since the Toyota production system engages in small-lot production, frequent transport and delivery each day is necessary. Therefore, delivery times must be written explicitly on this Kanban.

Also, Toyota has no special warehouse; therefore, the receiving place must be written clearly on this Kanban. Sometimes in the space under the supplier's name, a notation is written such as "1•6•2," which means that this item must be delivered six times a day and the parts must be conveyed *two delivery times later* after the Kanban in question is brought to the supplier. Figure 2.4 is based on the actual supplier Kanban pictured in Figure 2.5.

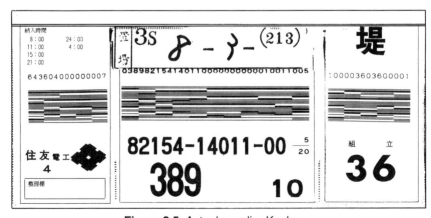

Figure 2.5. Actual supplier Kanban.

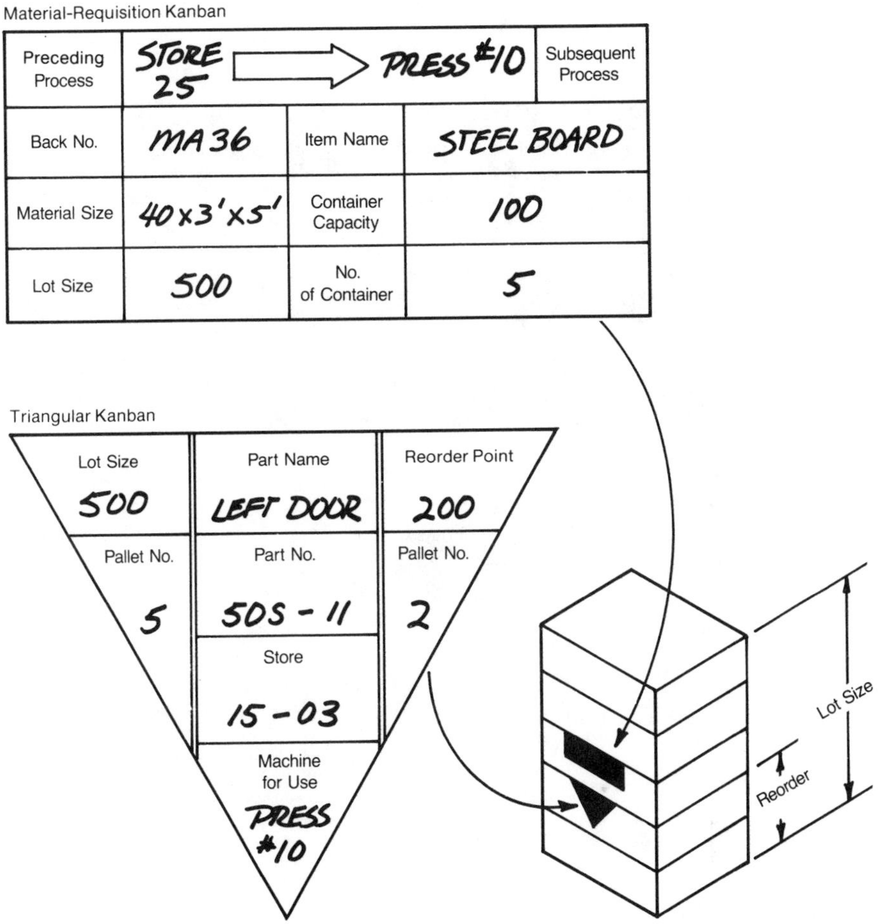

Material-Requisition Kanban

Preceding Process	STORE 25 ⟹ PRESS #10		Subsequent Process
Back No.	MA 36	Item Name	STEEL BOARD
Material Size	40×3'×5'	Container Capacity	100
Lot Size	500	No. of Container	5

Triangular Kanban

Lot Size	Part Name	Reorder Point
500	LEFT DOOR	200
Pallet No.	Part No.	Pallet No.
5	5OS - 11	2
	Store	
	15 - 03	
	Machine for Use	
	PRESS #10	

Figure 2.6. Signal Kanbans.

Next, to specify lot production in the diecasting, punchpress, or forging processes, a *signal* Kanban is used. As seen in Figure 2.6, a signal Kanban is tagged to a box within the lot. If withdrawals are made down to the tagged position of this Kanban, the production order must be set in motion.

Of the two types of signal Kanbans, the first one is a *triangular* Kanban. In Figure 2.6, the triangular-shaped Kanban orders punchpress process #10 to produce 500 units of a left door when the containing boxes are withdrawn down to the last two boxes; that is, the reorder point is two boxes or 200 units of a left door. Figure 2.7 shows a triangular Kanban for a blacket cab mounting. A triangular Kanban is made from a metal sheet and is fairly heavy.

The second type of the signal Kanban is rectangular-shaped and called a *material-requisition* Kanban. In Figure 2.6, press process #10 must go to store 25

Figure 2.7. Triangular Kanban for a blacket cab mounting.

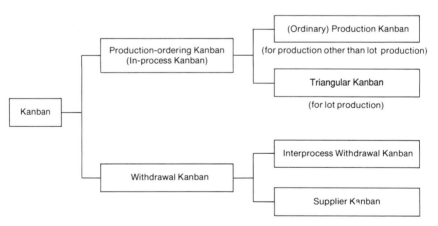

Figure 2.8. Framework of the main types of Kanbans.

to withdraw 500 units of a steel board when the left doors were brought to the body welding line by two boxes. In this example, the reorder point for material requirements is three boxes of a left door.

See Figure 2.8 for a classification of the main types of Kanbans.

How to Use Various Kanbans

Figure 2.9 shows how the withdrawal Kanban and the production-ordering Kanban are used. Starting from the subsequent process, the various steps utilizing the Kanban are:

1. The carrier of the subsequent process goes to the store of the preceding process with the withdrawal Kanbans kept in his withdrawal Kanban post (i.e., receiving box or file) and the empty pallets (containers) on a forklift or jeep. He does this at regular predetermined times.

2. When the subsequent process carrier withdraws the parts at store A, he detaches the production-ordering Kanbans which were attached to the physical units in the pallets (note that each pallet has one sheet of Kanban) and places these Kanbans in the Kanban receiving post. He also leaves the empty pallets at the place designated by the preceding process people.

3. For each production-ordering Kanban that he detached, he attaches in its place one of his withdrawal Kanbans. When exchanging the two types of Kanbans, he carefully compares the withdrawal Kanban with the production-ordering Kanban for consistency.

4. When work begins in the subsequent process, the withdrawal Kanban must be put in the withdrawal Kanban post.

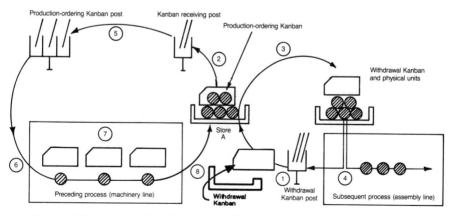

Figure 2.9. Steps involved in using a withdrawal and a production-ordering Kanban.

5. In the preceding process, the production-ordering Kanban should be collected from the Kanban receiving post at a certain point in time or when a certain number of units have been produced and must be placed in the production-ordering Kanban post in the same sequence in which it had been detached at store A.

6. Produce the parts according to the ordinal sequence of the production ordering Kanbans in the post.

7. The physical units and the Kanban must move as a pair when processed.

8. When the physical units are completed in this process, they and the production-ordering Kanban are placed in store A, so that the carrier from the subsequent process can withdraw them at any time.

Such a chain of two Kanbans must exist continuously in many of the preceding processes. As a result, every process will receive the necessary kinds of units at a necessary time in the necessary quantities, so that the JIT ideal is realized in every process. The chain of Kanbans will help realize line balancing for each process to produce its output in accordance with the cycle time (Figure 2.10).

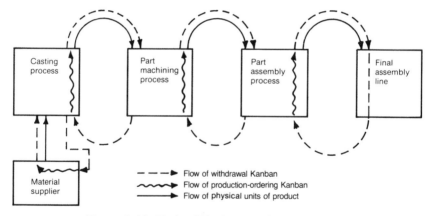

Figure 2.10. Chain of Kanbans and physical units.

Two Methods of Utilizing Production-Ordering Kanbans
One method for using production-ordering Kanbans is shown in Figure 2.11; it is used to issue many sheets of production-ordering Kanbans. Each sheet of the Kanban corresponds to container capacity. Production is undertaken according to the ordinal sequence in which the Kanbans were detached from the containers. Where many different kinds of parts exist, Kanbans are circulated in a manner depicted in Figure 2.11. The classified frames in the Kanban post and the classified labels at the store of finished goods is also shown.

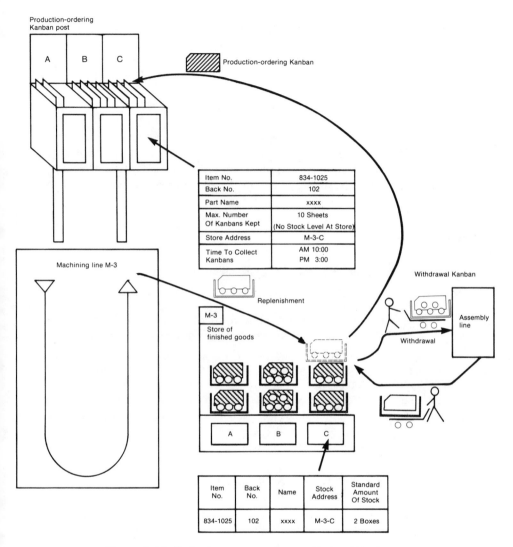

Figure 2.11. Ordinal sequence of many kinds of Kanbans.

The second method uses the single sheet of a signal Kanban (Figure 2.6). In the pressing department, for example, the production quantity is so large and the production velocity so rapid that the signal Kanban is used.

The signal Kanban can be tagged onto the edge of a pallet. At the store, it should be tagged at the position of the reorder point. When the goods at the store are withdrawn and the pallets are picked up, the signal Kanban should be moved to the reorder point instructions post. When it is moved to the dispatching post, operations will begin.

According to the ordering point system, when the reorder point and lot size are determined, there is no need to worry about daily production planning and follow-up. Simply keep watch on the timing of orders. This timing is automatically explicit when using the triangular Kanban which orders production and the rectangular Kanban which instructs material requisitions.

If several kinds of parts are produced at a certain process, these triangular Kanbans can instruct automatically what kind of part should be processed first. At some suppliers and also at some processes of Toyota, the triangular Kanban is used as a support for the ordinary production-ordering Kanbans. In this case, each individual part box contains its own production-ordering Kanban, and at the same time the triangular Kanban is tagged and positioned at the reorder point of the piled boxes.

Kanban Rules

In order to realize the JIT purpose of Kanban, the following rules must be followed:

Rule 1. The subsequent process should withdraw the necessary products from the preceding process in the necessary quantities at the necessary point in time.

If the production manager alone wished to introduce the Kanban system into the factory, his position would be so weak that he could not implement this first Kanban rule. To implement this rule, the top management of the company must win over all workers and should also make a critical decision to upset the previous flow of production, transport, and delivery. This decision will probably be met with much resistance because Rule 1 requires a complete change of the existing production system.

The following subrules will also accompany this rule:

• Any withdrawal without a Kanban should be prohibited.
• Any withdrawal which is greater than the number of Kanbans should be prohibited.
• A Kanban should always be attached to the physical product.

It should be noted that as prerequisites of the Kanban system, the following conditions should be incorporated into the production system: smoothing of production, layout of processes, and standardization of jobs.

The smoothing of production, or leveled daily production, is a necessary condition for a small-lot withdrawal and a small-lot production of subsequent processes, and is most important for implementing Rule 1. For example, if only the Kanban system is applied to withdrawing the parts from outside subcontracted companies without any smoothed production in the production line of the manufacturer, then the Kanban will be a very dangerous weapon and its original purpose will be lost. Subcontractors need a large amount of inventory, equipment, and manpower to respond to fluctuating demands from the manufacturer.

To use an example from Chapter 1, in the Corona assembly line, sedans are assembled and conveyed every one unit interval, while hardtops and wagons are assembled and conveyed in three unit intervals. The final output is then: sedan, hardtop, sedan, wagon, sedan, hardtop, etc.

However, even if Rule 1 was applied, JIT production could not easily be attained because Kanban itself is merely a dispatching means for actual production actions during each day at each process. Before entering the phase of dispatching the jobs by Kanban, overall planning throughout the plant must be made in advance. For this purpose, Toyota will inform each process and each supplier each month of a predetermined monthly production quantity for the next month's production so each process and each supplier in turn can prepare in advance its cycle time, necessary work force, necessary number of materials, and required improvement point, etc. Based on such overall plans, all processes in the plant can start to apply the Rule 1 simultaneously from the first day of each month.

Concerning withdrawal methods by Kanban, two additional features should be mentioned. At Toyota, there are two kinds of withdrawal systems: the *constant quantity, but inconstant cycle* withdrawal system, and the *constant cycle, but inconstant quantity* withdrawal system. Details of these systems are discussed in Chapter 19; here, two examples will be explained: the method for conveying a set of various parts in constant quantities and the method for conveying parts at a regular time with a round-tour mixed-loading system.

Whirligig. A whirligig beetle is an insect that whirls on the surface of water very swiftly. The carrier in the Toyota factory is also called the whirligig ("Mizusumashi"), because he travels between preceding processes and subsequent processes again and again. For example, when the parts necessary for assembling a small lot of accelerators (five units is a lot size) need to be withdrawn, the carrier will go around various stores at the various machining processes and withdraw the parts necessary to make a set of five accelerators. The whirligig conveyance is a representative example of withdrawing the parts in constant quantities as a set.

Constant Cycle and Round-Tour Mixed-Loading System. The round-tour mixed-loading system is used by the subcontractor. As far as withdrawals from subcontracted companies are concerned, it is the subcontractor who usually delivers its product to the company. Consequently, the carrying hours become important because of the frequent deliveries due to small-lot production.

For example, four subcontracted companies, A, B, C and D, are located in one area and must bring their products to Toyota four times a day in small lot sizes. Although such frequent delivery can decrease the level of inventory remarkably, it is unfeasible for each of the subcontractors because of high distribution costs.

So, the first delivery at 9 a.m. could be made by subcontractor A, also picking up on the way products from companies B, C, and D on A's truck. The second delivery at 11 p.m. could be made by company B similarly picking up the products of A, C, and D on the way. The third delivery at 2 p.m. would be made by C company. This is called the constant cycle, round-tour mixed loading system.

In the United States, however, this system may be hard to apply in some cases. Since America is so wide in a geographical sense, sometimes subcontracted company A might be very far from other subcontractors B, C, or D. In order to implement the Kanban system in such a situation, some additional strategies must be developed, such as exploring the possibilities of hiring subcontractors closer to the manufacturer, decreasing the rate of dependence on subcontractors, or withdrawing parts with a fairly large lot size. Also, in order for the suppliers to respond to frequent withdrawals by the main company, they should adopt the Toyota production system and shorten their production lead time.

Rule 2. The preceding process should produce its products in the quantities withdrawn by the subsequent process.

When Kanban Rules 1 and 2 are observed, all production processes are combined so they become a kind of conveyor line. The balancing of the production timing among all processes will be maintained by strictly observing these two rules. If problems occur in any of the processes, the whole process might stop, but the balance among processes is still maintained. Therefore, the Toyota production system is a structure which realizes such an ideal conveyor line system, and Kanban is a means of connecting all the processes. As a result, the inventory kept by each preceding process will be minimized.

The subrules for the second rule follow:

• Production greater than the number of sheets of Kanbans must be prohibited.
• When various kinds of parts are to be produced in the preceding process, their production should follow the original sequence in which each kind of Kanban has been delivered.

Since the subsequent process will require in a single unit or in a small lot size to attain smoothed production, the preceding process must make frequent setups according to the frequent requisitions by the subsequent process. Therefore, the preceding process should make each setup very quick.

Rule 3. Defective products should never be convened to the subsequent process.

The Kanban system itself will be destroyed unless this third rule is followed. If some defective items were discovered by the subsequent process, then the subsequent process itself makes its line stop because it does not have any extra units of inventory, and it sends those defective items back to the preceding process. Such line stoppage of the subsequent process is very obvious and visible to everyone. The system is based on the idea of Autonomation described in Chapter 1. Its purpose is simply to prevent recurrence of such defects.

The meaning of defective is expanded to include defective operations. A defective operation is a job for which standardization is not fully attained and inefficiencies then exist in manual operations, routines, and labor hours. Such inefficiencies would likely cause the production of defective items as well. Therefore, these defective operations must be eliminated to assure rhythmic withdrawals from the preceding process. The standardization of jobs is, therefore, one of the prerequisites of a Kanban system.

Rule 4. The number of Kanbans should be minimized.

Since the number of Kanbans expresses the maximum inventory of a part, it should be kept as small as possible. Toyota recognizes the inventory level increase as the origin of all kinds of wastes.

The final authority to change the number of Kanbans is delegated to the supervisor of each process. If he improves his process by decreasing the lot size and shortening the lead time, then his necessary number of Kanbans can be decreased. Such improvements in his process will contribute to the observance of Rule 4. If it is desired to inspire improved managerial ability, authority to determine the number of Kanbans must first be delegated.

The total number of each Kanban is kept constant. Therefore, when the daily average demand has increased, the lead time should be reduced. This requires the reduction of the *cycle time* of a standard operations routine by changing the allocation of workers in the line. However, because the number of Kanbans is fixed, a workshop incapable of such improvements will suffer line-stops or force the use of overtime. At Toyota, it is virtually impossible for workers to hide production problems in their workshop, for the Kanban system actually visualizes trouble in the form of line-stops or overtime, and will swiftly generate improvement activities to solve the problem. Shops might increase the safety stock or the total number of Kanbans to adapt to demand increase. As a result, the size of safety inventory can be an indicator of the shop's ability.

In case of a demand decrease, the cycle time of the standard operations routine will be increased. However, the probable idle time of workers must be avoided by reducing the number of workers from the line. Details of how to determine the number of Kanbans is discussed in Chapter 19.

Rule 5. Kanban should be used to adapt to small fluctuations in demand (fine-tuning of production by Kanban).

Fine-tuning of production by Kanban refers to the Kanban system's most remarkable feature: its adaptability to sudden demand changes or exigencies of production.

To illustrate what is meant by adaptability, we will first examine the problems faced by companies using ordinary control systems: i.e., companies not using Kanban. These companies lack the means to deal smoothly with sudden, unexpected demand changes. The ordinary control system centrally determines production schedules and issues them simultaneously to production processes; therefore, sudden demand changes will require at least a seven- to ten-day interval before schedules can be revised and reissued to the factory—the time interval for the computer to compile and calculate updated data. As a result, the various production processes will be faced from time to time with abrupt, jolting changes in production requirements; these problems will be compounded by the processes' lack of smoothed production.

Companies using the Kanban system, on the other hand, do not issue detailed production schedules simultaneously to the preceding processes during a month; each process can only know what to produce when the production-ordering Kanban is detached from the container at its store. Only the final assembly line receives a sequence schedule for a day's production, and this schedule is displayed on a computer which specifies each unit to be assembled next. As a result, even though the predetermined monthly plan demanded manufacture of six units of A and four units of B in a day, this proportion may be reversed at day's end. No one has instructed the plan changes to all processes; instead, each change has arisen naturally from market demand and exigencies of production, according to the number of Kanbans detached.

Here we see the meaning of *fine-tuned production*. Where Kanban is used, and production is leveled, it becomes easy to react to changes in the market by producing a few more units than the number predetermined by schedule. For example, 100 units a day must be produced as part of the predetermined plan for January, but on January 10th we find that 120 units per day would be necessary for February. According to Toyota's approach, we will adapt to the change by producing 105 or 107 units daily from January 11th on, instead of keeping at the 100 unit rate for a week or ten-day interval required for the production schedule to be revised—as is the case in ordinary production control systems. Moreover, we will not feel the changed plan, since production at each process is always subject to instruction by Kanban.

Such fine tuning of production by Kanban can only adapt to small fluctuations in demand. According to Toyota, demand variations of around 10 percent can be handled by changing only the frequency of Kanban transfers without revising the total number of Kanban.

In the case of fairly large seasonal changes in demand, or an increase or decrease in actual monthly demand over the predetermined load or the preceding month's load, all of the production lines must be rearranged. That is, the cycle time of each workshop must be recomputed and correspondingly the number of workers in each process must be changed. Otherwise, the total number of each Kanban must be increased or decreased.

In order to cope with the bottom and the peak in variation of demand during the year, top management has to make a decision either to level the sales volume for the whole year, or construct a flexible plan for rearranging all the production lines corresponding to seasonal changes during the year.

Lastly, concerning the adaptability of Kanban, it should be noted that the Kanban can be used also for parts in unstable use, although the safety stock will be somewhat greater in this case. For example, small iron pieces called balance weights must be attached to the drive shaft of a car by a worker to prevent any irregularity in its gyration. There are five kinds of balance weights, and they must be selected according to the grade of irregularity in the rotation of a shaft. If the rotation is even, no balance weight is necessary. If the rotation is irregular, one or more weights must be attached. Therefore, the demand for these five kinds of balance weights is entirely unstable and cannot be leveled at all.

In Toyota, however, a Kanban is attached to these balance weights, too. Since the inventory levels of the five kinds of balance weights will not increase more than the total number of each Kanban, the inventory levels and order quantities become measurable, and the safety inventory also can be reasonably controlled.

Although the Kanban transfer is made at a regular point in time, the number of Kanban for each kind of balance weights will somewhat fluctuate depending on the demand change. However, if we wish to minimize such fluctuations of Kanban, we have to improve the manufacturing process itself in some way.

OTHER TYPES OF KANBANS

Express Kanban. An express Kanban is issued when there is a shortage of a part. Although both the withdrawal Kanban and the production-ordering Kanban exist for this type of problem, the express Kanban is issued only in extraordinary situations and should be collected just after its use (Figure 2.12).

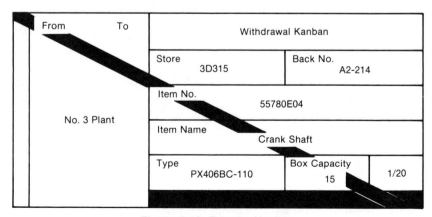

Figure 2.12. Express Kanban.

As an example, imagine a situation where the carrier for a subsequent process (assembly line) goes to the store of a preceding process (machining line) and finds that part B has not been sufficiently replenished and is in dire shortage (Figure 2.13). In such a case, the following steps will be taken:

1. The carrier issues the express Kanban for the part B and puts it in the express Kanban post (often called the *red post*) beside the production ordering Kanban post at the machining process.

2. At the same time, the carrier pushes a button for the machining line making the part B. The button used to call various machining lines is installed on a board beside the production-ordering Kanban post.

3. On an electric light board called *Andon,* a light corresponding to part B will be activated, indicating a spur in part B's production.

4. At that point of the line where the light has come on, the worker must produce the part B immediately, and bring it to the subsequent process (assembly line) himself with apology for its shortage. If the red lamp disappears immediately, the worker will be praised.

Emergency Kanban. An emergency Kanban will be issued temporarily when some inventory is required to make up for defective units, machine troubles, extra insertions, or a spurt in a weekend operation. This Kanban also takes the form of either a withdrawal Kanban or a production Kanban, and must be collected just after its use (Figure 2.14).

Job-Order Kanban. While all the aforementioned Kanbans will be applied to the line of recurrently produced products, a *job-order* Kanban is prepared for a job-order production line and is issued for each job order (Figure 2.15).

Through Kanban. If two or more processes are so closely connected with each other that they can be seen as a single process, there is no need to exchange Kanbans between these adjacent processes. In such a case, a common sheet of Kanban is used by these plural processes. Such Kanban is called a *through* Kanban (or *tunnel* Kanban), and is similar to the "through ticket" used between two adjacent railways. This Kanban can be used in those machining lines where each piece of a product produced at a line can be conveyed immediately to the next line by a chute one at a time. Or, this Kanban can be used in process plants such as heat treatment, electroplating, scouring, or painting.

Common Kanban. A withdrawal Kanban can also be used as a production-ordering Kanban if the distance between two processes is very short and one supervisor is supervising both processes.

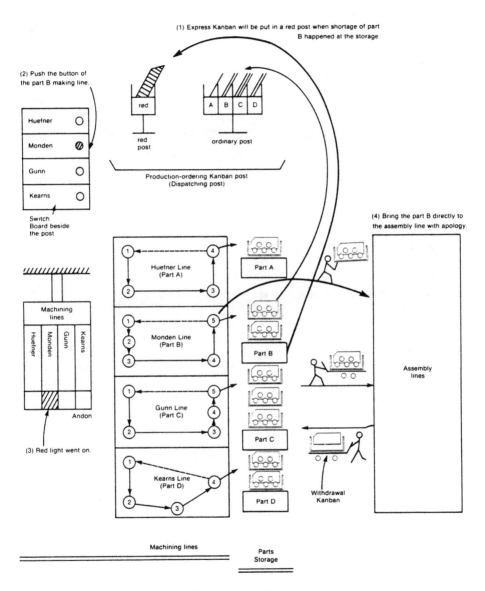

Figure 2.13. How express Kanban is used.

The carrier of the subsequent process will bring the empty boxes and the *common* Kanbans to the store of the preceding process. Then, he will bring the Kanbans to the Kanban receiving post (Figure 2.9), and withdraw as many boxes as the number of Kanbans brought. However, he need not exchange Kanbans at the store.

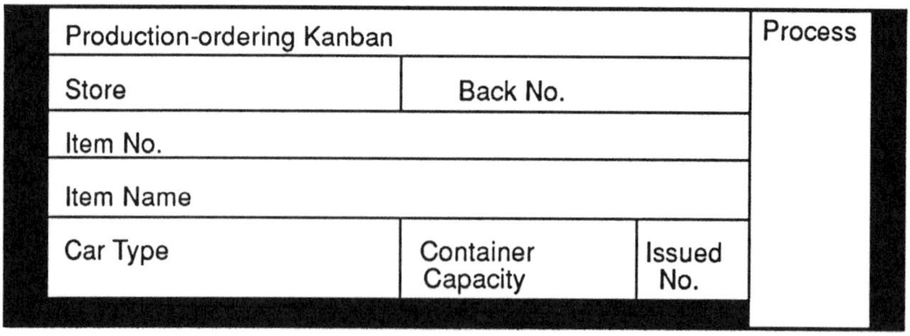

Production-ordering Kanban			Process
Store	Back No.		
Item No.			
Item Name			
Car Type	Container Capacity	Issued No.	

Figure 2.14. Emergency Kanban.

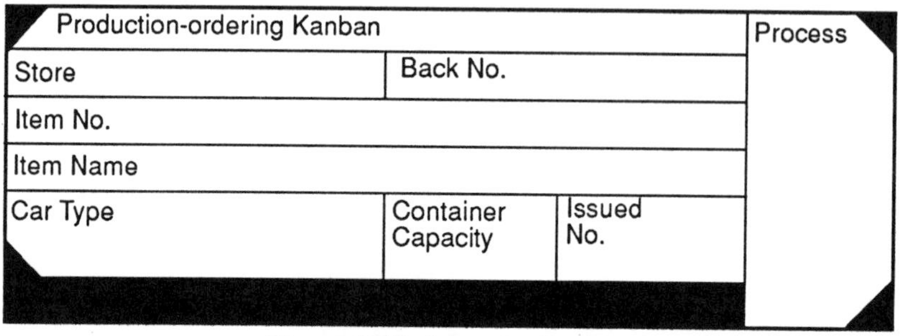

Production-ordering Kanban			Process
Store	Back No.		
Item No.			
Item Name			
Car Type	Container Capacity	Issued No.	

Figure 2.15. Job-order Kanban.

Cart or Truck as a Kanban. Kanban is often very effective when used in combination with a cart. In the Honsha plant of Toyota, in order for the final assembly line to withdraw large unit parts such as engines or transmissions, a cart is used which can load only a limited quantity.

In this case, the cart itself also plays a role as a Kanban. In other words, when the number of transmissions at the side of the final assembly line is decreased to a certain reorder point (say three or five pieces), then immediately the people engaged in putting transmissions into cars will bring the empty cart to the preceding process, i.e., to the transmission assembly process and withdraw a cart loaded with the necessary transmissions in exchange for the empty cart.

Although a Kanban must be attached to the parts as a rule, the number of carts in this case has the same meaning as the number of Kanbans. The subassembly line (transmission department) cannot continue to make its product unless an empty cart remains, thereby preventing excessive production.

As another example, at the Obu plant of the Toyoda Automatic Loom Works, Ltd. (a supplier of Toyota), the foundry equipment casts the cylinder blocks, crankshafts, and motor cases, etc. In this plant, raw materials such as pig iron and scrap iron are conveyed by a truck from the suppliers to input them into the cupola (furnace). No container or boxes exist to count and load these materials. In this case, the truck is regarded as a sheet of Kanban.

Label. A chain conveyor is often used to convey the parts to the assembly line by hanging the parts on hangers. A label specifying which parts, how many and when the parts will be hung is attached to each hanger with a smoothed interval. In this case, a label is used as a kind of Kanban, though not actually called Kanban, to instruct the worker putting various parts on the hanger from the parts store or the worker assembling various parts at the subassembly line. As a result, the subassembly process can produce only the parts required. A hanger with a label is called a *reserved seat* at Toyota.

A label is also applied to the final assembly line to instruct the sequence schedule of mixed models to be assembled (Figures 2.16 and 2.17).

Assembly no.						
				Destination		
Car type						
	AJ56P–KFH					

Rear spring	Rear axle	Booster	Steering lock	Collapsible handle
	S	**M**	**A**	
Def. gear ratio	Free wheel fab.	Electric systems	Exhaust	Transfer
400				
Alternator	Air cleaner	Oil cooler	Heater & air con.	Front winch
500Z			**H**	
Cold-climate oil	Altitude compensation	LLC	Fan	Rear hook
			D	
EDIC				Cold-climate destination
A				

Figure 2.16. Sample of a label used at the final assembly line.

Figure 2.17. Samples of labels (broadcasts).

Full-Work System. Among automated machining or assembly processes where there are no workers, how is it possible for the preceding machine to produce units only in the quantity withdrawn? Differences exist in the capacity and speed of production among various machines, and the preceding machine might continue its processing without considering any problems which might occur in the subsequent machining process.

The *full-work system* is employed with automated machining processes. For example, preceding machine A and subsequent machine B are connected to each other and the standard inventory level of work in process on machine B is six units. If machine B has only four units in process, machine A automatically begins to operate and produce its output until six units are placed in machine B. When machine B is full with the predetermined quantity (six units), a limit switch automatically stops the operation of machine A. In this way, the standard quantity of work is always placed in each process, thus preventing unnecessary processing in the preceding process (Figure 2.18). Because such eiectric control by a limit switch has come from the idea of a Kanban in a workplace where there are laborers and processes situated far from each other, the full-work system is also called an *electric* Kanban.

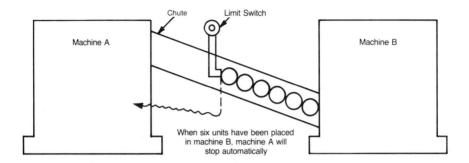

Figure 2.18. Full-work system.

As another example, suppose the blanking machine (the machine which punches the sheet metal) produces 90 units per minute, whereas the pressing machine in the punching and bending process produces only 60 units per minute. Due to its high capacity, usually the blanking machine operates only during the first two-thirds of the month and is idle the last third. But this method may produce unnecessary inventory in the blanking machine.

Suppose then, that the blanking machine was directly connected to the pressing machine and the magazine was set between the two. If the magazine becomes full with punched metals, the blanking machine stops automatically. If only a few units remain in the magazine, the blanking machine automatically starts to operate again. In other words, the blanking machine operates for about two minutes, then rests for about a minute.

At Toyota, in order to attain line balancing with regard to production quantities, intermittent operation by the full-work system is adopted in all the production lines. This system leads to the following advantages:

• Elimination of unnecessary inventory of work-in-progress.
• Grasping the overall capacity of production lines and disclosing the bottleneck process.
• Shortening of the lead time.
• Minimization of the final product inventory.
• Prompt adaptability to changes in demand.

3
Supplier Kanban and the Sequence Schedule Used by Suppliers

Sometimes a very powerful manufacturer may instruct his suppliers to bring their parts Just-in-time (JIT). In this case, if the manufacturer applied the Kanban system to his vendors without changing his own production systems, the Kanban system would be a demon to the vendors. Although the Kanban system is a very effective means to realize the JIT concept, it should not be applied to suppliers without corresponding changes in the overall production system of the user company. The Kanban system is merely a subsystem of the Toyota production system; the Toyota production system requires an overall rearrangement of existing production systems.

If the subsequent process withdraws parts with large variance in terms of quantity or timing, the preceding process must necessarily prepare slack capacities of manpower, facility, and inventory. In the same way, since the paternal manufacturer is connecting to the supplier through the Kanban system, the supplier would suffer if the manufacturer ordered parts in a fluctuating manner. Thus, an effort must be made to minimize the fluctuation of production in the final assembly line of the paternal manufacturer.

In 1950, the Honsha plant of Toyota began to install a line-balancing scheme between the final assembly line and machining lines. Then, the Kanban system was developed and gradually spread into further preceding processes. As a result, since 1962 the Kanban system has been applied to *all* of Toyota's plants. Thus, it was in 1962 that Toyota began to apply Kanban to its suppliers. By 1970, Toyota had applied Kanban to 60 percent of its vendors. As of 1982, Toyota has applied its *supplier* Kanban to 98 percent of its vendors, although still only 50 percent of the vendors are using *in-process* Kanban (or, *production-ordering* Kanban) in their own plants.

This chapter will cover the following topics:

• Monthly information and daily information provided to the supplier
• Later replenishment system by Kanban
• Sequenced withdrawal system by the sequence schedule table
• Problems and countermeasures in applying Kanban to the subcontractors
• How supplier Kanban should be circulated within the paternal manufacturer

The author collected data for this chapter by interviewing and observing Aisin Seiki Company, Ltd., one of the largest suppliers to Toyota.

MONTHLY INFORMATION AND DAILY INFORMATION

Toyota provides two kinds of information to its suppliers: The first is a predetermined monthly production plan which is communicated to the supplier in the middle of the preceding month. Using this predetermined monthly production plan, the supplier will determine the following planning dates:

1. Cycle time of each process
2. Standard operations routine which rearranges the allocation of workers appropriate to the cycle time at each process
3 Quantities of parts and materials to be ordered to subsuppliers
4. Number of each Kanban for subsuppliers

The second type of information is daily information, which specifies the actual number of units to be supplied to the customer company (i.e., Toyota). This daily information takes on two different forms: a Kanban or a sequence schedule table (often called a unit order table). These two forms of information are applied alternatively, depending on the withdrawal methods of Toyota.

Toyota uses two types of withdrawal methods: a *later replenishment* system, and a *sequenced withdrawal* system. The later replenishment system ("Ato-Hoju") is a method of using a supplier Kanban. Beside the assembly line at Toyota are many boxes which contain parts and supplier Kanban. As the parts are used by the assembly line these boxes will become empty, and then at a regular time the empty boxes and their supplier Kanbans will be conveyed to each respective supplier by truck. From the supplier's store of finished parts, other boxes filled with parts will be withdrawn by the truck.

Let's consider the sequenced withdrawal system. In some cases Toyota may provide a supplier with the sequence schedule for many varieties of finished parts, enabling Toyota to withdraw various parts in a sequence conforming to its sequence schedule for mixed model assembly line. Such a system is called the sequenced withdrawal system ("Junjo-Biki"). For example if the sequence schedule of various automobiles at Toyota's final assembly line is

$$[A - B - A - C - A - B - A - C - ...]$$

then the sequence schedule of various transmissions to be subassembled by the supplier must be

$$[Ta - Tb - Ta - Tc - Ta - Tb - Ta - Tc - ...]$$

where *Ta* means the transmission for car A.

LATER REPLENISHMENT SYSTEM BY KANBAN

How the Supplier Kanban Should Be Applied to the Supplier
As depicted in Figure 3.1, the flow of a supplier Kanban consists of two steps:

1. At 8 a.m., the driver of a truck conveys the supplier Kanban to the supplier. This truck also conveys the empty boxes to the supplier.

2. When the truck arrives at the store of the supplier, the driver hands out the supplier Kanban to the store workers. Then, the driver immediately mans another truck already bearing the part and its Kanbans, and drives back to Toyota. In this situation, two matters should be noted:

   a. *The supplier Kanban and the supplier's production lead time.* The number of the supplier Kanban brought to the supplier's store at 8 a.m. does not necessarily correspond to the boxes which the driver brings back to Toyota at 8 a.m. For example, if the parts are conveyed twice a day (8 a.m. and 10 p.m.), we can assume that the supplier Kanban contained in the filled boxes at 8 a.m. this morning is the same Kanban brought at 10 p.m. last night. (See the remarks on the supplier Kanban in Figure 3.1. The time needed for loading the parts on the truck has been omitted to simplify the figure.)

   b. *How to use trucks for Kanban system: the three-truck system.* The diagrammed situation must involve three trucks. One truck is being driven by the driver, while the other trucks are stationed at Toyota's store for unloading the delivered parts and at the supplier's store for loading the parts. Three people participate: the truck driver and two workers engaged in simultaneous loading and unloading.

Advantages of this conveyance system include:

- Shortened conveyance time between the supplier and the paternal maker for the driver has no waiting time, loading time, or unloading time at each store. As a result, the total lead time will be shortened. In other words, the system can eliminate the driver's idle time, since other people load and unload while another truck is on the road.

- While this system's required three trucks have three times the depreciation costs of one truck, the actual duration period is three times one truck. In the long run the system will not increase production costs. On the other hand, if parts are conveyed by only one truck, more than two persons are needed for loading and unloading to reduce total conveyance time as much as possible. These additional workers will increase production costs.

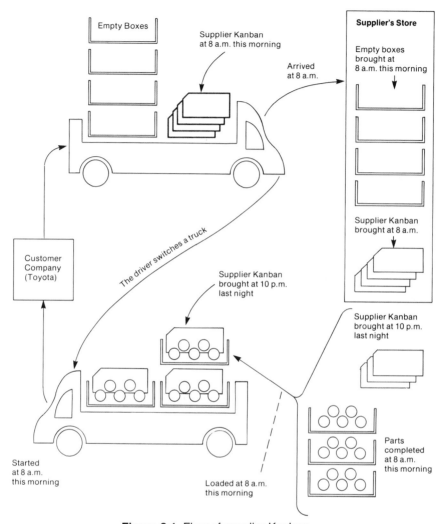

Figure 3.1. Flow of supplier Kanban.

• Although the Kanban system requires frequent conveyances, the merits of reducing inventory are immeasurably greater than the increased conveyance costs. Further, the reader should consider the benefits of the mixed loading, traveling conveyance system that Toyota applies to plural suppliers, as explained in Chapter 2.

How the In-Process Kanban Will Circulate in the Supplier's Plant

Suppose again that parts will be withdrawn by the automaker twice a day: 8 a.m. and 10 p.m. To correspond to this time schedule, the production ordering post for a manufacturing process is divided into two frames as depicted in Figure 3.2.

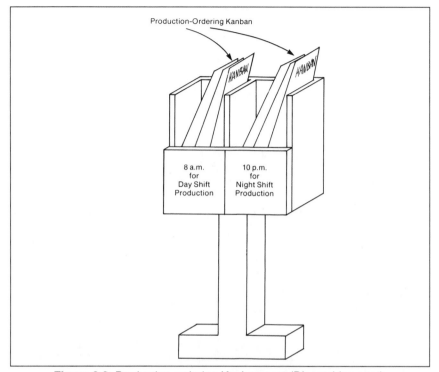

Figure 3.2. Production-ordering Kanban post (Dispatching post).

The 8 a.m. file contains as many production Kanbans as the number of customer Kanbans brought at 8 a.m., and will instruct production during the day shift. The production of parts will be completed at the latest by 10 p.m. that night, and the parts will be loaded on the truck at 10 p.m. to deliver to Toyota.

The 10 p.m. file contains as many production Kanbans as the number of customer Kanbans brought at 10 p.m., and will instruct the production for the night shift.

The required parts will be finished at the latest by 8 a.m. the next morning, and again will be loaded on the truck at 8 a.m. for delivery to Toyota. (Note that for simplicity loading time allowances are not included.) These operations are seen in Figure 3.3.

How the paternal company determines the total number of supplier Kanbans is detailed in Chapter 19. The number of supplier Kanbans which a supplier dispatches to the second step subsupplier is determined by applying the same formula. These formulas are calculated by computer. Also, the formula determining the total number of in-process Kanbans is explained in Chapter 19.

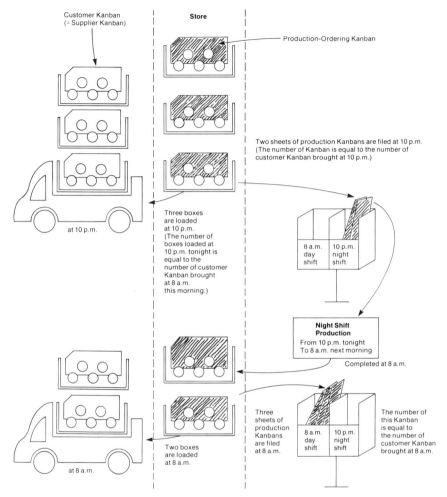

Figure 3.3. Flow of customer Kanban and in-process Kanban.

SEQUENCED WITHDRAWAL SYSTEM BY THE SEQUENCE SCHEDULE TABLE

Once a day, Toyota communicates the sequence schedule for various parts to the computer office of the vendor's plant. In some cases this sequence information will be recorded on a supplier's diskette allowing the computer to print out labels specifying the details of the parts to be assembled one by one on the supplier's assembly line. (The details of this EDP system used by a supplier are described in Chapter 20.)

The Shiroyama plant of Aisin Seiki Company, Ltd. (a Toyota supplier), for example, previously relied on a magnetic tape delivered by Toyota, which

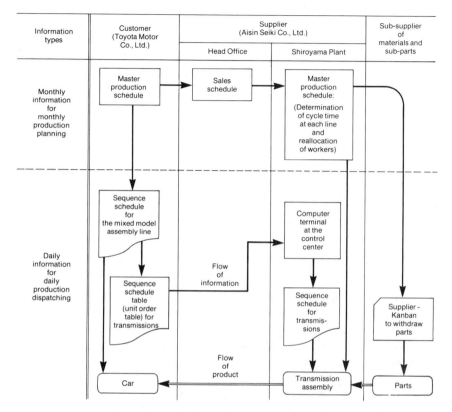

Figure 3.4. Information system under the sequenced withdrawal system.

specified the sequence schedule for the day's production of transmissions. Currently, however, an on-line computer system between the Shiroyama plant and Toyota communicates the sequence schedule in a real time manner. This is based on value-added network (VAN). This sequence schedule table is called the *unit order table* and is communicated to the assembly line on every hour (16 times a day), four hours before the delivery to Toyota. Notice how short lead time is! This information flow is depicted in Figure 3.4.

Both the later replenishment system and the sequenced withdrawal system are applied not only to the parts of a supplier, but also to the parts produced internally within Toyota Motor Corporation. For example, when Toyota's Honsha plant withdraws engines produced at Toyota's Kamigo plant, the sequenced withdrawal system is applied to the Kamigo plant.

In order to transmit the sequence schedule within Toyota's plants, a computer terminal has been installed in all of the plants. Formerly, Toyota used an interwriter (a type of fax machine), and the paper tape was electronically transmitted to the subassemblies.

Store Space and a Variety of Products
In order to reduce the inventory level of a store, it is also necessary to minimize the store's space size. However, the present state of the JIT production system by Kanban necessarily assumes that some amount of inventory exists at the store of parts completed by the previous process. The reasons follow:

• When the *constant quantity and inconstant cycle withdrawal system* is used, the preceding process must have some inventory of finished parts to adapt to any irregular timing of withdrawals. The timing of withdrawals must necessarily be irregular under this system because of fluctuating *demands in the outside market.*

• When the *constant cycle and inconstant quantity withdrawal system* is used, the preceding process must again have some inventory to adapt to inconstant quantities of withdrawals by the subsequent process. Again, under this system, the withdrawn quantity must fluctuate because of the vagaries of customer demand.

Therefore, the ideal of nonstock productions has not yet been realized under the present state of the JIT approach at Toyota, although inventory level has been very well controlled by the Kanban itself. Of course, if the ideal of invisible conveyor belt lines is realized throughout the plant, it follows that the nonstock production or *Just-on-time* production is attained. Still production at Toyota is far from this ultimate ideal, and the term *Just-in-time* is more appropriate for the present situation than the term *Just-on-time.*

At Toyota's Kamigo plant, for example, the store of finished products (engines) is classified for delivery to its various client plants and companies. On the other hand, if the store is classified for a broad variety of finished parts, the total quantities of parts will increase. Therefore, if the size of the part is quite large (for example, transmissions or engines), and its varieties are many, the sequenced withdrawal system must be applied to minimize the store space. However, if the part size is small, the later replenishment system will be applied.

If the geographical distance between the car assembly line and the engine assembly line is very large, then Kanban must be used. This is because the finally adjusted sequence schedule will be determined just when the painted body is introduced to the car assembly line (see details in Chapter 21).

How the Sequence Schedule Is Used in the Assembly Lines of a Supplier
Let us first examine the production situation at the Shiroyama plant of Aisin Seiki Company, Ltd. Its major products and their monthly production volumes (as of 1981) can be seen in Table 3.1. The production character of these products—large variety and short runs—is depicted in Figure 3.5.

Table 3.1. Major products and their monthly production volume.

Products	Volume	Customers
Manual transmission (T/M)	20,000	Toyota Motor Co., Ltd. Daihatsu Kogyo Co., Ltd.
Semi-automatic transmission (for the automobile) (ATM)	3,000	Suzuki Motor Co., Ltd.
Semi-automatic transmission (for the industrial vehicle) (T/C)	1,000	Toyota Automatic Loom Works Co., Ltd. International Harvester Co.
Power steering (P/S)	2,500	Toyota Motor Co., Ltd. Hino Motors Co., Ltd.

Now we will consider how the Shiroyama plant is coping with such productions of large variety and short runs. Considering the design process, it is possible to expand a basic model transmission to adapt to the large variety of cars in which they will be used (Figure 3.6).

This design process is incorporated into the various assembly lines as seen in Figure 3.7. The assembly line is divided into two parts (main and sub) and storage for half-finished and finished transmissions are installed. This divided assembly line responds to the many varieties of customer's orders. The lead time from the half-finished parts store to the finished parts store is only 15 minutes, and the conveyance to Toyota takes one hour. As a result, these assembly lines can respond to the large variety of orders demanded by Toyota—orders whose sequence information is introduced only four hours before the delivery.

At the head of the subassembly line, a label will be fastened to each transmission one by one, and these labels will sequence the 74 varieties of transmissions completed by the main assembly line. Meanwhile, each semifinished transmission at the main assembly line will receive its own Kanban, and successive production of the ten basic transmission types will be ordered by these Kanbans.

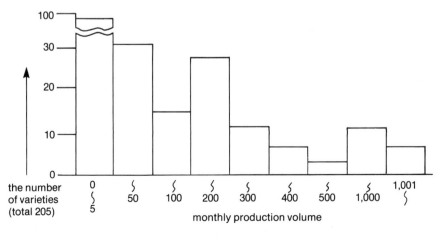

Figure 3.5. Production character of a large variety and short run operation.

Model	basic	4 speeds 5 speeds	engine gasoline diesel	frame truck bus	steering right left	final model
Variety	1	2	8	■ ■ ■	■ ■ ■	74

Figure 3.6. Design process from a basic model to the final models.

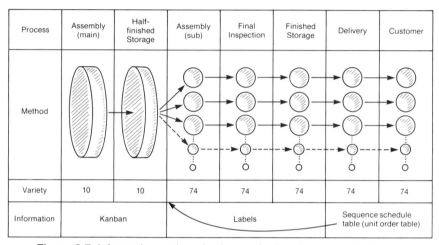

Process	Assembly (main)	Half-finished Storage	Assembly (sub)	Final Inspection	Finished Storage	Delivery	Customer
Method							
Variety	10	10	74	74	74	74	74
Information	Kanban		Labels			Sequence schedule table (unit order table)	

Figure 3.7. Information and production method on the assembly lines.

It must be emphasized here that the transmission is a unique example; while in most cases one Kanban will dispatch several—perhaps five—units which will be placed in one pallet, in the case of the transmission, each unit receives its own Kanban. The reason for this is that although each transmission is a large unit in itself, production must be able to respond to the large variety of demand.

PROBLEMS AND COUNTERMEASURES IN APPLYING THE KANBAN SYSTEM TO SUBCONTRACTORS

There must be some discrepancy between the quantities of parts the paternal company specifies in its monthly predetermined production plan and the quantities it actually orders during the month (based on Kanban or the sequence schedule table). This discrepancy is usually about ten percent. However, there is no concept of plan revision in the operating processes of the plants because only production information in the form of Kanban or labels is given in a real time manner.

Concerned by the discrepancy and other related problems which might occur in the transactions between a paternal manufacturer and its subcontractors, the Japanese Communist Party, along with the Japanese Government's Fair Trade Commission, has strongly criticized the Toyota system. The following sections will address their criticism and guidance as well as Toyota's countermeasures, together with the author's opinion on this problem.

Criticism By the Communist Party Against the Toyota Production System

The Taylor System was once opposed by American labor unions contending that scientific management neglected humanity and regarded man as a machine. Indeed, so intense did the dispute become that the United States found it necessary to investigate the subject through a special committee.

Now, just as scientific management once became an issue of the U.S. House of Representatives, the Toyota production system has come under the scrutiny of the Japanese House.

In 1977, just four years after the first oil shock hit Japan in late 1973, and when most Japanese companies were still suffering from its effects and the consequent inflation of yen currency, Michiko Tanaka, a member of the House of Representatives and also a member of the Japan Communist Party questioned Premier Takeo Fukuda about the Toyota production system as follows:

> The management situation of medium and small enterprises is so severe that it can hardly be compared with big companies. However, the supplementary budget at this time restricts the amount of loans and cannot offer a promising future to the minor companies.
>
> Especially severe are the problems faced by subcontractors, who supply sixty percent of manufacturers. For example, the Toyota Motor Company, Ltd. has earned the current profit of 210 billion yen (about $1 billion). Behind this huge profit how many subcontractors have dropped tears? Toyota's completely rationalized production system strictly instructs its subcontractors to deliver the required parts within today or by tomorrow. Therefore, there is no excessive parts inventory at Toyota, and thus there is no warehouse and no sleeping funds invested in the inventory.
>
> However, subcontractors are in a precarious situation if they occupy positions as low as the third, fourth or fifth steps in the vertical line among manufacturers. The reason is if they cannot deliver their parts just in time for the needs of the paternal company, the contracts will be cancelled. Thus, they must engage in estimated production, and if their estimates were mistaken, they have to undertake all the loss themselves. Though payment remains unchanged or is actually decreased, the subcontractors must put up with severe conditions to get their contracts.
>
> Moreover, a serious matter which cannot go unnoticed is that this Toyota system is now prevailing among many industries and a vast number of subcontractors are likely to fall victims to this system. If this practice of bullying the subcontractors is left unrestricted, the Japanese economy will be thrown into chaos.
>
> You have said that you will initiate a compassionate policy in behalf of medium and small enterprises, but how do you cope with these very wicked methods which take a superior position? I would like to hear your belief. (Proceedings at the Japanese House of Representatives, No. 4: October 7, 1977, p. 63.)

Fukuda responded as follows:

> Now, concerning your opinion on Toyota's rationalized production system, I hear that the Fair Trade Commission is now guiding the company. The government will also give assurance that the paternal manufacturer will not force its rationalization at the sacrifice of the subcontractor's interests. This is my conviction. (Proceedings, op. cit. p. 65.)

GUIDANCE BY THE FAIR TRADE COMMISSION BASED ON THE SUBCONTRACTORS LAW AND THE ANTI-MONOPOLY LAW

Thus, the Fair Trade Commission and the Small and Medium Enterprises agency of the government in Japan have guided the paternal manufacturers not to violate the Subcontractor's Law and the Anti-Monopoly Law. The Subcontractor's Law is an abbreviation of the "Anti-Deferment-of-Payment-to-the-Subcontractor's Law." This law was established in 1956 to maintain a fair subcontracting trade and to guard the subcontractors' interests.

The problematic points of the Kanban system which concerned the Fair Trade Commission were as follows:

1.When production is managed by the Kanban system the ordering time is obscure. According to the Toyota production system, it is only during the last 11 days of a previous month that a supplier will be notified of the predetermined monthly production plan concerning specific items, quantities, dates and times, etc. On the other hand, the Kanban system and the sequence schedule specify similar information. Therefore, the ordering time is not obvious: is it the time specified by predetermined monthly production plan, or by the Kanban and the sequence schedule?

However, according to the Subcontractor's Law (Article III), even though the ordering action by a paternal maker is an informal notification, the point in time when the instruction is concretely made is regarded as the ordering time.

2.According to the Kanban system there must be some discrepancy between the monthly quantity that is informally ordered and the quantity actually delivered by Kanban dispatchings. In other words, the essence of the Kanban system lies in fine tuning production or making minor adaptations to demand changes.

When the quantity of goods dispatched by the Kanbans turns out to be smaller than the quantity originally ordered by the monthly informally communicated master production schedule, the difference must be regarded as the rejection of acceptance, because Article I states that the actual order occurs when the supplier receives instructions from the informal production table.

In addition, the Subcontractor's Law (Article IV-I-1), prohibits the paternal manufacturer from rejecting all or part of the delivered goods it has ordered.

3. The Kanban delivery system should not be forced on the supplier. According to the Japanese Anti-Monopoly Law (Article 19): "A business company must not use unfair trading methods." In 1953, as an example of unfair trading methods, the following action was cited: "Realizing its superior position in regard to a dependent company, a business company must not trade with conditions exceptionally unfavorable to the other company in the light of normal business conventions."

Therefore, when applying the Kanban system to its supplier, a paternal company must secure an agreement with the subcontractor, and should never force implementation in a one-sided manner. In the trading contract, it should be noted that without such agreement the Kanban system will not be applied. Also, even if the subcontractor agrees to the application of Kanban, it must receive an adequate preparation period in order for it to adjust to the new system. Further, the paternal company should not urge the introduction of Kanban on vendors without adjusting the technical prerequisites of its own plant and without having full knowledge about the whole Toyota production system.

The other possible detrimental effects that Kanban may have on the subcontractor follow (referring to the paper of Mr. Hyogo Kikuchi, subcontract section manager of the Fair Trade Commission).

Most of the first-step subcontractors that adopted the Kanban system are enjoying the same advantages as Toyota. However, the second, third or fourth preceding step subcontractors may suffer from certain detrimental effects for which, essentially, the paternal companies are responsible. These detriments are:

• The subcontractors may have to increase their inventory to achieve the expected production, since they have to deliver parts as quickly as possible in response to withdrawal by Kanban. They may also have to utilize overtime to cope with the unexpected.

Such increase of inventory in the stores of subcontractors is a consequence similar to situation effected by the Cock System (or, "On-the-Premises Warehouse System") which was popular in Japan after World War II. In the Cock System, a subcontractor will hold a certain amount of its finished parts inventory and bear the risk himself by borrowing a part of the paternal maker's factory. Thus, the paternal maker could use the necessary items in the necessary quantities at the necessary time (JIT), and could issue the order sheet at the time of withdrawal. This system was criticized as a violation of the Subcontractor's Law, and the paternal manufacturers were dissuaded from its use.

• Notwithstanding standard increases in the quantity of monthly delivery, application of the Kanban system will increase overall conveyance times. The resulting increases in conveyance expenses will obviously increase the subcontractor's overall costs.

- The most important prerequisite of JIT production is production smoothing, or small lot production. When implemented by a large, paternal manufacturer, this process requires the installment of multipurpose machines and speedy setup actions. However, this brings up the subcontractor's obligation to install the same multi-purpose machines and improved setup actions in order to supply the part at the price which the user company has calculated based on its own smoothed, well-equipped production.

How Toyota Is Coping with Criticism
The main problem pointed out by the Fair Trade Commission was the discrepancy between quantities ordered by the predetermined monthly production plan and the daily Kanban or sequence schedule instructions.

Toyota countered this problem as follows:

- Toyota is trying to hold the aforementioned discrepancies down to less than ten percent of the monthly plan, and is requesting that suppliers allow this much difference.
- Since a model of an automobile will usually be produced for about four years, the supplier will not suffer seriously from monthly fluctuations, for these fluctuations are averaged out over many months.
- Toyota is promising its suppliers that it will give advance notice when it is about to stop production of a certain model. At that time it will establish a compensation structure.
- Toyota is telling its suppliers not to start production until instructed by the Kanban. Therefore, overproduction is not likely to occur.
- In order for the supplier to adjust to order-oriented production, it must shorten production lead time. Toyota is teaching how to achieve such reductions.

As a result of these steps, there is almost no confusion among Toyota's suppliers caused by plan revisions ordered by Kanban. The author especially supports Toyota's countermeasure number two. When a dealer's demands are declining, the actual quantity of goods withdrawn by Kanban is likely to be less than the monthly predetermined quantity.

If Toyota was to withdraw this difference in quantity at the end of the month in question, the informally instructed quantity for the next month would be correspondingly smaller than the quantity previously forecasted, and as a result the subcontractor would be surprised to see a sudden, steep drop in his orders. This would never happen at Toyota. According to its production system, Toyota withdraws only the quantity which corresponds as closely as possible to actual demand during the month. To achieve this approach, the quantities ordered both by Kanban and by the monthly predetermined instruction must be smoothed in daily production levels. As a result, the supplier would not be confused by the sudden fall in the actual ordered units. The supplier could adapt to the demand change smoothly by fine-tuning each month. The most remarkable advantage of the Kanban system, the adaptation to demand change by smoothing the changes of a plan, will begin to function at this point.

In regard to the various problems cited by the subcontract section of the Fair Trade Commission, the author holds the following opinions:

• Concerning the supplier's risk of holding of a large inventory, most of this problem will be resolved if the paternal manufacturer completes the various prerequisites of the Kanban system, especially the smoothing of production. Therefore, if this problem does arise, the Kanban system is guiltless and the paternal company must be blamed.

On the other hand, suppose a supplier is supplying parts to several manufacturers and only some of the manufacturers are applying Kanban to the supplier. This supplier might have problems even if the manufacturers using Kanban are completing the prerequisite conditions. However, since so many Japanese industries have adopted Kanban, this problem is diminishing. The use of Kanban is especially widespread throughout the auto industry.

• As for the problem of increased conveyance costs due to more frequent withdrawals, it can be solved by the round-tour mixed loading system and the three-truck system explained earlier in this chapter.

If large geographic distances prevent the effective use of such systems, as in the case of the United States, the following approaches can be considered:

a. Instead of relying on subcontractors, the paternal manufacturer should incorporate parts producing processes in its own factory. In the United States, automobile makers do not rely on subcontractors as much as Japanese auto makers.

b. Instead of making frequent orders to suppliers in small lot sizes, the user company should order in fairly large lot sizes. This practice can be seen in the case of Japanese automakers sending parts to foreign countries for overseas production. Kawasaki Motors U.S.A. is a good example of a company that has adopted the Toyota production system in the United States (1979).

• As for the difficulty the subcontractor may face in offering a part at the instructed price, such a problem can be resolved if the subcontractor itself adopts the Toyota production system. This problem also relates to the first problem. Even if the paternal maker has smoothed its production, the subcontractor might not be able to decrease his inventory and at the same time handle frequent withdrawals unless he can change his dies quickly.

Although Toyota is making an effort to keep monthly discrepancies down below 10 percent, some of the suppliers have reported that differences may run to plus-or-minus 20 percent of the initial monthly plan. However, if they are able to adapt to such demand changes in their own processes, this discrepancy does not pose serious problems. For example, the Kariya plant of Aisin Seiki Company, Ltd., has 0.7 days of safety stock ready for delivery to the customer. This means that it delivers parts three times a day to its customer, while holding safety inventory equivalent to two deliveries per day (i.e., $2/3 = 0.7$). The level of safety stock indicates the supplier's ability to adapt.

Therefore, subcontractors must also rationalize their production systems. They should not succumb to the easy attitude that rationalization must only be carried out by paternal manufacturers, for rationalization decreases costs, and cost reduction is a shared obligation of both manufacturers and subcontractors.

Figure 3.8 shows that most of the big suppliers of Toyota were once part of the Toyota Motor Corporation. Since each of them can be seen as simply another production process of the Toyota plant, the aforementioned problems do not exist among these companies.

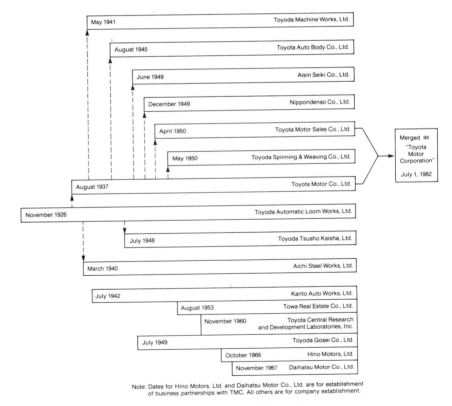

Note: Dates for Hino Motors, Ltd. and Daihatsu Motor Co., Ltd. are for establishment of business partnerships with TMC. All others are for company establishment.

Figure 3.8. Formation of the Toyota Group.

Mr. Taiichi Ohno, original developer of the Toyota production system, says:

> "In order to make the Toyota production system truly effective, we should recognize its limitations. Only if Toyota shares its destiny with surrounding cooperative manufacturers as a single community can it approach the perfect realization of this system. Therefore, Toyota is improving the physical capabilities of our cooperative manufacturers by sending our I.E. staffs to them."

In short, paternal manufacturers must teach suppliers to implement the Toyota system, and at the same time the supplier must also frankly accept such guidance in order to make real improvements. With the existence of such a give-and-take relationship, warehouses are actually disappearing from the yards of Toyota's cooperative companies, including the second and third steps vendors.

It must be added, however, that it is somewhat difficult for a supplier to introduce a Kanban system independently unless its paternal company dispatches the supplier Kanban with smoothed order quantities.

Finally, another problem must be mentioned briefly: although there is no obvious resistance against the Toyota production system among Toyota's laborers, some people feel that this system will force the intensification of labor. At the present time it is difficult to justify such an argument with objective data. If we take into account the increasing number of suggestions per workers per year, we see that the humanity of laborers is well respected in this system. How Toyota has resolved the conflict between productivity and humanity will be discussed in Chapter 12. (Also see Muramatsu, Miyazaki, and Tanaka, 1980, 1981.) It is quite obvious that the Toyota production system cannot be implemented in a company or organization where a labor union opposes productivity increases. This point may be the critical condition which will restrict the application of the Toyota production system. Unless there is opposition from a labor union, this system can be applied to any company in any country.

SUPPLIER KANBAN CIRCULATION IN THE PATERNAL MANUFACTURER

The production line is usually situated a short distance from material or parts storage, and in such situations the following steps will be taken to request supplier's materials (each step number corresponds to the number in Figure 3.9):

1. When a worker at the production line sees a material box empty out, he will push the switch beside the line.
2. The material-calling Andon located beside the material store will activate a lamp just under the metal plate indicating the material in question.
3. At the same time, a large red light will come on at the material storage.
4. The material carrier at the store will watch the material-calling Andon to see which metal plate is lit.

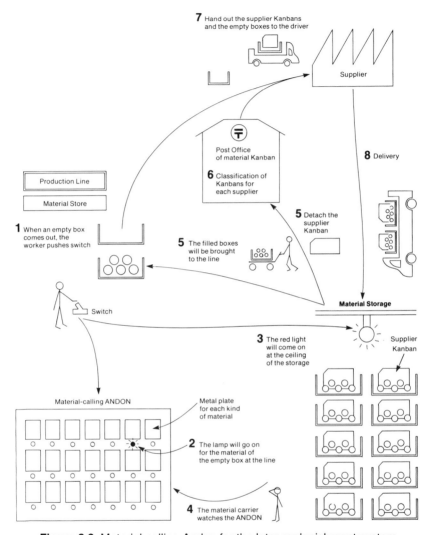

Figure 3.9. Material-calling Andon for the later-replenishment system.

5. Then, the carrier brings the box containing the material in question to the line. This box also contains the supplier Kanban, but the carrier must detach it before he brings the box to the production line.

6. The supplier Kanbans will be brought to a post office for supplier Kanbans, where these Kanbans will be classified for each supplier in the same way as a post office will classify letters for each address.

7. The processed and classified supplier Kanban will be given to the truck driver for subsequent delivery to the supplier. The empty boxes have already been loaded on the driver's truck.

The metal plate for each kind of material, which is part of the material-calling Andon, is essentially a kind of *withdrawal* Kanban. At the Aisin Seiki Company, Ltd., this metal plate is called Kanban, and there is no Kanban in the material boxes beside the production line. However, although the author saw similar metal plates at the Honsha plant of Toyota, Toyota does not call this metal plate a Kanban. Each material box beside the line contains a standard supplier Kanban.

The Honsha plant of Daihatsu Motor Company, Ltd., which has a business partnership with Toyota, is also using a plate-sliding file as depicted in Figure 3.10. In this plant, the metal plate, which a lamp has highlighted, will be placed in a plate-sliding file according to the order of its lamp's activation. Then, the carrier will withdraw the plate from the bottom of this sliding file, collect the materials designated by the plates from various stores in the plant, and bring them to the line. The material-calling Andon or the metal-plate board has various forms in different companies. Each company devises its own forms. The details of the material-calling Andon and metal plate will be explained as a *hired-taxi system* in Chapter 21.

The inside of the post office for supplier Kanbans is shown in Figure 3.11. The post office is located either beside or inside the material storage. Recently, however, companies have begun sorting the supplier Kanbans by computer.

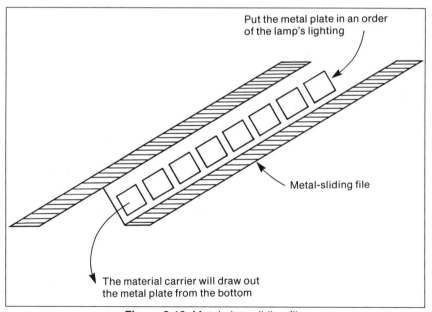

Put the metal plate in an order of the lamp's lighting

Metal-sliding file

The material carrier will draw out the metal plate from the bottom

Figure 3.10. Metal plate sliding file.

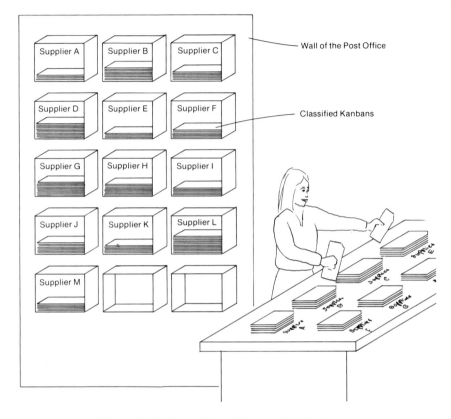

Figure 3.11. Post office of the supplier Kanbans.

STRUCTURE OF THE SUPPLIER KANBAN SORTING OFFICE

An office used for classifying supplier Kanbans is managed as follows:

Step 1: When the first part is picked from the parts box on the production line, the worker places the parts Kanban in the Kanban post beside the line. (This is the usual method, whereas Step 5 in the previous section is somewhat specialized.)

Step 2: The Kanbans are brought to the Kanban sorting office from the Kanban post once every hour.

Step 3: The Kanban sorting office uses a machine to automatically sort various supplier Kanbans by supplier.

Step 4: The sorted supplier Kanbans are shelved on the wall of the office which is partitioned for each supplier.

When a truck from a parts maker arrives the Kanban kept in the classified shelves is not actually handed out to the driver directly. The arrival of trucks is irregular due to traffic on the way, and thus the number of Kanbans received is also irregular. When the truck arrives late, the number of Kanbans received is higher, but if the truck is early the number of Kanbans received is smaller. As a result, the quantity of parts withdrawn from a supplier is widely influenced by early and late arrival of trucks. This prevents smoothed production for the suppliers and the manufacturers.

For diminishing such fluctuations caused by traffic problems, a method has been devised to have one more sorting shelf on the wall near the entrance of the sorting office. The shelf mentioned in step 4 is at the back of the office. A card listing vendor names who receive Kanbans is hung beside the second shelf near the entrance and replaced every hour. The supplier Kanbans of vendors listed on this card only are placed in the second shelf. The truck driver is given his Kanbans from this shelf at the entrance (see Figure 3.12). Therefore, if the driver of the truck comes early, he will not be given any Kanbans until his designated time. If he arrives late, he will receive only the number of Kanbans that he would have received if he had arrived at his designated time.

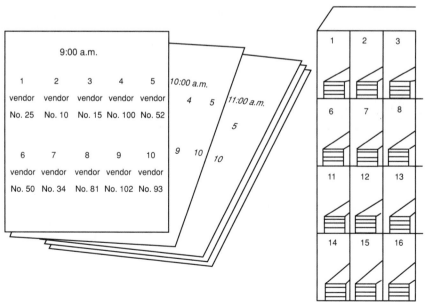

Figure 3.12. Hourly card listing of vendors' names in the supplier Kanban sorting office.

Inventory Quantity of Purchased Parts

At a Daihatsu body-welding plant the inventory quantity of purchased parts that are supplied twice a day is the amount of one delivery unit plus the safety stock. The quantity of parts arriving five times a day equals one delivery, or one fifth of a daily supply, plus the safety inventory.

At Toyota Shatai, a car-body assembly plant, the delivery cycle is 1-10-6. This means that the inventory quantity equals a *one-time* delivery plus safety stock, a daily total of *ten* deliveries is made, and a delivery ordered by Kanban is set off by a run *six* times after the Kanban was dispatched to Toyota Shatai. Travel time from the body maker (located in Nagoya City) to the welding plant is three hours. Yet, trouble on the road sometimes causes the units already started and units in transit to arrive at the plant at one time. In such a case it is possible by phone to get Toyota Shatai to stop the next run, but it is impossible to stop the parts already on their way to the plant.

Generally speaking, the inventory for a quarter shift's use, that is for two or three operations, is to be stocked according to the purchased parts. However, when the increased production of a specified model is expected, or during a heavy snow season, the inventory is increased.

The number of Kanbans is adjusted monthly in accordance with the production volume for each month. If complications arise at the supplier's office resulting in a delay in supply, what should be done? Two common reasons for delay in supply are: 1) misapplication of the Kanban, and 2) trouble in the supplier facility.

The first case may need an explanation. A supplier located in the country is often small-sized and its production capacity may be insufficient to adapt to manufacturer demands conveyed via Kanbans. However, the forecasted requirements of each type of model are communicated three months in advance to the supplier from the plant on a rolling basis every month. Moreover, confirmations of the actual order are made twice in the month just previous to taking delivery. Therefore, the supplier should be able to avoid delay due to its limited capacity by producing and stocking the necessary inventory during previous months.

In contrast, if a supplier is located nearby, the maker may dispatch special carriers to the supplier or ask them to bring the parts quickly by taxi. Even if a supplier's plant is located in Nagoya City, small parts such as bis and bearings can be carried on a bullet train ("shin-kan sen train") and the maker (Daihatsu) has only to wait its arrival at Shin-Osaka Station.

Incidentally, the deliveries from Nagoya District to the plant at Daihatsu are done at ten minute intervals and seven or eight transportation firms are used. In addition, the maximum number of delivery runs from one particular supplier is 20 times a day.

Practical Examples of Delivery System and Delivery Cycle

The Kyoto plant of Japan Sheet Glass Company, Ltd. has about 500 employees and produces about 600,000 to 700,000 square meters of glass monthly. The delivery to Toyota is made based on the Kanban system; however, the Kanban system is not used inside the plant. The characteristics of the Kanban system in this plant are depicted in Figure 3.13.

Japan Sheet Glass Company, Ltd. contracts with a transportation firm to deliver Kanbans from Toyota. (In fact, this transportation company is one of many companies affiliated with Toyota.) Once delivered, the Kanbans are put into a Kanban post divided into many sections for each supply run. In the plant's shipping area, products are stored for shipment and are separated by a Kanban for each run. A Kanban is then inserted into each pallet containing products, one Kanban to a pallet. If the total number of pallets is different from the number of Kanbans, Toyota will have to hold excess stock. To avoid this problem, pallets are checked to ensure that the appropriate Kanbans are attached.

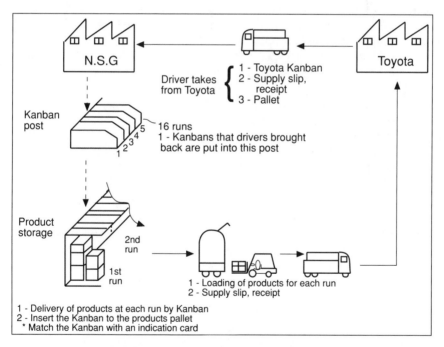

Figure 3.13. Circulation of supplier Kanban.

Number of Supply Runs and Delivery Schedule of Each Plant

Now let's describe the number of delivery runs to each Toyota plant. The Tsutsumi plant, for example, is supplied 16 times a day, and the units (glass) are unloaded at two places in the plant. The Motomachi plant is supplied 10 times a day at three places. Details for number of deliveries to each plant are shown in Figure 3.14.

The total number of runs to each plant amounts to 39. If all of these runs were done individually, the transport cost would be compounded and quite expensive. Since an 11-ton truck is used for these deliveries, its capacity is more than one run. Therefore, a schedule of 20 runs total was devised. Destinations and runs were combined based on proximity, quantity, and load weight. The combination of destinations is shown in Figure 3.15.

This timetable is based on the 16 runs to Tsutsumi plant combined with runs to Motomachi plant and Takaoka plant. For example, the first run to Tsutsumi is combined with the first run to Motomachi. Again, the second run to Tsutsumi is combined with the second run to Motomachi. Then, the third run is combined with the first run to Takaoka.

The four runs to the Tahara plant of Toyota are added to this timetable as independent runs because the plant is in an isolated location. Since the loaded quantity of the three runs to Hino Motorcycle Company is not very much, they are included in the 16 runs to Tsutsumi and are conveyed with the third, eighth, and eleventh runs to Tsutsumi.

The delivery cycle to each plant is written on the right side of this timetable. Although we have mentioned the delivery cycle before in Chapter 2 (see Figure 2.4), let's consider it again with actual examples. The former numbers 1 and 16 of the first two numbers in the delivery cycle for Tsutsumi plant (1-16-16) show that there are 16 delivery runs to Tsutsumi everyday. The last number, 16, means that the delivery issued by a supplier Kanban is actually carried out 16 runs after the supplier Kanban arrives at the glass plant. In the case of the Tahara plant, the delivery cycle is 1-4-5. This means the delivery is four times a day, but the delivery is five runs after the Kanban arrives.

The supply to Tsutsumi, instructed by a supplier Kanban brought back to Toyota with the first run, is delivered by the next day's first run to Tsutsumi. The last number in the delivery cycle is determined by the distance between the Toyota plant and the supplier plant, rather than the production lead time of the supplier plant. In short, conveyance time is the chief cause. Therefore, a parts plant near Toyota could supply in a cycle of 1-16-4.

Kanban System and Adaptation to Emergency

How can the Kanban system adapt to emergencies? The plant is 200 kilometers away from Toyota and it takes 3.5 hours one way by truck. If complications arise on the way, the JIT supply to Toyota becomes impossible and Toyota will be forced to stop operations. Take, for example, heavy snowfall in Sekigahara or traffic congestion on a national holiday. To deal with emergencies the plant has storage areas called "stations" 30 minutes away from the plant. In winter, inventory is stored in these storage areas for two days, and one day during other seasons. This is the safety inventory. Moreover, to avoid a delay in production,

Number of runs to each Toyota plant/day		
1	to	Tsutsumi plant .... 16 runs (2 places)
2	to	Motomachi plant .... 10 runs (3 places)
3	to	Takaoka plant .... 6 runs (3 places)
4	to	Tahara plant .... 4 runs (4 places)
5	to	Hino plant .... 3 runs (1 place)

Figure 3.14. Number of delivery times to each plant.

Number of deliveries to each plant				Departure from Japan Sheet Glass Co., Ltd.	Arrival at Toyota	Arrival time of Kanban	* Delivery cycle of each plant
Tsutsumi	Motomachi	Takaoka	Tahara				
1	1			3:20	8:00	13:30	1 - Tsutsumi plant 1 - 16 - 16
2	2			5:10	9:10	15:20	
3		1		4:10	8:20	14:20	
4	3			7:40	11:30	17:30	2 - Motomachi plant 1 - 10 - 10
5		2		7:20	11:20	17:30	
6	4			11:10	14:10	23:20	
7	5			12:20	15:50	24:30	3 - Takaoka plant 1 - 6 - 6
8		3		11:50	15:20	1:00	
9	6			14:20	21:00	2:30	
10	7			16:10	22:10	4:20	4 - Tahara plant 1 - 4 - 5
11		4		15:10	21:20	3:20	
12	8			18:30	24:30	6:50	
13		5		18:20	24:20	6:30	5 - Hino 1 - 2 - 4
14	9			24:10	3:40	10:20	
15	10			1:20	4:50	11:30	
16		6		1:50	4:20	11:00	
			1	21:00	7:50	7:00	
			2	5:00	12:50	15:00	
			3	10:00	20:50	20:00	
			4	16:00	1:50	4:00	

Note: This delivery schedule is based on the cycle to theTsutsumi plant. Delivery to Motomachi and Takaoka are set within it and to Hino is relayed in Toyoda City then delivered by Toyota's run.

Figure 3.15. Delivery schedule for Toyota.

there is another storage area within the plant beside the shipping storage area for the exclusive use of Kanbans described previously. This holds stock for 0.6 months.

For the Kanban system to be completely effective, conditions in the production process of suppliers are very important. Suppliers must be flexible and adapt to fluctuations in production when orders are given from Toyota. Machine breakdown, for example, must not occur in the supplier's plant. Unless the plant maintains a high actual operating rate, the Kanban system does not work properly.

A strategy is necessary to deal with the problems of hazardous weather conditions and traffic conditions. Alternate driving routes have been established for these occurrences. Additionally, the plants have their own three-step process for assessing and dealing with delays and emergencies. They are:

Step 1 - Caution: If less than a two-hour delay is expected, the trouble can be solved by consulting with the transportation company.

Step 2 - Warning: If there is a delay of more than two hours, the plant itself takes action and thus plays a central role.

Step 3 - Emergency: If there is a delay of more than three hours, emergency headquarters are established in this plant and the inventory in the "station" of the plant near Toyota is used.

Finally, when the Kanbans and units do not flow smoothly because of a problem within Toyota, although this is rare, the trouble is dealt with by adjusting the number of Kanbans from Toyota.

4
Smoothed Production Helps Toyota Adapt to Demand Changes and Reduce Inventory

The ultimate purpose of the Toyota production system is to increase profit by reducing costs. Cost reduction is achieved by eliminating waste; waste is exposed and eliminated by Just-in-time (JIT) production. In sales, the JIT concept will be realized by supplying the salable products in salable quantities only. This situation is characterized as production which is promptly adaptable to demand changes. As a result, excess inventories of finished products can be eliminated.

At Toyota, the means for adapting production to variable demand is called production smoothing. The concept of production smoothing is to diminish as much as possible the quantity variance in a production line. The following sections highlight two phases of the production smoothing process—*smoothing of the total production quantity* and *smoothing of every model's production quantity*—for better understanding.

SMOOTHING OF THE TOTAL PRODUCTION QUANTITY

Smoothing of the total production quantity is done to minimize the variance in total outputs between two sequential periods. In short, the goal of production smoothing is to produce the same amount of products every period (usually every day).

Although the demand for automobiles can change widely depending on the season thus affecting monthly production volumes, production smoothing allows daily production volumes to remain constant. For example, consider mass production of the Corolla. Initially, a per month quantitative production schedule is made, based on the demand forecast. This figure is then simply divided by the number of operating days in the month to get a daily production volume. In this manner, it may be feasible to develop a plan that would enable daily production of the desired number of cars. This is the *smoothing of the total production quantity*.

Using this concept, the priority is to maintain the daily production schedule for the Corolla model as a whole. Corolla models that vary from the basic model are not a consideration in this concept.

Another consideration is that the quantity of demand within a month is not constant. For example, demand for cars in the early part of a month may be high and then slack off during the latter part of the month. Under such a condition, if the same amount of cars is produced every day, reserve inventories would be needed to provide enough cars to meet the demand early in the month, while excess inventories would accumulate at the end of the month because of the reduced demand for cars. Consequently, the shorter the period of a master production plan, the better for executing *smoothing of the total production quantity;* i.e., a half-month plan is better than a monthly plan, while a weekly plan is even more desirable.

On the other hand, if the time span of the master production plan is too short, then smoothing of the total production quantity will disappear. In other words, if making a production plan according to actual orders that change daily, the function of smoothing of the total production quantity would produce just the averaged hourly production volume and would not level the total output in a month. Also, big fluctuations in the daily production volume force the plant to change its quantitative work force every day, thus leading to waste of work force especially at a plant where daily worker transfer is unfeasible. After all, smoothing of the total production quantity is meant to level the daily amount of products flowing as much as possible by anticipating peaks and valleys in demand. It is necessary for avoiding overall waste in an entire production system.

There are two kinds of waste. First, in plants where products are created in various quantities, the plant's facilities, people, inventories, and other elements necessary for production are prepared and set up for peak demand as the standard. As a result, during a period of short runs, the plant is likely to display waste in the forms of work force and inventories, when compared with a peak period. This waste arises from *uneven periods of demand.*

The second type of waste occurs in processes (specifically final assembly lines) where the smoothing of the total production quantity has not been implemented yet and production occurs in a variant way. Since under the pull system a preceding process properly prepares its units in quantities corresponding to the peak quantity withdrawn by the subsequent process, it follows that excessive work force and inventory build-up would occur. Here, the waste occurs *between processes.*

Variances in the total production quantity in a final assembly line at Toyota force related parts makers to retain excessive work force and inventories because the pull system (Kanban) connects processes at Toyota with external cooperative enterprises. To practice smoothing the total production quantity without occurrence of waste between processes, the final assembly line and all processes must produce products according to the cycle time. This means balancing between processes (synchronization) will be completely realized if every preceding process finishes at the same pace within the averaged cycle time for all specifications. The average cycle time for the whole operation is calculated by dividing the number of actual operating hours per day (480 minutes or 960 minutes) by the averaged daily production volume in the final assembly line. It is obvious from Figure 4.1 that the number of workers required corresponds to this cycle time. (Figure 4.1 shows the master production plan with two-week intervals at the motorbike plant of Kawasaki Heavy Industry.) In this figure, the worker transfer within a line is made every half month.

MARCH												
Date	1	2	3	...	14	15	16	17	18	...	30	31
Production quantity	250	245	245	...	250	250	205	200	200	...	205	205
Total number of workers	54	54	54	...	54	54	44	44	44	...	44	44
Number of attendants	52	52	53	...	51	52	41	42	43	...	42	41
Line stop time (min.)	88	80	53	...	90	87	83	80	75	...	84	78
Cycle time (sec./unit)	121	120	120	...	121	121	140	144	144	...	140	140

Figure 4.1. Master production plan divided into two-week intervals.

Demand Fluctuation and Production Capacity Plan

The work force layout in Figure 4.1 is for March, the month in which customer demand is at its peak. According to the schedule, the predetermined production volume per day from the first to the fifteenth of the month was 250 cars, while from the sixteenth to the thirty-first it was decreased to around 200. Therefore, 54 workers were assigned for the early part of the month and 44 were assigned for the latter part of the month. In the figure, 54 workers had been scheduled to work on March 2 but only 52 workers actually reported, causing the line to stop for 80 minutes that day. The line stop time is apt to increase proportionally to the number of absentees.

Adapting to increased demand. In the latter part of the month, each line is informed of the daily average quantity for the next month for each variety. This information and other planning data is calculated by a computer in the central production control department.

Once a production process receives its monthly schedule for average daily production, it must adapt its operations to the new information. For example, the load on a machine ordinarily is set at approximately 90 percent of its full capacity, and each worker, operating as a multi-function worker, might handle as many as ten machines. When demand increases, temporary workers are hired and each worker handles less than ten machines, thereby enabling 100 percent utilization of machine capacity. (It is, however, necessary to have machines on which even a newly hired, unskilled laborer will be able to become fully proficient within three days.) On assembly lines, for example, if a single worker has handled the job within a two-minute cycle time, he will be able to handle the same job within a one-minute cycle time when the number of temporary workers is increased. As a result, the production quantity can be doubled. This approach will also be applied to long-range plans for additional man and machine capacities.

Toyota can adapt to a relatively short-term increase in demand, by introducing early attendance and overtime, which can fill up unscheduled hours between the first shift (8 a.m. – 5 p.m.) and the second shift (9 p.m. – 6 a.m.). Doing so allows for an increase in production capacity of up to 37.5% (which is equal to 6 additional working hours / 16 regular working hours). Moreover, various improvements within each process produce extra time that can be used during a period of increased demand.

Adapting to decreased demand. Adapting to decreased demand is considerably more difficult than adapting to an increase in demand. In parts manufacturing processes, the number of machines handled by each worker will increase, because temporary workers will be dismissed. On the assembly line, cycle time will increase due to the reduced demand quantity. How then should surplus manpower be utilized? Toyota believes that it is better to let extra workers take a rest than to produce unnecessary stock. The following are examples of activities that may be organized during a slack period:

• Transfer workers to other lines for which demand increased.
• Decrease overtime.
• Use a paid holiday.
• Conduct quality control circle meetings.
• Practice set-up actions.
• Conduct maintenance and repair of machines.
• Manufacture improved tools and instruments.
• Conduct plant maintenance and upkeep.
• Manufacture parts previously purchased from suppliers.

Although the most important goal is improving the process to meet demands with a minimum number of workers, Toyota does not consider it necessary to minimize the number of machines. Their theory is to have the required machine capacity for peak demand and hire additional workers (temporary or seasonal) when needed so that effective production capacity can be easily expanded. Most Japanese manufacturing companies, including Toyota, employ many temporary workers.

SMOOTHING EACH MODEL'S PRODUCTION QUANTITY

Smoothing a model's production quantity is an expansion on the idea of smoothing the total production quantity. Realizing that automobiles have thousands of specifications for various combinations of body types (i.e., sedans, hardtops, wagons, etc.), what would happen if the final assembly line produced one body type all day long? For example, consider the efficiency of a final assembly line that produces sedans one day, hardtops the next, and vans the day after that. A preceding process making the parts for sedans would have work to do one day, but not again for two days. The same would be true of the lines dedicated to vans and hardtops. However, if every subassembly line completed its full production capacity of all types of stock every day with no stoppage of operations, the quantity of finished parts would be very large—about three or four times the quantity produced by smoothed production. The waste of overproduction in preceding processes or subassemblies is considerable. It becomes apparent then that smoothing of every model's production quantity is required.

Suppose 16,800 Corollas must be produced in a month which has 20 operating days. Ninety-six hundred sedans (A), 4800 hardtops (B), and 2400 wagons (C) are needed. Under a two-shift operation per day, each shift will have to produce 240 sedans, 120 hardtops, and 60 wagons per day. (See Figure 4.2.) Here, the cycle time is determined by dividing the production volume per shift by 480 minutes. According to this calculation, one product A has to be produced in 2 minutes and one product B in 4 minutes. Thus, on average, one car of any type must be produced in 1.14 minutes.

	Monthly output	Output per shift	Cycle time
A	9,600 units	240 units	2' = 480/240
B	4,800 units	120 units	4' = 480/120
C	2,400 units	60 units	8' = 480/60
	16,800 units/month	420 units/shift	1.14' = 480 min/420 units

Figure 4.2. Smoothing of each model's production quantity and cycle time.

In short, the purpose of smoothing every model's production quantity is to check variances in the flow of each product variety between periods (days). The aim is to level the quantity of parts consumed and produced each period because if great variances existed in the daily consumed quantity of parts of a specified variety, the subassembly lines in question would have to hold huge excess inventories and work force.

Sequence Schedule for Introducing Models

All product varieties can be produced according to the average cycle time of all varieties as long as each model's cycle time is considered when determining the sequence of each model. Figure 4.3 depicts sequence scheduling for the smoothed production of Toyota.

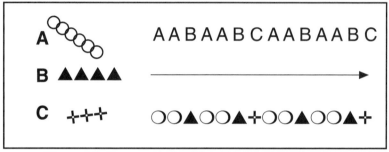

Figure 4.3. Sequence scheduling smoothed production.

Figure 4.4 illustrates lot (batch) production in which production occurs at the line's own peculiar speed, rather than at the speed dictated by market demand. This type of production can cause variances in the necessary volumes of each subassembly part. However, even using lot production, many companies are able to achieve smoothing of production by using a daily production quantity. This is true in plants where the required number of products is conveyed to the retail store once a day as is the delivery of necessary parts to the company. As a result, the amount of parts to be supplied does not change much. Companies that employ lot production will probably never achieve the ultimate in smoothed production—responding to sales velocity of each product sold in the marketplace. To illustrate this point, consider the following example.

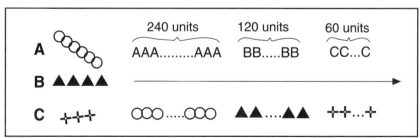

Figure 4.4. Lot (batch) production.

Assuming that the lot production method is being used, suppose a plant introduces the Kanban system and forces its cooperative makers to deliver the necessary parts hourly. Parts makers will suffer from large variances in quantity withdrawn each hour. Unless the quantity becomes constant, the parts makers must prepare extra stock to adapt to the hourly order.

At Toyota, the concept of smoothed production is also applied to the difference in man hours it takes to produce different cars on the same line. Toyota classifies the various cars on a production line by man hours required for each type of product into three groups: large, medium, and small. Each of these groups is further identified by a specific color: red, white, or yellow.

Suppose the man hours needed to produce A, B, and C on the same line are 70 minutes, 50 minutes, and 60 minutes, respectively. If the cars are produced in a certain sequence, i.e., A, B, C, A, B, C, the line would not stop because the average cycle time of this line is 60 minutes. See Figure 4.5. However, if product A (Figure 4.6) is lot produced, this 60-minute cycle time line will not be able to complete it because A needs a 70-minute cycle time. This would cause the line to stop. In order to prevent the line from stopping, the number of workers would have to be increased to complete the work within 70 minutes, the peak operation cycle time.

Man hours can also be smoothed in the same way as is the sequence of vehicles. This point will be explained further in the goal chasing method described in Chapter 16.

Incidentally, what has brought about the smoothing of each model's production quantity is a tendency to produce vehicles corresponding to the diversification of needs in the marketplace. In other words, if the market had not demanded such diversification, smoothing of the total production quantity alone would have satisfied demand changes. Nevertheless, as the diverse specifications production increases, realizing the smoothing of each model's production quantity becomes more difficult.

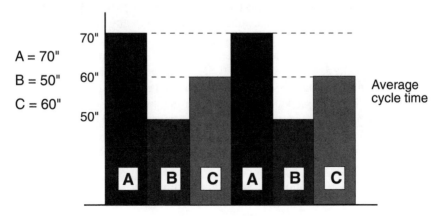

Figure 4.5. Sequence schedule that enables assembly within the average cycle time.

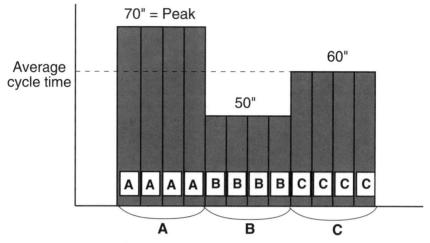

Figure 4.6. Sequence schedule that causes line stoppage.

First of all, as the number of diverse models increases, the number of lots also increases as do setup actions for each preceding process. Conversely, if decreases in frequent setups at preceding processes are desired, the lot sizes would have to be increased at each preceding process and considerable stockpiles of parts inventory would result.

Two Phases of Production Smoothing
Figure 4.7 shows the analysis of the two phases of production smoothing. The first phase shows the adaptation to monthly demand changes during a year (monthly adaptation), and the second phase shows adaptation to daily demand changes during a month (daily adaptation). The first phase, monthly adaptation, will be achieved by monthly production planning—the preparation of a master production schedule instructing the averaged daily production level of each process in the plant. This master production schedule is based on a monthly demand forecast.

The next phase, daily adaptation, is made possible by daily production dispatching. Here, the role of the Kanban system is needed for production smoothing because daily production dispatching can only be achieved by using a pulling system. The Kanban system and sequence schedule provide that system. Only when a sequence schedule is prepared for the mixed-model assembly line can Toyota make smoothed withdrawals from its suppliers and subassemblies.

Details of an information system concerning the monthly production schedule and determining daily production dispatching will be described in Chapter 5.

Flexible Machinery Supporting Smoothed Production
Since production smoothing requires production of many varieties of products on the same line each day, it necessarily gets more complicated and difficult to

achieve as variety is promoted in the marketplace. Fortunately, Toyota has developed facilities to resolve the conflict between market variety and the ideal of production smoothing, i.e., multi-function machines in the line. The exclusive-purpose machine is a powerful means of reducing mass-production costs, but it is not suitable for varied short-run productions. Thus, it is necessary to add minimal apparatus and tools to such exclusive machines, turning them into the type of multi-purpose machines required in Toyota plants.

Another mechanical means for supporting the smoothing of production is the flexible manufacturing system (FMS). Narrowly defined, FMS is an automatic production system consisting of an automatic machining instrument, an automatic conveyance instrument, a material handling instrument, and a microcomputer system which controls these instruments. The FMS's function is to automatically control alteration in specifications, machining time, lot size, etc. by using the production schedule program memorized in the microcomputer.

Introduction of FMS enables a factory to respond to many varieties and short-run productions by means of hardware. However, such progress in hardware can sometimes require significant investment in facilities to support production. In such cases, the system may create some problems for medium and small manufacturers.

COMPARISON OF THE KANBAN SYSTEM WITH MRP

From the viewpoint of adapting production to demand changes during a month, material requirement planning (MRP) and the Kanban system both aim to realize JIT production. MRP is a system which uses bills of material, inventory, open order data, lead time, and master production schedules to calculate requirements for materials.

For the MRP technique, the concept of a *time bucket* is very important. A time bucket is a specifically allotted period of time in which a certain quantity of units must be produced. In a sense, the time bucket concept can be seen in the Kanban system in one day; yet a typical MRP time bucket will entail at least a week. Furthermore, MRP necessitates the *time phasing* concept which requires making up an inter-bucket schedule that dispatches parts to a product by using lead time data.

The Kanban system does not essentially require this time-phasing concept since it is based on smoothed production. However, the delivery cycle must often be considered in determining the number of Kanbans based on the lead time of the production process. (Refer to Figure 2.4 and Chapter 19.) In the case of very short production runs where smoothing of production is very difficult, MRP may be more appropriate.

As seen in Figure 4.7, the Kanban system requires that an overall production schedule be circulated throughout the plant before actual production begins. Such an overall plan in MRP is called a *master schedule*. This master schedule is very

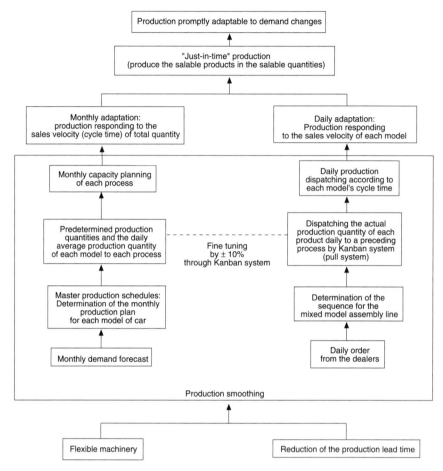

Figure 4.7. Framework of Toyota's production smoothing.

important for MRP because it is a target to be rigorously maintained. In the Kanban system, the overall plan does not strictly target production, but merely sets up a loose framework that prepares the plant-wide arrangement of materials and workers at each process.

Consequently, in the MRP system, a review must be made at the end of every planned production interval—or bucket—that compares planned production with actual performance. If the review discovers a discrepancy between planned and actual performances, remedial action must be taken. Since these are bucket sizes of at least a week, the master schedule must be revised weekly.

The Kanban system does not require any comparisons between planned and actual performance at the end of a production interval, i.e., one day, because such comparisons must necessarily evolve out of the daily actual production process and the daily dispatching of production by Kanban. If the daily production plan—the sequence schedule—requires revision, such revision will be based on the dealer's daily orders and will reflect daily market conditions. Furthermore, since the Kanbans actually flow backward through the plant from the final assembly line to the preceding process, only the final assembly line needs to be notified of any changes in sequence for the entire plant's production to be modified autonomously and in a decentralized way within every process. Hence, the Kanban system is characterized as a *pull system,* while other means of dispatching production information, such as MRP, are characterized as *push systems,* where the push comes from a central planning office.

However, the Kanban system can be compatible with MRP. After MRP creates the master schedule, the Kanban system could be applied as a dispatching tool of production within each bucket. Yamaha Motor Company, Ltd. is employing this system which they have named Pan Yamaha Manufacturing Control (PYMAC).

5

The Information System Between Toyota, Its Dealers, and Parts Manufacturers

In this chapter, the information system which links Toyota to its dealers and parts manufacturers will be examined. The first topic is how dealers transmit sales data to Toyota and how Toyota processes this data. How Toyota informs its suppliers of the parts and materials needed to produce specific vehicles will be discussed next, and lastly, a description of the information system within Nissan Motor Company, which is a rival car manufacturer of Toyota, will be given.

THE ORDER ENTRY INFORMATION SYSTEM

Toyota plans its production in two steps. The first step is preparing a monthly production plan, which consists of a *master production schedule* and a *parts requirement forecast* table. The second step is developing a daily production order after deciding the product delivery schedule and the sequenced schedule of production.

Monthly Production System
Master production schedule and parts requirement forecast. In order to make the master production schedule and the parts requirement forecast, managers create a monthly sales plan. Both domestic and foreign sales departments are involved in this planning. Every month, the domestic sales department receives information estimating the demand for the following three months. The estimates are listed according to models (car model lines) and major specifications. The major model specifications are determined by the combination of different body types, engine sizes, transmission types, grades of models, etc. The foreign sales department also receives estimated demand data from its foreign dealers in the same manner as the domestic sales department.

In addition to this sales data, Toyota managers take into consideration the production capacity of their plants when developing the production plan. First, production smoothing is planned for the most recent month (dividing the total number of cars for each model line by the total number of working days in a month). This is called the *master production schedule.*

The Material Requirement Plan (MRP) is then prepared based on the master production schedule, using a bill of materials. This method is used by all car manufacturers whether they call this process MRP or not. Required materials and parts calculated by MRP are then sent to each Toyota plant and each subcontract parts manufacturer. This is the *parts requirement forecast.* However, as will be discussed later in this chapter, each parts manufacturer is not required to follow this parts requirement forecast for their daily production. Variations in the production order are reflected through Toyota's Kanban system.

Daily Production System
The product delivery schedule and sequence schedule. Toyota's daily production schedule is determined by the product delivery schedule and the sequence schedule. Daily production information is sent from dealers and processed as follows:

1. A 10-day order is sent to Toyota's sales division from dealers.
2. A daily order (daily alteration if necessary) is sent to Toyota's sales division from dealers.
3. Toyota's sales division sends the daily order to Toyota's manufacturing division.
4. A daily sequenced production schedule is created and sent to Toyota plants and suppliers.

These four steps are described in detail below.

Step 1. Each dealer sends Toyota's sales division the 10-day order specifications for each model as ordered by customers, including color and option preferences. The accumulated quantity of three days of the 10-day order cannot exceed the production volume determined by the monthly master production schedule. This 10-day order is sent by computer seven to eight days before the beginning of each 10-day order period (see Figure 5.1). Then, based on the 10-day order, the daily production quantity for each line and each plant is planned. This means modifi-

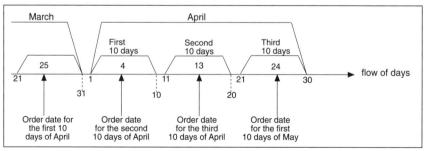

Figure 5.1. 10-day order from the dealer.

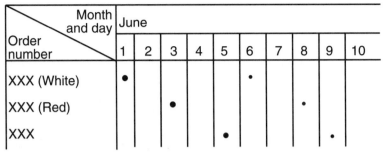

Order number \ Month and day	June									
	1	2	3	4	5	6	7	8	9	10
XXX (White)	●					●				
XXX (Red)			●					●		
XXX					●				●	

Figure 5.2. Delivery schedule.

cation of the master production schedule and an update to the delivery schedule as shown in Figure 5.2.

Step 2. Statistically, Toyota can expect changes to the 10-day order to be in the plus or minus 10 percent range (maximum 23 percent). For example, as Figure 5.2 shows, when receiving the actual order for a white car instead of a red car, Toyota must change its production and delivery schedules from producing a red car to a white car. This process is called *daily alteration* and is done four days before the roll-off of the final product from the assembly line.

Step 3. Toyota sales division's computer system divides dealer orders into categories for different types of models, bodies, engine sizes, transmissions, body colors, etc. The sales division then sends this information to the manufacturing division three days before the roll-off of the final product. It is very important for the manufacturing division to receive this information so that required daily production can be determined.

Step 4. After receiving the daily orders from Toyota's sales division, the manufacturing division prepares the sequenced production schedule for the mixed model assembly line. The final assembly line is informed of the sequenced production schedule only two days before the roll-off of the final product. It should be noted that this sequenced schedule is revised and sent to the assembly line every day. Figure 5.3 illustrates the flow of the order and production information from step 2 to step 4.

The four-step ordering process allows the final product to be rolled off the assembly line just four days after dealers send in their orders. To further facilitate speedy production, Toyota limits the actual production lead time between the welding line and the final assembly line to one day. On the other hand, delivery and shipping lead times vary because of differences in the geographical locations of dealers.

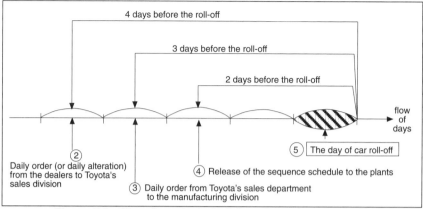

Figure 5.3. Steps from dealer's daily order to the car roll-off.

The Sequenced Production Schedule

All workers in the final assembly line only need to know what kind of car they are to assemble. To obtain this information, computer printers and displays are installed at the final assembly line. The sequenced production schedule determines the order of models to be assembled and is sent from the central computer to the printers and displays in an on-line real time manner. Printers are used for the sequenced production schedule because printed documents are needed at the final assembly line. In other assembly functions where a written document is not needed, only displays are used.

In addition to this information, the computer terminals provide specification labels which are attached to the car body. Each worker in the final assembly line can build the exact specification of each model demanded by using parts described on the label. Other parts assembly lines and suppliers who produce large unit parts, such as engines or transmissions, also use the label and sequenced production schedule to facilitate sequenced withdrawal of parts. The remaining lines, such as the casting line, machining line, etc., as well as suppliers, use Kanbans (*later replenishment system*) to control their production quantities.

On-Line System at the Distribution Stage

For the automobile manufacturer, reduction of the overall lead time—from reception of customer orders at the dealer to the distribution of a car to the customer—is crucial in order to meet the customer's satisfaction. This is partially done by reducing the dealer order processing time.

Before Toyota installed a computer system, dealers sent both 10-day orders and daily alterations to Toyota by telex. With this system, it took at least three weeks, and sometimes as much as two months, for dealers to receive the cars they ordered.

Toyota developed its current on-line system which enables it to reduce the ordering process and promptly respond to customers' demands. Toyota's dealer network system uses a new fiber optic cable route that was installed throughout Japan by Japan's leading domestic phone company, NTT. This system links the mainframe of Toyota's head office and Nagoya branch office (Toyota's sales division) with terminals at every dealership. Initially, this network system was installed only among the four major Japanese Toyota sales companies (Tokyo Toyopet, Osaka Toyopet, Aichi Toyota Motor, and Kanagawa Toyota Motors). In January 1968, when Toyota began to produce its luxury car, "Crown," it initiated an ordering process using the on-line system, and gradually expanded this system throughout the country.

This system has three types of functions: real-time processing, file transmission, and electronic mailing. To utilize these functions at dealerships that had different computer systems, Toyota developed and installed a business protocol at each dealer which allowed for Open System Interconnection (OSI).

Using the network system, Toyota was able to improve its operations in many areas. First, Toyota now knows inventory information at all dealers, and dealers can move stock to other dealers as required. Second, Toyota can apply a flexible delivery schedule in that it can quickly change the delivery destination as required. For example, automobiles to be shipped to dealer A can easily be shipped to dealer B instead. Third, Toyota can inform the dealers which model is in high demand and which model is not. By providing this information, Toyota can advise dealers of their purchase plan. This procedure is similar to a point of sale (POS) system, which is used in supermarkets and department stores. The C90 office at Toyota is in charge of communication between dealers and Toyota.

THE INFORMATION SYSTEM BETWEEN TOYOTA AND PARTS MANUFACTURERS

Parts Requirement Forecast Table

Toyota sends a three-month production schedule, called a *parts requirement forecast table,* to its parts suppliers. Information about actual parts supplied during the most recent month is provided as a final forecast and recorded on a daily basis. The forecast for the remaining two months is estimated. (Figure 5.4 does not show the two-month forecast because of space limitations.)

In all likelihood, these estimates will change from day-to-day. Additionally, the actual production volume is sometimes increased or decreased from the volume depicted in the forecast table. These adjustments to the production forecast are made via the Kanban system as a fine-tuning measure.

The quantity of different parts to be supplied is projected in the parts requirement forecast table shown in Figure 5.4. As a specific example, the instructions for part C follow:

To supplier XXXX

PARTS REQUIREMENT FORECAST (FOR MAY)   Prepared April 22, 1992

Parts	Delivery Cycle			Number of Kanban	Difference with the Former Time	Number of part box per day (10 units/box)									Requirement Forecast for May
	day	times	later			Day 1	2	3	6	7	Day 8	29	30	Day 31	
A	1	14	3	4	-1	8	8	0	8	8	8	8	8	8	1,718
B	1	14	3	3	0	6	5	0	5	5	5	5	5	4	1,020
C	1	10	2	3	-1	7	7	0	7	7	7	7	7	7	1,600
D	1	14	2	19	3	44	44	0	45	44	44	44	44	44	9,761
E	1	14	3	2	-1	5	5	0	5	5	5	5	5	5	1,141
F	1	10	2	1	0	1	0	0	0	0	1	1	0	0	94

Figure 5.4. Parts Requirement Forecast Table.

• Estimated quantities.
  – Total quantity to be withdrawn in May = 1,600
  – Total quantity to be withdrawn in June = 1,600*
  – Total quantity to be withdrawn in July = 1,700*

  * Forecasted quantities for June and July are not shown. The total quantity to be withdrawn in May is a finally determined number provided the adjustment by the Kanban system during the current production is excluded.

• Parts per box. Each box contains ten parts.

• Quantity of boxes per day. The number of boxes to be supplied daily in May is indicated. Note that in May the supplier's daily production of part C is a smoothed (constant) number of boxes per day, where

$$\left(\frac{\text{Total number withdrawn in May} = 1,600}{\text{The number of parts/box} = 10} \right) \times \left(\frac{1}{\text{Total working days} = 22} \right)$$

  = 7 boxes per day

• Kanban information:
  – Delivery frequency of Kanbans. Kanbans are delivered ten times a day, and finished parts should be delivered to Toyota two delivery times after the supplier has received the Kanbans. Therefore, the delivery cycle of parts C is 1-10-2.

  – Number of Kanbans. This specifies the total number of Kanbans used for the part by Toyota. For item C, three Kanbans are used.

  – Differences with the former time. For part C, Kanbans are delivered every other delivery time. A difference of "-1" means that at delivery time *t*, the parts corresponding to two kanbans are supplied. But at point in time *t+2*, parts corresponding to only one Kanban are supplied (see Figure 5.5).

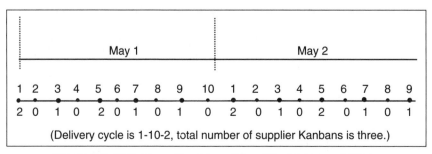

Figure 5.5. Delivery cycle and number of Kanbans per delivery.

Network System Within Toyota Group Using VAN
Using VAN, a network system has been built between Toyota and the major suppliers in the Toyota group, such as Nippon Denso, Toyota Fabric, and Toyota Automatic Loom Works. This network is called TNS-S. Recently, Toyota built an on-line network to communicate with outside contract automobile body makers, such as Toyota Body, Kanto Auto, and Daihatsu Motor.

The communication link within Toyota groups using VAN allows the parts requirement forecast table and the sequenced production schedule to be sent through the computer system. In addition, Toyota's assembly plants can send the sequenced production schedule to in-house engine plants through a telecommunications line.

The system also solved the problem that outside body makers had because they were unable to send timely information through the old computer system to a parts maker who was also a Toyota contractor. The system allows Toyota and the outside body maker to send parts requirement information simultaneously to parts manufacturers.

The Parts Distribution System
This communication networks is actually Toyota's Strategic Information System (SIS), also called the Toyota Network System (TNS), and consists of the following six subsystems:

1. TNS-D—Network between Toyota and dealers.
2. TNS-B—Network between Toyota and body makers.
3. TNS-S—Network between Toyota and suppliers.
4. New ALC system—The New Assembly Line Control System which is a portion of Toyota's in-house CIM, which will be described in Chapter Six.
5. Information System at sales companies.
6. TNS-O—Network between Toyota and overseas plants and dealers.

By having this information network, Toyota can adapt to the market demand very quickly as a whole synchronous organization whose members are the automaker (Toyota), dealers (domestic and overseas), suppliers and body makers, etc. In other words, Toyota can respond to the changes in market demands (in terms of preferences of customers, products, variety, and quantity, etc.) in each stage of development—sales, manufacturing, and parts purchasing.

Recently, a transportation company opened a warehouse between Toyota and its parts suppliers. This warehouse functions as a distribution center, and every part demanded by Kanban is distributed from its stock on an hourly basis. The inventory in this distribution center is only for one to two days consumption. It is important to mention that the warehouse stores parts from various parts suppliers. The warehouse functions like a dam, where water from various small streams (parts makers) is pooled for one to two days consumption, and then poured as a mixed load into one big stream (Toyota) on an hourly basis. Figure 5.6 describes

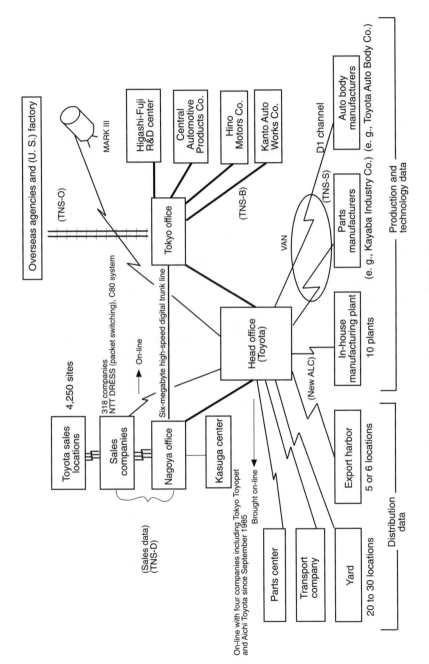

5.6. Strategic Information System (SIS) of Toyota.

the whole information network system among Toyota, its dealers, parts manufacturers, body makers, etc.

PRODUCTION PLANNING SYSTEM IN NISSAN

Nissan has a production planning system which is very similar to Toyota's (see Figure 5.7). The system consists of production planning for domestic and export sales. Production planning for domestic sales will be the focus here.

First, Nissan develops annual and semi-annual production plans. For example, total production volume for its Blue Bird model is determined based on the company's profit plan or sales plan which is based on manager's sales forecasts.

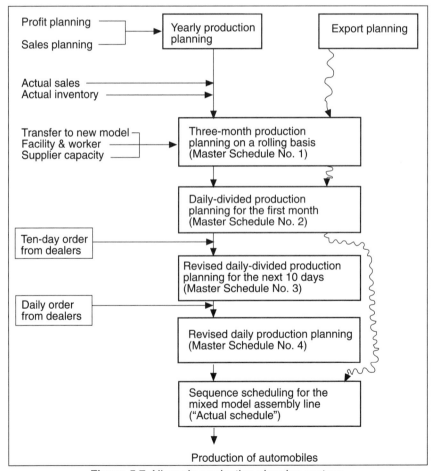

Figure 5.7. Nissan's production planning system.

Next, a three-month production plan, called a *Master Schedule No. 1,* is developed. Production plan information on Master Schedule No. 1 is estimated based on the actual sales volume and the inventory levels of the prior period, and considers the feasibility of using new technologies, facilities, work forces, and parts suppliers. This schedule also takes into consideration the monthly demand forecast data from dealerships.

One month before a big seasonal demand, such as March (the season of personnel transfers) or July (the month of bonus payments), the plants have to produce additional automobiles for the following month's increased sales, in addition to the demand for the current month. This type of planned inventory is also included in Master Schedule No. 1.

Master Schedule No. 2 contains the daily production volume of the most recent month of the three-month production schedule. (Total production volume of the most recent month divided by the total working days in the month.)

Based on this plan, the required work force for production is allocated to each production process. The total necessary work force is calculated, and an overtime work schedule (if needed) is determined. Then, an allocation of the available work force for each operating day is performed. Once this work schedule is determined, it cannot be changed during the month since the total production volume is fixed by Master Schedule No. 1. The above production plans are based on sales forecast studied by Nissan.

After these steps, dealers contribute important data for production planning. Dealers send the 10-day orders outlining demand for color options, etc. This 10-day order includes sales forecasts and final demand by customers. Combining the 10-day order and the Master Schedule No. 2, Nissan makes *Master Schedule No. 3.* Since the 10-day order in essence acts as an adjustment function to the three-month sales forecast, Master Schedule No. 3 cannot differ much from Master Schedule No. 2.

Next, each dealer sends a daily order alteration which adjusts the 10-day order previously sent to Nissan from the dealers. For most models, the range of the adjustment should be maintained at about 20 to 50 percent. However, there are some models which dealers can change without limitation. In this regard, Nissan seems to have a superior system to Toyota because by their flexibility in accepting order changes, Nissan's production can be closer to their customers' needs. Nissan receives the daily order alteration four days before the end of the assembly period.

Information included in the daily order alterations is used to develop *Master Schedule No. 4,* the daily production schedule. Based on this daily production schedule, Nissan estimates necessary parts using MRP, and submits orders to their parts suppliers. This is the most different aspect of Nissan's system when compared to Toyota's system because Toyota estimates parts based on a Kanban system.

Finally, the actual schedule is provided daily to the assembly line to determine the sequence of the models to be produced. Figure 5.7 illustrates how the four master schedules are related. Also as Figure 5.7 shows, the production schedule for exported cars does not require steps 3 and 4. The different geographic locations of export destinations and the associated lead time for delivery precludes exact adjustments to the production schedule.

Nissan's Ordering Systems From Parts Suppliers
Nissan sends four different types of information to its suppliers. This information is an *estimate* calculated in accordance with the four master schedules mentioned before (see Figure 5.8, part 1). The *actual* delivery order follows using four forms of production orders (see Figure 5.8, part 2).

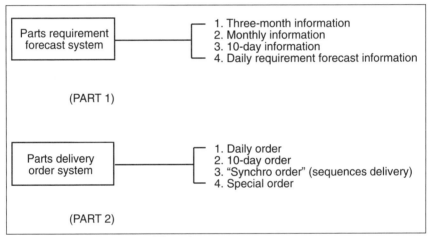

Figure 5.8. Nissan's parts procurement system.

Daily Order. At Nissan, daily delivery is adopted for 80 percent of the parts supply items. The daily parts order is made one day after dealers send daily order alternations (four days before the final roll off). With this system, all necessary parts are delivered to the plants four days before the beginning of trim-in.

After receiving daily order alterations, Nissan determines its final daily production schedule. Then, using the daily production schedule and MRP, each necessary part is ordered. Toyota has implemented its decentralized production system with a pull-through system using the Kanban. Since each part's production is controlled by Kanban, centralized production control is unnecessary during the month. On the other hand, at Nissan, all delivery order planning is made in the central office. The central office calculates the necessary parts to order using MRP and sends this information to its parts suppliers. Usually, daily orders are delivered eight separate times each day.

10-Day Order. Followed by the 10-day production schedule (Master Schedule No. 3), the 10-day parts supply order is used to order small parts, in particular, standardized common parts necessary for North American transplants. Also, for some very small suppliers, who may not have computer terminals, the 10-day order is used instead of the daily delivery order because frequent communication through the computer system is required.

Synchronized Order. The synchronized supply order has the same function as the sequenced production schedule used by Toyota. It determines the sequence of various parts to the assembly line. Information about the type of parts necessary for a specific car is provided on the label (*broadcast*) of the car in the trimming line. The same information is sent simultaneously to the parts suppliers.

It is ideal for the parts suppliers to deliver required parts to Nissan plants just before Nissan's workers use the last part in the storage. Because each parts supplier delivers its product every hour (16 times a day), the average inventory level in the Nissan plant is about the volume of 30 minutes consumption. Also, the parts delivered by synchronized order are delivered directly to the assembly lines instead of being delivered to the parts warehouse or to parts inspectors. The total through-put time is about four to six hours after each car is conveyed to the trimming line. However, because the synchronized order is placed at the time of the trim-in, this system is not available for parts, which are distributed from suppliers who are located a considerable distance from Nissan's plant. For the synchronized order system to be effective, each parts supplier has to be located relatively close to the Nissan's plants.

Special Order. The special order is a system that places orders on a monthly basis. This system is used primarily for models that are not in high demand. For instance, only 80 President model cars (Nissan's luxury model) are produced each month, which is an average of four per day. Because of the limited number of vehicles produced, Nissan does not allow daily dealer alterations for this model. Consequently, parts orders are placed monthly and are not updated on a daily basis as with other models.

6
Computer Control System in an Automobile Factory

CENTRALIZED CONTROL SYSTEM AND DECENTRALIZED CONTROL SYSTEM

An assembly line of automobiles consists of a body-welding process, a painting process, an assembly process, and a detection process. To control these processes, a *centralized control system* and a *decentralized control system* have been established. The following section discusses the problems of the former and the necessity of the latter.

The centralized control system in Toyota's assembly line has terminals (printers, card readers, sequencers, robots, etc.) at every body-welding, painting, and final assembly process. Each terminal is linked directly to an upper-layer computer on a line direct linking system. This upper-layer computer controls the operations of all the terminals. Therefore, the load on the upper-layer computer's central processing unit (CPU) becomes very high. Installing just one more new terminal may require re-examining the entire computer system. Sometimes, the installation of a new terminal is inadvisable. For instance, if the performance of the existing stable system becomes ineffective after installation of a new terminal, it is considered infeasible to install this additional terminal.

The introduction of new automatic machines, robots, and micro-computer systems, for the goal of automating an assembly line, must often be abandoned due to the difficulty in connecting with the upper-layer computer. If the introduction of these new terminals is realized, it will likely become a local stand-alone operation, and the total coordinated automation in the factory will not be accomplished.

With this in mind, Japanese motor companies are currently adopting a more flexible system allowing for easy expansion of a computer system within a factory. This decentralized control system has the flexibility to adapt promptly, not only to diversification of specifications, but also to the many developments of new products or model changes.

The decentralized control system (or *diversified autonomous control system*) makes it possible to easily expand an assembly line control system. Under this control system, the upper-layer computer can concentrate on management of the entire factory by controlling the line computers located at each process: body-welding, painting, and the final assembly process. Also, the line computers at each process will control the terminals at each process.

The decentralized control system may be considered as a hierarchical control system. The upper-layer computer coordinates several of its subsystems, while the subsystems' computers themselves control other subsystems autonomously.

STRUCTURE OF A HIERARCHICAL DECENTRALIZED CONTROL SYSTEM

As described in the previous section, the decentralized control system coordinates subsystems while maintaining the autonomy of each subsystem. This can be called a *hierarchical decentralized control system* or *harmonious decentralized control system.*

Kanto Auto Works, Inc., a member of the Toyota Group, has the following hierarchical control system which is also illustrated in Figure 6.1.

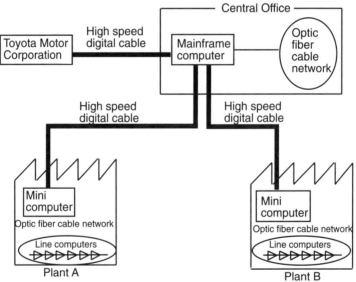

Figure 6.1. Hierarchical decentralized control system and company-wide network.

1. A *host computer* for clerical calculations is installed at the central office and is connected by high speed digital cable to mini computers in every plant.

2. The *mini computer,* used for production control in each plant, is joined to respective work stations installed in the body-welding, painting, and assembly process by means of an optic fiber cable.

3. The *work station*, or *line computer,* for each process works as the production line control system. This line computer is connected with card readers, printers, robots, and Andon, etc., through a *line controller PC* located at each workplace.

This case has been introduced by H. Takahashi and H. Kubota of Kanto Auto Works (1990). Toyota also has a similar system which will be discussed later. An overview of the hierarchical control system functions, described above, is shown in Figure 6.2. The functions of a line computer are illustrated in Figure 6.3 (Y. Okada and T. Sasaki 1986).

Each plant within this company has an Assembly Line Control (ALC) room equipped with a mini computer. An assembly sequence schedule and a file on each car's specifications (specs) is transmitted daily to the mini computer from a host computer at the central office. The mini computer sends daily production plan data to the line computer at each process. After receiving the production plan data, each line computer controls its operations autonomously (without relying on the mini computer in the ALC room). Only information about completed items in each process is transmitted in real time to the upper level mini computer. The following section covers actual control conditions in each process, step by step, in the body-welding, painting, assembly, and detection check processes.

Control System for the Body-Welding Process
The body-welding process work station gives instructions for beginning operations according to a sequence schedule of models. At the same time, a card printer issues a *body identification number card* which is then hung on each auto body. The data on the card is read by a card reader installed in the process. The card reader accesses the file on the line computer to retrieve the auto body's specifications. This will be transmitted to a line controller at the workplace as an operation instruction. The card reader also collects data about completed items at each welding line.

A magnetic card printer is installed at the beginning of the body line and prints a magnetic card containing instructions from the line computer (Figure 6.4). The magnetic card with the body type I.D. number is attached to the auto body at the beginning of the line. This is not a Kanban but a card with a magnetized portion on the lower part, like a passenger train ticket used for an automatic ticket-examining machine. When the card is inserted into the card reader at the end of each process, a control room operator can recognize immediately which process was being performed at that moment, through a display on the computer.

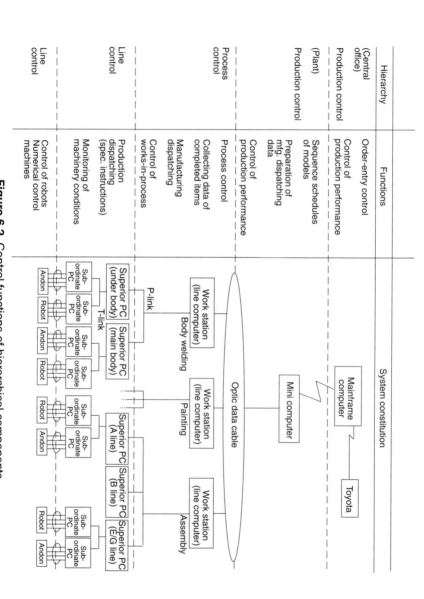

Hierarchy	Functions	System constitution
(Central office)	Order-entry control	
Production control	Control of production performance	
(Plant)	Sequence schedules of models	
Production control	Preparation of mfg. dispatching data	
	Control of production performance	
Process control	Process control	
	Collecting data of completed items	
	Manufacturing dispatching	
	Control of works-in-process	
Line control	Production dispatching (spec. instructions)	
	Monitoring of machinery conditions	
Line control	Control of robots Numerical control machines	

Figure 6.2. Control functions of hierarchical components.

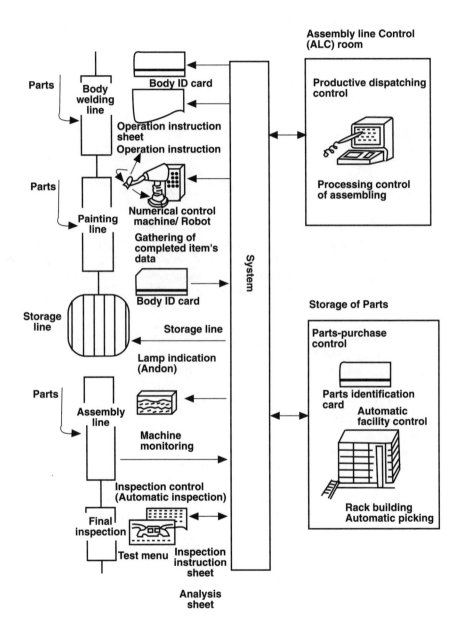

Figure 6.3. Functions of a line computer at each process.

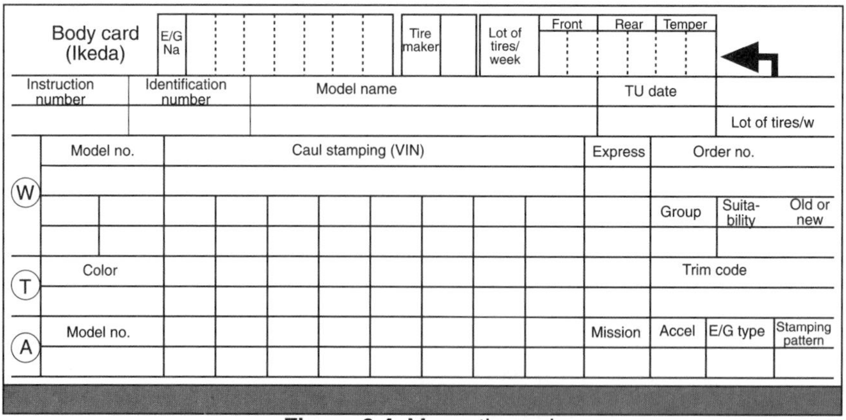

Body card (Ikeda)	E/G Na						Tire maker	Lot of tires/ week	Front	Rear	Temper	◀
Instruction number	Identification number	Model name							TU date			
												Lot of tires/w
	Model no.	Caul stamping (VIN)						Express		Order no.		
(W)									Group	Suita-bility	Old or new	
(T)	Color								Trim code			
(A)	Model no.							Mission	Accel	E/G type	Stamping pattern	

Figure 6.4. Magnetic card.

At the same time, the body-welding line computer controls equipment through a line controller PC at the workplace. This equipment control enables welding machines to automatically select necessary parts as they are needed in accordance with the sequence schedule. These parts are then carried to the line. The control also includes the automatic changeover (automatic setup) of welding equipment on the line.

Control System for the Painting Process

In the painting process a card reader is connected with each line computer. This machine reads the card and prints an operation instruction sheet for workers at the workplace. In addition to the magnetic card, a card-like wireless instrument, called an *I.D. card* (identification card), has been used to detect the actual passage of each body in each line of the painting process. Since the I.D. card has greater memory capacity than the magnetic card, Toyota has been using it in the painting line and also in the assembly line where it is called an *I.D. tag.*

The I.D. card number corresponds to the auto body I.D. number. The I.D. card can inform, on a real time basis, which painting procedure the auto body has completed. The I.D. card is heat resistant and is not adversely affected by the painting process. When painting is completed, an operator switches the I.D. card off so that it will stop sending a message. The I.D. card is also used to control the automatic machines and painting robots according to the specs of each auto body.

The following are two types of model sequence controls that are also conducted: the first model sequence control is a body-entry-and-exit control in a storage line installed between a middle-painting process and an over-painting process. At this point, the auto bodies exiting from the middle-painting process are placed in order so that all auto bodies to be painted the same color will successively enter the over-painting process. This minimizes both wasted paint and loss of time due to setups each time the paint color is changed.

The second model sequence control is also a body-entry-and-exit control in the painted-body storage line located at the end of the painting process. At this stage the balance of assembly time is considered and the previous sequence of auto bodies is altered to allow for the optimum entry into the final assembly line. Toyota is, at this point, applying expert systems using a set of rules concerning the "Succession and Interval Control" rules that will be discussed in Chapter 17.

If an auto body is poorly painted, it is rejected and kept aside. Consequently, the model sequence in the painting line is likely to be out of order, and an auto body that is to be painted again, as in the case of a two-tone color, will disrupt the order. Thus, it is best to determine the sequence for these situations when the order has been completed and the painted auto bodies are suspended in the air waiting for introduction into the assembly line. This final order may still be rescheduled prior to entering the assembly line due to insertion of painted auto body inventory stocked in the storage line.

For processes that have rework due to imperfections, a new sequence schedule is required. At the stage of suspending a painted body, the confirmed final sequence schedule is transmitted to the ALC room where the sequence schedule is then transmitted to the engine and seat factories. Prompt transmittal of this information is important because subsequent processes happen very quickly. For instance, in an assembly line, it usually takes about two and one-half hours for the auto body to arrive at the point of engine installation.

Control System for the Assembly Line
When an auto body is put on the assembly line, the card on the body is read and an *operation instruction label* (also called a trim-parts instruction sheet) is printed out. Information about assembly specs of each model is electronically recorded in the form of images (pictures or symbols) rather than the English alphabet. A sheet of image information (operation instruction label) for each auto body is provided to the assembly line in the production sequence. This enables even a new-hire to manage operations in the assembly line. Figure 6.5 is an illustration of an operation instruction label at the engine assembly line of Kubota, Inc.

This instruction label is attached to the edge of the car hood. All operators at each process must work in accordance with the instructions on the label. (See also Figure 2.17.)

Since an auto assembly line consists of almost one hundred processes, it is impossible to write on one sheet of labels the complete information of all processes. Thus, various labels are printed at several points along the line. At the same time, operation instruction labels are issued to subassembly lines, such as an engine assembly line, a tire assembly line, and a seat assembly line, in a synchronized manner with the main assembly line.

In addition to operation instruction labels, specifications are also conveyed by lamps located on part shelves. These lamps are activated through a *multiplex electric transmission loop* which is a PC network connected with a work station

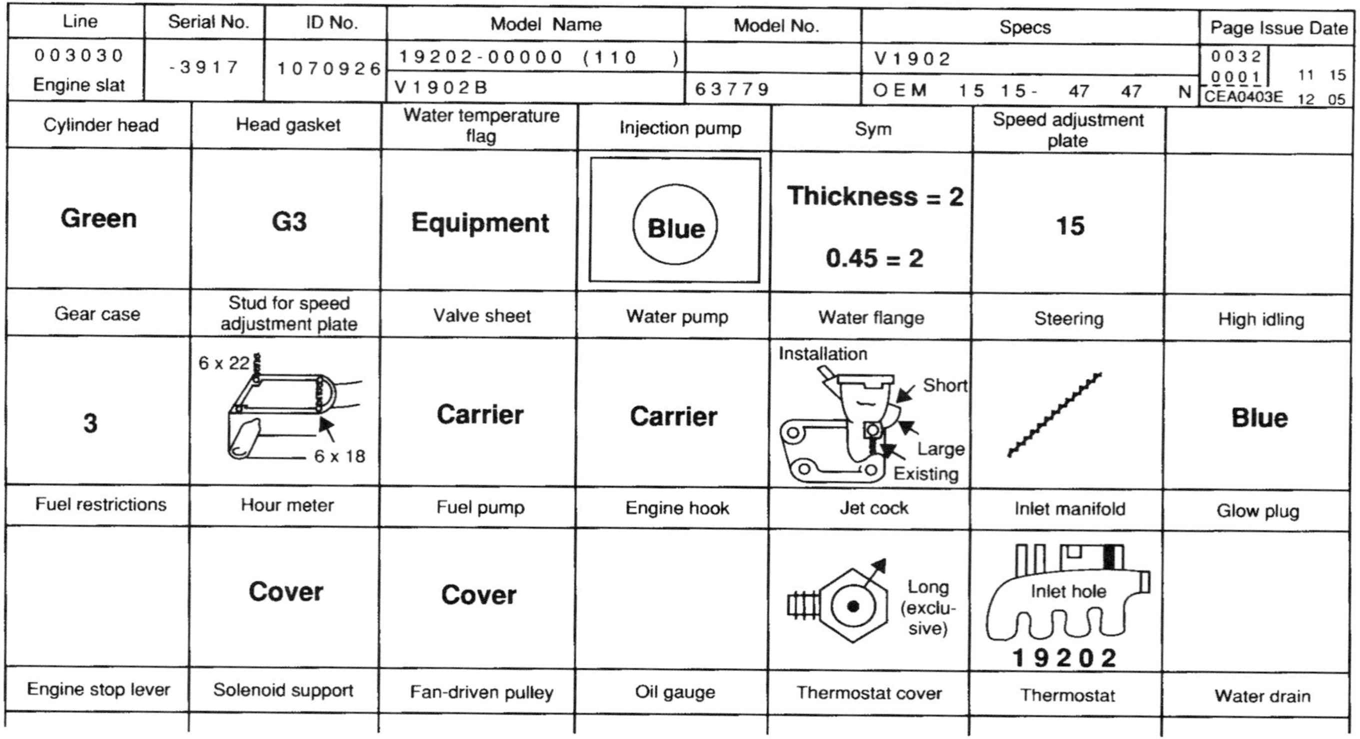

Figure 6.5. Operation instruction sheet.

Line	Serial No.	ID No.	Model Name	Model No.	Specs	Page	Issue	Date
003030	-3917	1070926	19202-00000 (110　)	63779	V1902	0032		
Engine slat			V1902B		OEM V1902 15 15- 47 47 N	0001	11	15
						CEA0403E	12	05

Cylinder head	Head gasket	Water temperature flag	Injection pump	Speed adjustment plate
Green	G3	Equipment	(Blue)	Thickness = 2 0.45 = 2 15
3	Cover Cover	Carrier	Carrier	
Gear case	Stud for speed adjustment plate (6 x 22, 6 x 18)	Valve sheet	Water pump	Water flange — Installation: Short / Large Existing / Long (exclusive) Steering High idling
Fuel restrictions	Hour meter	Fuel pump	Engine hook	Jet cock Inlet manifold Glow plug
Engine stop lever	Solenoid support	Fan-driven pulley	Oil gauge	Thermostat cover Thermostat (Inlet hole 19202, Blue) Water drain

Figure 6.5. Operation instruction sheet. (Source: p. 37 of Takahashi, M. "Mixed Production of Truckter Factory," *Kojokanri,* Vol. 35, No. 1. Jan. 1989)

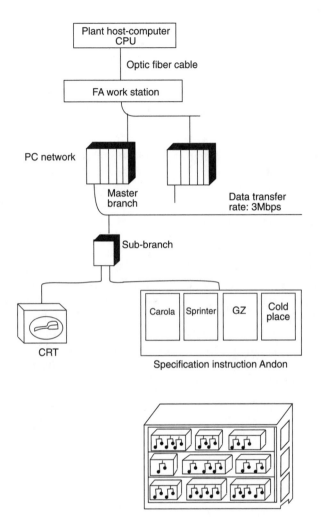

	Specification instruction Andon	
	CRT display	Specification instruction Andon
Outline	Colors, shapes, part, etc. are displayed on the CRT.	Lamp display showing body type, specs, and parts of a specified car.
	1 place	33 places

Figure 6.6. Production dispatching through Andon.

at the assembly process. The loop is constructed by a master-node unit and many sub-node units (10 to 200) joined in a row with one twisted wire. As various lamps are switched on, operators are instructed which parts to select. Also, through the loop, gasoline and engine oil are provided by an automatic machine according to each specification. The Andon is also informed of the specification through this loop (see Figure 6.6). The Andon is used not only for the purpose of detecting trouble but also for giving specs to workers.

Functions of ALC Rooms in Plant and Central Office
It has previously been mentioned that a host computer (mini computer) is placed in the ALC room of a plant and is connected to the work station of each process through a local area network (LAN) by an optic fiber cable. In the ALC room, access is always available to actual passed items of various processes. These can be observed on the display in the ALC room. Any revision of a production dispatching plan is transmitted from the ALC room to line computers at the respective processes (see Figure 6.7).

The mainframe host computer in the central office is informed of both the final detection data and the actual passed items of each process in real time from a plant host computer (mini computer). This information is transmitted to and memorized by the mainframe computer in a batch-processed format.

This central host computer is connected with the production management division, the executive room, and the production technology division through an LAN within the central office (Figure 6.8).

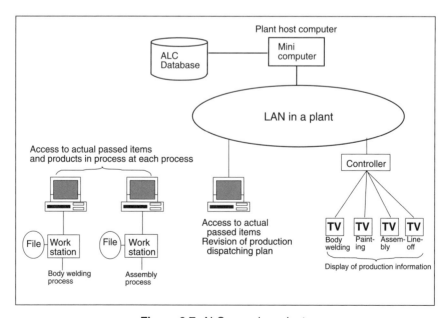

Figure 6.7. ALC room in a plant.

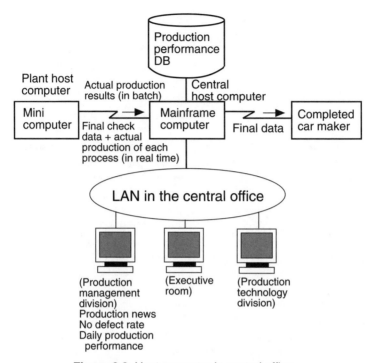

Figure 6.8. Host computer in central office.

NEW ALC SYSTEM AT TOYOTA

The centralized assembly line control system Toyota installed in 1966 was eventually transformed to the hierarchical style described in the beginning of this chapter. In 1989, Toyota introduced the new ALC (Assembly Line Control) System in the Tahara plant and has expanded this system to all their plants. (Many of the points below are attributed to the 1990 report by Fukumoto of Toyota.)

The new ALC System is a decentralized hierarchical system which places great emphasis on two basic concepts of the Toyota production system:

1. Flexibility and expansion of the system, and
2. Just-in-time delivery of production information in response to plant needs based on the pull system.

Initially, the central office installed a large IBM host computer which performed as a data bank, controlling and saving company wide production information. For example, the mixed model sequence schedule is determined and stored in the data bank. This enables a smoothed withdrawal of parts, alteration and cancellation of the schedule, and the gathering of production performance data. The host computer is always ready to respond in a timely manner to requests for information from the plant. The central office also conducts other related systems, such as accounting, cost accounting, budget control, and quality control.

Toyota is adopting the Fujitsu FACOM A-50 and A-60 as plant host computers. The FACOM A-50, called Gateway, receives sequence schedule information from an IBM central host computer through cables and then converts and transmits this information to the FACOM A-60, a file server. The file server requests the production information from the central host computer, and also controls the progress of the cars at each process in the plant.

At Toyota, the role of each processes' line computer is extremely autonomous. An I.D. tag requesting production information from the file server is attached to the cart of a vehicle on the line. The file server writes the information on the I.D. tag through an I.D. writer positioned on the line so the vehicle and its production information are united. The most significant and unique feature of Toyota's new ALC System is that exchanges of information are carried out in a pull system manner, so that each plant, line, and process can always utilize the necessary information at the necessary time.

As the vehicle flows on the line, an antenna on the line reads its I.D. tag at the necessary points. Robots and automatic machines are properly assigned the production instructions for the vehicle by means of the line controller. Toyota's new ALC System is illustrated in Figure 6.9.

New ALC System Development

At Toyota, several divisions have systematically organized project teams and promoted development of the new ALC System. These are the Information System Division, F.A. System Department of the Production Technology Division, Inspection Division, Facilities Division, and Plant Manufacturing Division (Figure 6.10).

The Information System Division and the F.A. System Department of the Production Technology Division played chief roles; the former engaged in building the functions of a central host computer and each plant host computer, while the latter contributed to the introduction of terminal robots and automatic machines. The Inspection Division participated in the area of quality assurance, and the Plant Manufacturing Division dispatched a member of the Production Management Department at the conception building stage. The project team was composed of section chiefs from each of these divisions and people from Fujitsu were asked to participate as special partners.

As seen in Figure 6.11, as soon as the designing policy was determined, the Tahara plant was chosen and asked to be a pilot model plant. After receiving their informal okay, the endorsement of top management was obtained through a formal "Ringi" procedure (i.e., circulation of the signature approval documents among the top executives). Initial endorsement and cheerleading came from those

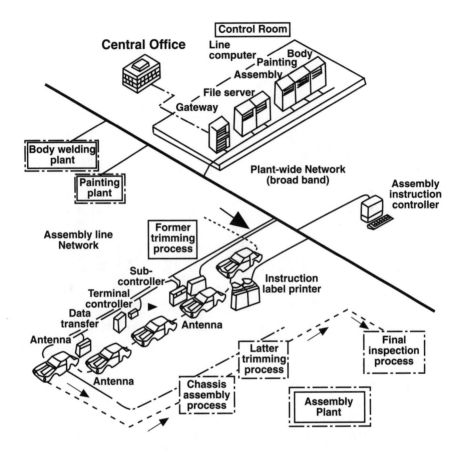

Figure 6.9. The new ALC system.

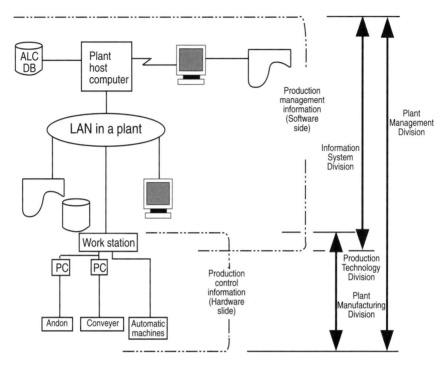

Figure 6.10. Apportionment of system development functions.

who were at the forefront of controlling the system because they feared they would not be able to adapt to plant needs if the company were to remain as it was.

Finally, a mention of the relationship between the system described in this chapter and computer-integrated manufacturing (CIM) is in order. The computer control system introduced here is composed of computer-aided manufacturing (CAM) which gives instructions to the automatic processing and assembly machines and computer-aided planning (CAP) which designates production schedule information. Computer-aided design (CAD) is also applied to product design, process design, and process layout. CAM, CAP, and CAD are all integral components of the overall computer integrated manufacturing system utilized by Toyota.

▷ Phase I ... Pilot study plant: Tahara plant
　　Step 1 ... establish basic system
　　Step 2 ... improvement of system functions and its extensions to the whole plant

		Information System Division	Production Technology Division	Inspection Division	Mfg. Division	Facilities Division
'88		4 Suggestion of promoting the automation				
	Step 1	5 Determination of reconstruction policy				
					7 Pre-negotiation to the plant	
		8 In-house authorization				
		11 Launching the project including computer-makers				
'89	Step 2	5 Introduction to Lexus line				
		8 Introduction to Celica line				
'90		11 Step 1 Evaluation and development plan				
		12 Extension to the whole plant				

▷ Phase II ... Introduction to the other plants

Figure 6.11. Promotion schedule.

7

How Toyota Shortened
Production Lead Time

FOUR ADVANTAGES OF SHORTENING LEAD TIME

Promptly adapting to meet the actual daily demand for various kinds of automobiles is the purpose of Just-in-time (JIT) production. Also, production of various products and parts must be scheduled in a constant quantity every day to stabilize the daily work at Toyota's plants and their part suppliers. Having the flexibility to respond to market demand and the stability of smoothed production requires shortening of the production lead time (the time interval from production dispatching to delivery of completed products).

Furthermore, a 10 percent discrepancy exists between production quantities ordered by the predetermined monthly plan and the quantities dispatched daily by Kanban and the sequence schedule. This discrepancy may cause problems such as excessive inventory or work force. To prevent the occurrence of such problems, Toyota must start production immediately when a dealer's order is received. Suppliers especially must command rapid means of production, once the order arrives. If they try to anticipate demand by producing parts in advance of receiving an order, they stand to suffer from having a surplus of inventory at month's end. Of course, production on such short notice requires a remarkable shortening of lead time so that an engine cast at 8 a.m., for example, will be ready for installation in a finished car rolling off the assembly line at 5 p.m.

The following advantages can be attributed to this shortening of the production lead time:

- Toyota can achieve a job-order oriented production that requires only a short period to deliver a particular car to the customer.
- The company can adapt very quickly to changes in demand in the middle of the month, so the inventory of finished products maintained by Toyota's sales division can be minimized.
- Work-in-process inventory can be significantly decreased by minimizing unbalanced production timing among the various processes and also by reducing the lot size.

• When a model change is introduced, the amount of "dead" stock on hand is minimal.

The production lead time of any product, assuming production takes place in a multi-process factory, consists of three components: processing time for supply lots, waiting time between processes, and conveyance time between processes. How Toyota minimizes the time required for each of these components is the main topic of this chapter, but before discussing this problem let us first examine these components.

COMPONENTS OF PRODUCTION LEAD TIME IN A NARROW SENSE

In a narrow sense, the lead time consists of queue time before processing, setup time, run time, wait time after processing, and move time. The components of production lead time are shown in Figure 7.1.

Figure 7.2 illustrates the relationship between these components in a multi-process production. Using process 2 in Figure 7.2 as an example, queue time before processing (B_2) is the time span that workers or materials have to wait before processing. Wait time after processing(I_2) is the time that inventory must wait before being conveyed to the next process. Although there are two types of wait times, let's regard both of them as the same for the time being. Also, let's regard the setup time plus the run time (P_2) as processing time in a general sense. As such, the components of production lead time could be narrowed down further into three categories: processing time of products, wait time, and move time.

To achieve ideal JIT production, each of these components should be shortened. Figure 7.3 shows how the respective components of production lead time can be shortened.

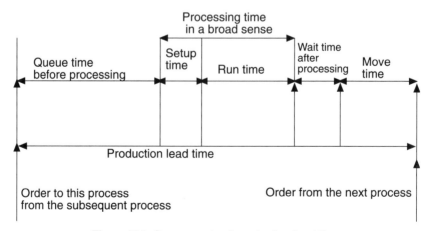

Figure 7.1. Components of production lead time.

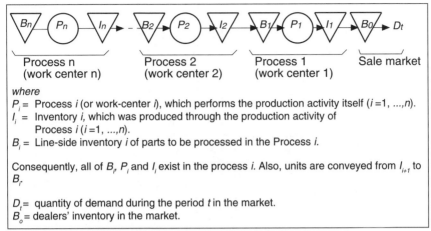

Figure 7.2. A chain of multi-process production.

SHORTENING PROCESSING TIME THROUGH SINGLE PRODUCTION AND CONVEYANCE

As a first step in reducing lead time, Toyota has refined the moving assembly concept of the conveyor system which characterizes the Ford System. This conveyor system, in its standard form, operates in accordance with a certain time interval in which one unit of a finished automobile will roll off the terminal point of the final assembly line. The operation time and conveyance time of every process in this line must be equalized. To do so, the assembly line must be divided to make the operation times of each workplace the same and have them start and end at precisely the same time. Also, the conveyance times between workplaces on the line must be equalized so that they too start and end at the same time. In the Ford System, the belt conveyor is used to make this equalization.

The basic idea of the Toyota production system is based on a similar conveyor concept. According to the conveyor system, a unit of finished automobile can be produced in every cycle time, and simultaneously each unit of the output of any process in this line will be sent on to the next process. The cycle time consists of the equalized operation time and conveyance time. In Toyota, such a production flow is called *single-unit production and conveyance* ("Ikko-Nagashi" in Japanese).

Although this single-unit flow of production concept is now quite prevalent in most companies' assembly line systems, processes for making parts supplied to the assembly line are usually based on lot production. Moreover, their lot size is still fairly large. Toyota, however, has extended the idea of single-unit flow to processes such as machining, welding, pressing, etc. Even if a process does not involve single unit production, the operation is still limited to small lot production. In this manner, all Toyota plants use an integrated single-unit flow of production, which is all connected to the assembly line. In this sense the Toyota production system is an extension of the idea behind the Ford System.

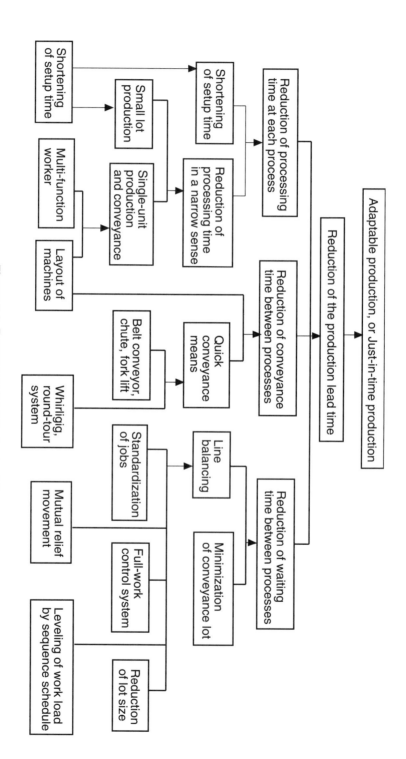

Figure 7.3. Framework for reducing lead time.

Multi-Function Workers

To achieve the single unit production goal, Toyota prepared new workplace layouts allowing for multi-process holding by multi-function workers. The machine layout was changed so that each worker could handle several different types of machines at the same time.

In the gear manufacturing process, for example, each worker attends to 16 machines. Unlike many typical production situations where a worker would interface with only one type of machine, the Toyota set up involves 16 machines performing different types of operations (grinding, cutting, etc.). The laborer, as a multi-function worker, first picks up one unit of a gear brought from the preceding process and sets it on the first machine. At the same time, he detaches another gear already processed by this machine and puts it on a chute to roll in front of the next machine. Then, while he is walking to the second machine, he pushes a switch between the first and second machines to start the first machine. He performs a similar operation on the second machine, and then moves to the third machine pushing a button again to start the second machine and so on, until he has worked on all 16 machines and finally returns to his initial process. This is done in exactly the cycle time necessary, so one unit of a finished gear will be completed in five minutes.

With this method, only one item of stock is involved in the work-in-process in each machine, and the goal of single-unit production and conveyance is realized between different types of machines. The inventory level is minimized and production lead time is shortened. Such shortened lead time helps Toyota promptly adapt to demand changes or customer orders.

On the other hand, in the typical machining plant, a turner handles only a lathe and a driller handles only the drilling machine. The layout of machinery often consists of 50 or 100 stands of lathes that are laid out as a block. After the turning process is finished, the output must be sent as a large lot to the drilling process. Then after the drilling operations, the output must be brought to the milling process in a large-lot quantity, and so on. Even though each process uses a belt conveyor, the output does not flow as a single-unit production conveyance. This is a traditional job shop type of machine layout.

Although large-lot production can minimize the average unit cost, it will increase the inventory level of each department and also increase the total production lead time. This makes prompt adaptation to customer orders in the middle of the month infeasible.

Under the requirements of smoothed production, all processes in Toyota must ideally produce and convey only one piece corresponding to each single unit that is coming off the final assembly line. In addition, each process must ideally have one piece in stock, both between machines and between processes. In short, all workshops must ideally avoid all lot production and lot conveyance. Although Toyota has succeeded in reducing lot size, some processes still remain which are operated with lot production and lot conveyance. Figure 7.4 shows an overall outline of Toyota's production processes.

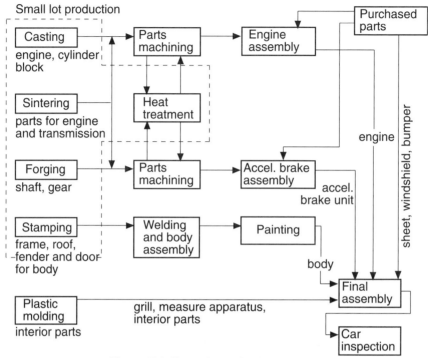

Figure 7.4. Toyota's production process.

Outline of Toyota's Plants

The processes can be roughly classified into five categories. These five categories are:

- *Casting and pressing.* Includes the casting process, which is mainly the foundry of engines, the sintering process for parts, the forging process for shafts and gears, and the pressing process for bodies. These processes involve lot production because they have large scale automated plants. Some of them, however, have fairly small lot sizes (mostly for two shifts' use) because of speedy setup actions.

- *Parts machining.* Engaged mainly in small lot production or single-unit production and conveyance.

- *Parts assembling.* Workshops to assemble engines or accelerator and brake units. These processes are engaged in single-unit production and conveyance.

- *Body welding.* Workshops that weld pressed parts, assemble them for a car body, brass, sand, and finally paint these parts. One-piece production and conveyance is the method used in these processes.

- *Final assembly line.* Operated by one-piece production and conveyance directed by the sequence schedule. Withdrawal Kanbans are attached to parts in racks beside the final assembly line so that the workers can easily pick them up. Parts such as engines, accelerator units, and brake units are attached to the auto body here, and various measurement apparatuses, sheets, windshields and bumpers, etc., are also attached here. After inspection, the automobile will be conveyed to the holding yard of Toyota's sales division.

Shortening Processing Time through Small-Sized Lot Production

In processes such as casting, forging, and stamping that use lot production (also called batch production), lot size must be reduced to shorten processing time. It is very simple logic that reduction of the lot size leads to shortening of production hours. Suppose processing time per unit of part A is one minute and the lot size is 3,000, then the total processing time amounts to 50 hours. However, by reducing the lot size to 300, that is one-tenth of the initial lot size, its processing time can be only five hours. In this example, the processing time of part A has decreased to five hours from 50 hours just by reducing the lot size. This simple logic is basic to shortening the lead time by reducing the lot size.

In the previous example, however, since 3,000 units of part A are needed, production of the small lot size (300) must be repeated 10 times. Additionally, parts B and C, needed at the same time, are also produced in small lot sizes. Therefore, during the 10 production runs for part A, the production of parts B and C must be inserted.

Also, if the setup time in changeover of the lots is kept constant, the total setup time will increase in proportion to the increased number of changes of the lots. Therefore, the setup time must also be shortened when lot sizes are reduced.

In the previous example, suppose the setup time is one hour and processing time per unit is one minute. In this case, if the production lot is 3,000 units, the total production time (setup time + total processing time = one hour + [one minute $\times$ 3,000]) required is 51 hours. However, by shortening the setup time to six minutes, or one-tenth of the initial setup time, the production lot size can be reduced to 300, or one-tenth of the initial lot size. The reason is that even if the production is repeated 10 times with lot sizes of 300, the total production time and output will be the same as before. In short, the total production time is still 51 hours (6 minutes + [one minute $\times$ 300] $\times$ 10).

In general, if the setup time was reduced to 1/N of the initial time, the lot size could be reduced to 1/N of its initial size without changing the loading rate of the process in question.

Advantages of Small Lots in the Production of Different Products

Again, assume there are three kinds of parts: A, B, and C. The processing time of any part, per unit, is one minute and the setup time of alternating the lots is one hour. Further, the lot size of any part is 3,000. Then, to get these three kinds of parts requires a total production time of 153 hours (51 hours $\times$ 3).

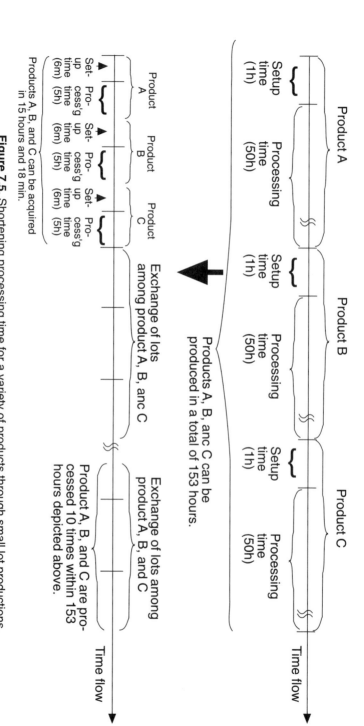

Product A | Product B | Product C

Setup time (1h) | Processing time (50h) | Setup time (1h) | Processing time (50h) | Setup time (1h) | Processing time (50h)

Time flow

Products A, B, anc C can be produced in a total of 153 hours.

Product A | Product B | Product C

Set-up time (6m) | Pro-cess'g time (5h) | Set-up time (6m) | Pro-cess'g time (5h) | Set-up time (6m) | Pro-cess'g time (5h)

Exchange of lots among product A, B, anc C

Exchange of lots among product A, B, and C

Product A, B, and C are pro-cessed 10 times within 153 hours depicted above.

Time flow

Products A, B, and C can be acquired in 15 hours and 18 min.

Figure 7.5. Shortening processing time for a variety of products through small lot productions.

Here, if the lot sizes of parts A, B, and C were reduced to one-tenth of their initial size and the setup time is reduced to one-tenth of its initial time, the necessary time to produce these three kinds of parts would be only 15 hours and 18 minutes, when it had taken 153 hours before. Figure 7.5 illustrates this example.

In this manner, shortening the processing time without decreasing productivity will be accomplished by reducing setup time and lot size. This is especially effective when many varieties of products are produced.

Control Chart of Lot Size Reduction
As has always been the case in automobile manufacturing, the lot size of stamped parts of an automobile is fairly big. Therefore, a lot size reduction control chart, as seen in Figure 7.6, is recommended.

In this figure, the lot size quantity is plotted on the vertical axis (ordinate) and the lot size quantity divided by the quantity used per shift is plotted on the horizontal axis (abscissa). The abscissa shows how many shifts can use the quantity of parts provided by one lot. Since a lot size covering more than three shifts is too big, the vertical line at the abscissa value 3 has been drawn. A horizontal line crossing the ordinate value 1,000 is drawn as a standard. Then various stamping parts are plotted in the figure. At first, most of them appeared in the right upper part, but a control target is set so as to bring them one by-one to the left lower part. An example target, as seen in the Figure 7.6, is to bring the marks for parts A and B to the spot the two arrows are pointing to.

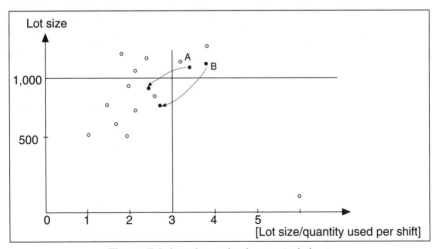

Figure 7.6. Lot size reduction control chart.

SHORTENING WAITING TIME AND CONVEYANCE TIME

How to Balance Each Process

Waiting time is defined as the time spent by parts-in-process waiting to be processed and assembled, or by completed products waiting to be withdrawn by a subsequent process; it excludes the conveyance time. The first type of waiting times is often caused by a delay in a preceding process making the subsequent process wait. The second is often caused by a delay in a subsequent process making the preceding process wait. The latter arises in many cases under a pull system like Kanban. Both causes are the results of unbalanced production time between processes.

Under the push system, a large-sized lot in the preceding process may force the subsequent process to wait. In such a case under the pull system, the preceding process is contrarily apt to produce intermittently, repeatedly stopping and starting its production without smoothing. To shorten the wait time in this process, line balancing must be achieved. The first priority is to achieve production of the same quantity in the same amount of time in each process. Although the cycle time must be the same in all processes on the assembly line, there will be some variance in the actual operation time among processes depending on minor differences in workers' skills and capabilities. To minimize these differences, standardization of actions or operating routines is very important, and the supervisor or foreman must train workers to master the standard routines (see Chapter 10).

At the same time, what Toyota calls *mutual relief movement* should be applied to make up for delays in some processes. At Toyota, the point connecting two workers or two processes is designed so that the workers will be able to help each other. This point is similar to the baton touch zone in relay races of track and field events. For example, when one part is completed by a team of workers in a certain line, the part must be handed on like a baton to the next worker. If the person in the subsequent process is delayed, the preceding worker should set up and take off the work on the subsequent machine. When the subsequent worker returns to his initial position, the preceding worker should hand the work to him immediately and go back to the preceding process. This same system would apply in reverse if the preceding worker was delayed. Friendships may be cultivated through such teamwork under the mutual relief system.

The most serious problem with regard to line balancing is the existence of capacity differences among the machines used in each process. The *full-work control system* described in Chapter 2 is used to cope with such capacity differences.

Shortening Waiting Time Caused by Pre-Process Lot Size

To shorten the waiting time caused by a big lot size in the preceding process the conveyance lot size need only be minimized (unless there are many varieties of parts). This approach allows production with a large lot size for certain kinds of products, but it also requires that the product be conveyed to the subsequent process in minimal units. In other words, even if the product lot is made up of six hundred units, when one unit is completed, it should be conveyed immediately to the next process.

The effect of this approach is illustrated by the following example. Suppose there are three processes and each takes one minute to produce one unit. One unit of a product will require three minutes to go through the three processes. If six hundred units must be produced, one process requires six hundred minutes, or ten hours, and all three processes will take 30 hours. However, if each single unit is conveyed to the subsequent process as soon as it has been processed by the preceding process, then processes 2 and 3 can operate at the same time as process 1. Process 2 will have to wait while process 1 is finishing the first unit, but only for one minute. Process 3 will also have to wait while process 2 is finishing its first unit, but again only for one minute. To produce six hundred units through these three processes, the total time required is:

$$600 \text{ minutes} + 1 \text{ minute} + 1 \text{ minute} = 602 \text{ minutes}.$$

This relationship is depicted in Figure 7.7. However, if process 1 and 2 each had one unit of inventory of finished output of its process on hand at the beginning of each month, the above waiting time of one minute each would disappear. Then it would be necessary to spend only six hundred minutes to produce six hundred units in the three processes.

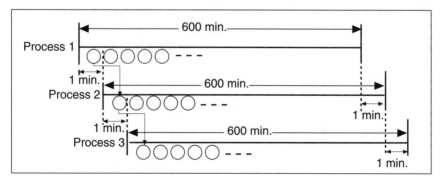

Figure 7.7. Relationship between processes and processing times.

In a case in which lot production and lot conveyance are applied to *n* processes, the total processing time = *n T,* where *T* = processing time in each process. But if single-unit conveyance is applied to *n* processes with each preceding process having output a single unit of finished inventory, the total processing time will be only *T*; that is, it will be shortened by *1/n*.

If the conveyance lot is only a single unit, however, the frequency of delivery must be increased, and the problem of minimizing conveyance time arises.

Two Steps for Conveyance Improvement
Improvement of the conveyance operation can be achieved in two steps: layout of machines and adoption of quick conveyance means. The layout of different kinds of machines should be in accordance with the flow of processes instead of by machine type. If there are many kinds of products, common or similar processes for these various products should be grouped together. Next, quick means of conveyance such as the belt conveyor, or chute, or fork lift should be used to connect the processes. The use of the whirligig beetle system and round-tour mixed-loading system by the subcontractor will help promote the continuous flow of products among processes.

BROAD APPROACH TO REDUCING PRODUCTION LEAD TIME

The Japanese JIT production system is aimed at flexible adaptation to fluctuations in demand quantity and variety in the market. Here the term "flexible" means "with short production lead time." The production lead time is the total completion time of every operation necessary for producing the merchandise. The necessary operations to produce products are: demand analysis, planning and designing of products, preparations of facilities (production engineering), manufacturing, and distribution of products to customers.

The JIT goal can be achieved by considering all necessary lead time required for each of the operations. Figure 7.8 shows the system of operations directly related to production.

Five Principles for the Ideal Factory Automation
By looking at the entire production system operation, it will be possible to supply timely, well-made products demanded by customers. The products will be the best in terms of quality, function, and price.

For example, in the development of a new product, it is necessary to promptly grasp the need of the market and quickly connect it to development of the product. For this purpose, establishing new organization structures will be required. Changing organizational structure to a flatter type of hierarchy and simplifying the decision-making steps will allow for quick adaptation. This new structure will enable prompt decision making on both clerical and management levels. An information network between departments and using computer-aided design

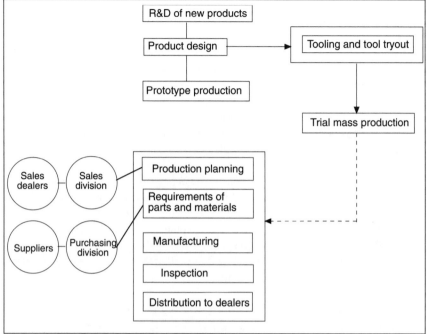

Figure 7.8. System of operations surrounding production.

(CAD) and computer-aided manufacturing (CAM) to aid in shortening the designing lead time would also be beneficial.

Here let us consider in detail production preparation and manufacturing systems. Production preparation involves preparing production facilities, conveyance machinery, and storage equipment (automatic warehouses), etc. and is usually assigned to the Production Engineering Department. On the other hand, the manufacturing system is a production control system mainly aimed at creating the smooth flow of products throughout the plant. The Production Management Department is usually responsible for the components within the manufacturing system.

Within the production preparation system, tooling and tooling tryout are obvious candidates for reducing lead time. If the problem is approached from the perspective of JIT production control, it is possible to reduce manufacturing lead time as well.

From the JIT point of view, the following facility preparations would be required:

• *Install multiple compact facilities to enable small lot size production.* Production via large-lot sizes is apt to create huge inventories between processes because the parts will have to sit and wait before being processed by the next process. A longer run time is also required to finish processing the large lot. As a result, the inventory of completed products becomes a large lot as well.

For example, in an aluminum foil factory, an annealing furnace softens coils of pressed aluminum foil and then removes the residual oil which collects on the aluminum foil. A small coil of aluminum foil can be heated in a day, but a wide coil requires several days heating. The furnace was installed in the age of small varieties and large runs. It was expected to heat large-lot sizes on a wide aluminum coil, but as already mentioned, this process requires a long time. Under such a condition, the process becomes a bottleneck and a detriment to the shortening of the whole production lead time.

- *Develop a technology for shortening chemical reaction time.* The delay of a process operation is often caused by slow chemical reactions. The reaction in eliminating oil from the aluminum foil in the annealing furnace is one such example. Another example can be found in pharmaceutical or cosmetic plants. If a chemical reaction time for inspecting finished products takes too long to complete, then a bottleneck will occur at the end of the process and create delays for all preceding processes within the plant.

- *Eliminate excessively speedy facilities.* Raising the processing speed at each process is important for reducing the run time. However, the process speed is sufficient if it is within the cycle time determined by the demand in the market place. Therefore, facilities that can produce products piece-by-piece according to the cycle time should be installed. The product cycle time will vary depending on the type and market conditions of each industry.

- *Connect machines so products can flow rapidly.* Machines or processes should be joined in a conveyor-like system or a cellular layout, rather than in a job shop or functional layout. This is done by building up a transfer line with many machines. The transfer line should contain buffer inventories stored at several places between machines. These buffer inventories can prevent an immediate line-stop when a single machine in the line breaks down. The buffer inventories are replenished by the "pull system" (a concept of the Kanban system of JIT production).

    Note: Under a large-lot production scheme, the pull system will not make any sense because it will neither shorten the production lead time nor reduce the inventory. This is why the pull system should only be adopted for small lot production.

• *Plan flexible manufacturing systems (FMS) for the future.* Consider how FMS should be in the future. Presently, there are three types of FMS. One type is a flexible machining cell (FMC), which is a cell constructed by a machining center (or turning center), a robot, and a palette pool. Another type of FMS places machining centers in a flow line, and the third FMS is of the job shop variety (also called random access FMS). In this type of FMS, various work pieces are conveyed at random and identified at a particular machine where they are set up and processed. This FMS also facilitates automatic exchange of tools and control of work-in-process inventory.

Of these three kinds of FMS, the FMS with the flow line is the most desirable for use with the JIT production system. However, the FMS in use today do manage to perform flexible processing for a group of similar parts. If a production technology is developed which enables flexible processing even among different types of parts, the flow-line type FMS will make it possible to process various products with a short lead time. The author is expecting such an FMS will be invented.

Concerning the manufacturing system, lead times can be broken down into the following types as depicted in Figure 7.9 (see next page):

L_1 = lead time of data processing (from demand forecasting to production dispatching)
L_2 = lead time of the manufacturing activity itself
L_3 = lead time of delivering completed products to customers

Shortening each of these lead times will depend on the market movement, flexibly adapting to market fluctuations, and reducing costs as much as possible. The Toyota production system works on shortening an L_2 type of lead time.

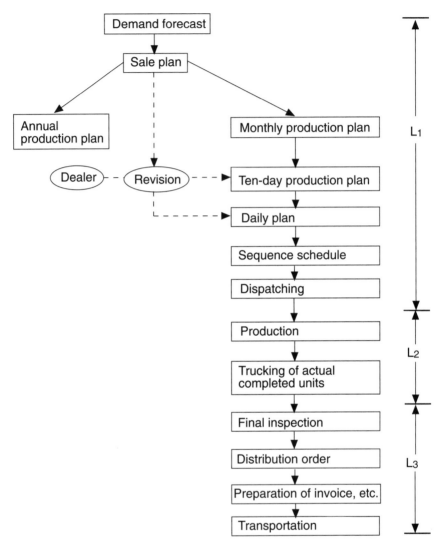

Figure 7.9. Three types of lead time in a manufacturing system.

8
Reduction of Setup Time— Concepts and Techniques

In 1970, Toyota succeeded in shortening the setup time of an 800-ton punch press for the hood and fender to three minutes. This is called a *single setup,* meaning that the setup time has a single-digit number of minutes (within nine minutes, 59 seconds). At present the setup time has, in many cases, been reduced to less than a minute, or *one-touch setup.* Before 1981, American and European companies often spent from two to several hours, or at worst, an entire day on a setup action.

The need for Toyota to develop such an incredibly short setup time was recognized by Taiichi Ohno, former vice president of the company, who realized that by shortening setup time Toyota could minimize lot size and therefore reduce the stock of finished and intermediate products.

Through small-lot production, the production lead time of various kinds of products can be shortened, and the company can adapt to customer orders and demand changes very promptly. Even if the types of cars and delivery dates are changed in the middle of the month, Toyota can adapt quickly. From this viewpoint, too, the inventory of finished and intermediate products can be reduced.

The ratio of machinery utilization to its full capacity will be increased because of the reduced setup time. It should be noted, however, that the machinery utilization rate is allowed to be low since overproduction is considered to lead to waste, a worse situation than a low utilization rate. The minimization of stocks, job-order oriented production, and prompt adaptability to demand change are the most important advantages of a single setup.

The single setup is an innovative concept invented by the Japanese in the field of industrial engineering. This idea was developed by Shigeo Shingo, a consultant at Toyota, and is now common knowledge in IE theory and practices of the world. The single setup should not be considered a technique. It is a concept that requires a change in attitude by all the people in a factory. In Japanese companies, the shortening of setup time is promoted not by the IE staff, but through the activities of small groups of direct laborers called quality control (QC) circles or ZD (zero defect) groups. Achievement of improved setup time and the attendant morale boost enable workers to take on similar challenges in other areas of the factory; this is an important side benefit of shortening setup time.

SETUP CONCEPTS

To shorten the setup time, four major concepts must first be recognized. Six techniques for applying these concepts are described herein. Most of these techniques were devised for applying concepts 2 and 3. To examine each concept and technique, the setup actions for the punch press operation will be used as a main example, but the same approach can be applied to all kinds of machines.

Concept 1: Separate the internal setup from the external setup. Internal setup refers to those setup actions that inevitably require that the machine be stopped. External setup refers to actions that can be taken while the machine is operating. In the case of a punch press, these actions can be taken before or after changing the die.

These two kinds of actions must be rigorously separated. That is, once the machine is stopped, the worker should never depart from it to handle any part of the external setup.

In the external setup, the dies, tools, and materials must be perfectly prepared beside the machine, and any needed repairs to the dies should have been made in advance. In the internal setup, only the removal and setting of dies must be done.

Concept 2: Convert as much as possible of the internal setup to the external setup. This is the most important concept regarding the single setup. Examples include:

• The die heights of a punch press or a molding machine can be standardized by using the liner (spacer) so that stroke adjustment will be unnecessary (Figure 8.1).
• The die-casting machine can be preheated using the waste heat of the furnace that belongs to this machine. This means the trial shot to warm up the metal mold in the die casting machine can be eliminated.

Concept 3: Eliminate the adjustment process. The process of adjustment in the setup actions usually takes about 50 percent to 70 percent of the total internal setup time. Reducing this adjustment time is very important to shortening the total setup time.

Adjustment is usually considered to be essential and to require highly developed skills, but these are mistaken notions. Setting operations such as moving the limit switch from the 100 mm position to the 150 mm position might be necessary. But once the limit switch has been moved to a certain position, further repetitive revision of the setting positions should be eliminated. Setting is a concept that should be considered independently of adjustment. Examples include:

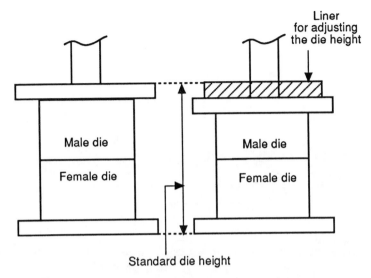

Figure 8.1. Using a liner to standardize die height.

- The maker of a punch press may produce a machine that is adjustable to various buyers' die-height requirements. But each particular company (each user) could standardize its die height at a certain size so that the stroking adjustment could be omitted (Figure 8.1)

- Suppose the molding machine requires a different stroke of the knockout depending on the die used, so the position of the limit switch needs changing to adjust the stroke. In order to find the right position, adjustment is always necessary. In such a situation, instead of only the one limit switch, five limit switches can be installed at the five required positions. Furthermore, in the new device, electric current can be made to flow only to the necessary limit switch at a certain point in time with one touch handling. As a result, the necessity to adjust the position is completely eliminated (Figure 8.2).

- To exchange the dies on the stamping machine, a revolving table car can be prepared. The idea behind this revolving table car is the same as the principle of a revolver (gun). The procedures follow (Figure 8.3):

    a. Detach the no. 1 die from the die holder of the press (production by this die is finished).
    b. Push the table car to approach the press and then fix the stopper.
    c. Put the no. 1 die on the table car.
    d. Revolve only the upper part of the table car to set the no. 2 die on to the bolster.
    e. Detach the table car stopper, pull the table car far from the press and at the same time set the no. 2 die on the press.

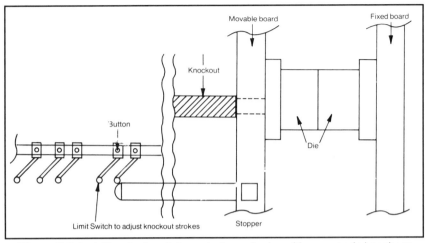

Figure 8.2. Installing limit switches at all required positions speeds knockout stroke adjustment.

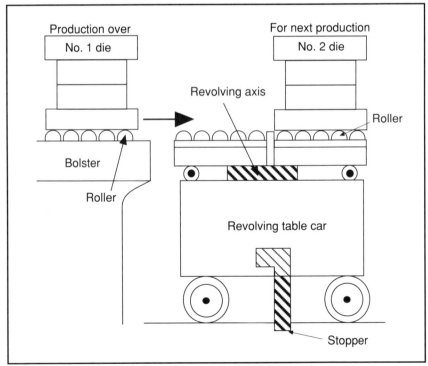

Figure 8.3. Revolving table car.

It should again be emphasized that although the machine might be capable of changing positions continuously, only a few finite, stepwise positions are needed. The example of the five discrete limit switches (Figure 8.2) is based on this idea. The number of setting positions needed in actual operations is quite limited. Such a system can be described as the *finite-settings built-in system*. This system will enable one-touch setup.

Concept 4: Abolish the setup step itself. To completely do away with the setup, two approaches can be taken: one, use uniform product design and use the same part for various products; two, produce the various parts at the same time. The latter can be achieved by two methods. The first method is the set system. For example, on the single die of the punch press, two different shapes of parts A and B were carved as a set. These two parts are separated after continuously punching both shapes at the same time.

The second method is to press the multiple parts in parallel using less expensive multiple machines. For example, one department uses a normal jack for a pressing function instead of the punch press. In this department, each worker handles this small jack while he is engaged in other jobs as a multi-functional worker. This jack is attached to a small motor for use and can perform the same function as a heavy punch press. If several jacks of this kind are available, they could be used in parallel for producing various types of parts.

Concept Application

The following are six techniques for applying the four concepts explained before.

Technique 1: Standardize the external setup actions. The operations for preparing the dies, tools, and materials should be made into routines and standardized. Such standardized operations should be written on paper and pasted on the wall for workers to see. Then the workers should train themselves to master the routines.

Technique 2: Standardize only the necessary portions of the machine. If the size and shape of all the dies is completely standardized, the setup time will be shortened tremendously. This, however, would cost a great deal. Therefore, only the portion of the function necessary for setups is standardized. The liner explained under Concept 2 (Figure 8.l) for equalizing the die height is one example of this technique.

If the height of the die-holders were standardized, the exchange of fastening tools and adjustments could be eliminated (Figure 8.4).

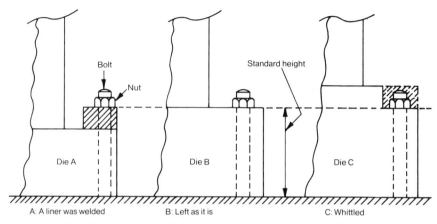

Figure 8.4. Standardizing die-holder height reduces the need to exchange fastening tools.

Technique 3: Use a quick fastener. Usually, a bolt is the most popular fastening tool. But because a bolt fastens at the final turning of the nut and can loosen at the first turn, a convenient fastening tool that would allow only a single turning of the nut should be devised. Some examples are the use of the pear-shaped hole, the U-shaped washer, and the chipped nut and bolt as shown in Figure 8.5.

A coil-winding operation was carried out by a certain company. The wound coil used to be pulled out after the nut and washer were removed. To shorten the time required to pull out a coil, the outside diameter of the nut was set at a size smaller than the inside diameter of the coil and a U-shaped washer was used. The coil could then be detached very quickly by loosening the nut by only one turn, pulling out the U-shaped washer, and then pulling out the coil without removing the nut.

There were 12 bolts on the surrounding edge of the furnace. But the bolt hole of the lid was altered to a pear shape, and the U-shaped washer was used. As a result, when the nut is loosened by only one turn, the U-shaped washer should be pulled out and the lid must be turned to the left so that the lid can open through the bigger part of the pear-shaped holes without detaching the nuts from the bolts.

Three portions of the outside of the bolt must be chipped off, and corresponding to these portions, the screw of the nut inside also must be chipped off in three places. Then, when the nut is pushed down by matching the screw portions of the nut to the chipped portions of the bolt, the nut can fasten the machine in only one turn.

A cassette system that utilizes the setting-in idea will enable setup within a minute, or one-touch setup. An example is shown in Figure 8.6. The sliding guide block shown in the figure was also devised and the size of the die holder was standardized. Figure 8.6 also illustrates a device for die installation using a mountain-shaped guide.

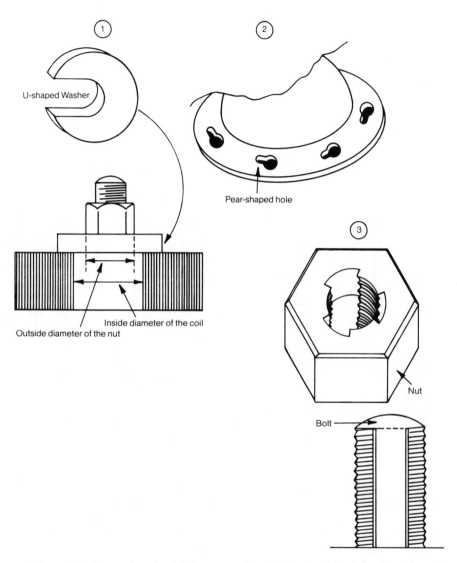

U-shaped Washer

Pear-shaped hole

Inside diameter of the coil

Outside diameter of the nut

Nut

Bolt

Figure 8.5. Examples of quick fasteners (Technique 3): 1) U-shaped washer; 2) Pear-shaped bolt hole; 3) Nut and bolt with corresponding portions chipped off.

Technique 4: Use a supplementary tool. It takes a lot of time to attach a die or a bite directly to the punch press or the chuck of a lathe. Therefore, the die or bites should be attached to the supplementary tool in the external setup phase, and then in the internal setup phase this tool can be set in the machine at one touch. For this method, the supplementary tools must be standardized. The revolving table car in Figure 8.3 is another example of this technique.

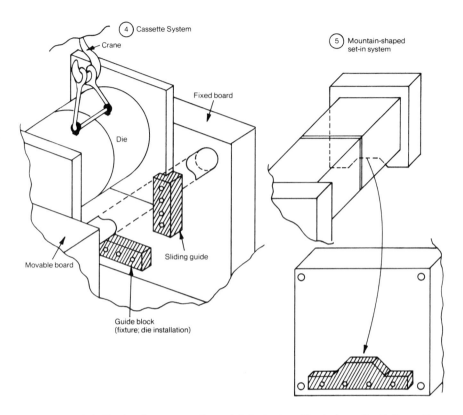

Figure 8.6. Setting-in systems for quick fastening (Technique 3): 4) Cassette system with sliding guide block; 5) Die-installation device with mountain-shaped guide.

Technique 5: Use parallel operations. The large punch press or the large molding machine will have many attachment positions on its left and right sides as well as on its front and back sides. The setup actions for such a machine will take one worker a long time. However, if parallel operations by two persons were applied to such a machine, wasteful movements could be eliminated and the setup time reduced. Even though the total number of labor hours for the setup was not changed, the effective operating hours of the machine could be increased. If a setup time of one hour were reduced to three minutes, the second worker would be needed for this process for only three minutes. Therefore, specialists in setup actions are trained on the punch press, and they cooperate with the machine operators.

Technique 6: Use a mechanical setup system. To attach the die, oil pressure or air pressure could be used for fastening at several positions at a time by the one-touch method. Also, the die heights of a punch press could be adjusted by an electrically operated mechanism. However, although such mechanisms are very convenient, an expensive investment in them would be "putting the cart before the horse."

Although Toyota has reduced the setup time to less than ten minutes, that shortened time is the internal setup time. The external setup still requires half an hour or one hour even at Toyota. Without this time span, the die for the next lot cannot be changed. As a result, the lot size or the number of setups per day at Toyota is essentially constrained by the time span of external setup.

In conclusion, for American and European companies, as well as companies of any other country, application of the Toyota production system might pose some difficulties, such as labor union or geographical problems. However, the approaches to reducing the setup time described here can definitely be applied in any company and will reduce in-process inventory and also shorten the production lead time, although not as greatly as they would if accompanied by the Kanban system. Reducing the setup times of many machines would be one of the easiest ways to introduce the Toyota production system.

9

Practical Procedure for Reducing Setup Time

In the previous chapter, we learned the importance of and need for reducing setup time—that is, using a small-lot production to shorten lead time. This chapter discusses an implementation program for reducing setup time. The program basically promotes improvement activities which reduce setup time. An organizational promotion plan for the program is described in the final section.

ANALYZING SETUP ACTIONS

To shorten setup time, it is important to first recognize the current conditions about setup actions within the plant. Although most plant managers and section heads are concerned about reducing setup time, they usually leave setup operations in the hands of floor workers. As a result, they are often unaware of the actual setup conditions themselves. Although exact timing of the current setup actions may have never been measured, workers—when asked—will guess that a setup action takes "about" two hours to two and one-half hours. The key word here is *about*. In reality, the setup actions are likely to be out of control. However, if management began to pay attention to setup actions and operators, and take and record exact measurements, opportunities for improvement could be identified.

The following problems may exist when setup actions are lengthy or if setup time varies greatly:

1. Setup completion is uncertain.
2. Setup procedure has not been standardized.
3. Procedure is not observed properly.
4. Materials, tools, and jigs are not prepared before setup operations start.
5. Attaching and detaching actions are lengthy.
6. The number of adjustment operations is high.
7. Setup actions have not been properly appraised.

These problems can be improved through daily investigation and repeated questioning of setup conditions at the actual work place. The following example from Daihatsu Industry illustrates this point (M. Yutani 1990, T. Morimatsu 1988, and T. Soukura 1987).

First, the standard operations routine sheet for all processes in the stamping section must be examined. For this example, the Daihatsu automatic tandem line (Figure 9.1) will be used. The process and standard operations routine depicted in Figure 9.2 illustrate that the following problems can arise in the stamping line:

1. Operation loads among processes are unequal.
2. Delay in the operation time for machine B-1 causes a delay in the subsequent process.
3. Opening the safety fence to exchange the T/O attachment for machine B-1 increases the setup time.

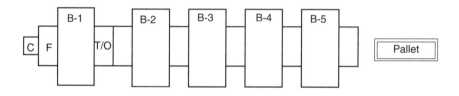

C: Cranesaver (stand to place materials)
F: Feeder (equipment used to provide work material)
T/O: Turnover (equipment used to turn over work material)

Figure 9.1. Daihatsu's automatic tandem line.

Once identified, the problem spot is videotaped for precise motions and time constraints. Alternative methods should be tested until the best alternative is identified. Once implemented, the new method should be documented on the standard operations routine sheet. The same approach should be applied to each problematic process. Figure 9.3 illustrates the sequence for researching setup actions.

PROCEDURE FOR SETUP IMPROVEMENTS

In addition to video taping and conducting time and motion studies of setup actions, there are four more procedures for attaining setup improvements. The first step is to separate the *internal setup* from the *external setup*. The second step is to shorten the internal setup time by improving operations. The third step is to promote further reduction in internal setup time through equipment improvement, and the fourth step is the challenge to reduce the setup time to zero. Each of these steps is detailed in sequence in Figure 9.4.

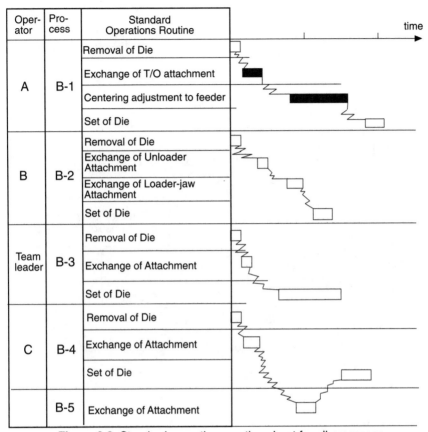

Oper-ator	Pro-cess	Standard Operations Routine	time
A	B-1	Removal of Die	
		Exchange of T/O attachment	
		Centering adjustment to feeder	
		Set of Die	
B	B-2	Removal of Die	
		Exchange of Unloader Attachment	
		Exchange of Loader-jaw Attachment	
		Set of Die	
Team leader	B-3	Removal of Die	
		Exchange of Attachment	
		Set of Die	
C	B-4	Removal of Die	
		Exchange of Attachment	
		Set of Die	
	B-5	Exchange of Attachment	

Figure 9.2. Standard operations routine sheet for all processes.

Step One: Differentiation of external and internal setup

Internal setup refers to actions that require the machine to be stopped; external setup refers to actions that can be performed while the machine is operating. The main objective in this step is to separate the internal setup from the external setup, and to convert as much internal setup as possible to external setup.

For conversion of internal setups to external setups and to decrease external setup time, the following four points are essential:

1. Pre-arrange jigs, tools, dies, and materials.
2. Maintain good operating condition for dies.
3. Create operating tables for the external setup.
4. Maintain tidiness in storage area for detached jigs and dies.

The most important of these four points is the last one: maintaining a tidy storage area for tools, jigs, and dies. Tools stored in a disorderly manner in a

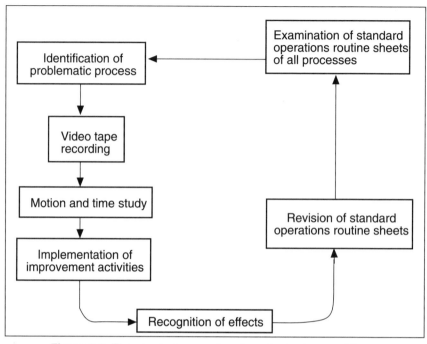

Figure 9.3. The research procedure for actual setup conditions.

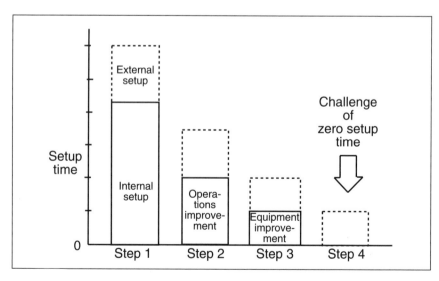

Figure 9.4. Steps to improving setup time.

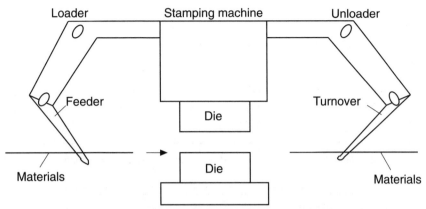

Figure 9.5. Sketch of automatic stamping machine.

toolbox will cause workers to waste time searching for needed tools—a typical wasteful operation creating no additional value.

For example, Figure 9.5 is a sketch of an automatic stamping machine. As shown, feeder and turnover attachments must be exchanged as the configuration of the material to be fed into the machine is rotated. Several changes have been made to convert internal setup actions to external ones. Figure 9.6 shows the internal setup action prior to the improvement. The unloader attachments were kept at a tool storage area away from the stamping machine causing the operator to go to the storage area to retrieve the tools. The setup was improved by locating unloader attachments just outside the safety fence near the stamping machine with the intention of converting the test from an internal setup to an external one. However, it still required time to retrieve the tools from outside the fence. Thus, to shorten the travel time, a doorway was made in the safety fence enabling advance preparation of tools (an external setup).

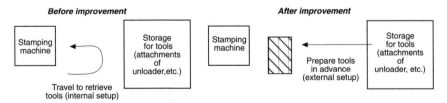

Figure 9.6. Example of conversion from internal setup to external setup.

Step Two: Operations improvement
For the internal setup which cannot be converted to external setup, emphasis is placed on shortening internal setup by continuously improving and monitoring operations. The following are key areas for continuous improvement:

• Keep tool and die storage areas tidy and organized
• Monitor effects of changing operations routine
• Monitor work force needs for each operation
• Monitor the necessity of each operation

Continuous examination of these areas will make improvement opportunities apparent. For instance, Figure 9.7 illustrates an example of operations improvement. The top portion of the figure shows the transfer of materials on a cranesaver

Objective of improvement	Route revision for material transfer on cranesaver

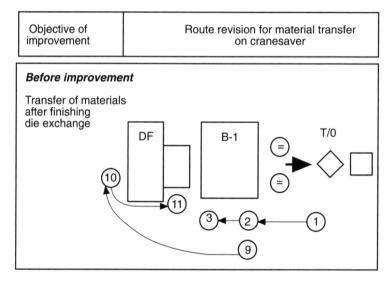

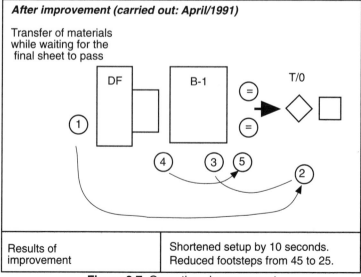

Results of improvement	Shortened setup by 10 seconds. Reduced footsteps from 45 to 25.

Figure 9.7. Operations improvement.

in front of a feeder prior to revising the route. As shown, the materials were usually transferred *after* the exchange of die was completed. By revising (improving) the route (as shown in the lower portion of the figure), the materials can be transferred from point 1 to point 2 *while waiting* for the unloader to unload the last stamped sheet. Then the die is exchanged. The result is a decrease in footsteps and a reduced setup time.

Step Three: Equipment improvement
Suppose that all the methods to shorten the setup time have been performed within the limits of operational improvements. The next strategy would be to improve the equipment. Following are several ways to do so.

- Organize external setups and modify equipment so that a variety of setups can be selected with the touch of a button. Also, recycle heat from machining operations and use for preheating ovens, etc.
- Modify equipment structure or invent tools enabling a setup and setoff reduction. Also, examine the devices for transporting the die or jig in and out of the machine area.
- Eliminate adjustments needed to set the height or position of dies or jigs by using a limit switch and converting from manual to automatic adjustments.
- Revise the standard operations routine sheet and provide training as equipment is improved.

It is important to note that setup actions usually take about 50 to 70 percent of the total internal setup time. Reducing this time is critical to shortening overall setup time.

Equipment improvement also includes the mechanization of manual operations, such as fastening a bolt by oil pressure instead of by hand. Moreover, since many stamping machine setup attachments are fairly heavy and are usually lifted by workers, lightweight attachments should be developed as part of the equipment improvement program.

The following is an example of an equipment improvement at Daihatsu which has made it possible to reduce the adjustment time of feeder centering. As seen in Figure 9.8, position setting of the side guides is adjusted by turning a handle. Because the width of both side guides differs depending on each die, the handle usually had to be turned numerous times to make the correct adjustment. As an improvement, this position-setting action was converted to an external setup by using an automated motor.

Step Four: Zero setup
The ideal time required for setup is zero. To realize zero setup, a common part should be used for various products. This could be achieved in the development and design stage of new models. For other ideas and methods, see Concept Four of the previous chapter.

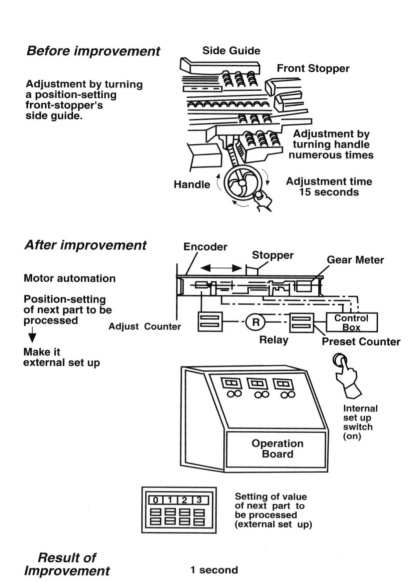

Before improvement

Adjustment by turning a position-setting front-stopper's side guide.

Side Guide

Front Stopper

Adjustment by turning handle numerous times

Handle

Adjustment time 15 seconds

After improvement

Motor automation

Position-setting of next part to be processed
↓
Make it external set up

Encoder

Stopper

Gear Meter

Adjust Counter

R

Relay

Control Box

Preset Counter

Operation Board

Internal set up switch (on)

0 1 1 2 3

Setting of value of next part to be processed (external set up)

Result of Improvement

1 second

Figure 9.8. Shortening of adjustment time for feeder centering.

It is customary to enter the revised setup actions in the standard operations routine sheet after they have been made. Yet these revisions should not be regarded as the accurate or everlasting ones. Instead, they should be considered the best operating criteria for the time being and be subject to change for the purpose of improvement.

INFORMING OPERATORS OF IMPROVEMENTS

Naturally, there will be either delay or rapid progress in actual setup actions when compared with the standard routine. Operators are informed of the change during setup operations in the following way.

Figure 9.9 shows an Andon which is hung from the ceiling at a stamping section in Daihatsu. The light is divided into 11 parts with the middle four parts indicating the progress of setup operations. Each of these four parts specifies the passage of one fourth of the standard setup time with the last part indicating that the setup should be near completion. Responding to the progress, each part is lit in sequence.

The other four parts on the right-hand side are numbered according to each process. If something abnormal happens in a process, the part representing that process is lit. The remaining three lamps on the left side of the Andon are used as trouble indicators for dies and machines.

Each stamping line has an Andon overhead where setup progress and problems can be monitored and easily seen by everyone. Most operators, however, are too busy with their respective setup actions to notice and respond to Andon stimuli. Therefore, it is a supervisor's responsibility to pay attention to the Andon and immediately respond to trouble indicators.

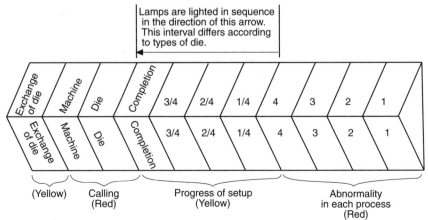

Figure 9.9. "Andon" showing the progress of operations.

Music For Standardization

Daihatsu also uses another method for monitoring setup progress. It allows operators to concentrate on their work, yet be informed of the progress at the same time. This method uses music.

Four different melodies corresponding to each of the four steps of setup actions within a plant are played (see Figure 9.10). During the first step, "For Elise" is played over the speakers; during the second step "Sakura Sakura" (cherry blossoms) is played; during the third step "Murano Kajiya" (blacksmith of a village) is played and when setup should be completed, "Lorelei" can be heard within the plant. If the setup operations are not completed by the time "Lorelei" is played, it means that the target time for completion has expired.

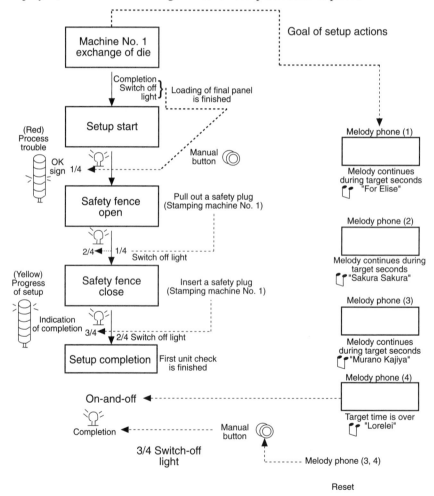

Figure 9.10. Setup sequence introduced by various melodies.

Preventing Temporary Line Stoppage After Setup

Even though setup actions may have been improved through the previously mentioned continuous improvement procedures, a stamping machine often stops immediately after a new setup (or startup). (See Figure 9.11.) This delay is most likely caused by the die itself rather than the other equipment. The quality maintenance (QM) of dies is important for improving a facility's actual operating rate. A temporary line stoppage just after setup is the same as spending a long time for the setup itself.

The initial step to maintaining the quality of dies is to classify different defect conditions into five categories:

1. unevenness
2. baking
3. wrinkle
4. break
5. wrap

The next step is to find the cause (or quality component) of each defect category on the die. For example, a wrap on a stamped part is due to the disparity between upper die and lower die which is usually caused by poor connections between the slide plate and a slide guide. To keep the system running smoothly,

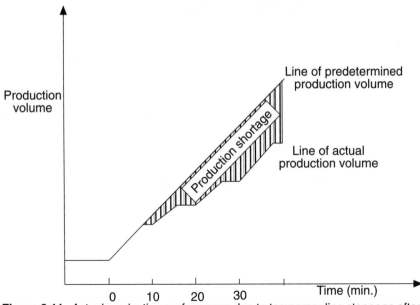

Figure 9.11. Actual production performance due to temporary line stoppage after setup actions.

the guides would have to be checked constantly. Another example is baking which results from the lack of a blankholder (an area where dies are chipped off as the upper die meets with a lower die).

Obviously, it is far more beneficial to produce quality dies rather than repairing a die after a defect occurs. For this reason, it is essential to detect any defective processes and establish the cause up front.

Other maintenance tasks are performed by professionals who service and repair the equipment and by the operators themselves. Operators perform what is called self-managed maintenance which includes activities like cleaning and lubricating. The professionals perform maintenance activities on a scheduled basis while operators perform their maintenance activities more frequently.

These continuous improvement efforts at Daihatsu resulted in lot sizes being reduced from 100 to 67; setup time being decreased from 12 minutes to 6.4 minutes, and manpower requirements per setup being decreased from 6.3 people to 3.3 people. These results are summarized in Figure 9.12.

Points of evaluation	1983	1988
Lot size Setup time Operators per setup	100 12 min. 6.3 people	67 6.4 min. 3.3 people

Figure 9.12. Effects of setup improvement.

ORGANIZATION STRUCTURE FOR PROMOTING SETUP TIME REDUCTION

Daihatsu began encountering the problems of prolonged setup time and increased setup operations when the need arose to stamp many varieties of products in small lot sizes and when automated lines were implemented to cut down on manpower. An improvement project team made up of many workers in the stamping department was formed to solve these two problems. Figure 9.13 shows the organizational structure of the group and each member's role.

People from other segments of the company were included to obtain objective input. The plant engineering staff answered technical questions, and senior and upper management organized the team, supported recommendations, followed up on implementation, and finally evaluated the effectiveness of the group.

The project team members felt a certain amount of pride and pleasure in brainstorming, gathering and analyzing data, and formulating a solution to the problem. A successful solution arrived at through group involvement is a catalyst for continuous improvement programs.

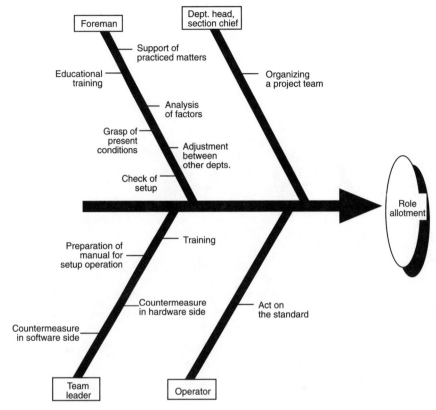

Figure 9.13. Organization of the improvement group and its member's roles.

10
Standard Operations
Can Attain Balanced Production
with Minimum Labor

The ultimate purpose of the Toyota production system is to reduce costs relating to production. To do so, Toyota tries to eliminate production inefficiencies such as unnecessary inventories and workers.

Standard operations are aimed at using a minimum number of workers for production. The first goal of standard operations is to achieve high productivity through strenuous work. Strenuous work at Toyota, however, does not mean forcing the workers to work very hard; instead, it means working efficiently without any wasteful motions. A standardized order of the various operations to be performed by each worker, called the *standard operations routine*, is important in facilitating this first goal.

The second goal of Toyota's standard operations is to achieve line balancing among all processes in terms of production timing. In this case, the cycle time concept should be built into standard operations.

The third and final goal is that only the minimum quantity of work-in-process will qualify as *standard quantity of work-in-process*, or the minimum number of units necessary for the standard operations to be performed by workers. This standard quantity helps eliminate excessive in-process inventories.

To attain these three goals, standard operations consists of the cycle time, standard operations routine, and standard quantity of work-in-process (Figure 10.1).

In furthering these goals, production is set to eliminate accidents and defective production. As a result, the routine and positions to check the safety and quality of products are also standardized. Thus, safety precautions and product quality are subgoals of Toyota's standard operations.

DETERMINING THE COMPONENTS OF STANDARD OPERATIONS

The components of standard operations are determined mainly by the foreman (supervisor). The foreman determines the labor hours required to produce one unit at each machine and also the order of various operations to be performed by each worker. Generally in other companies such standard operations are determined by the IE staff.

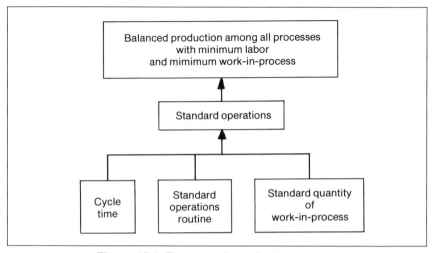

Figure 10.1. Elements of standard operations.

Toyota's method might seem unscientific; however, the foreman has an intimate knowledge of past performances of workers. In addition, the typical foreman also uses IE techniques, such as time and motion studies; therefore, such factors as the determined motion speed can be regarded as appropriate even by an impartial observer. Also, in order to teach the worker to understand and follow the standards completely, the foreman himself must master and recognize the standards perfectly.

Standard operations are determined in the following manner:

1. Determine the cycle time.
2. Determine the completion time per unit.
3. Determine the standard operations routine.
4. Determine the standard quantity of work-in-process.
5. Prepare the standard operations sheet.

Determining the Cycle Time
The cycle time or tact is the time span in which one unit of a product must be produced. This cycle time is determined by the required daily quantity of output and the effective daily operating time in the following manner:

$$\text{Cycle Time} = \frac{\text{Effective Daily Operating Time}}{\text{Required Daily Quantity of Output}}$$

The effective daily operating time should not be reduced for any allowances due to machine breakdowns, idle time awaiting materials, rework, or for fatigue and rest time. Also, the necessary quantity of output should not be increased to allow for defective output. By viewing as unnecessary the time spent in producing defective items, such time is visible when it occurs in a process, making it possible to take immediate action to improve the process. The cycle time can be rather long compared to other companies which make allowances for fatigue time and defective items when determining the cycle time. Moreover, since it is necessary to determine both the number of different operations and the number of workers needed to produce a single unit of output within the cycle time, the number of workers in any department at Toyota's factory can be decreased if the cycle time is relatively longer.

Sometimes, the cycle time is determined erroneously by using the current machine capacity and labor capacity. Although this gives a probable time span for producing one unit of output, it does not give the necessary time span needed for repositioning the workers. To be sure that the cycle time is determined properly, the effective daily operating time and the required daily output must be used.

Determining the Completion Time Per Unit

The completion time per unit of output has to be determined at each process and for each part. This time unit is always written on the *part production capacity sheet* which is filled out for each part (Figure 10.2).

The *manual operation time* and the *machine automatic processing time* are both measured by a stopwatch. The manual operation time should not include the walking time at the process. The speed and the level of skill required for each manual operation are determined by the foreman.

The *completion time per unit* in the basic time column is the time required for a single unit to be processed. If two units are processed simultaneously, or one unit in every few units is inspected for quality control, the completion time per unit will be written in the reference column.

In the tool exchange column, the *exchange units* specify the number of units to be produced before changing the bite or tool. The *exchange time* refers to the setup time.

The production capacity in the extreme right-hand column is computed by the following formula:

$$N = \frac{T}{C + m}, \text{ or } \frac{T - mN}{C},$$

where mN = summation of total setup time

Formula Notations:
N = Production capacity in terms of units of output
C = Completion time per unit
m = Setup time per unit
T = Total operation time

Part production capacity sheet

Item no.	Item name	Necessary quantity per day	Worker's name

Order of processes	Description of operations	Machine no.	Basic time — Manual operation time (min. / sec.)	Basic time — Machine processing time (min. / sec.)	Basic time — Completion time per unit (min. / sec.)	Tool's exchange — Exchange units	Tool's exchange — Exchange time	Production capacity (960 min) units	References — manual operation ——— machine processing ··········
1	center drill	CD-300	07	1 20	1 27	80	1'00"	655	
2	chamfer	KA-350	09	1 35	1 44	20	30"	549	
3	ream	KB-400	09	1 25	1 34	50	30"	606	
4	ream	KC-450	10	1 18	1 28	40	30"	643	
2-1	mill	MS-100	(20)	(2 10)	(2 20)	1,000	7'00"	820	
2-2	mill	MS-101	(15)	(2 10)	(2 15)	1,000	7'00"		
	(two stands of machines)		18						
3	bore	BA-235 (two units processing at a time)	(08)	(50)	(58)	500	5'00"	1,947	
4	gauge (1/5) (one unit inspection in every five units)		04 (18)		29				
	total		09						

References:

$$\left[\begin{array}{c}\text{manual operation}\\\text{time per unit}\end{array}\right] = \frac{20'' + 15''}{2} = 17.5'' \to 18''$$

$$\left[\begin{array}{c}\text{manual operation}\\\text{time per unit}\end{array}\right] = \frac{8''}{2} = 4''$$

$$\left[\begin{array}{c}\text{manual operation}\\\text{time per unit}\end{array}\right] = \frac{18''}{2} = 9''$$

Figure 10.2. Part production capacity sheet.

Determining the Standard Operations Routine

After determining the cycle time and the manual operation time per unit for each operation, the number of different operations that each worker should be assigned must be calculated. In other words, the standard operations routine of each individual worker must be determined.

The *standard operations routine* is the order of actions that each worker must perform within a given cycle time. This routine serves two purposes. First, it provides the worker with the order or routine to pick up work, put it on the machine, and detach it after processing. Second, it gives the sequence of operations that the multi-functioned worker must perform at various machines within a cycle time.

At this point, it is important to differentiate between the order of process and the operations routine because these two orders are not identical in many cases. If the operations routine is simple, it can be determined directly from the part production capacity sheet (Figure 10.2). In this case, the order of processes is actually identical with the operations routine. If the routine is complicated, however, it may not be easy to determine whether the automatic processing time of a certain machine will be finished before the worker handles the same machine in the next cycle of the tact time. As a result, the standard operations routine sheet is used to determine the exact operations routine (Figure 10.3).

The procedure to prepare the standard operations routine sheet follows:

1. The cycle time is drawn with a red line on the operations time dimension of the sheet.

2. The approximate range of processes which one worker can handle should be predetermined. The total operations time, which is approximately equal to the cycle time in red, should be computed using the part production capacity sheet (Figure 10.2). Some slack time for walking between machines must be allowed. The walking time should be measured using a stopwatch and recorded on some memo.

3. The manual operation and machine processing times for the first machine are first drawn on this sheet by copying the data from the part production capacity sheet.

4. Next, the second operation of this worker must be determined. It should be remembered that the order of processes is not necessarily identical to the operations routine. Also, the walking distance between machines, the point at which product quality is checked, and specific safety precautions must be taken into account at this stage. If some walking time is necessary, its time must be drawn on the sheet by a wavy line from the ending point of the preceding manual operation time to the beginning point of the subsequent manual operation time.

| Item no. | 3561-4630 | Standard Operations Routine Sheet | | Date | Oct. 15, '81 | Necessary quantity per day | 240 units | Manual operation —— |
| Process name | Machining: part 2 | No. 1 | | Worker's position & name | | Cycle time | 2 min. | Machine processing – – – Walking ⁓⁓⁓ |

Order of operations	Names of operations	Time Manual	Time Machine	Operations Time ('': sec. ': min.)
1	Pick up the material from the pallet	01"	—	
2	CD-300: center drill	07"	1'20"	
3	KA-350: chamfer	09"	1'35"	
4	KB-400: ream	09"	1'25"	
5	KC-450: ream	10"	1'18"	
6	NE-200	08"	50"	
7	GR-101	05"	—	
8	SA-130	07"	1'10"	
9	JI-500	10"	1'30"	
10	HU-400	12"	55"	
11	Wash, attach the nipple, put in the pallet	20"	—	

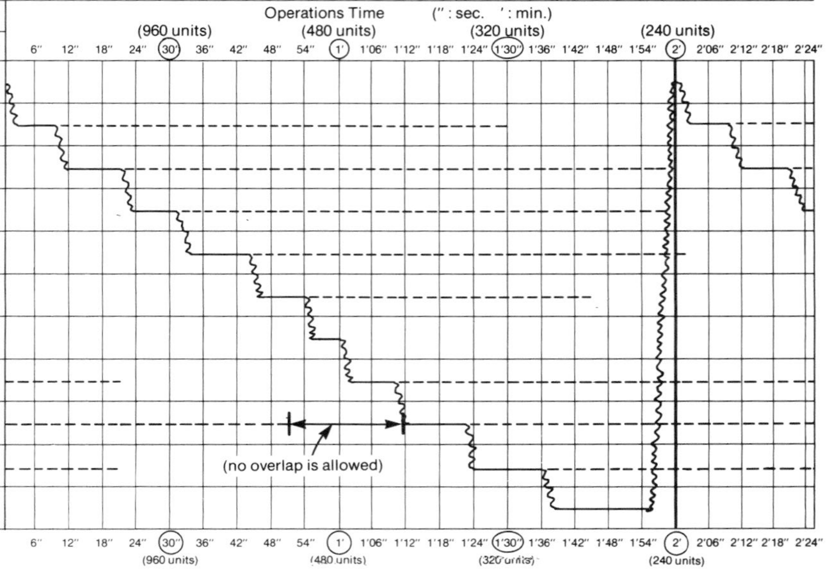

(no overlap is allowed)

Timeline scale: 6" 12" 18" 24"(960 units) 30" 36" 42" 48" 54"(480 units) 1' 1'06" 1'12" 1'18" 1'24"(320 units) 1'30" 1'36" 1'42" 1'48" 1'54"(240 units) 2' 2'06" 2'12" 2'18" 2'24"

Figure 10.3. Standard operations routine sheet.

5. Steps 3 and 4 are repeated until the whole operations routine can be determined. When performing these steps, if the dotted line of machine processing time reaches the solid line of the next manual operation, the operations sequence is not feasible and some other sequence must be chosen.

6. Since the operations routine was plotted to cover all of the estimated number of processes at step 2, the routine must be completed at the initial operation of the next cycle. If walking time is necessary for this winding up, a wavy line must be drawn.

7. If the final wind-up point meets the red line of cycle time, the operations routine is an appropriate mix. If the final operation ends before the cycle time line, consider whether more operations can be added. If the final operation overflows the cycle time line, ways to shorten the overflow must be considered. This could be achieved by improving various operations of this worker.

8. Finally, the foreman should actually try to perform the final standard operations routine. If the foreman can comfortably finish it within the cycle time, the routine can then be taught to the workers.

The allocations of various operations among workers must be such that each worker can finish all of his assigned operations within the specified cycle time. Also, the layout of processes must be such that each worker has the same cycle so that production line balancing among various processes can be realized. A simplified scheme of this allocation of operations and layout of processes is shown in Figure 10.4.

If there is too much waiting time at the end of the operations routine in Figure 10.3, a double cycle time could be set in order to have simultaneous operations by two or three workers subject to the same operations routine. This helps to eliminate slack in the cycle time (Figure 10.5). Otherwise, by an improvement in the operations of the process in question, one more operation could be inserted into the cycle time.

Yo-i-don System

"Yo-i-don" means *ready, set, go*. The Yo-i-don system is a method for balancing the production timing (synchronization) among various processes where there is no conveyor belt. It can also be used as a method of measuring the production capacity of each process.

Let's examine in detail the Yo-i-don system using Andon. In a body welding plant of Daihatsu Motor Company (a partner of Toyota), there are six *underbody* processes ($U_1, U_2, ... U_6$), six *side-body* processes ($S_1, S_2, ... , S_6$), and four *main-body* processes ($M_1, M_2, ...M_4$), as depicted in Figure 10.6. By companies, the body welding plant is also called a sheet-metal factory, a body assembly line, or simply a body line.

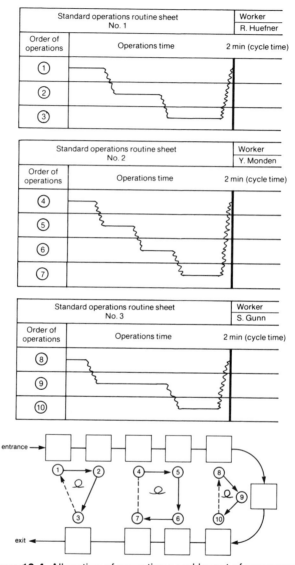

Figure 10.4. Allocation of operations and layout of processes.

The body welding plant must produce one unit of its product in three minutes, thirty-five seconds (the cycle time of this factory). By dividing this cycle time into three equal portions accumulatively as 1/3, 2/3, and 3/3 when time elapses, the standard time per unit of a product for completing each process is established. The table in Figure 10.7 is called "Andon"; it is hung high from the factory ceiling for all workers to see.

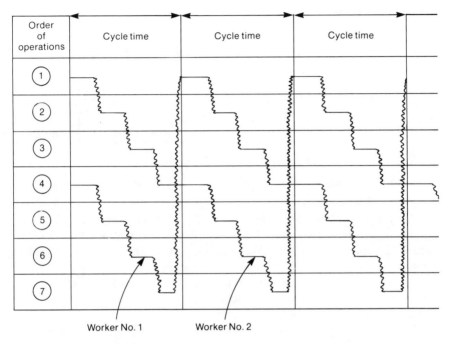

Figure 10.5. Double cycle time for use by two workers.

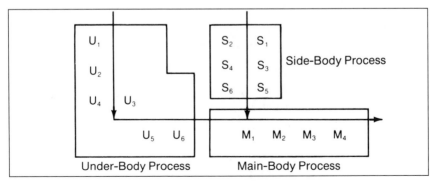

Figure 10.6. Process in a body welding plant.

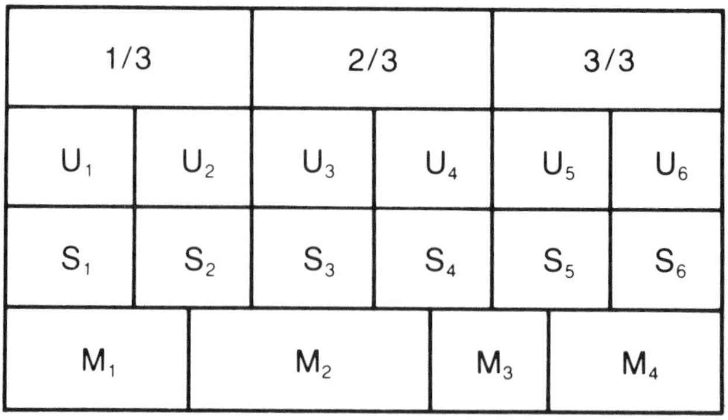

1/3		2/3		3/3	
U_1	U_2	U_3	U_4	U_5	U_6
S_1	S_2	S_3	S_4	S_5	S_6
M_1		M_2		M_3	M_4

Figure 10.7. Andon of the body plant.

The workers of under-body processes must complete their operations from U_1 to U_6 within three minutes, thirty-five seconds, and the laborers of the side-body processes also must finish their jobs from S_1 to S_6 within this time period. And, the workers in the main-body processes must complete their processes from M_1 through M_4 within the cycle time. At the starting point of a cycle, each worker sets the work to the first process he must handle. If each worker finishes his operations at all his responsible processes and transfers the finished work to the next process within the cycle time, then this body welding plant as a whole can produce one unit of finished product per three minutes, thirty-five seconds.

The worker in each process will push his button when his job is finished, and after three minutes, thirty-five seconds have passed, the red lamp on Andon will only go on automatically at those processes where the job is not yet completed. Since the red lamp indicates a delay in processing, the whole line stops operation while a red lamp is on.

For example, the red lamp might be turned on at processes U_4, S_5, and M_2. When this happens, the supervisor or nearby workers help the workers at these processes finish up their jobs. In most cases, all red lamps will go out within 10 seconds.

At this stage, the next cycle time will start, and again the operations in all processes start together. This is called Yo-i-don, which will realize the balanced production among all processes. It utilizes Andon, cycle time, and the multi-process holding for a single-piece production and conveyance. The Andon in this case is also called the *process-completion display board,* which is at times apart from the usual Andon board at Toyota.

In a sense, the Yo-i-don system is a modification of the so-called "Tact system." Under the ordinary Tact system, the supervisor will oversee the whole process, and when all workers finish their respective jobs, he signals to move the product of each process to the next process. However, under the Yo-i-don system at Toyota, such a function is replaced by the Andon. However, new considerations and expectations must be made for the introduction of welding robots, conveyor belts between processes, and central computer systems controlling the body-welding lines.

One Shot Setup

Machine sequencing is an important consideration in complex operation routines. If there are many different machines laid out in succession, how should the setup problem be handled?

Suppose, for example, that there are four different kinds of machines such as a bending machine (W), a punch press (X), a welding machine (Y), and a boring machine (Z) in succession at a certain machining process (Figure 10.8). Assume that these four machines are handled by a multi-functioned worker and although he is now processing part A, he must next process part B in this multi-machinery process.

In order to change production from part A to part B in this situation, the worker will never setup these four machines after finishing the processing of all of part A at these machines. Such an approach would consume an appreciable amount of production lead time.

Instead, the worker should begin the setup of part B while part A is still in process. Note that only a single unit of a part can flow through each machine within a cycle time. Therefore, when the last unit of part A has been processed at the first machine W, "air" should be sent to machine W. While "air" is flowing through machine W, the setup action can be performed for this machine. In other words, machine W can be setup within a given cycle time.

As a result, all of these four machines can be setup by sacrificing production of just one piece of part B. If all of these four machines are handled by one multi-functioned worker, all of the machines can be setup within four cycle times. If each machine is handled separately by each different worker, all four machines can be setup in one cycle time of the first case. At Toyota, such a setup approach is called *one shot setup* (Figure 10.8).

Determining the Standard Quantity of Work-in-Process

The standard quantity of work-in-process is the minimum necessary quantity of work-in-process within the production line; it consists principally of the work laid out and held between machines. It also includes the work attached to each machine. However, the inventory at the store of completed products of the line cannot be regarded as the standard holding quantity.

Without this quantity of work, the predetermined rhythmic operations of various machines in this line cannot be achieved. The actual standard holding quantity varies according to the following differences in machine layouts and operations routines:

- If the operations routine is in accordance with the order of process flow, only the work attached to each machine is necessary; it will not be necessary to hold work between machines. (Consider 7 → 8 in Figure 10.9.)

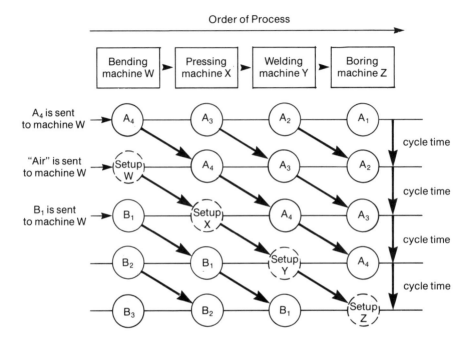

Figure 10.8. One shot setup.

- However, if the operations routine is in an opposite direction to the order of processing, it must be necessary to hold at least one piece of work between machines. (Consider $8 \rightarrow 7$ in Figure 10.9.)

Moreover, when determining the standard quantity of work held, the following points should also be taken into consideration:

- The quantity necessary for checking the product quality at necessary positions of the process.
- The quantity necessary to be held until the temperature of a unit from the preceding machine goes down to a certain level.

The standard quantity held should be kept as small as possible. Besides reducing holding costs, visual control in checking the product quality and improving the process would be made easier because defects would be more evident.

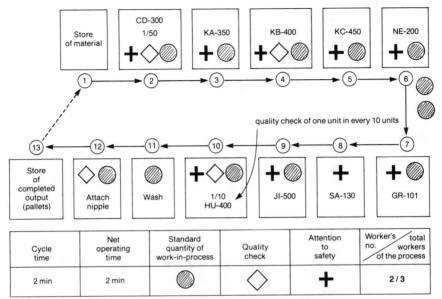

Figure 10.9. Standard operations sheet.

Preparing the Standard Operations Sheet

The standard operations sheet is the final item needed for standardizing the operations at Toyota. This sheet (Figure 10.9) contains the following items:

- Cycle time
- Operations routine
- Standard quantity of work-in-process
- Net operating time
- Positions to check product quality
- Positions to pay attention to worker safety

When a standard operations sheet is displayed where each worker of the process can see it, it can be useful for visual control in the following three areas:

1. It is a guideline for each worker to keep his standardized operations routine.
2. It helps the foreman or supervisor check to be sure each worker is following standard operations.
3. It allows the superior manager to evaluate the supervisor's ability, since standard operations must be revised frequently by improving operations of the process. If the unrevised standard operations sheet was up for a long time, the manager would note that the supervisor is not making an attempt to improve operations.

PROPER TRAINING AND FOLLOW-UP: THE KEY TO IMPLEMENTING A SUCCESSFUL SYSTEM

Once the standard operations were set by the supervisor (foreman), he must be able to perform these operations perfectly, and then instruct his workers to do so. The supervisor should not only teach the operations, but also explain the reasons the standards must be kept (i.e., the goals of standard operations). This provides the workers with the incentive to take responsibility for product quality.

In order to ensure that the workers thoroughly understand the standards, two sheets called the *operations keypoints note* and the *operations guidance note* are prepared and conveyed to the workers. The operations keypoints note describes the important points of each operation in the standard operations routine, while the operations guidance note will explain the details of each operation at each line and also methods for checking product quality. They also contain the data provided by the standard operations sheet. These sheets are also posted in each process.

The supervisor must always observe firsthand whether the standards are being followed in his department. If the standards are not being kept, he should immediately instruct the workers in the proper procedures. If the standards themselves are faulty, they must be revised promptly.

An electric board shows the actual and scheduled cumulative quantities of outputs at the completion of each cycle time in every process. The supervisor must check the results of implementing the standard operations, and if something abnormal is found in the process, he must investigate the reasons and take remedial actions. The supervisor's remedial actions are regarded as current control or operational control, but his performance in each month can be evaluated by the traditional budgetary control system.

Finally, it is important to revise the standard operations regularly, since they are always imperfect and operations improvements are always required in a process. The most fundamental idea behind the Toyota production system is summed up in the statement:

> Progress of a company can be achieved only by continuous efforts on the part of *all* members of the company to improve their activities.

11
Machine Layout, Multi-Function Workers, and Job Rotation Help Realize Flexible Workshops

Toyota manufactures a variety of automobiles with many different specifications. Each type of car is always subject to fluctuations in demand. For example, the demand of car A might decrease, while at the same time, car B might increase in its demand. Therefore, the work load at each car line in the plant must be frequently evaluated and periodically changed. Continuing an example, a number of workers at the line for car A would have to be transferred to the line for car B so that each line can adapt to the change in demand with the minimum necessary number of workers.

Moreover, even though the demand of all types of products may be reduced simultaneously because of a general economic depression or some foreign export restriction, the company should still be able to reduce the number of workers at any line by taking out temporary workers or extra workers coming from related companies.

Shojinka: Meeting Demand through Flexibility

Attaining flexibility in the number of workers at a workshop to adapt to demand changes is called *Shojinka*. In other words, Shojinka in the Toyota production system means to alter (decrease or increase) the number of workers at a shop when the production demand has changed (decreased or increased).

Shojinka has an especially significant meaning when the number of workers must be reduced due to a decrease in demand. For example, at a line, five workers perform jobs which produce a certain number of units. If the production quantity of this line was reduced to 80%, the number of workers must be reduced to four $(5 \times 0.80 = 4)$ if the demand decreased to 20%, the number of workers would then be reduced to one.

Obviously, then, Shojinka is equivalent to increasing productivity by the adjustment and rescheduling of human resources. What was called a flexible workshop in the title of this chapter is essentially a workshop which is achieving Shojinka. In order to realize the Shojinka concept, three factors are prerequisite:

1. Proper design of machinery layout.
2. A versatile and well-trained worker; i.e. a multi-function worker.
3. Continuous evaluation and periodic revisions of the standard operations routine.

The machinery layout for Shojinka at Toyota is combined U-form lines. Under this layout, the range of jobs for which each worker is responsible can be widened or narrowed very easily. However, this layout assumes the existence of multi-functioned workers.

Multi-functioned workers at Toyota are cultivated through the unique *job rotation system*. And, finally, the revision of the standard operations routine can be made through continuous improvements in manual jobs and machineries. The purpose of such improvements is to reduce the necessary number of workers even in the period of increased demand.

The relationship among these important prerequisites is shown in Figure 11.1. This chapter is devoted to explaining the factors affecting the widening or narrowing of the range of jobs for each worker.

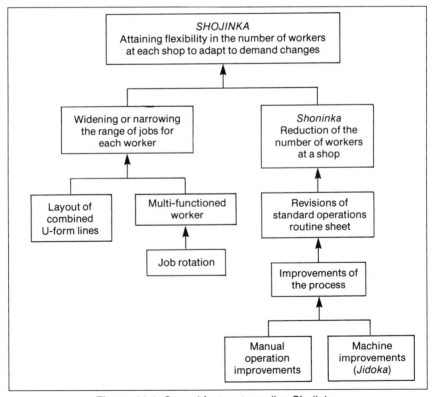

Figure 11.1. Causal factors to realize Shojinka.

LAYOUT DESIGN: THE U-TURN LAYOUT

The essence of the U-turn format is that the entrance and exit of a line are at the same position. The U-turn layout has several variations, such as the concave (⊔) and circle forms (Figure 11.2). The most remarkable and important advantage of this layout is the flexibility to increase or decrease the necessary number of workers when adapting to the changes in production quantities (changes in demand). This can be realized by adding or reducing the number of workers in the inner area of the U-shaped workplace (Figure 11.2).

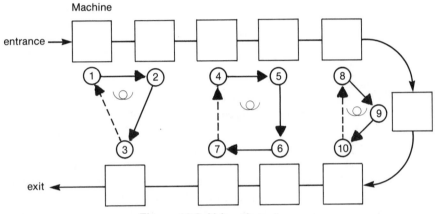

Figure 11.2. U-form layout.

Just-in-time pulling production also can be achieved in each process. The unit of material can pass into the entrance of the process when one unit of output leaves through the exit. Since such operations are performed by the same worker, the quantity of work-in-process within the layout can always be constant. At the same time, by keeping a standard inventory quantity at each machine, the unbalanced operations among workers will be visualized, so that improvements in the process can be evoked.

Finally, the U-turn format allows regions or areas to be developed for specific worker operations. Systems using automatic large scale machines often have workers located only at the entrance and exit. A chain hanger is one such example. If the positions for loading and unloading the material are different, two persons will always be needed, and each worker often has idle time or waiting time. However, if the loading and unloading positions are set at the same point of line, one worker can handle both the entrance and exit jobs.

Improper Layouts
Improper layouts which Toyota has avoided can be divided into three major categories: bird cages, isolated islands, and linear layouts.

Bird cage layouts. The simplest form of machine layout calls for one worker assigned to one type of machine. This type of layout has a major disadvantage: the worker has waiting time after he has loaded the work piece into the machine and the part is in process. To avoid such waiting times, two or more stands containing the same type of machine can be laid out around the worker (Figure 11.3). This type of layout is called a bird cage layout; they are usually triangular, rectangular, or rhombic in shape.

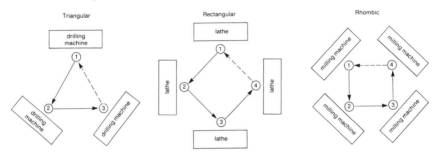

Figure 11.3. Types of bird cage layouts.

By making each worker handle multiple machines of the same type, the production quantity per worker can be increased. Although this method is much improved over the single machine layout, the production quantity per worker increases; thus, the inventory of semi-finished or intermediate inventory produced at each station also increases. As a result, production balancing between stations is difficult to achieve and these semi-finished products cannot flow smoothly and continuously through the various production processes. *Synchronization* among stations is hardly achieved. In turn, the lead time to produce finished goods rises dramatically.

Isolated island layouts. In order to avoid excessive intermediate inventories from each station and decrease the conveyance time, the layout of machines must be improved to increase the speed of producing a finished product. Therefore, the layout of machines should be in accordance with the sequential order of processing a part (see Figure 11.4). This layout assumes the existence of a multi-function worker, and enables a continuous, smooth flow of products among different types of machines; it also ensures a continuous walking route with the least distance for each worker. This type of layout is called an *isolated island layout*.

Toyota rejects all types of the isolated island layout because of the following disadvantages:

• When the entire factory is under this layout, workers are separated from one another and, as such, cannot help each other. It is difficult to attain total balancing of production among the various processes. Unnecessary inventory

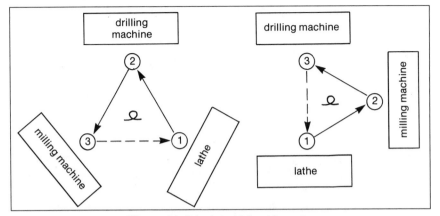

Figure 11.4. Isolated island layouts.

still occurs among different processes. The mutual relief movement (Chapter 7) cannot be applied to isolated islands.

- Since unnecessary inventory can exist among isolated islands, worker waiting time will be absorbed in producing this inventory. Thus, the reallocation of operations among workers to respond to the changes in demand is difficult in this process.

The layout of the isolated island is based on the methods engineering theory that a worker should never walk at all while working at a certain position. Such an idea was held even by Henry Ford. This idea is correct when productivity is viewed from the efficiency of individual workers; however, it is incorrect when viewed from line balancing within a whole factory and from minimizing the total number of laborers.

Concerning the isolated island, the way of using a conveyor is also important. A conveyor is often used only to convey products from place A to place B. In this case, the worker at place A is separated from the worker at place B, and therefore they cannot help each other with the job. Toyota will remove the conveyor in such cases.

Linear layouts. To overcome the demerits of an isolated island layout, different types of machines can be laid out in a linear form (Figure 11.5). Under this layout,

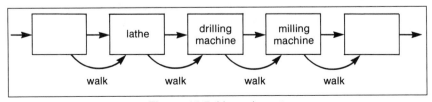

Figure 11.5. Linear layout.

workers must walk between machines. This is one of the typical characteristics of Toyota's layout.

Using this linear layout, one of the major disadvantages of isolated islands (unnecessary stocking of outputs among processes) can be eliminated, thereby allowing products to flow smoothly and quickly among machines. One problem that cannot be eliminated using the linear layout, however, is the inability of reallocating operations among workers to adapt to changes in demand.

Another problem associated with this system is that when machines are set out in a linear form, each line is independent from other lines. In this situation, the repositioning of operations among workers in accordance with the demand for products often requires a fractional number of workers, such as 8.5 persons. Since 0.5 manpower is not possible, it must be rounded up to one person. As a result, the worker will have some amount of waiting time, or excessive production will occur.

As an example, one unit has been produced in a two-minute cycle time by only one worker. Assume that the demand of cars was increased and that the cycle time was reduced to 1.5 minutes per unit. In this case, if a worker can normally finish half of the total jobs for making one unit of product within one minute, then an additional worker must be introduced to this process to complete the other half of the total jobs. As a result, each of the two workers in this process must have 0.5 minutes of waiting time in every cycle time. Or, if the first worker performed more jobs in 1.5 minutes without any idle time, the second worker must have one full minute of idle time.

Combining U-form Lines

In order to overcome this problem of fractional numbers of workers, Toyota eventually decided to combine several U-form lines into one integrated line. Using this combined layout, the allocation of operations among workers in response to variations in production quantities of automobiles can be accomplished by following the procedures of setting the standard operations routine.

The following example will show how Shojinka can be attained using this concept. Suppose there is a combined process which consists of six different lines (A-F), and each line is manufacturing a different gear (Figure 11.6). According to the monthly demand of products in January, the cycle time of this combined process was one minute per unit. Under this cycle time, eight persons were working in this process (Figure 11.7), and the walking route of each worker is described by the arrow line.

In February, however, the monthly demand for products was decreased and the process cycle time was increased to 1.2 minutes per unit. As a result, all operations of this combined line were reallocated among the workers and each worker now had to undertake more operations than in January. Figure 11.8 shows that the walking route of each worker was expanded under the new allocation of operations. In this case, worker 1 will do as an additional job some of the

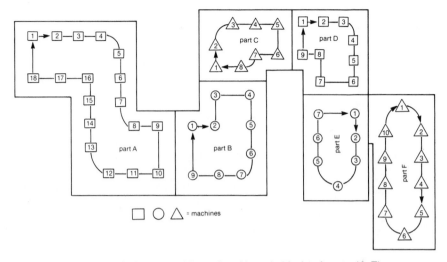

Figure 11.6. Combined line of making six kinds of parts (A-F).

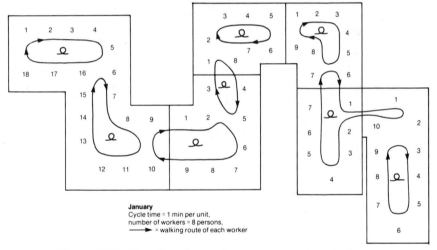

Figure 11.7. Allocation of operations among workers in January.

operations which worker 2 was doing in January. Worker 2 will also undertake an additional job which was previously accomplished by worker 3 in January. The result of expanding the walking route of each worker is that workers 7 and 8 can be omitted from this combined line. Thus, the fractional manpower which might have occurred in a linear form layout was absorbed in various individual lines under this combined layout.

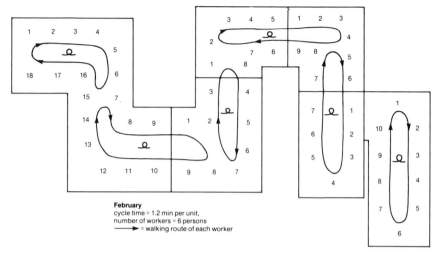

Figure 11.8. Allocation of operations among workers in February.

ATTAINING SHOJINKA THROUGH MULTI-FUNCTION WORKERS

Figure 11.1 showed that the ability to widen or narrow the range of jobs performed by each worker is a key ingredient in achieving Shojinka. Carefully-designed machine layouts help develop this ability, but machine layouts alone cannot achieve Shojinka.

Remember that the true meaning of Shojinka is the ability to quickly alter the number of workers at each shop to adapt to changes in demand. When viewed from the side of the individual worker, Shojinka demands that the worker be able to respond to changes in cycle time, operations routines, and in many cases, the duties of individual jobs. In order to respond quickly, the worker must be multi-functioned; that is, he must be trained to be a skilled worker for any type of job and at any process.

Cultivating Multi-Function Workers through Job Rotation

Obviously, cultivating or training the individual worker to become multi-functioned is an important part of achieving Shojinka. Toyota cultivates their workers using a system called *job rotation,* where each worker rotates through and performs every job in his workshop. After a period, the individual worker develops proficiency in each job and thereby becomes a multi-functioned worker.

The job rotation system consists of three major parts. First, each manager and supervisor must rotate through every job and prove their own abilities to the general workers in the shop. Second, each worker within the shop is rotated through and trained to perform each job in the shop. The final step is scheduling the workers through job rotation at a frequency of several times each day.

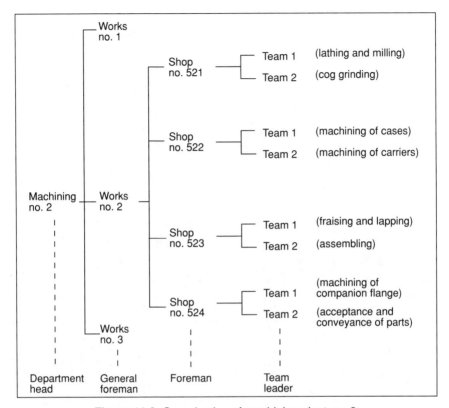

Figure 11.9. Organization of machining plant no. 2.

Toyota first implemented a job rotation plan at their Tsutsumi Factory (Machining Plant No. 2) where rear-wheel differential carriers are processed and assembled. The organization of the plant is shown in Figure 11.9. Notice that at each work's shop and line there are general foremen, foremen, and line chiefs, respectively. General workers are the responsibility of each line chief with a total of 220 employees working at the plant. Rotation of workers among jobs was implemented following the three steps previously discussed.

Step 1: Rotation of supervisors. In order to cultivate general laborers into multi-function workers, the managers and supervisors must first display themselves as models or examples of the multi-functioned worker. As a result, all of the general foremen, foremen, and line chiefs (about 60 persons total) were rotated among each work's shop and line in this plant. The foremen were transferred among shops of the same works. Since the rotation of all managers and supervisors took three years to accomplish, the job rotation plan was implemented as part of a long-range planning program.

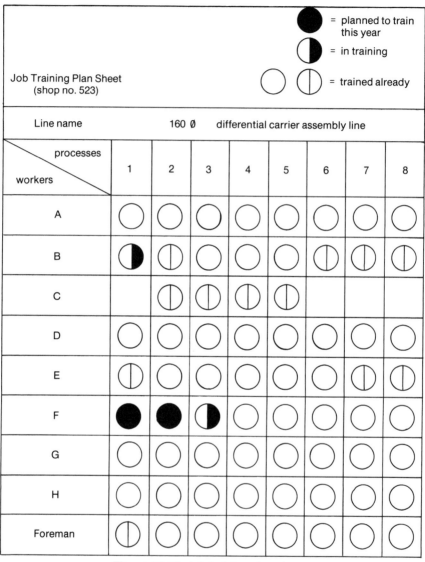

Figure 11.10. Job training plan sheet.

Step 2: Rotation of workers within each shop. To accomplish this step, a job-training plan must be scheduled for general workers as was planned for shop number 523 in Figure 11.10. This plan was set by the general foreman so that every worker in his shop could master any kind of operation at every process in the shop.

To promote the training plan, a multi-function worker rate for each shop must be formulated using the following formula:

$$\frac{\sum_{i=1}^{n} \text{number of processes each worker } (i) \text{ has mastered}}{\text{total number of processes within the shop} \times n}$$

where n = total number of workers at the shop.

Toyota's goal for this rate was 60% for the first year (1977), 80% for the second year (1978), and 100% for the third year (1979). However, the actual average rate attained in 1979 at the Tsutsumi Plant was 55%. This low figure was due to the physical health and strength of the typical worker, the number of extra workers from outside-related companies, and the number of temporary seasonal and newly-employed laborers. The actual training time for a worker to master each job usually varies from several days through several weeks.

Step 3: Job rotation several times per day. When the aforementioned multi-function worker rate became high, Shojinka could be realized, and job rotation could be made every week, or in many cases every day. In some advanced cases, all workers could be rotated among all processes of the line in two- or four-hour intervals.

An example of this advanced job rotation occurred in line 2 of shop number 523. In this line, the 160 Ø differential carriers are assembled by eight workers (excluding the line chief as a relief man) within its cycle time of 26 seconds. The layout and standard operations routine of each worker are depicted in Figure 11.11. Keep in mind that each process means the standard operations routine, or in other words, the walking route of each worker. Such a walking route will not change unless the cycle time of this line is changed.

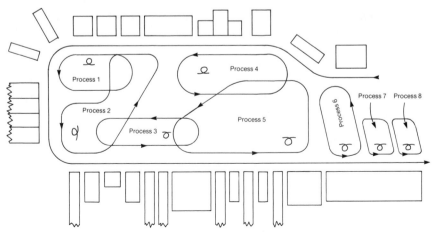

Figure 11.11. Layout and standard operation routines.

Process No.	Contents of the job at each process	Characteristic of operations	Manual operations time	Fatigue rank
1	Differential case	Skill of finger work is required	26"	4
2	Cover assy	Skill and knowledge of quality check are required	26"	5
3	Can adjust	Long walking distance	26"	3
4	Ring gear assy	Finger work, and heavy work by right arm	26"	1
5	Pre-load adjustment	Long walking distance with heavy material	26"	2
6	Bearing assy	Sensitivity of hand and finger is required	26"	6
7	Back-rush holding	Skilled work, and heavy work by waist and arms	26"	7
8	Rock-bolt assy	Waiting time of 2 sec. exists	24"	8

Figure 11.12. Job characteristics and fatigue rank of each process.

The manual operations time to complete one unit at each process was about 26 seconds for all workers except at process 8. The job characteristic and fatigue rank of each process in this line are described in Figure 11.12. The grade of fatigue at each process will be different depending on differences of the operations contents.

Job rotation at shop 523 is accomplished in intervals of two hours. First, a predetermined job rotation schedule must be planned for the five days of the following week. When planning this type of schedule, it should be noted that the allocation of the various processes among workers must be fair; also, the training program for the newcomer must also be considered.

Each morning, the general foreman listens again to the health conditions and desires of all workers, and also reexamines the proper way to introduce extra workers onto the line. Finally, he determines the job rotation schedule (Figure 11.13).

In this job rotation schedule, the following conditions of the workers H, B, and C should be considered:

• Worker H is a veteran, but sickly.
• Worker C is a long-term extra worker from outside of the company.
• Worker B is still in a training stage for process 1.

Job-Rotation Schedule   (shop no. 523)

Times of rotation	Line name / Time interval / Process no.	160 Ø differential carrier assembly line							
		1	2	3	4	5	6	7	8
1	8AM - 10AM	A	B	C	D	E	F	G	H
2	10AM - 12AM	G	A	B	C	D	H	E	F
3	1PM - 3PM	E	G	C	A	B	F	D	H
4	3PM - 5PM	D	C	G	B	A	H	F	E
5	5PM - 7PM	B	D	C	F	E	A	G	H

Figure 11.13. Job rotation schedule for workers (A-H).

Therefore, when worker B works at process 1 in his fifth rotation time, veteran worker D will support him as a nearby worker.

At this shop, all workers except C and H will engage in different kinds of jobs in each two-hour interval. Since this workshop has a smaller cycle time (twenty-six seconds), the worker must have a narrower range of jobs; this is the principal reason for assigning a two-hour interval to this shop. In the event the cycle time was longer, however, workers could handle a wider range of jobs, and thus a four-hour interval could be applied. Some shops even have eight hour intervals (or, one-day interval).

Additional Advantages of Job Rotation
Among the advantages of job rotation documented by Toyota at their Tsutsumi Plant include:

- The workers' attitudes are refreshed and muscle fatigue can be prevented; as a result, workers are more attentive and careful in avoiding labor accidents. The frequency of shop accidents is actually decreasing at this plant.
- The feeling of unfairness that veterans must have heavy work will disappear. Also, at the beginning of each rotation, there is conversation between rotating workers. Through these conversations, the human relationship between workers improves, and the mutual relief movement will be further promoted.
- Since senior workers and supervisors teach their own skills and knowledge to their younger workers and subordinates, the skills and know-how are dispersed throughout the shop and kept on standard operations sheets.
- Since each worker participates in every process within the shop, he feels responsible for all goals of the shop, such as safety, quality, cost, and also production quantity.
- At new shops and processes, all people (irrespective of supervisors or subordinate workers) take a fresh approach and, through this new viewpoint, can isolate problems or points for improvements. Thus, ideas and suggestions to improve the process will increase remarkably.

The various benefits can best be summarized with the simple words: respect for humans. This is a considerably different attitude from traditional schemes where mass production yields a division of labor and, in turn, specialization of labor, simplification of jobs, and, finally, human alienation.

Importance of the Line Chief: Giving Rest Time and Job Rotation to Workers

One of the most important elements affecting the success of the job rotation system is the role of the line chief. Aside from guidance, the line chief also allows workers to take rest time while still permitting job rotation. The line chief or foreman can always replace a worker in the line, whether the worker is taking a rest or exchanging jobs with another worker.

Suppose worker A wishes to take a rest (or another kind of job). At this time, he calls his line chief or foreman and explains his desire. The line chief will then take worker A's job, and worker A can take a rest. After taking a rest, worker A may go to worker B and ask to exchange jobs. Worker B then leaves his process and worker A engages in B's job. If worker B does not want to have a rest, he may request to change jobs with another worker. The other worker can in turn take a rest when worker B takes his new job.

In this way any worker can take a rest and still exchange his job with another worker. This process can occur quite freely whenever a worker desires, even though the job rotation schedule (Figure 11.13) has been established and there is no allowance for a rest time in the standard operations routine sheet.

America vs. Japan: The Multi-Function Worker

The multi-functioned worker is not unique to Toyota; in fact, the concept of the multi-function worker is prevalent in many companies throughout Japan. A question that comes to mind is: "How can the multi-function worker be prevalent in Japanese companies but hardly exist in American companies?" To understand the reason for this difference, it is best to analyze a case study involving a company that seems typical of the American business climate: the Caterpillar Tractor Company, for example. In its large-parts machine line for the type D-8 tractor, there are various kinds of jobs and numerous workers (Figure 11.14).

Labor grade	Kinds of jobs	Number of workers
A	Sweeper	1
B	Cleaner	1
C	Production scraper	2
D	Mill	5
E	Multi-driller	1
F	Multi-driller	1
F	Radial-driller	10
G	Boring machinist	5
H	Salvage welder	5
H	Salvage welder	5

Figure 11.14. Job types at a machining line in the Caterpillar Tractor Company.

The left side of Figure 11.4 displays the labor grade for the job (letters A-H). The rank of each labor grade increases with ascending letters of the alphabet. A wage rate per hour is determined for each labor grade. Even for the same kind of job, such as multi-driller, there are separate ranks and wage rates—in this case grades E and F. Figure 11.15 shows the basic hourly wage rate for each labor grade.

Labor grade	Pay raise steps 1	2	3	4
A	4.69			
B	4.69	4.77		
C	4.77	4.86		
D	4.86	4.96		
E	4.86	4.96	5.07	
F	4.96	5.07	5.35	
G	5.07	5.19	5.35	
H	5.07	5.19	5.35	5.57
J	5.19	5.35	5.57	5.83
K	5.35	5.57	5.83	6.15
L	5.57	5.83	6.15	6.49

Figure 11.15. Hourly basic wage rate of each labor grade (as of 1976; dollar unit).

Figure 11.14 shows that there are some laborers who work specifically as a sweeper, cleaner, or production scraper. These classes of workers seem unusual in Japanese eyes, because in Japan it is quite natural that the individual driller or welder sweeps his own area, as well as setting up and scraping his workpiece. In the Caterpillar Tractor Company, the boring machinist specializes only in boring, and he has his own wage rate based on his labor grade.

The facts here show the following features about the American business community:

- In American companies, job classification is excessive compared with Japanese companies. This seems to be based on an American ideology for standardization, which has resulted in an extremely fine division of labor.
- Most American workers are single-function workers. Even if the worker is versatile, he still works as a specialist of a certain type of job. This seems partly based on the fact that there are many kinds of craft unions in the same factory.

Such excessive classification and specialization in jobs increases the cost of products. For example, suppose that an electric welding operation needed only 20 seconds to make one unit, and the job must be done at a specific welding place. If one part is made each minute of cycle time, the welder will process this part in

20 seconds and have a waiting time of forty seconds; otherwise, the worker will engage in lot production, which creates a large inventory from the welding process. This creates a long lead time as a whole.

Other reasons why the multi-function worker has not been cultivated in American companies are:

- Wage systems based on labor grades.
- Lack of on-the-job training programs for cultivating blue-collar workers into multi-function workers.
- Difficulty of transferring blue-collar workers among the various kinds of jobs in a plant.

Looking at the first of these factors, the wage rate of each labor grade cannot be increased once it has reached its final step (Figure 11.15). After that step, the only pay raises possible are those designed to overcome inflation. In order for blue-collar workers to increase their wages beyond this point, they must take either of two approaches: change job type within the same company or change companies.

The first approach, changing jobs within the same company, has two negative aspects. First, American companies rarely give on-the-job training (like Toyota's Job Rotation System) to blue-collar workers. At the Caterpillar Tractor Company, for example, a sweeper (Figure 11.14) will remain in his present job unless he personally studies to become a driller or boring machinist.

Second, and more important, American companies rarely transfer blue collar workers among various kinds of jobs within the same company as Japanese companies do. For example, the management of the Caterpillar Tractor Company appear very reluctant to implement a job rotation system for the following reasons:

- Without a vacancy at the job in question, transfer cannot take place.
- Without a proposal or request from some worker, management cannot determine who should be transferred.
- The transfer of workers is normally determined automatically in accordance with seniority out of those workers desiring transfers.
- Many workers requesting transfers often want to take simpler, easier jobs.

As a result of these negative aspects, American workers seeking to increase their wage rates quite often will transfer to another company. This is best observed by the labor mobility rates for Japan and the United States. The labor mobility rate is essentially a percentage of the total work force that changes companies (enter or leave). During 1978, the average monthly labor mobility rate for Japan was 1.4%, while the rate for the U.S. was 3.9%. Therefore, the annual rate for the U.S. was 47%, nearly 2.8 times the rate for Japan. This seems to indicate that nearly one half of the U.S. labor moves to a new company each year.

Japanese Business Climate: Ideal for the Multi-Function Worker

In Japan, a laborer's wages are basically connected to each individual worker, not to a specific labor grade. His wage rate will be increased mainly on the number of years he has been employed by the company. Also, the typical Japanese company teaches many different jobs to workers by means of on-the-job training programs. These wage rates and OJT systems help motivate workers to stay in the same company until retirement. As a result, a multi-function worker can be developed that is also loyal to the company.

The labor-grade wage system has not been adopted in Japan as a principal criterion to determine wages. Although this wage system is partially adopted, the pay-raise period is very long; this is partly based on the Japanese value of group consciousness. Also, the typical Japanese firm has only an enterprise union in each company, instead of having many different craft unions in one plant.

The life-time employment system kept by Japanese management is another strong factor to explain why typical Japanese employees are motivated to be versatile workers. Under this employment system, the company often has a favorable return on investment in educating the laborer as a multi-function worker.

At Toyota, overtime work seems to be a buffer for keeping such stable employment. By realizing Shoninka and Shojinka, Toyota has only the minimum number of workers necessary at each workshop, and all workers usually realize overtime. If demands were decreased or robotics were introduced, the overtime would be decreased without dismissing or laying off any workers.

Moreover, seasonal part-time workers and business groups are behind the life-time employment system. Firms within a certain business group will help each other; in this way, a depressed company can transfer its workers to prosperous companies within the business group. The Japanese business environment undoubtedly supports this type of employment system.

The Japanese employment system, wage system, the system of transferring workers among various departments, and the OJT system for cultivating versatile workers are all based on the principal Japanese value of group consciousness. For the purpose of attaining total system effectiveness in a society which had no additional frontiers, excessive individualism had to be restrained. Only an educational system would be effective in changing the social value over a long period of time.

12

Improvement Activities
Help Reduce the Work Force
and Increase Worker Morale

The Toyota production system attempts to increase productivity and reduce manufacturing costs. Unlike other such systems, however, it reaches its goal without a loss in the human dignity of the worker. As has often been pointed out in connection with the conveyor belt system developed by Henry Ford, attempts to increase productivity are usually accompanied by an increased demand on the individual worker. To increase productivity, one must either maintain the same level of production while reducing the size of the work force or produce more and more with the existing number of workers. Traditionally, either alternative has involved an unacceptable sacrifice in human terms—a dehumanization of the worker. At Toyota, however, the conflict between productivity and human concerns has been resolved by initiating positive improvements at every workplace through small groups called *quality control circles* (QC circles).

The improvements are varied: refinement of manual operations to eliminate wasted motion, introduction of new or improved machinery to avoid the uneconomical use of manpower, and improved economy in the use of materials and supplies. All three types of improvements are evolved by means of small group meetings in which a suggestion system similar to that employed in other countries plays a prominent part.

In addition, the Kanban system also functions to promote improvements in productivity. In all likelihood, it is the only production control system that also provides a motivation for improved productivity. Figure 12.1 shows the relationships between the Kanban system, various improvements in the workplace, quality control circles, and increased productivity and morale.

IMPROVEMENTS IN MANUAL OPERATIONS

In any factory, all manual operations fall into one of the following three categories:

- *Pure waste*—Unnecessary actions which should be eliminated immediately; i.e., waiting time, stacking of intermediate products, and *double transfers* (Figure 12.2).

177

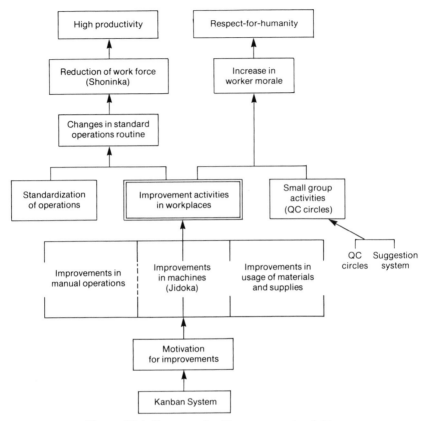

Figure 12.1. Framework of improvement activities.

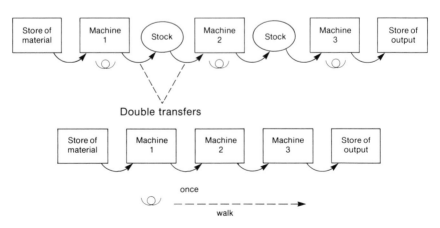

Figure 12.2. Elimination of double transfer.

- *Operations without value added*—Operations that are essentially wasteful but may be necessary under the current operating procedures. They include walking long distances to pick up parts, unpacking vendor parcels, shifting a tool from one hand to another, etc. To eliminate such operations, it would be necessary to make changes in the layout of the line or arrange for vendor items to be delivered unpackaged—none may be practical at the present time.

- *Net operations to increase value added*—Conversion or processing operations that increase the value of raw materials or semi-finished products by adding manual labor; i.e., subassembly of parts, forging raw material, tempering gears, painting body work, etc.

Also, remedial operations—operations to repair or remove defective products, tools, or equipment—are found in all factories.

Net operations to increase value added typically constitute only a small portion of total operations, but most of these serve only to increase costs (Figure 12.3). By raising the percentage of net operations to increase value added, labor required per unit can be reduced, thus reducing the number of workers at each workplace. The first step is to eliminate pure waste. Next, reduce operations without value added as far as possible without incurring unreasonable costs. Finally, examine even net operations to increase value added to see if they can be further increased as a proportion of total operations by introducing some type of automatic machinery to take the place of operations currently being carried out by hand.

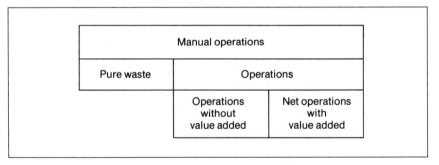

Figure 12.3. Categories of operations.

REDUCTION OF THE WORK FORCE

When making improvements to reduce the number of workers on its combined U-form lines, Toyota eliminates wasteful operations, reallocates operations, and reduces the work force. These three steps are really parts of a cyclical process: elimination of purely wasteful operations (waiting time) immediately leads to reallocation of operations among workers at the workplace and a partial reduction in the work force. The three steps may be repeated several times before all possible improvements to the line have been made (Figure 12.4).

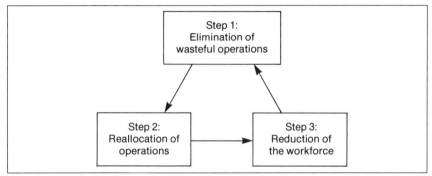

Figure 12.4. Cycle for reducing the number of workers.

The first step toward reducing the number of workers is to determine the waiting time for each worker and revise the standard operations routine to eliminate it. Waiting time is often hidden behind overproduction and so never comes to light. In such cases, large amounts of inventory are behind or between processes. As a result, actions such as moving and stacking inventory, which occupy much of a worker's waiting time, are often regarded as part of his job. At Toyota, however, such actions are classified as a waste of overproduction, and the Kanban system, which serves to reduce inventory levels, makes the waste of overproduction obvious. Kanban plays an important a role in eliminating wasteful operations by standardizing operations.

To illustrate how eliminating waiting time and reallocating operations leads to a reduction in the work force, consider the following example. Seven workers, A through G, are all working at the same workplace. The standard operating time for the operations assigned to each worker must be measured. By subtracting the standard operating time for each worker from the cycle time, waiting time during each cycle for each worker can be determined. If, for example, the cycle time is one minute per unit of production and the total standard operations assigned to worker A take 0.9 minutes, he will have 0.1 minutes of waiting time. In most cases, each of the other workers will also have waiting times of varying length (Figure 12.5).

To eliminate waiting time, some of worker B's operations must be transferred to worker A, some of worker C's operations to worker B, and so forth until enough operations have been reallocated to eliminate the waiting time for workers A through E. At this point, worker G's job will have been eliminated altogether (Figure 12.6).

When reallocating operations among workers—either to bring about improvements in manual operations or to compensate for changes in production levels—the following three rules should be observed:

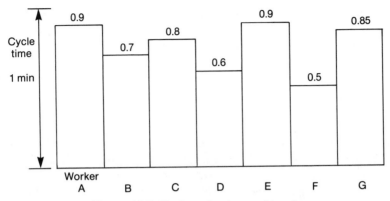

Figure 12.5. Each worker has waiting time.

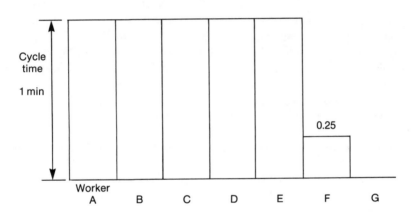

Figure 12.6. Reallocation of operations among workers.

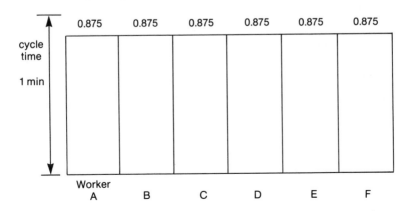

Figure 12.7. Wrong allocation of operations.

1. When the waiting time for each worker is being measured, he should stand without doing anything at all after finishing the operations assigned to him. If worker B, for example, finishes his job in 0.7 minutes he should simply stand idle at his work station for the remaining 0.3 minutes. In this way, everyone will be able to see that he has free time, and there will be less resistance if he is assigned one or two more jobs.

2. When reducing the number of workers at a workplace, the best worker(s) should always be removed first. If a dull or unskilled worker is moved, he may resist, his morale may suffer, and he may never develop into a skilled worker. An outstanding worker, by contrast, is usually more willing to be moved since he has more self-confidence and may welcome the opportunity to learn other jobs in the factory.

3. After operations have been reallocated to workers A through E, the 0.75 minutes of waiting time for worker F should not be disposed of by distributing it equally among the six workers remaining on the line. If it were, it would simply be hidden again, since each worker would slow down his work pace to accommodate his share of the waiting time. Also, there would be resistance when it came time to revise the standard operations routine again (Figure 12.7). Instead, a return to step 1 is necessary to see if further improvements can be made in the line to eliminate the fractional operations left for worker F.

All three types of manual operations must be examined, including net operations to increase value added which might be omitted through introduction of an automatic machine. At this state, however, it is important to choose the least expensive plan, since only 0.25 minutes of manual operating time needs omitting. Less expensive improvements include:

- Move parts supplies closer to the worker or introduce chutes to shorten walking distances.
- Use smaller pallets that can be placed beside workers who need only a small number of parts at a time.
- Redesign a tool to eliminate the wasted motion in changing it from one hand to the other.
- Make it easier to pick up tools by hanging them in racks with their handles uppermost.
- Introduce some simple tools to streamline operations.
- When a worker operates more than one machine, locate the on/off switch between the two machines so it can be pushed while the operator is walking from one machine to the other.

By means of one or more of the aforementioned devices, it should be possible to eliminate the 0.25 minutes of operating time remaining for worker F and so remove him from the line. Thus, in our example, it would be possible to eliminate two out of seven workers. Look at the line again for previously overlooked wasteful operations and attempt to remove another worker by eliminating other operations without value added. Improvements to the line at this point are difficult; some improvements that are intrinsically worthwhile may be held in reserve until a sales or model change makes it possible to alter the cycle time or the design of the workplace.

IMPROVEMENTS IN MACHINERY

In any manufacturing process, two kinds of improvements exist: improvements in manual operations and improvements in machinery. The first involves definition of standard operations, reallocation of operations among workers, relocation of stored parts and semi-finished products, etc. The second type of improvement involves introduction of new equipment such as robots and automatic machines. At Toyota, improvements in manual operations are always undertaken before making improvements in machinery. The reasons follow:

- From a cost-benefit standpoint, machine improvement may not pay. Remember that the purpose of any improvement is to reduce the number of workers. If the same purpose can be achieved through improvements in manual operations, it will not pay to install a new schedule.

- Changes in manual operations can be reversed if necessary, while those in machinery cannot. Thus, if a machine improvement ends in failure, the machine is a total loss. The cost of improvements in manual operations, on the other hand, are at least partially recoverable.

- Improvements to machinery often fail if they are made before improvements in manual operations. Since an automatic machine is inflexible in its operation, it can be successfully integrated into a line only if all manual operations have already been standardized. Otherwise, improper processing of the work piece and operation of the machine may result in any unacceptable number of defective parts and the machine itself may break down frequently. If an automatic punch press, for example, was installed where the wrong types of material might be placed in the machine, the die could be permanently damaged and the machine along with it. As a result, it would be necessary to assign a watchman to the machine and its value as a labor-saving improvement would be reduced considerably.

Policies in Promoting Jidoka

Autonomation or "Jidoka" is essentially improving machinery to reduce the number of workers. There are two problems, however, that should be considered when promoting Jidoka:

1. Even if the introduction of an automatic machine reduces manpower require-ments by 0.9 persons, it cannot actually reduce the number of workers on the line unless the remaining 0.1 person (which is often the watchman for the machine) can also be eliminated. As a result, introduction of the machine serves only to increase manufacturing costs and thus the cost of the product. To put the matter a different way, a reduction in the man hours required to produce a unit ("Shoryokuka") is not the same thing as a reduction in the work force. For this reason, a true reduction in the work force is called "Shoninka" at Toyota to distinguish it from Shoryokuka. Only Shoninka can reduce the cost of an automobile.

2. Jidoka often has the undesirable effect of fixing the number of workers who must be employed at a given workplace; i.e., while Jidoka replaces manual operations, it may also require a certain number of workers to help the machine by performing operations that cannot be automated. As a result, the same number of workers must always be present to operate the machine regardless of production quantity. At Toyota, this phenomenon is called a *quorum system* ("Te-i-in-se-i"), which is an undesirable phenomenon in any business.

In both respects, then, introduction of Jidoka may actually limit the ability to reduce the number of workers—a matter of some concern, since it is always essential to be able to reduce the work force, especially when demand decreases. How can the two problems be solved? How can Shojinka (flexibility in the number of workers) be maintained when introducing Jidoka? Toyota has two policies:

1. Automatic machines should be introduced only when a strong need exists, not simply because the manual operation in question can be replaced by a machine.

2. The work stations at a machine should always be located as close together as possible, especially when the machine occupies a large area, as is the case with a transfer machine. Too often, the work stations are widely separated, and each worker's operation time at the machine per cycle is fractional. As a result, it is impossible to combine fractional manpower operations into integer operations when the work force must be reduced.

JOB IMPROVEMENTS AND RESPECT FOR HUMANITY

When making job improvements, respect for humanity can be maintained by observing the following rules:

Give workers valuable jobs. Reductions in the work force are sometimes regarded as a way of forcing hard work on workers without consideration for their humanity. This criticism, however, is based on a misunderstanding of the nature of job improvements or in cases where the wrong procedure has been adopted. When operations at a workshop are improved, each worker must understand that the elimination of wasteful actions will never lead to harder work. Instead, the goal of the improvement program is to increase the number of net operations with added value that can be performed with the same amount of labor. For example, suppose a worker on a trimming line must walk five or six steps to pick up a part and climb in and out of the car several times during each cycle. The function of job improvement is to eliminate such wasteful actions and use the time instead to perform net operations with added value, thus reducing the total standard operations time and the number of workers. Unless this point is fully understood, the Toyota production system is hard to apply, especially in an environment where the labor union is strong.

At Toyota, then, respect for humanity is a matter of allying human energy with meaningful, effective operations by abolishing wasteful operations. If a worker feels that his job is important and his work significant, his morale will be high; if he sees that his time is wasted on insignificant jobs, his morale will suffer as well as his work.

Keep the lines of communication within the organization open. The approach used to promote job improvements is very important. A mere injunction to "Reduce the number of workers!" or "Improve the process!" is not enough to solve the problem. Every workshop has its problems and workers are usually interested in solving them. A worker may complain, for example, that his operation is hard to do because of crowded conditions at his work station or that the machine is hard to adjust and leaks oil. When the worker notifies his supervisor about such problems, however, the supervisor may not pay attention or repair personnel may not attend to the problem on a timely basis. When this happens, an exceptional worker may try to solve the problem himself—and fail, especially if the solution requires that a machine be redesigned or modified. In most cases, however, the worker will simply lodge a complaint with the labor union and resistance to the manager will come out. (A representative case is described in Runcie 1980.) If, on the other hand, the supervisor responds quickly and effectively, the worker will trust his supervisor and feel that he has an active role in efforts to improve the shop.

A relationship of trust and credibility is most important in promoting improvements. In order to establish such a relationship, however, the formal lines of communication from the lower level workers through to the foreman and general foreman up to the superintendent must be well drawn and open since any problem must be solved through these channels. If the supervisors and IE staff respect proposals from the workshop and promote improvements together with workers, each individual in the factory will have high morale and an awareness of his role in improvement activities. No one will feel alienated, and every worker will feel that his work is an important part of his life.

THE SUGGESTION SYSTEM

Although the stated purpose of any suggestion system is to draw upon the ideas of all employees to improve company operations, its real purpose is often quite different. In such cases, the suggestion system is intended simply to give an employee the sense that he is recognized by his company or his superior, or to build loyalty and company pride by allowing him to draw up plans as if he were a member of management. In other words, the real purpose of a suggestion system in most companies is labor or personnel management.

At Toyota, however, both the purpose and spirit of its suggestion system are expressed in the slogan: "Good products, good ideas"—that is, its goal is to draw upon the ideas of all employees in order to improve product quality and reduce costs so the company can continue to grow in the world automobile market. This is not to say that Toyota is oblivious to the effect of a suggestion system on labor relations, but it is some index of the seriousness with which Toyota takes its employees' suggestions that most of the improvement activities described in this chapter were initiated through a company-wide suggestion system.

Individual improvement schemes are devised and introduced by an individual worker or by *QC circles* composed of workers at each workplace led by the supervisor. When one of the members of the group calls a problem to the attention of the supervisor, the supervisor takes the following steps:

1. *Define the problem.* In considering the problem, the supervisor should attempt to determine the exact nature of the difficulty and its effect(s) on other operations and workers.

2. *Examine the problem.* Present conditions must be examined in detail to determine the causes of the problem. In the process, other related problems may also come to light.

3. *Generate ideas.* The supervisor should encourage the worker to generate ideas for solving the problem. For example, suppose a worker has pointed out that it takes him a great deal of time to count the number of units on a pallet and that the pallet often contains several different kinds of parts. The worker might then suggest that frames be installed in the pallet to make it easier for him to count

the number of parts it contains and to separate one kind of part from another (Figure 12.8). Or an equally good solution may be evolved by the group as a whole. In either case, the supervisor should always show respect for his subordinates' ideas.

4. *Summarize ideas.* The supervisor should summarize the various proposed solutions to the problem and allow his subordinates to select the best scheme.

5. *Submit the proposal.* One member of the group should write the selected scheme on a suggestion sheet and put it in the suggestion box. Although many suggestions for improvements are generated by means of QC circles, individual ideas for improvements can be submitted at any time without consulting with the supervisor or another group member. Nor is it necessary for a problem to arise in order for the group to operate as a source for suggested improvements.

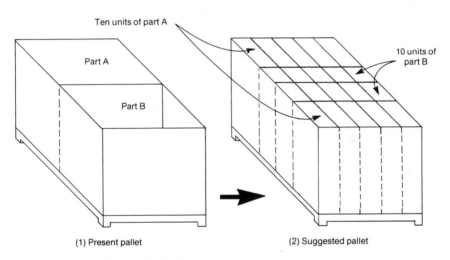

Figure 12.8. Example of suggestion scheme.

Toyota uses the following check list of topics for QC circle meetings:

Improvements in manual operations:
1. Is it appropriate to store materials, tools, and products in the present way?
2. Is there any easier way to manage machine handling or machine processing?
3. Can you make your job easier and more efficient by changing the layout of machines and conveyance facilities?

Savings in materials and supplies:
1. Are oil, grease, and other supplies being used efficiently?
2. Is there anything that can be done to reduce leakage of steam, air, oil, etc.?
3. Can you reduce the consumption of materials and supplies by improving materials, machining methods, and jigs?

Improving efficiency in the engineering department and in offices:
1. Are there jobs in your office that overlap?
2. Are there any jobs that could be eliminated?
3. Could you improve the present voucher system?
4. Could your job be standardized?

Improving the work environment to increase safety and prevent dangerous accidents:
1. Are the lighting, ventilation, and temperature conditions good?
2. Are dust, gas, and bad odors fully removed from the work area?
3. Is your safety equipment appropriate: Does it function well?

Improving efficiency and uniformity of the automobile itself:
1. Can the quality of the automobile be improved by changing its design and manufacture?
2. Is there any way to increase the uniformity of the product?

Although the procedure for proposing improvements is much the same at Toyota as it is in America and European countries, the system for evaluating the proposals is quite different and far more effective because it is carried out in a rapid and orderly fashion. The assessment of proposals follows the path through the organization shown in Figure 12.9 and consists of the following steps:

1. All suggestions are gathered at the plant office on the first day of each month and recorded in the suggestion ledger.
2. Each Plant Sectional Committee examines the suggestions by the twentieth of the month and determines which plans deserve rewards of 5,000 yen or less.
3. The Plant Committee or Department Committee then examines plans which deserve a reward of at least 6,000 yen.
4. Plans which deserve a reward of at least 20,000 yen are examined professionally by a corporate-wide Suggestion Committee.
5. An official announcement of the results of the examination is published in the evaluation result table and in the Toyota newspaper.

All plans that have been adopted are implemented immediately. In some cases, a plan will be designated "pending" and examined again the following month. Other plans, designated "reference," may be improved by committee

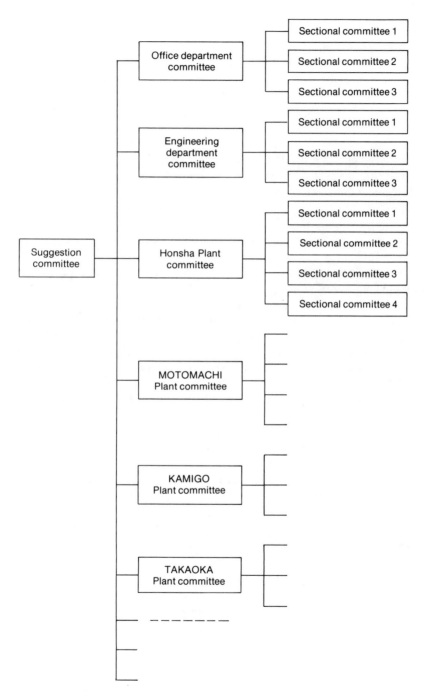

Figure 12.9. Organization of suggestion system committees.

members or managers and used later. If any type of plan contains patentable material, the committee notifies the person responsible for the suggestion and then submits the plan to an Invention Committee for appropriate action. All patents are applied for under the company name. The rewards are usually kept by each group and used for recreational activities such as trips or fishing parties.

In addition to monetary rewards, other kinds of commendations are awarded:

- For outstanding proposals, the company gives a testimonial to the person or persons responsible at a ceremony held each month.
- On a yearly basis, commendations are awarded to the person with the largest total amount of rewards, the largest average reward per suggestion, etc.
- Any employee who has been given yearly commendations for three years in a row is given a special testimonial and a commemorative gift.
- A yearly testimonial and trophy can also be awarded to outstanding groups.

The suggestion system at Toyota was introduced in June, 1951. Figure 12.10 shows the number of proposals in recent years. It does not show, however, that there were about 53,500 workers at Toyota in 1984, including office workers. Thus, after 1984, each worker suggested an average of more than 40 improvement plans each year, most of which (95%) have been adopted. After 1987, however, Toyota began to put more emphasis on the quality of proposals instead of on the number of proposals resulting in the average number of proposals per person decreasing to 30.

In summary, the suggestion system has the following advantages:

- The system operates through individual workers or QC circles where the supervisor of each group can give his subordinates' problems and proposals sincere and immediate attention.
- Proposals are examined every month on an orderly schedule and the results are announced immediately.
- The evaluation process establishes a close relationship between workers and the professional staff. For example, if a suggested improvement involves a change in design, a professional engineer will examine it immediately.

KANBAN AND IMPROVEMENT ACTIVITIES

Everyone wants to take it easy, and, in this respect, the Japanese are no different from people in other countries. When inventory levels are high, things seem to go better for everyone: if a machine breaks down or the number of defective parts increases suddenly, subsequent operations need not stop so long as there is sufficient stock in inventory; and when the required number of units are not produced during regular working hours, it is usually unnecessary to schedule overtime in order to meet production goals. As long as problems like these are

Year	Number of Suggestions	Number of Suggestions/ person	Participation Rate (%)	Adoption Rate (%)
1976	463,442	10.6	83	83
1977	454,552	10.6	86	86
1978	527,718	12.2	89	88
1979	575,861	13.3	91	92
1980	859,039	19.2	92	93
1981	1,412,565	31.2	93	93
1982	1,905,642	38.8	94	95
1983	1,655,868	31.5	94	95
1984	2,149,744	40.2	95	96
1985	2,453,105	45.6	95	96
1986	2,648,710	47.7	95	96
1987	1,831,560	--	--	96
1988	1,903,858	--	--	96

Figure 12.10. Number of proposals in recent years.

hidden behind high inventory levels, however, they cannot be identified and eliminated. As a result, they will continue to be responsible for various kinds of waste: wasted time, wasted labor, wasted material, etc.

By contrast, when inventory is minimized by Just-in-time withdrawals under the Kanban system, such problems are impossible to ignore. If, for example, a machine breaks down or begins producing defective parts, the whole line will stop and the supervisor must be called in. In many cases, it will be necessary to schedule overtime hours in order to make up for lost production time. As a result, activities to correct the problems will take place in the appropriate QC group, plans for improvements will be devised, and productivity will rise. The function of the Kanban system is not merely to control production levels. Its more important role lies in its ability to stimulate improvements in operations that eliminate waste and improve productivity. Figure 12.11 shows the relationship between the Kanban system and improvement activities.

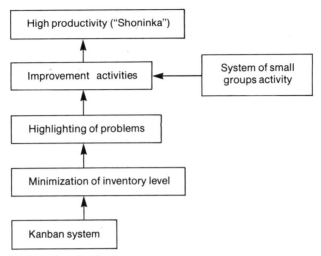

Figure 12.11. Relationship between Kanban system and improvement activities.

In recent years, Toyota has expanded its improvement activities to all departments, including indirect divisions. In 1980, Toyota had 48,000 employees, 20,000 of whom were manual laborers in factories. The performance of the remaining 28,000 people, in indirect departments, however, had an important effect on what happened in the workplace. The jobs at departments such as quality control, cost control, product design, and production control, for example, all affected the performance of direct departments. Thus, in correcting individual problems at the workplace, Toyota has more than once found it necessary to make improvements in indirect departments as well. As a result, improvement activities in manufacturing operations have brought with them company-wide improvements.

Reductions in the work force brought about by workshop improvements may seem to be antagonistic to the worker's dignity since they take up the slack created by waiting time and wasted action. However, allowing the worker to take it easy or giving him high wages does not necessarily provide him an opportunity to realize his worth. On the contrary, that end can be better served by providing the worker with a sense that his work is worthwhile and allowing him to work with his superior and coworkers to solve the problems they encounter.

QC CIRCLES

A *quality control circle,* or *QC circle,* is a small group of workers that study quality control concepts and techniques spontaneously and continuously in order to provide solutions to problems in their workplace. At Toyota, the ultimate purpose of QC circle activities is to promote a worker's sense of responsibility, provide a vehicle to achieve working goals, enable each worker to be accepted and recognized, and allow improvement and growth in a worker's technical abilities. The purpose of the QC circle is somewhat different from that of the suggestion system outlined previously. The evaluation for QC circle activities is hardly made in terms of the monetary amount of improved effects, but rather by how positive the circle is acting, how well the subject (topic) is pursued, and to what degree the members are participating.

Structure of the QC Circle

The QC circles at Toyota have a direct relationship with the formal organization of the workplace; therefore, all employees must participate in some QC circles. The QC circles are made up of a team leader ("Hancho") and his subordinate workmen (Figure 12.12). The QC circle may take the form of a *united circle* where members of other circles participate, or a *mini-circle* which consists of a subgroup of members from the entire circle, depending on the topic to be solved. The supervisor or section head ("Kocho") and the foreman ("Kumicho") act as advisor and subadvisor, respectively.

Each plant or division has its own QC promoting committee (Figure 12.13). At Toyota, QC circle activities are supported by the highest responsible person at each plant. The personnel division and the education division recently have begun promoting QC circle activities. As of 1981, about 4,600 groups of QC circles were active at Toyota; each group averaged 6.4 members.

QC Topics and Achievements

The subjects QC circles select as problems to be solved are not confined to product quality; cost reduction, maintenance, safety, industrial pollution, and alternative resources are considered as well. In 1981, the subject breakdown was: product quality, 35%; maintenance, 15%; cost reduction, 30%; and safety, 20%. The number of achieved topics in each circle averaged 3.4 per year. Since the economic effect itself is not the only purpose, 3~4 subjects are settled as a goal to be achieved each year.

The number of circle meetings actually held was 6.7 times per year for each topic, and each topic required an average of 6.4 hours. Therefore, each meeting was approximately one hour in length. It is considered best at Toyota to have the circle meeting two or three times each month and approximately thirty minutes to one hour in duration. Figure 12.14 details how QC circles are implemented.

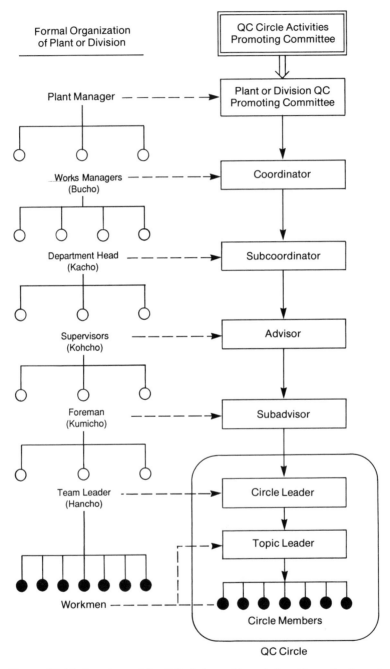

Figure 12.12. Structure of the QC circle and its relationship to the formal organization.

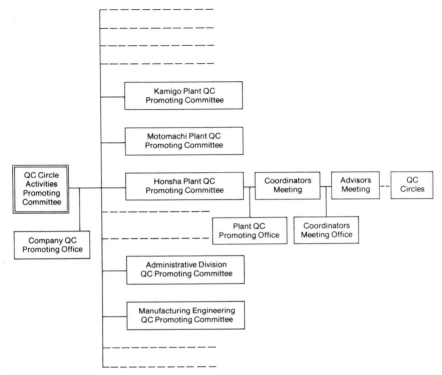

Figure 12.13. Organization for promoting QC circle activities.

Commendation Systems

The commendation systems at Toyota consist of three classes: topics commendation, QC circle commendation, and QC circle-Toyota prize. Each class includes various levels of awards.

The *topics commendation* awards the individual topic which was registered by each circle. When the topic has been completed, it may be awarded the *effort prize*. This is a monetary reward given each month or every other month. One third of the topics commendations are awarded the *advisor prize,* and one third of the advisor prize winners will be given the *coordinator prize.* These awards are given every six months.

One topic will be awarded to the plant promoting committee commendation for each workshop within the plant. Furthermore, each plant committee will recommend about four topics (responding to quality, costs, maintenance, and safety) to receive the *Gold prize* and the *Silver prize* given by the company. Because there are thirteen plants and divisions and four topics are recommended, about 150 circles are usually awarded Gold or Silver prizes twice a year.

Awards are announced following each QC circle's presentations are made at the plant. The *QC circle commendation* awards the overall performance of a circle's one-year activities. This class of commendations also includes the advisor prize, coordinator prize, and plant committee prize.

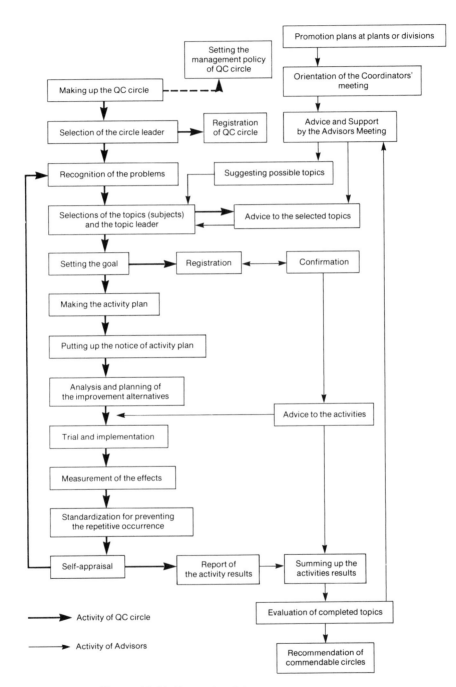

Figure 12.14. Promoting QC circle activities.

A circle that has performed excellent activities for three years will be requested by the works manager to summarize its activities and give a presentation at the *plant-wide presentation contest*. Then, at the *first selection contest* production control managers from 13 plants and divisions will hear 13 presentations and select five circles as the final candidates for the *QC circle-Toyota prize*. These five circles must make presentations before the chairman of the company QC promoting committee and the engineering vice-president. Eight circles not given the Toyota prize can still be awarded the *Excellence prize.*

Two circles out of the five Toyota prize winners will then participate in the regional QC circle contest outside the Toyota Motor Corporation. Then, if passed, they will participate in the *All-Japan QC Circles Contest.*

The suggestion system previously described in this chapter is different from the QC circle's commendation system. However, the monetary reward from the suggestion system will be given if the QC circle proposes improvement techniques. In this case, because the suggestion plan is the circle's proposal, the reward will be saved by the circle and used for its own purposes, such as a softball game or fishing contest.

Education Systems for QC Circles
At Toyota, several education programs promote QC circle activities. The following courses are held on a continuous basis:

- *Problem-solving course* for the foreman and supervisor.
- *Advisor course* for the department head and supervisor. (These two courses are also open to the supplier's employees.)
- *Trainer course* for department heads. The department heads must take this course when they are promoted.
- Various presentation contests within and without the company.
- Shipboard school which goes to Hong Kong or Formosa.
- Inspection tour for field supervisors which goes to the U.S. or Europe for three weeks.

13
5S—Foundation for Improvements

Various opportunities exist in a plant that are often overlooked and left untouched in spite of their potential to make profits. These include, for instance, limiting the production of defects, the margin of operation efficiency (man-hour), excess inventories, and missed delivery deadlines. These overlooked opportunities, or slack, are referred to as "Muda" in Japanese. Muda is essentially the waste of manpower, outputs, money, space, time, information, etc.

American economists recognize this as "organizational slack," which was first described by R.M. Cyert and J.C. March (1963). In prosperous times, such slack is usually left as it is. But, during recessions, when companies are struggling, emphasis is immediately placed on trying to improve organizational slack and profits. However, the Japanese feel that the cut into the organizational slack must be constantly executed whether in prosperous or adverse times. The continuous implementation of smaller improvement activities is the principle behind "Kaizen," an activity employed by many Japanese companies.

Kaizen, or "5S," is a method used to diminish the slack hidden in plants. 5S represents the Japanese words *Seiri, Seiton, Seison, Seiketsu,* and *Shitsuke,* which collectively translate to a cleanup activity at the work place.

Over time, various kinds of dirt can accumulate in the plants and offices within a company. *Dirt* in a plant includes unnecessary work-in-process (WIP) inventories; defective inventories; unnecessary jigs, tools, and measures; "inferior oil;" and unneeded carts, equipment, tables, etc. In an office, the unnecessary documents, reports, and stationers are *dirt* as well. 5S is the process of washing out all this dirt in order to be able to use the necessary things at the necessary time in the necessary quantity. By implementing 5S, the levels of quality, lead time, and cost reduction can be improved. These are the three main goals of production management. Mr. Hiroyuki Hirano believes that by promoting 5S, a plant can supply the products which customers want, in good quality, at a low cost, quickly, and safely, and thus increase company profits.

To achieve the aforementioned goals, the following "Muda," or slack, must be diminished:

1. Excessive setup time. It is time consuming to look for dies, jigs, or tools needed to perform setup for the next operation. Setup time can be reduced or eliminated by neatly arranging in advance the necessary materials for a particular setup operation.

2. Defective materials/products. Defects will become apparent in a clean plant. "Point photography," a concept which stimulates feelings of pride and shame in workers, is used to motivate workers to reduce defects. (Point photography will be discussed in more detail at the conclusion of this chapter.)

3. Cluttered work areas. Cleanliness and neatness at the workplace increase the efficiency of operations. Conveying products becomes easier after eliminating unnecessary materials on the floor. A clean work place raises worker morale, thereby increasing the attendance rate. In addition, since a clean facility reduces problems, the available operating time in a plant will also increase.

4. Missed delivery times. To deliver products just-in-time, the inputs for making products, such as manpower, materials, and facilities, must flow smoothly. Since the lack of necessary units will be more visible in a clean plant, orders to replenish necessary supplies will become more efficient and less time will be wasted waiting for materials.

5. Unsafe conditions. Improperly stacked loads, oil on the floor, etc., can cause injuries to workers and perhaps damage inventory, which will increase costs and delay delivery of products.

The 5S movement has several other merits to it. For example, it cultivates good human relationships in a firm and raises morale. A company, whose plants are clean and neat, will win the credibility of customers, suppliers, visitors, and applicants.

The components of 5S are defined as follows:

Seiri: **to clearly separate necessary things from unnecessary ones and abandon the latter.** As a means to practice Seiri, red rectangular labels (described later) are used so that only necessary things will remain within the plant.

Seiton: **to neatly arrange and identify things for ease of use.** The Japanese word "Seiton" literally translated means laying things out in an attractive manner. In the 5S context, it means arranging materials so that everyone is able to find them quickly. To realize this step, indicator plates are used to specify the name of each item and the address of its storage.

Seiso: **to always clean up; to maintain tidiness and cleanliness.** This is a basic cleanup process in which an area is swept with a broom and then wiped with a floor cloth. Since floors as well as windows and walls have to be cleaned, Seiso here is equivalent to the large scale cleanup activity carried out at the end of each year in Japanese households.

Although, such company-wide, large-scale cleanups are conducted several times a year, it is important for each work place to be cleaned daily. Such activities tend to reduce machine malfunctions caused by dirty oil, dust, and rubbish. For example, if a worker complains that a machine is malfunctioning, it does not necessarily mean that the machine needs a tune up. In fact, a program of work station housekeeping may be all that is necessary.

Seiketsu: **to constantly maintain the 3S mentioned above, Seiri, Seiton, and Seiso.** Keeping a clean workplace without rubbish or oil leakage is the activity of Seiketsu.

Shitsuke: **to have workers make a habit of always conforming to rules.** According to Dr. Eizaburo Nishibori (1985), Shitsuke is the most important discipline of the 5S. Therefore, a person who trains others must first exhibit superior behaviors.

Managers should not expect their subordinates to simply follow their designations; they should *inspire* their subordinates and expect their success rather than giving flat criticisms. Managers should listen to their subordinates' ideas and express encouragement by saying "your idea is interesting." Even when a fault is obvious, managers should teach subordinates to recognize the fault themselves and either make a suggestion or tolerate the failure. Managers who criticize subordinates without first giving them the opportunity to challenge themselves cannot cultivate proficient subordinates.

For 5S to be effective, workers must make a habit of placing things near at hand for easy access. Having only the knowledge of 5S is not enough; workers must also practice 5S over and over. It should become a spontaneous, natural act of their own volition rather than something they are forced to do.

Below are guidelines for practicing 5S. For these, the author is indebted to the splendid ideas of Mr. Hiroyuki Hirano (1990), Mr. Tomoo Sugiyama (1985), and others.

VISUAL CONTROL

For improvement activities to take place, every employee—from top management to terminal worker—must have and share a strong consciousness to eliminate the hidden wastes, abnormalities, and various other problems within the plant. These problems must be visible to every employee; hence, Seiri and Seiton are the first two steps toward improvement (see Figure 13.1).

To recognize wasted items, materials are separated into *necessary* and *unnecessary* stacks. Then, "visual Seiri" is attained by using red labels; "visual Seiton" is attained using indicator plates.

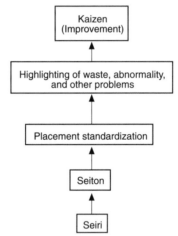

Figure 13.1. Seiri and Seiton: first steps of Kaizen.

Visual Seiri

In a plant, dirt will gather over time and allow wastes to build up. At Toyota, red labels are used to seal the wastes and expose them for what they are. They are then completely thrown away.

The red label technique consists of the following six steps which must be conducted about twice a year:

Step 1. Establishment of a red label project. There are two kinds of red label strategies: *the red label at each work place* and *the company-wide red label*. The former should be done every day, while the latter should be done only once or twice a year. The company-wide red label project is similar to the large-scale cleanups conducted in Japanese households at year end. For this company-wide red-labeling project, top management's enthusiasm is indispensable. The president should be the chair of the red label project.

Step 2. Determination of objects to be sealed. Items that need to be controlled and sealed by red labels are inventories, machinery, and space. Inventories include materials, WIP, parts, half-finished products, and finished products. Machinery includes machines, facilities, carts, pallets, jigs, tools, cutting instruments, tables, chairs, dies, vehicles, and equipment. Space represents the floors, passages, shelves, and storages.

Step 3. Determination of labeling criteria. Although the instructions are to seal the unnecessary items with red labels, it is sometimes difficult to determine which items are unnecessary. Therefore, specific criterion must be developed to draw a sharp line between the necessary items and the unnecessary ones. In general, parts, materials, and machines, etc. which will not be used during the upcoming month will be regarded as redundant. As Seiri proceeds, this time criteria may be reduced to the upcoming week.

Step 4. Preparation of labels. Figure 13.2 shows labels containing the date, name of the checker, item classification, item name, quantity, department name, actions, and reasons to be sealed (e.g., defective units, noncritical units, or

Model	SZ-250P
Product name	door
Lot size	40
Quantity	1 pallet
Process	door welding
	Sep. 2 / 1990
Reasons	Dent

(The actual size is 5" x 5".)

Classification	1. Facilities 2. Jigs and tools 3. Measures 4. Materials 5. Parts 6. Works in-process 7. Half-finished products 8. Completed products 9. Sub-materials 10. Clerical supplies 11. Documents
Item name	
Number	
Quantity	
Reasons	unnecessary, defective
Department	
Date	

Figure 13.2. Standard red labels.

unnecessary units). Even if it is difficult to judge whether or not to seal an item, the red label should be applied. All red labeled items will be grouped and evaluated one more time before being disposed.

Step 5. Labeling. A member of the management staff should do the actual labeling. They are able to assess conditions more objectively than would a person directly in charge of the workplace.

Step 6. Evaluation of sealed items and recommended actions. Sealed inventories are classified into four groups: defects, dead stock, staying items, and leftover materials. At this stage, the defects and dead stock (i.e., old models no longer used) should be thrown out, whereas staying items (excess inventories) should be transferred to the red label storage. The leftover materials (scraps) should be examined for usability. Unusable leftover material is discarded, while the usable parts are placed in red label storage.

After finishing the sealing process, the results should be summarized in a *list of unnecessary inventories* and a *list of unnecessary facilities* as shown in Figure 13.3. Each list should conclude with a recommendation for action and/or counter-measure.

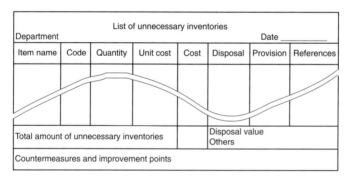

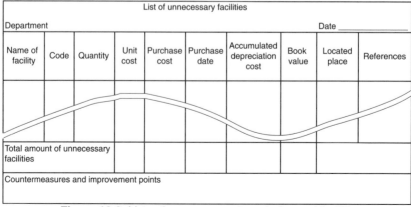

Figure 13.3. Lists of unnecessary inventories and facilities.

Indicator Plate for Visual Seiton

After the red labeling elimination process, only necessary items are left. The next step is to distinctly show where (position), what (item), and how many (quantity) materials exist so they can be easily recognized.

Visual Seiton allows workers to easily identify and retrieve tools and materials and then readily return them to a location near the point of use. Indicator plates are used to facilitate ease of location and retrieval of needed materials. The following steps are taken before indicator plates are attached to materials:

1. Decide item placement
2. Prepare containers
3. Indicate the position for each item
4. Indicate the item code and its quantity
5. Make Seiton a habit

Step 1. Decide item placement. The principle behind determining a location for each item is to define the items that are used frequently and then place them around the workers who use them. Other less frequently used items are placed farther away. Additionally, items should be located at a height between a worker's shoulders and waste. This method decreases the amount of time and energy spent walking to and from storage areas.

Step 2. Prepare the container. After deciding on the space, containers such as boxes, cabinets, shelves, palettes, etc., must be prepared. However, purchasing new containers should be absolutely avoided since the ultimate objective is to reduce space and minimize the size and quantity of inventories.

Step 3. Indicate the position for each item. Indicator plates containing *place codes* are created and hung from the ceiling. The place code is the address of the item's location. It is made up of the *place address* and the *spot address* (see Figure 13.4). In addition to these indicator plates, more specific *spot plates* are placed on each shelf.

Step 4. Indicate the item code and its quantity. Item codes and quantities are specified on the item itself via an *item code tag* and on the shelf the item occupies via an *item code plate*. The application of these item code plates is similar to the system for assigning parking spaces in a parking lot. In this example, each car's number plate corresponds to the item code tag. Item code plates correspond to those placed at the head of each parking spot showing the owner's name and plate number (see Figure 13.5).

As for the quantity indication, the maximum (lot size) and minimum (reorder point) quantities of inventories are specified. Instead of using written numbers for these quantities, it is better to express the desired quantity visually by drawing a

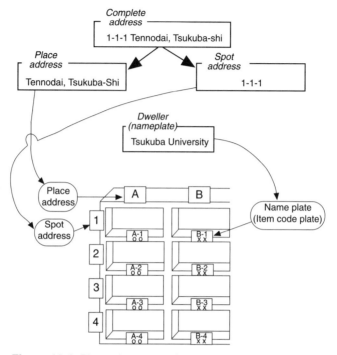

Figure 13.4. Place plate, spot plate, and item code plate.

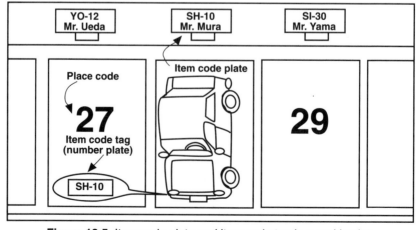

Figure 13.5. Item code plate and item code tag in a parking lot.

conspicuous colored line at the proper position. This will enable the operator to obtain the maximum and minimum quantity level at a glance without having to read every written number (see Figure 13.6).

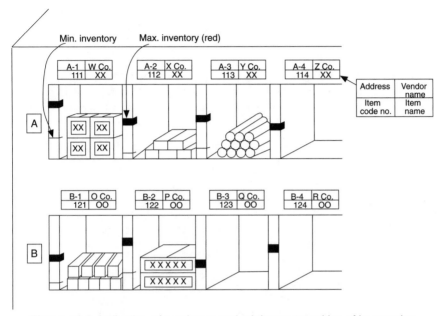

Figure 13.6. Indication of maximum and minimum quantities of inventories.

Step 5. Make Seiton a habit. To continuously maintain order in a plant, Seiri and Seiton must be performed adequately. These actions include visual separation of necessary and unnecessary materials, organization of frequently used stock at nearby places, and the use of place code plates, item code plates, and quantity indicator lines.

PRACTICAL RULES FOR SEITON

Seiton of WIP

Seiri and Seiton are typically applied to WIP. The Toyota production system specifically emphasizes the importance of inventory reduction. Improvement activities will progress easily only if the existence of wastes, abnormalities, or problems are perceived by everyone in the entire plant. These problems include excessive WIP inventories, defective units, and inventories whose completion is held up by machine troubles at subsequent assembly stations.

So that any operator can recognize the occurrence of abnormalities, item placement is standardized by using indicator plates. For example, a quick glance will enable anyone to easily notice whether or not boxes of a certain item are where they should be, or if they have exceeded the limit line of maximum quantity.

Rules of Seiton for WIP will be discussed below.

Rule 1: First-In, First-Out. In Seiton, it is very important to correctly load and setup the WIP. The principle of First-In, First-Out (FIFO) must be observed so that things put in first can be taken out and used first. FIFO is preferred over another rule of loading, Last-In First-Out (LIFO), where new parts are piled over old ones. Under LIFO, only the new parts are used and the old ones remain at the bottom, unused, which can create a potential quality control problem.

When loading stock via a forklift, the position of each pallet will be determined by the direction of the fork. Therefore, if pallets are placed in the direction as shown in Figure 13.7a, they could not be withdrawn according to FIFO. A space of passage for carriers must be made as in Figure 13.7b. The storage racks should be broad in width and short in depth like a chest of drawers, or have many entrances and short-depth.

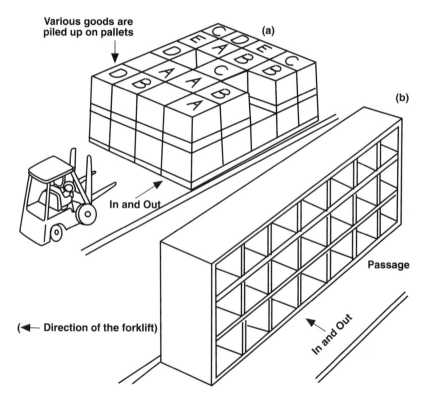

Figure 13.7. "First-In, First-Out" requires broad width and short depth.

Rule 2: Setup for easy handling. It is said that 30 to 40 percent of processing costs and 80 to 90 percent of processing time is spent on material handling. Therefore, improvement in material handling is very important for efficient plant operation. Using a *material handling index of liveliness,* as shown in Figure 13.8, can help determine the best method of conveyance, i.e., pallet, cart, fork lift, etc.

Classification	Index of liveliness	Number of required tasks	Variety of required tasks				Conditions
			Group	Raise	Lift up	Bring	
In bulk	0	4	O	O	O	O	Left in bulk directly on the floor or tables
Unified in a box or batch	1	3	--	O	O	O	Placed in a container or grouped in a bundle
In box with bolsters	2	2	--	--	O	O	Raised by pallets or skids
On a carriage	3	1	--	--	--	O	Set on carriages or something with castors
On the move	4	0	--	--	--	--	Moving by conveyor, chute, or carriages

Figure 13.8. Material-handling index of liveliness.

The index of liveliness is calculated by classifying the number of required tasks into five levels of activity. Then, the sum of the levels is divided by the number of steps in the process (see Figure 13.9).

With this index, material handling activity can be analyzed as shown in Figure 13.9. If the averaged index of liveliness is less than 0.5, containers, pallets, and carts should be prepared instead of putting items directly on the floor. If the average index is less than 1.3, many more uses of the pallets, carts, and forklifts are recommended.

Rule 3: Regard stock space as part of manufacturing line. Since a tremendous variety of parts, materials, jigs, and tools exists, it is necessary to position them for easy access by their users. If the user is working in a job-shop situation, parts should be stored based on the similarity of their functions. If the user is mass producing a product, parts should be arranged and stored according to the production line.

In either method, however, it is important to clearly separate defective items from good ones and make them strikingly different. Hence, storage for defects should be red-colored, located outside the product lines, and placed piece-by-piece.

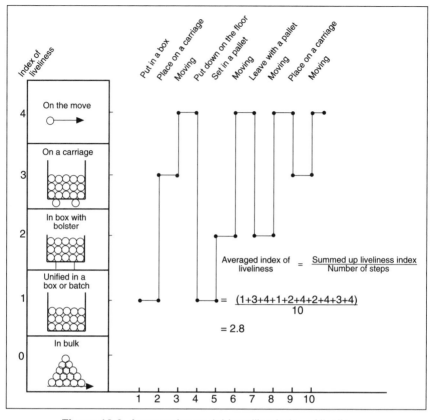

Figure 13.9. Averaged material-handling index of liveliness.

Seiton of Jigs and Tools

Perhaps the most used items in an automobile manufacturing plant are tools and jigs, and there are many varieties of each. As already discussed, it is important to have these items neatly arranged in close proximity to the worker, but it is just as important to devise a way for the worker to return these materials with ease after each use. Following are some considerations for accomplishing this goal:

Point 1: Can jigs and tools be eliminated? Consider whether or not a function can be performed effectively without jigs or tools. For instance, suppose a screw is currently tightened using a wrench. If the screw can be modified into a switch shape, the function can be performed by hand instead.

Point 2: Can the variety of jigs and tools be decreased? Consider whether the variety of fastening operations can be consolidated into a smaller variety by standardizing at the design stage.

Point 3: Are tools positioned ergonomically? Wasted motion and the possibility of injury to the worker can be avoided by placing frequently used items between the worker's waist and shoulders.

Point 4: Can the worker easily identify storage places for tools? Tracing the outline of a tool or jig on the place where it is to be stored allows the worker to easily recognize where to return the item. This is one of three approaches toward satisfying Seiton as it relates to storing tools (see Figures 13.10 and 13.11).

Another method, *blindfold returns,* where items are placed into sacks rather than hung on a peg board in a specified location, allows the worker to release the tool in an approximate position without having to follow it with his eyes.

The third alternative is perhaps the most ideal method because it allows workers to immediately and unconsciously return tools. This is the method of suspending tools on cables hung from the ceiling.

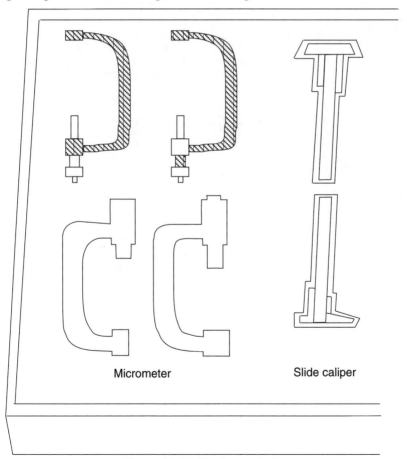

Micrometer   Slide caliper

Figure 13.10. Tracing control.

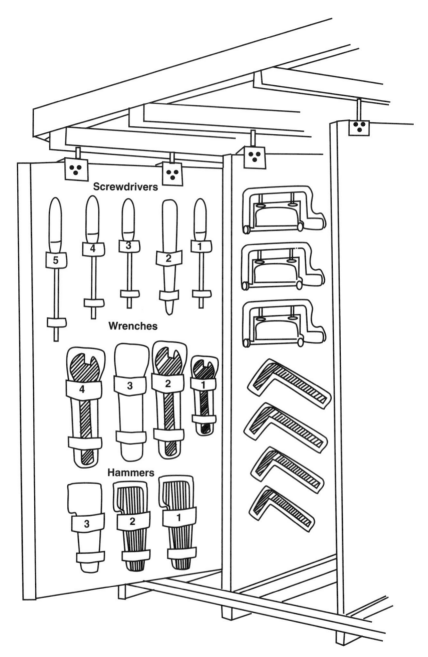

Figure 13.11. Blindfold return and a drawing cabinet exclusively for tools.

Seiton of the Cutting Instruments, Measures, and Oil

Storage of cutting instruments such as drills, taps, grinders, etc., should be determined based on how frequently the instruments are used. If the instruments are used at many machines for mass production, the product line system (previously discussed) would be most suitable. On the other hand, if used in a job shop situation, the instruments should be stored according to their function.

Since these instruments have sharp edges, careful attention to how they are stored is important. Adequate space between blades should be provided in order to protect the blades and for ease of maintenance (oiling). Figure 13.12 illustrates how and on what type of surface cutting instruments should be stored.

Other sensitive tools such as calipers, gauges, micrometers, straight rulers, etc., require special attention as well. To keep these measuring tools accurate, it is imperative to protect them from dust, dirt, and vibration. Some will require oiling to protect from rust. The straight ruler should be hung up in a perpendicular position to avoid warping.

Many types and grades of oil are used in manufacturing plants. Often the oil arrives in large containers and is then transferred to smaller, more manageable containers. To avoid mix up, a color coding system should be implemented. Oil drums and their respective oil feeders should be painted or marked with the same color. Also, the filling station should be marked with the same color as the drum and feeder.

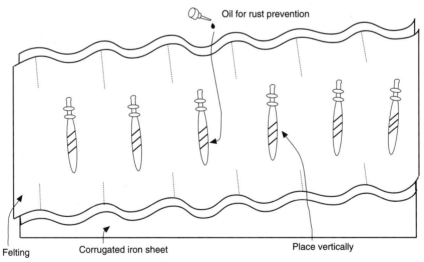

Oil for rust prevention

Felting   Corrugated iron sheet   Place vertically

Figure 13.12. Maintenance of cutting instruments.

Visual Controls for Limit Standards

Visual indicators are extremely effective when used for control limits because they are easily recognized by everyone with just a glance. Some examples are described below.

- A meter-zone indication is used to separate a danger zone from a normal zone. The indicator can be a color or a line. The zone method is also used to indicate the minimum allowable stock quantity of WIP.

- Fit marks are lines that are drawn on, for example, from the head of a bolt to a nut at the properly fastened position. When the respective parts of the line on the bolt and the nut do not coincide with each other, then the bolt is loose. This idea has wide applications.

- To maintain a certain level or condition, a needle can be used to mark each control limit on every measure. When the needle crosses over the limit point, abnormal conditions will become apparent. A mark on the oil-level window of an oil stove is one such example.

- Spot marks and stop lines are used for marking the position of an item and for depicting the position to stop. For example, in order to adjust the center of a die, a center pin or a spot mark indicates the die's accurate position on the pressing table.

- Separation lines drawn with white paint or vinyl tape divide passageways and workplace areas thus maintaining the high level of safety within a plant. Similar lines should also be used to indicate storage locations of carts, products in process, jigs, instruments, and cleanup tools.

Seiso, Seiketsu, Shitsuke

The latter three terms in 5S are closely interrelated. "Seiso," to continually maintain tidiness within the plant, depends on "Seiketsu" which is to standardize cleanup activities so that these actions are specific and easy to perform. "Shitsuke" is the method used to motivate workers to continually perform and participate in Seiso and Seiketsu activities.

Daily preventative maintenance activities and general cleanup activities can reveal the following conditions on the shop floors:

- rubbish
- water and oil leaks
- tires marks
- dust scattered by cutting materials

Once revealed, it is necessary to investigate the causes and origination of the dirt and then implement a system of future prevention.

Countermeasures against dirtiness must be taken at the source. For example, if tire tracks from a forklift are found on the floor it can be deduced that abrupt starts and sudden stops are the cause. A placard stating, "Sudden starts and stops generate dirt," may help to prevent future tire track conditions. Forklifts can also be equipped with a tire-washing brush or a mop for cleaning the passages.

Perhaps the largest source of dirt in workplaces comes from cutting instruments (i.e., dust, oil, cutting solution, etc.). As seen in Figure 13.13, most covers installed around a grinder for collecting the dust are inappropriate. The needed improvement can be seen by testing the grinder with a piece of chalk. When ground, the chalk will show the area that should be covered to collect dust particles. In addition to installing a cover that will collect the dust at the point of grinding, dust can also be controlled by covering the legs of the machines. By doing so, cleanup work under machines and tables should become easier and faster—perhaps by as much as 50 percent. Note that covers must be designed for easy removal when performing machine maintenance activities (see Figure 13.14).

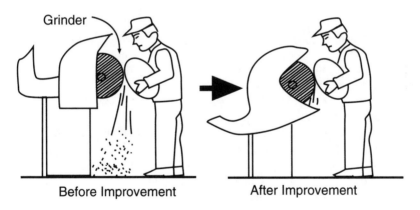

Before Improvement   After Improvement

Figure 13.13. Use of dust collecting covers.

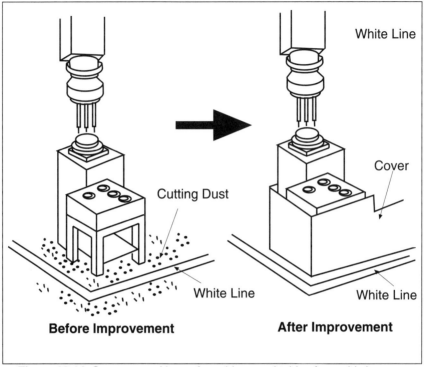

White Line

Cutting Dust

Cover

White Line

White Line

Before Improvement

After Improvement

Figure 13.14. Cover around legs of machines and tables for rapid clean up.

"Shitsuke," motivating workers to perform maintenance and continuous improvement activities, is considered the most difficult component of 5S. Japanese workers are expected to exercise *self control*—instead of being controlled by management—for this activity.

Initially the Japanese followed the Western belief that control could be achieved by setting a goal for the worker and then rewarding, or "giving a carrot," if the goal was met. If the goal was not met, discipline, or "a stick," would be offered. However, Japanese workers did not respond as expected. Instead, they were offended by the strict orders to comply.

Subsequently, the notion of *self control* was implemented. Management's role here was just to inform their subordinates of the purposes of their jobs, and entrust them with all the details of the job. The result was subordinates who not only produced things, but who also had a sense of responsibility for the quality of the products they made.

It was found that the emotions of pride and shame influenced Japanese workers more than the "carrot and stick" incentive system. The worker's conscience was the motivator. Workers are evaluated based upon the comparison between their own present and past performances and between theirs and other workers' performances. In other words, the desire to improve oneself and a sense of rivalry were used to motivate people to control themselves. A suggestion system was also implemented as a source of limitless power for improvement activities.

The Japanese administrative system is very collective in that workers have a feeling that their superior is one that works together with the company. Although they are merely told of the purpose of their work, each subordinate is conscious of the necessity to perform self control to become part of the team. Under such a condition, challenging and competitive spirits serve as strong motivators for improvement.

Motivation to improve, or Shitsuke, is the essence of the Japanese management system.

PROMOTION OF 5S SYSTEM

Promoting 5S depends on top management's decisions. When implementing any continuous improvement process such as 5S there will be those in management who have doubts about whether the process will succeed. They will say , "How much indeed will the productivity increase?" or "How much will 5S contribute to the actual profits?"

Before implementing a process like 5S, people's ways of thinking and their attitudes toward work must first be changed. All members of the company must have a sufficient understanding of its real meaning and purpose, and they must integrate their understandings through company-wide or workplace-wide seminars. It is also useful to hang some banners with slogans such as: "Clean workplaces are created by using the power of everyone," or "There is no waste in a clean workplace," etc.

Since 5S activities require long-term continuous efforts, it is necessary for the entire company to understand its purpose. Some members of management may think that they have nothing to do with Seiri and Seiton, etc., regarding them as matters of the floor-level workplace. This is the reason the existing organizational structure in a company should be utilized in promoting 5S throughout the entire plant.

Success or failure of 5S depends on top management's wishes and whether or not the initiative was taken. Establishment of a 5S project should be chaired by the top management, and a leader of each workplace must be the first to practice it and exhibit a good example. If management and work place leaders show a strong commitment to 5S, their subordinates will too and 5S will be successful.

Point Photography

In conclusion, *point photographing,* a method that is considered to be a strong motivational tool for 5S, will be introduced.

Point photography is the practice of taking pictures of the same position of the workplace from the same direction by the same camera before and after the application of 5S. These photographs are then shown to workers to be compared. Point photography works because of the feelings of pride or shame evoked when workers see the comparisons. Special effort should be made to photograph areas that workers especially do not wish to be seen by others, such as facilities with oil leaks, scattered cutting dust, disorganized tools, and any other unsafe spots.

A *point photographing chart,* depicted in Figure 13.15 (see next page), is used to display the pictures. It contains a space for the date the picture was taken, a column for evaluation by safety patrols or others, and a space for advice from a superior or humorous comments from other colleagues.

Each time an improvement is made, a picture should be taken and posted next to the last photo taken to show a chronological series of improvements. If the date of point photographing is known in advance and can be clearly noted on the chart, it becomes a goal and will help raise workers' desire to show improvements by that date. These charts are also used by superiors for evaluation purposes.

Point photography is a remarkable stimulant to workers and enables management to effectively continue with improvement activities. Through point photography, workers can visually see the pride or shame of their workmanship. Realization that improvement is needed becomes a spontaneous reaction to an embarrassing photograph. Conversely, if the point photography reveals that the rules of 5S have been followed, the worker has set a good example and is looked up to by his colleagues.

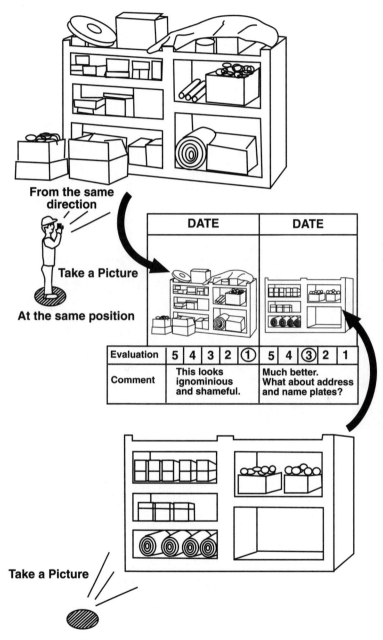

From the same direction

Take a Picture

At the same position

	DATE	DATE
Evaluation	5 4 3 2 ①	5 4 ③ 2 1
Comment	This looks ignominious and shameful.	Much better. What about address and name plates?

Take a Picture

Figure 13.15. Point photography method.

14
"Autonomous Defects Control" Assures Product Quality

In Japan, quality control (QC) or quality assurance (QA) is defined as the development, design, manufacture, and service of products that will satisfy the consumer's needs at the lowest possible cost. As the definition implies, the customer's satisfaction with product quality is an end in itself at Toyota. At the same time, however, product quality is an indispensable part of the Toyota production system, since without quality control the continuous flow of production (synchronization) would be impossible.

The evolution of the Japanese approach to quality control and its application to specific needs and problems with the Toyota production system will be examined in this chapter. As Figure 14.1 shows, quality control began with independent inspectors and statistical sampling methods but soon moved to a "self-inspection of all units" method which is based on autonomous control of defects within the manufacturing process itself. Quality control has now become a company-wide concern that extends outward from manufacturing to Toyota's functional management units.

Until 1949, quality control activities in Japan were largely a matter of rigorous inspections carried out by specialized inspectors: an approach that has been all but abandoned in present-day quality control programs. Today in Japan, fewer than five percent of factory employees are inspectors, and in the top companies fewer than one percent. By contrast, in America and Europe, where quality control activities are seldom entrusted to workers on the line, nearly ten percent of all factory employees are inspectors.

In Japan, inspections by specialized inspectors have been minimized for a number of reasons: inspectors whose activities stand outside the manufacturing process perform operations with no value added and thus add to production costs without increasing productivity. Also, feedback from the inspectors to the manufacturing process usually takes so long that defective parts or products continue to be produced for some time after a problem is discovered.

Under the present system, the manufacturer or manufacturing process is itself responsible for quality control; those who most directly produce defective parts are immediately aware of problems and are charged with the responsibility for

221

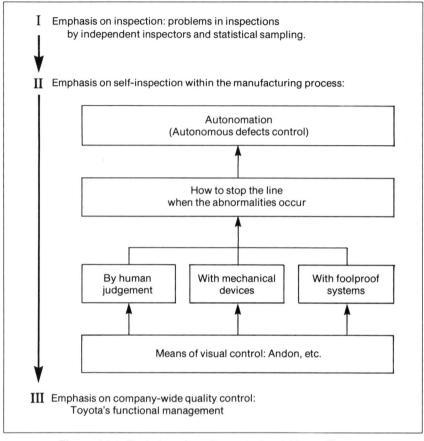

Figure 14.1. Evolution of quality control activities at Toyota.

correcting them. As a result, few inspection procedures are assigned to specialized inspectors; usually the final inspections are made from the point of view of the consumer or management and are not inspections for defects that would affect the flow of production.

STATISTICAL QUALITY CONTROL

Statistical quality control (SQC) originated in America in the 1930s as an industrial application of the control chart devised by Dr. W. A. Shewhart. It was introduced to Japanese industry after World War II, largely as the result of a lecture tour by Dr. W. E. Deming in 1950.

Although statistical quality control is still an important technique in Japanese QC systems, it too has certain drawbacks:

- In SQC, the acceptable quality level (AQL) which determines products that are passed but are of the minimum acceptable quality, is fixed at 0.5% or 1.0%. Either level, however, is unsatisfactory from the point of view of companies that aim for very high producer quality; e.g., a defect rate of one in a million. At Toyota, for example, the goal of quality control is to obtain one hundred percent good units or a defect rate of zero. The reason for this is quite simple: even though Toyota may produce and sell millions of automobiles, an individual customer buys only one. If his car has defects, he will think—and tell his friends—that Toyotas are "pieces of junk."

- Under the Toyota production system, excess inventory is a type of waste and thus is not permitted. Furthermore, Just-in-time (JIT) production or the ability to meet demand changes with a minimum of lead time also makes it necessary to minimize inventory. If defective workpieces occur at any stage in the process, the flow of production will be interrupted and the entire line will stop.

For both reasons, then, Toyota is unable to rely on statistical sampling alone and has been forced instead to devise inexpensive means of conducting inspections for all units ("total inspection") to ensure zero defects.

Statistical sampling is still practiced at certain departments where lot production takes place. At a high-speed automatic punch press, for example, where lots of 50 or 100 units are kept in a chute, only the first and last units in the chute are inspected. If both units are good, *all* units in the chute are considered good. If the last unit is defective, however, a search will be made for the first defective unit in the chute, all defective units in the chute will be removed, and remedial action taken. So that no lot will escape inspection, the punch press is set to stop automatically at the end of each lot.

Use of statistical sampling is in effect a total inspection since it is used only when an operation has been fully stabilized through careful maintenance of equipment and tools and sporadic defects do not occur. In such cases, the distribution of the product's data variation (6 × the standard deviation) will be relatively small compared to the designed tolerance, and the bias of the data mean from the central value of the designed specification will also be small (Figure 14.2). Under such conditions, the sampling inspection plan will guarantee the quality of all units in the chute.

In effect, then, all units inspection or its equivalent has been substituted for ordinary statistical sampling, just as inspections within the manufacturing process itself have been developed to replace inspections by independent inspectors. In both cases, more traditional methods of quality control have been replaced by self-inspection of all units in the interest of further reducing the number of defective units. This approach to quality control is called "Jidoka" or "Autonomation."

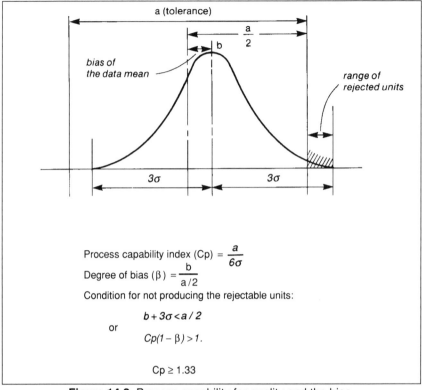

Process capability index $(Cp) = \dfrac{a}{6\sigma}$

Degree of bias $(\beta) = \dfrac{b}{a/2}$

Condition for not producing the rejectable units:

$$b + 3\sigma < a/2$$

or

$$Cp(1 - \beta) > 1.$$

$$Cp \geq 1.33$$

Figure 14.2. Process capability for quality and the bias.

AUTONOMATION

In Japanese, Jidoka has two meanings and is written with two different ideograms (Figure 14.3). One ideogram means automation in the usual sense: to change from a manual process to a machine process. With this kind of automation, the machine operates by itself once the switch is thrown but has no feedback mechanism for detecting errors and no device for stopping the process if a malfunction occurs. Because this type of automation can lead to large numbers of defective parts in the event of a machine malfunction, it is considered unsatisfactory.

Jidoka =
$$\begin{cases} 1. \; 自動化 \; = \text{Automation} \\ 2. \; 自働化 \; = \text{Autonomation} \end{cases}$$

Figure 14.3. Two meanings of Jidoka.

The second meaning of Jidoka is *automatic control of defects,* a meaning coined by Toyota. To distinguish between the two meanings of Jidoka, Toyota often refers to the second type of Jidoka as "Ninben-no-aru" Jidoka or, literally translated, *automation with a human mind.* Jidoka translates to autonomation in English.

Although autonomation often involves some type of automation, it is not limited to machine processes. It can be used in conjunction with manual operations as well. This is a different point from the Detroit technique called "Feedback Automation." In either case, it is predominantly a technique for detecting and correcting production defects and always incorporates a mechanism to detect abnormalities or defects, and a mechanism to stop the line or machine when abnormalities or defects occur.

In short, autonomation at Toyota always involves quality control since it makes it impossible for defective parts to pass unnoticed through the line. When a defect occurs, the line stops, forcing immediate attention to the problem, an investigation into its causes, and initiation of corrective action to prevent similar defects from occurring again. Autonomation also has other equally important components and effects: cost reduction, adaptable production, and increased respect for humanity (Figure 14.4).

Cost reduction through decreases in the work force. With equipment designed to stop automatically when the required quantity has been produced or when a defect occurs, there is no need for the worker to oversee machine operations. As a result, manual operations can be separated from machine operations, and a worker who has finished his work at machine A can go on to operate machine B while machine A is still running. Autonomation thus plays an important role in refining the standard operating routine: the worker's ability to handle more than one machine at a time makes it possible to reduce the workforce and thus the cost of production.

Adaptability to changes in demand. Since all machines stop automatically when they have produced the required number of parts and produce only good parts, autonomation eliminates excess inventory and thus makes possible JIT production and ready adaptability to changes in demand.

Respect for humanity. Since quality control based on autonomation calls immediate attention to defects or problems in the production process, it stimulates improvement activities and thus increases respect for humanity.

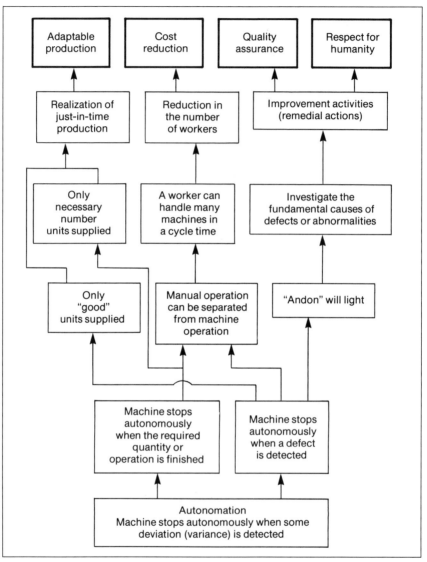

Figure 14.4. How autonomation attains its purposes.

Autonomation and the Toyota Production System

Having examined the purposes of autonomation, we next consider its application to the Toyota production system; i.e., the specific types of devices used to stop the line when defects occur, the techniques employed to accustom the workers to autonomated production, and the means for monitoring production and correcting abnormalities when they occur.

Methods for Stopping the Line

In general, there are two ways to stop the line when abnormalities occur: by relying on human judgment and by means of automatic devices.

Each worker has the power and the responsibility to stop the line if all operations are not or cannot be performed in accordance with the standard operations routine. The causes are either a reduction in the number of workers (Shojinka), which results in a cycle time that is too short, or defective units produced at the preceding process, making it necessary for the worker at the next process to stop the line. If, for example, it takes a worker 80 seconds to complete his assigned operations and his cycle time is 70 seconds, he must stop the line for ten seconds at each cycle. Otherwise, he will be unable to finish his work and defects will occur. When the line stops, supervisors and engineers must investigate the problem and undertake improvement activities in order to reduce the actual operations time from 80 to 70 seconds. Such activities may include elimination of wasteful actions, shortening of walking distances, etc.

Defective units produced at the preceding process usually appear when reductions in intermediate inventory under the Kanban system or reductions in the workforce, make it impossible to replace the defective units from inventory or repair them during waiting time. As a result, the line must stop when the defects appear, which calls attention to the problem and presents an opportunity for further improvement activities. Design defects, for example, or a continually omitted operation at the previous process may surface in this way (Figure 14.5).

With line stoppages due to defective units or revisions of the standard operations routine, the supervisor's responsibility is twofold. First, he must teach the workers to stop the line whenever defects occur so that only good units are delivered. Second, he must discover and correct the cause of the defects that have stopped the line. In the case of defective workpieces delivered from the preceding process, for example, he must return the parts to the previous station, investigate the cause of the problem, and, if necessary, institute changes to prevent the defects from occurring again.

The key to preventing defects via human judgment is that every worker has the power to stop the line. In this respect Toyota's production system is not only more effective in controlling quality than Henry Ford's conveyor line, but more humanistic as well.

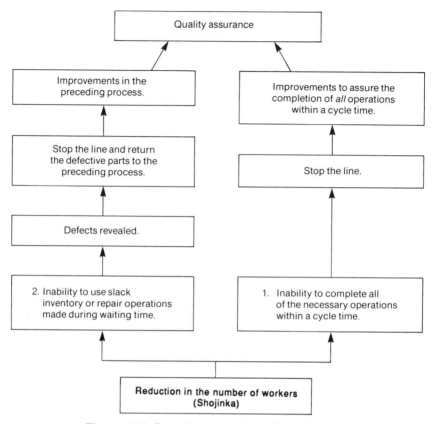

Figure 14.5. Causal relationships in line stoppages.

At Toyota, worker morale is often so high that workers sometimes fail to stop the line when they should, and may even enter the next process to complete their assigned operations; i.e., they force themselves to finish their jobs in spite of the supervisor's instructions to stop the line if they are delayed or become tired.

Similar problems may also develop with part-time or seasonal full-time workers who often send products on without installing all of the parts or without fully tightening fasteners. In either case, quality control methods based on human judgment alone may fail as a result of the worker's reluctance to slow production and call attention to himself by stopping the line. A series of devices were installed to stop the line automatically if the worker fails to complete his assigned operation in the allotted time.

Mechanical Checks in Aid of Human Judgment

On one line, for example, the workers carry out their operation while walking along beneath an overhead conveyor. Between processes is a mat like those that open doors automatically in supermarkets and airports. If the worker exceeds the distance allotted for completion of his work, he steps on the mat and the line stops. In a similar operation, the tool used to install lug nuts on wheels is suspended from an overhead rail and moves with the worker as he walks along the line. If the tool holder passes a certain point on the rail, the line stops automatically to prevent the worker from entering the next process to finish his job.

At first, workers resisted even such limited forms of automatic controls because they were forced to complete their jobs within the assigned cycle time. Thus, it was necessary for the supervisors to explain the purpose of the system and its advantages for the worker: to free him from the burden of wasted actions by identifying and correcting various problems in the line. As a result, the workers fully accepted the system, quality control improved, and the total time consumed by line stoppages was actually reduced.

Foolproof Systems for Stopping the Line

Foolproof systems are similar in operation to the mechanical checks described here and are widely used in both machine and manual operations. Unlike the mechanical checks, however, foolproof systems are used to eliminate defects that may occur due to an oversight on the worker's part, not to lack of time in the cycle or unwillingness to stop the line.

A foolproof system consists of a *detecting* instrument, a *restricting* tool, and a *signaling* device. The detecting instrument senses abnormalities or deviations in the workpiece or the process, the restricting tool stops the line, and the signaling device sounds a buzzer or lights a lamp to attract the worker's attention. In the packing process shown in Figure 14.6, for example, the lift or the product may be damaged if the product is off center on the pallet. To prevent this, a pair of limit switches detects the side-to-side position of the product and a pair of electric eyes checks its position front to rear. If the product is incorrectly positioned, a stopper prevents the pallet from continuing along the line to the lift and a buzzer sounds to call the problem to the worker's attention. In this case, the limit switches and electric eyes are the detecting instruments, the stopper is the restricting tool, and the buzzer is the signaling device.

Generally, detecting devices fall into one of three categories and are dictated by the type of foolproof method in use.

Contact method. Limit switches or electric eyes like the ones shown in Figure 14.6 are used to detect differences in the size or shape of the product and thus to check for the presence of specific types of defects. For the purpose of using the contact method, uniqueness of shape or size is sometimes intentionally designed into essentially similar parts. Devices that distinguish one color from another are also part of the contact method, even though the "contact" is made with reflected light instead of a limit switch or electric eye.

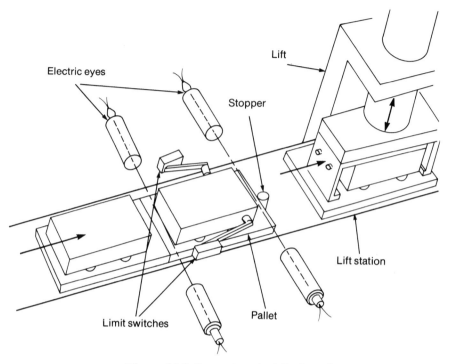

Figure 14.6. Contact method (foolproof).

Altogether method. Unlike the contact method, which is used mainly to check for the presence of a particular feature or to ensure that a specific step has been performed correctly, the altogether method is used to ensure that all parts of an operation have been successfully completed. An altogether system is used, for example, to be sure that the worker puts all of the required parts and an instruction sheet into the shipping box (Figure 14.7). To construct the foolproof, electric eyes were installed in front of each part bin so that the worker's hand interrupts the light beam when he removes a part or instruction sheet from its bin. Unless all of the beams have been interrupted, the stopper will not release the box and allow it to leave the worker's station.

Other processes controlled by the altogether method use a counter to prevent oversights. At a spot welding station, for example, a counter records the number of welds and sounds a buzzer if there is a discrepancy between the number it has counted and the number required.

Action step method. The action step method is so named because, unlike other foolproof methods, it requires the worker to perform a step which is not part of the operations on the product. Consider, for example, the station where metal fittings

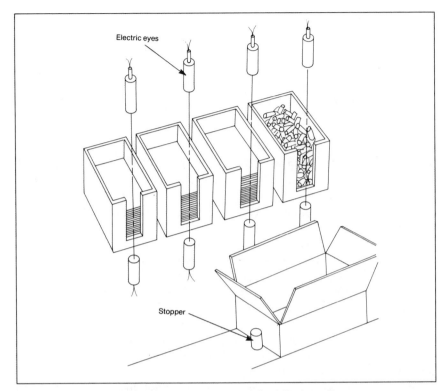

Figure 14.7. Altogether method (foolproof).

are attached to seats. Since the same department would often process as many as eight different kinds of seats in a mixed schedule, a Kanban was attached to each seat so that the worker would know which metal fittings to attach. Even so, improper metal fittings continued to be installed several times each month. As a result, the following action step foolproof system was devised: Kanbans attached to seats were designed with an aluminum strip across the bottom which, when inserted in a Kanban inserting box, activated a red light over the proper box of metal fittings and opened the box. The worker could then make no mistake in choosing the correct part.

The aforementioned is an example of the advantages of a foolproof system over methods based on human judgment alone. Both methods fulfill the major purposes of autonomation: quality assurance, cost reduction, realization of just-in-time delivery, and increased respect for humanity. Foolproof systems, however, not only guarantee product quality, but contribute to greater respect for humanity by relieving the worker of constant attention to worrisome details.

Visual Controls

In implementing autonomation, various visual controls monitor the state of the line and the flow of production. Some of the visual controls have been mentioned in connection with various types of quality control devices. Most foolproof systems, for example, use a light or some other type of signal to indicate an abnormality in the production run. Other visual controls include: Andon and call lights, standard operations sheets, Kanban tickets, digital display panels, and storage and stock plates.

Andon and call lights. Each assembly and machining line is equipped with a call light and an Andon board. The call light is used to call for a supervisor, maintenance worker, or general worker. Usually it has several different colors of lights, each of which is used to summon a different type of assistance. On most lines the call light is suspended from the ceiling or otherwise located so that supervisors and maintenance workers can see it easily.

Andon is a nickname for the indicator board that shows when a worker has stopped the line. As explained earlier, each worker at Toyota has a switch that enables him to stop the line in the event of a breakdown or a delay at his station. When this happens, a red lamp on the Andon over his line will light to indicate which process is responsible for the stoppage. The supervisor then goes immediately to the workstation to investigate the problem and take the necessary corrective action. Figure 14.8 shows a call light and Andon boards with the switch used to control the lamps. In the figure, the call lights are mounted on the Andon; at some stations, however, the two are installed at separate locations (Figure 14.9).

In many cases, the Andon has different colored lights to indicate the condition of the line. A green light, for example, indicates normal operation, a yellow light indicates that a worker is calling for help with a problem. If the trouble is not corrected, a red light will come on to show that the line has stopped. At other locations, Andon boards may have even more lights and use a different color code to indicate the condition of the line. The board usually has five colors with the following meanings:

Red	Machine trouble
White	End of a production run; the required quantity has been produced
Green	No work due to shortage of materials
Blue	Defective unit
Yellow	Setup required (includes tool changes, etc.)

All types of Andons are turned off when a supervisor or maintenance person arrives at the workstation responsible for the delay.

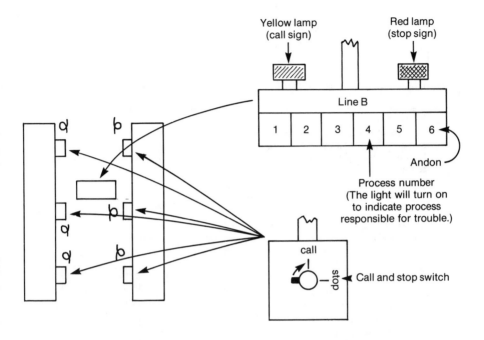

Figure 14.8. Call light, Andon, and stop switch.

Standard operations sheets and Kanban tickets. As explained in Chapter 10, a standard operation at Toyota consists of a cycle time; a standard operations routine, including assigned checks for quality and safety; and a standard quantity of work-in-process. All three of these elements are included in a standard operations sheet, which is posted at the line where each worker can easily see it. When a worker cannot perform his standard operations within the cycle time, he must stop the line and call for help to resolve the problem. The standard operations sheet thus works together with other types of visual controls to achieve standard operations, eliminate waste, and prevent defects.

Like the standard operations sheet, Kanban tickets also serve as a visual control over abnormalities in production. If, for example, products find their way into the storage area behind the line with no Kanban attached, it is a sign of overproduction that should be investigated immediately. Either the cycle time has been set too long, the worker has excessive waiting time, or the line has been stopped frequently at the next process. In any case, the absence of the Kanban should act as a signal for immediate investigation and elimination of the problem.

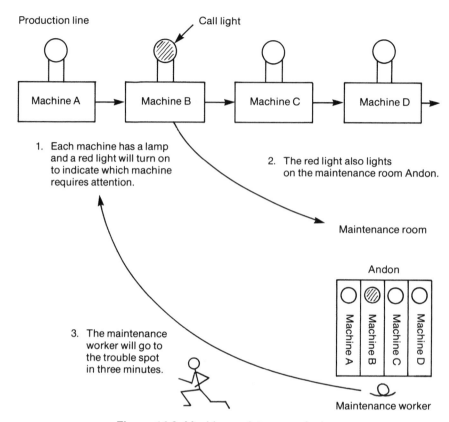

Figure 14.9. Machine-maintenance Andon.

In addition to their role in overproduction control, Kanban tickets serve other visual control functions as well. By checking the number of the production ordering Kanban, for example, the supervisor can tell which products are in process and determine whether overtime will be necessary or not.

Digital display panels. The pace of production is also shown in digital display panels which indicate both the day's production goal and a running count of the units produced so far. Thus, by watching the panels, everyone on the line can tell whether production is going too slowly to meet the day's goal and can work together to keep production on schedule. Like call lights and Andons, the digital display plates also serve to alert supervisors to problems and delays at various points along the line.

Store and stock indicator plates. Each storage location is assigned an "address" which is shown both on a plate over the storage location (Figure 14.10) and on the Kanban. As a result, carriers can always deliver parts to the proper location by

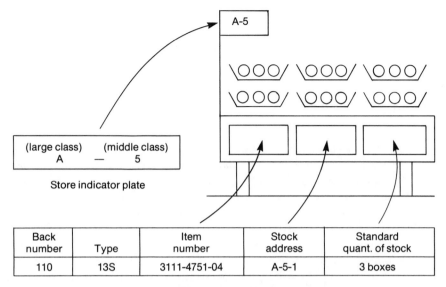

A-5

(large class) (middle class)
A — 5

Store indicator plate

Back number	Type	Item number	Stock address	Standard quant. of stock
110	13S	3111-4751-04	A-5-1	3 boxes

Stock indicator plate

Figure 14.10. Store plate and stock plate.

comparing the address on the Kanban to that on the store plate. In addition to the storage address, the stock plate also indicates the standard quantity of stock as an aid to inventory control.

While visual control systems are effective in achieving autonomation, they, like other quality control methods, function only to detect abnormalities (Figure 14.11). Remedial action to correct the defects or abnormalities remains in the hands of the supervisor and his workers, who must always follow a prescribed sequence of events: standardization of operations, detection of abnormalities, investigation of causes, improvement activities through QC circles, and restandardization of operations. Ultimately, however, the goal of autonomation

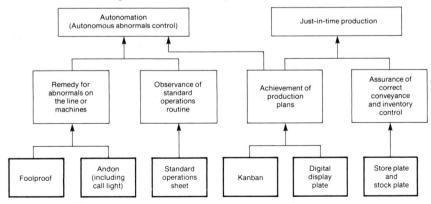

Figure 14.11. Framework of the visual control systems.

must be unmanned production, where even remedial action to correct defects is taken autonomously. Before going on to examine other types of quality control, it may be useful to look at robotics—its use and its potential impact on the Toyota production system.

ROBOTICS

Like their American counterparts, Japanese automobile manufacturers are installing industrial robots on a large scale, especially in processes that involve welding, painting, and machining of parts. The reasons are many, including: increased safety, increased product quality, and increased productivity with, of course, reduced costs. Where safety and product quality are concerned, the advantages of robotics are obvious. Robots can relieve human workers of hazardous jobs in areas where they are exposed to dangerous fumes and other environmental threats. Since robots can perform repetitive operations with high accuracy and without fatigue, they also contribute to improved quality control. Increased productivity, on the other hand, is less simple to assess.

At present, a skilled laborer in Japan earns about 4 million yen per year with annual increases of approximately six to seven percent. While wages continue to rise, the cost of the simplest robot is approximately two million yen. Even the most complex robots can be purchased for 15 to 20 million yen. Since a painting robot, for example, can do the work of 1.5 men, the long-term savings in labor costs from robotics are obvious and hard to ignore. In addition, robots are more easily adaptable to increased product diversity than a human labor force since they require fewer changes in the layout of processes when designs change. A production system composed of robots and machines, for example, can often be adapted to new models simply by a change in tools and a change in the robot's memory. With men-machine systems, on the other hand, a model change often involves large investments in new equipment and training for human operators.

Robots and the Toyota Production System

Whatever the impact of robotics on employee relations, it is important to see that its introduction is not an abandonment but a logical extension of the Toyota production system. In fact, the principal goals of robotics are fully in keeping with those of the system, which are, in general, cost reduction, quality assurance, flexible production, and respect for humanity. How robotics contributes to the first three goals has already been described. Its contribution to respect for humanity is not only to relieve human workers of risky, severe jobs but to extend in various ways the prevailing use of machines and technology in the Toyota production system—namely, to replace men with machines only when it will free the worker from repetitive tasks and make more time available for meaningful human action. In short, robots, like any other kind of technology must remain the tool of men and not the other way around.

COMPANY-WIDE QUALITY CONTROL

The phrase Total Quality Control (TQC) was first used by Dr. Feigenbaum of the United States in *Industrial Quality Control* magazine (May, 1957). According to Feigenbaum, all departments of a company, including marketing, design, production, inspection, and delivery must participate in QC.

Feigenbaum assigns the central role in promoting TQC to QC specialists. Japanese TQC, however, which is often called Company-Wide Quality Control (CWQC) to distinguish it from Feigenbaum's TQC, is not conducted by QC specialists. If it were, line employees in each department would very likely reject the suggestions of the QC staff because line connections are very strong in Japanese companies. Instead, QC is the responsibility of workers at every level and in every department of the organization, all of whom have studied QC techniques.

According to Dr. Kaoru Ishikawa, promoter of the Japanese QC movement, CWQC has the following three characteristics: all departments participate in QC, all types of employees participate in QC, and QC is fully integrated with other related company functions.

All Departments Participate in QC
To assure product quality, all departments—product planning, design, testing, purchasing, suppliers, manufacturing engineering, inspection, sales, service, etc.—must participate in QC activities. Quality analyses at the product development and product design stages, for example, are essential to establishing overall product quality, since it is impossible to correct errors made at either stage once the product reaches manufacturing and inspection departments. At the same time, however, each of the other departments also has an important role of its own to play. At this point, it may be useful to recall the definition of quality control with which the chapter began: in Japan, quality control (QC) or quality assurance (QA) is defined as the development, design, manufacture, and service of products that will satisfy the consumer's needs at the lowest possible cost.

Satisfaction of the consumer's needs is predominantly the concern of new product development and design, which must identify customer needs, such as high gas mileage and trouble-free performance, and be sure that the product satisfies them. Quality control at this level ensures that the Japanese automobile will continue to be popular throughout the world and thus, ultimately, that sales and profits will continue to be high. Quality control during manufacturing (through autonomation and other techniques described in this chapter) decreases production costs by reducing defects and thus guarantees both low cost to the consumer and company profitability. And finally, quality control in customer service in the after market is important for maintaining the automobile in good working order, thereby confirming the customer's confidence in the product and in the company. The same points are made in pamphlets issued by Toyota Motor Sales, USA.

All Employees Participate in QC

People at all levels of the organizational hierarchy participate in quality control—from the president of the company, the directors, and departmental managers to blue collar workers and salesmen. Furthermore, all suppliers, distributors, and other related companies also take part in QC activities.

Although the term "QC circle" is very popular in other countries, it should be recognized that QC circle activities are merely a part of CWQC. Without CWQC and without the obvious participation of top management, departmental managers and their staffs, QC circles would lose much of their effectiveness and might cease to exist altogether.

QC Is Fully Integrated with Other Related Company Functions

To be effective, quality control must be promoted together with cost management and production management techniques. These include profit planning, pricing, production and inventory control, and scheduling, each of which has a direct impact on quality control. Cost control techniques, for example, can help identify wasteful processes that can be improved or eliminated and can measure the effect of QC activities once undertaken. Pricing determines not only the level of quality built into the product but the customer's expectations about quality as well. And various kinds of production control data can be used to measure defect rates, establish target areas for QC activities, and promote QC in general.

15
Functional Management to Promote Company-Wide Quality Control and Cost Management

As described in Chapter 14, CWQC is possible only if quality control activities and quality-related functions are carried out in all departments and at all levels of management. Furthermore, the activities of each department must be planned so they are reinforced by other departments. Additionally, they will benefit from quality-related functions throughout the company. The responsibility for establishing communication links between the various departments at Toyota and ensuring cooperation in implementing QC programs is given to an organizational entity known as a *functional meeting*. Functional meetings do not serve as project teams or task forces. Rather, they are formally constituted, decision-making units whose power cuts across department lines and controls broad corporate functions. Consisting typically of department directors from all parts of the company, each functional meeting will consider such corporate-wide problems as cost management, production management, and quality assurance, respectively. The meeting participants then communicate their policy decision and plans for implementation to each department for action. Such management through functional meetings is called *functional management* ("Kinohbetsu Kanri") at Toyota.

In this chapter, we will examine the structural relationships between the functional meetings and the more formally developed organizations at Toyota, how business policy is made and administered through functional management, and some of the advantages to be gained from the functional management concept. Although the Toyota production system in a narrow sense does not include the product planning and design steps, the author includes functional management in the broad overview of the system. The reader should realize that the most important aspects for increasing productivity or decreasing costs and improving quality are the QC and cost reduction activities in the product development and design steps.

Historically, functional management is the outgrowth of a long process of trial and error. The QC Promoting Office at Toyota took the first steps toward CWQC in 1961 by defining various important functions to be performed by the company. Each department, in turn, collaborated to determine and arrange the contents of the functions. By the addition, integration, and abolition of these inputs, the defined functions were classified and selected into the two most necessary rules for the entire company: quality assurance and cost management. Rules were then established to define what kinds of activities each department must undertake to properly perform these two functions.

QUALITY ASSURANCE

Quality assurance, as defined in this rule at Toyota, is to assure that the quality of the product promotes satisfaction, reliability, and economy for the consumer. This rule outlines the activities of each department for quality assurance at all phases from product planning to sales and service. Further, the rule specifies *when* and *what* should be assured by *whom at where*.

The rule defines *when* as eight applicable steps in a series of business activities from planning through sales. The eight steps are:

- product planning,
- product design,
- manufacturing preparation,
- purchasing,
- manufacturing for sales,
- inspection,
- sales and service, and
- quality audit.

The term by *whom at where* means the specific department manager and the name of his department. *What* consists of items to be assured and the operations for assurance. Table 15.1 defines the quality assurance rule as it pertains to the steps in the business activities defined here and the primary operations of each department.

COST MANAGEMENT

Toyota utilizes cost management to develop and perform various activities to attain a specific profit goal, evaluate results, and take appropriate action as necessary. In other words, cost management is not simply confined to cost reduction. It also covers company-wide activities to acquire profit. This rule specifically outlines the activities of each department level to maintain cost management. The framework of this cost management evolves from the following four categories: target costing, capital investment planning, cost maintenance, and cost improvement (or *Kaizen costing*).

Target costing has been regarded as especially important because most of the cost is determined during the development stages of the product. A cost planning manual assigns primary responsibilities and tasks at each phase of product development. Establishing a target cost to be followed during all development stages promotes activities to reduce costs, while maintaining minimum quality standards.

Cost maintenance and cost improvement (*Kaizen costing*) are cost management processes at the manufacturing level. These are promoted by a company-wide budgeting system and the improvement activities described in Chapter 12. To maintain these functions, each department has its own departmental budgeting manual and cost improvement manual.

The contents of cost management activities are specified in detail in the cost management operations assignment manual. Table 15.2 summarizes the cost management rule with respect to related departments and cost management operations.

Relations Among Departments, Steps in Business Activities and Functions
In order to effectively promote functional management, it must be clearly understood how each step to be performed by each department contributes to its function. Because equal emphasis cannot be placed on all operations, each step must be graded for relative contribution. Thus, the right-hand column in Tables 15.1 and 15.2 describes the relative contribution for each managerial function, as noted by the following symbols:

◎ Defines factors with critical influence on the function

○ Defines factors with some influence that could be remedied in later steps

△ Defines factors with relatively small influence

Such assessments were made for all functions. The relationships between departments and functions are summarized in Table 15.3.

The final business purpose at Toyota is to maximize long-range profit under various economic and environmental constraints. This long-range profit will be defined and expressed as a concrete figure through long-range business planning. Therefore, each function must be carefully selected and organized to be helpful in attaining the long-range profit.

If the number of functions is too high, then each function will begin to interfere with other functions, frustrating attempts to produce a new product in a timely and cost effective manner. Further, too many functions will foster strong independence of certain functions to the point that each departmental manager might be enough to perform the function.

Conversely, if the number of functions is too small, too many departments will be related in a single function. Managing so many departments from a certain functional standpoint would be very complicated, if not impossible.

Toyota regards quality assurance and cost management as paramount functions, or *purpose functions,* and calls them the two pillars of functional management. Other functions are regarded as *means functions.* Thus, product planning

Table 15.1. Quality assurance summary.

Functional Steps	Person in Charge	Primary Operations For QA	Contribution

Product Planning	• Sales Department Manager
	• Product Planning Department Head
		1. Forecasts of demands and market share
		2. Obtain the quality to satisfy marketing needs
		  a. Set and assign proper quality target and cost target.
		  b. Prevent recurrence of important quality problems.
			△
			
			◎

Product Design	• Design Department Manager
	• Body-Design Department Manager
	• Engineering Department Managers
	• Product Design Department Manager
		1. Design of prototype vehicles
		  a. Meet quality target
		  b. Test and examine car for:
		    Performance
		    Safety
		    Low Pollution
		    Economy
		    Reliability
		2. Initial design to confirm necessary conditions for QA
			
			◎
			○
			
			○

Manufacturing Preparation	• Engineering Department Managers • QA Department Manager • Inspection Department Managers • Manufacturing Department Manager	1. Preparation of overall lines to satisfy design quality 2. Preparation of proper inspection methods 3. Evaluation of initial prototypes 4. Develop and evaluate a plan of initial and daily process control 5. Preparation of line capacities	◎ ○ ○ △ ◎
Purchasing	• Purchasing Department Managers • QA Department Manager • Inspection Department Managers	1. Confirmation of qualitative and quantitative capabilities of each supplier 2. Inspect initial parts supplied for product quality 3. Support in strengthening QA system of each supplier	△ △ △
Manufacturing	• Manufacturing Department Managers • Production Control Department Manager	1. Match product quality to established standards 2. Establish properly controlled lines 3. Maintain necessary line capacities and machine capacities	○ ○ ○
Inspection	• Inspection Department Manager • QA Department Manager	1. Inspect initial product for quality 2. Decision whether to deliver product for sale	○ ◎
Sales and Service	• Sales Department Manager • Export Department Manager • QA Department Manager	1. Prevention of quality decline in packaging, storage and delivery 2. Education and public relations for proper care and maintenance 3. Inspection of new cars 4. Feedback and analysis of quality information	○ △ △ ◎

Table 15.2. Cost management summary.

Functional Steps	Related Departments	Cost Management Operations	Contribution
Product Planning	• Corporate Planning • Product Planning Office • Production Engineering Departments • Accounting Departments	1. Set target cost based on new product planning and profit planning, then assign this target cost to various cost factors 2. Set target investment figures 3. Allocate target cost to various design departments of individual parts *(cost planning)* 4. Allocate target investment amounts to various investment planning departments *(capital budgeting)*	◎ ◎ ○ ○
Product Design	• Product Planning Office • Engineering Departments	1. Cost estimate based on prototype drawing 2. Evaluate possibility of attaining target costs 3. Take necessary steps to minimize deviations between target costs and estimated costs through Value Engineering (VE)	◎ ◎ ○
Manufacturing Preparation	• Product Planning Office • Engineering Departments • Manufacturing Engineering Departments • Production Control Department	1. Establish cost estimate by considering line preparation and investment plans 2. Evaluate possibility of attaining target costs 3. Take actions to minimize deviations 4. Evaluate facilities investment plans 5. Evaluate production plans, conditions and decisions to make or buy parts	◎ ◎ ◎ ○ ○
Purchasing	• Purchasing Departments	1. Evaluate procurement plans and purchasing conditions 2. Establish control of supplier prices (comparison of target reduction and actual reduction amounts, analyze variances and take appropriate action) 3. Investigate improvement of supplier costs (apply Value Analysis (VA), establish support to promote supplier cost improvement activities)	○ ○ ◎
Manufacturing Inspection	• Related Departments • Accounting Department	1. Instigate cost maintenance and improvements through: a. budgeting fixed costs (Manufacturing and Managerial Departments) b. cost improvements in primary projects (classified for each type of vehicle and cost factor) c. increased cost consciousness of employees through suggestions systems, case presentation seminars, reward or incentive programs, etc.	○ ○ ◎
Sales and Service	• Related Departments • Accounting Department	1. Measure actual costs of new products through overall evaluation 2. Participate in analyses and discussions at operations check, cost management functional meetings, cost meetings, and various committee meetings	○ ○

Business Activity	Related Departments	Functions					
		Quality	Cost	Engineering	Production	Business	Personnel
Product Planning	• Product Planning Department • Engineering Planning Department	◎	◎	○	△	◎	○
Product Design	• Laboratory • Design Department	◎	○	◎	○	○	○
Manufacturing Preparation	• Manufacturing Engineering Department • Manufacturing Planning Department	◎	◎	○	◎	△	○
Purchasing	• Purchasing Department • Purchasing Management Department	◎	◎	△	△	△	○
Manufacturing	• Motomachi plant • Honshu plant	◎	◎	△	◎	○	◎
Sales	• Sales Department • Export Department	◎	○	○	○	◎	○

Functional Management

Departmental Management

Table 15.3. Summary of various functional managements.

and product design are integrated into an engineering function; manufacturing preparation and manufacturing into a production function; and sales and purchasing into a business function.

As a result, six functions remain in the Toyota functional management system (Table 15.3). In summary, each function in new product development, manufacturing technique, and marketing philosophy is not identical with other functions in its character or priority.

ORGANIZATION OF THE FUNCTIONAL MANAGEMENT SYSTEM

At Toyota, each director of the company is responsible for a certain department. Since each department involves more than one function, each director must participate in multiple functions (Table 15.3). No single director is responsible for a single function; he serves as a member of a team. Conversely, not all department directors participate in all functions. This would create difficulties managing each functional meeting because of too many members. For example, although there are thirteen departments involved in product planning and product design, only one or two directors will attend a QA functional meeting.

As previously stated, the functional meeting is the only formal organizational unit in functional management. Each functional meeting is a chartered decision-making unit charged to plan, check, and decide remedial actions required to achieve a functional goal. Each individual department serves as a line unit to perform the actions dictated by the functional meeting.

Figure 15.1 details the framework of the top management organization at Toyota. Each department is managed by a managing director or common director, whereas each functional meeting consists of all directors, including six executive directors. Since each executive director is responsible for integrating the actions of various departments, he will participate as chairman in those functional meetings that have close relationships with his integrated departments. By necessity, even a vice president may participate in a functional meeting. A functional meeting typically numbers about ten members.

The quality assurance and cost management functional meetings are normally conducted once a month. Other functional meetings are usually held every other month. A functional meeting should not be convened without a significant agenda.

Functional meetings are positioned below the management meeting which consists of all managing directors and the standing auditor. The management meeting is an executive organization that gives final approval to the decision items of the functional meeting. However, the essential decision-making authority remains with each functional meeting because implementation of the decision begins at the functional meeting. As long as there are no special objections in the management meeting, the decision made by the functional meeting will be treated as a company decision.

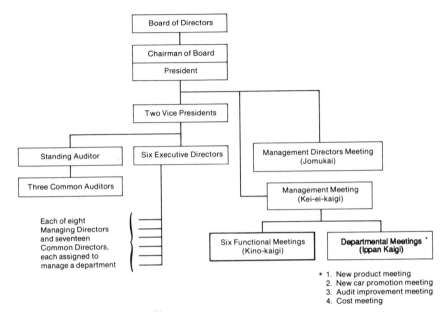

Figure 15.1. Framework of Toyota management organization (as of 1981).

The *departmental meetings* shown in Figure 15.1 provide each department with a vehicle to discuss implementation of decisions made by the functional meeting. Note that the departmental meeting is not positioned as a substructure of the functional meeting. As with the functional meetings, plans for implementation generated within departmental meetings are subject to review and approval by the management meeting.

Occasionally, a problem arises such as a need to achieve a certain quality characteristic within a short-term period that cannot be resolved by only one functional meeting. By necessity, man-hours and costs must increase to improve the quality. At this time, a *joint functional meeting* is found to combine quality and production functions. Further, in order to cope with a new legal restriction for safety and pollution, most of the functions, such as QA, cost, engineering, and production, must consider the restriction together. In this case, an *enlarged functional meeting* is formed to consider the problem. Note that these are not permanent organizational entities.

Another example involves a *cost management functional meeting*. Just after the oil shock in 1973, the profitability of the Toyota Corolla showed a marked decrease because of cost increases due to oil prices. At that time, the plant manager of Corolla made the following proposals to the cost functional meeting:

1. Promotion of a company-wide cost reduction movement for Corolla.

2. Organization of a Corolla Cost Reduction Committee chaired by the plant manager.

3. As substructures to this committee, organization of the following sectional meetings:
   a. production and assembly
   b. design and engineering
   c. purchasing

4. Establish a cost reduction of 10,000 yen (about $80) per automobile.

5. Goal to be achieved within six months.

Through a concerted effort by all departments based on the decisions of the cost management function meeting, the actual result of the plan was 128 percent attainment of the goal at the end of six months (May 1975).

Business Policy and Functional Management
Since the introduction of the CWQC concept, a business policy has been developed and published. The policy applies to the operations level and includes each function previously discussed. The six elements of the business policy are shown in Figure 15.2 and defined in the following paragraphs.

1. *Fundamental policy* is the business ethic principle, or fundamental directions, of the company. Once established, it will not change for many years. An example is "Toyota wishes to develop in the world by collecting all powers inside and outside the company." The expression is abstract, but represents a business philosophy of top management. The fundamental policy is used to guide long-range planning.

2. *Long-term goals* are goals to be attained within five years as an output of long-range planning. These goals are concrete figures expressed for production quality, sales quality, market share and ROI, etc.

3. *Long-term policy* is the strategy used to achieve the long-term goals, and is expressed in more concrete detail than the fundamental policy. It covers several items common to the overall company. For example: "In order to manage the overall company in a scientific manner, policies, goals, and plans must be prepared for each department and a control point must be clearly defined and directed."

4. *Annual slogan* is a means for Toyota to emphasize annual policies. It consists of two types of slogans. The first type remains the same every year, such as "Assure the quality in every Toyota." The second type emphasizes the policy for the year. For example, the slogan for 1974 just after the oil shock was "Build Toyotas for the changing age." Also: "It is time to use scarce resources effectively." The purpose of these slogans is to encourage a sound mental attitude in all employees.

5. Accepting the long-term goals described above, the *annual goals of each function* to be achieved within the current year must be expressed in specific figures. These goal figures are established for each function. Each functional meeting, in turn, decides how to achieve these goals. The items included as annual goals for each function follow:

   a. Overall company: ROI, production quantity, and market share.
   b. Production: Rate of reduced manpower to previous year's manpower level.
   c. Quality: Rate of reduction of problems in market.
   d. Cost: Total amount of costs to be reduced, plant and equipment investment amount, and margin rates of the preferentially developed automobiles.
   e. Safety, sanitation, and environment: Number of closures for holidays, etc., at business and plants.

6. Once annual goals are established for each function, a*nnual working plans of each function* must be determined by the appropriate functional meeting. Implementation of these working plans then becomes the responsibility of the department meeting.

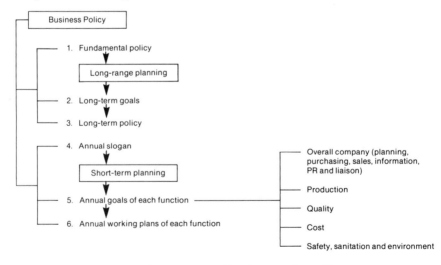

Figure 15.2. Six elements of business policy at Toyota.

Classification of the functions shown in Figure 15.2 is somewhat different than shown in Table 15.3 because the business policy must describe all the important topics to be achieved in the current year. The business function in Table 15.3 is incorporated into the overall company function shown in Figure 15.2, which also includes information and public relations. Further, although the safety, sanitation, and environment functions are not shown in Table 15.3, nor is there a functional meeting, safety and environment are included with the production functional meeting, while sanitation is included with both the production and personnel functions.

Business Policy Development

Formal announcement of the business policy at Toyota is made by the president in his New Year's greetings to the employees. Development plans of each function will then be issued to each department by the office of the functional meeting. Department policies and plans are then formulated by the department meeting.

After implementation of these plans, the results of actual performance will be evaluated during the middle and at the end of the current year. Feedback from these evaluations will be used to form the policies for the next year. Such checks and evaluations are made at three levels within the organization: operations checks of selected topics by top management, functional checks by each functional meeting chairman, and department checks by each department manager or director. Figure 15.3 shows the organization planning and control system employed at Toyota.

Critical Considerations for Functional Management

Four critical considerations demand special attention in order to achieve a successful functional management program:

1. Selection of important functions should be made using special caution to properly balance department participation. Having too many departments in the same functional meeting leads to confusion and difficulties in managing the meeting; too few member departments creates a need for many individual functions that will begin to overlap responsibilities, again creating confusion and management problems.

2. Functional management should not be regarded as an informal system. The position and guidelines of functional meetings in the top management scheme must be clearly defined. The function meeting must be given the necessary authority to implement its decisions as company policy.

3. Each line department must have a strong structure in place to execute the plans put forth by the various functional meetings.

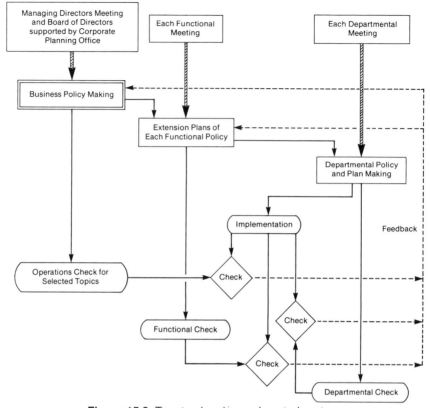

Figure 15.3. Toyota planning and control system.

4. The director in charge of each function is also responsible for an individual department. However, he must not view the function for his department alone, but rather formulate and direct the function for the overall company.

Advantages of Functional Management
Functional management as implemented at Toyota offers certain advantages not found in other management systems. For example:

• Both policies and implementation are decisive and rapidly instituted. This results because the functional meeting is a substantial decision-making entity with responsibilities and authority directed from top management. Additionally, communication to executing line departments is rapid since the members of the functional meeting are also directors responsible for the related departments.

- *Nemawashi* is unnecessary at Toyota. The original meaning of Nemawashi comes from the preparations for transplanting a large tree. You must dig around the roots and cut the big roots to influence small roots to run and secure new positions. Nemawashi, as applied to business, relates to the persuasion of related individuals, such as management executives, to accept a proposal before a formal decision meeting. At Toyota, the functional meeting itself becomes the Nemawashi negotiation.

- The functional meetings serve to greatly enhance communications and human relations among various departments because all sides are brought together to achieve a common goal.

- Communications from subordinate employees to the functional meetings are easily achieved because there is no need for Nemawashi. These employees need only to bring their suggestions and ideas to their department manager for discussion at the functional meeting.

PART III
QUANTITATIVE TECHNIQUES

16

Sequencing Method for the Mixed-Model Assembly Line to Realize Smoothed Production

The procedure for designing a mixed-model assembly line involves the following steps:

1. Determination of a cycle time.
2. Computation of a minimum number of processes.
3. Preparation of a diagram of integrated precedence relationships among elemental jobs.
4. Line balancing.
5. Determination of the sequence schedule for introducing various products to the line.
6. Determination of the length of the operations range of each process.

Chapter 16 deals with the fifth step: The problem of sequencing various car models on the line.

GOALS OF CONTROLLING THE ASSEMBLY LINE

The sequence of introducing models to the mixed-model assembly line is different due to the different goals or purposes of controlling the line. There are two goals:

1. Leveling the load (total assembly time) on each process within the line.
2. Keeping a constant speed in consuming each part on the line.

Chapter 16 is based on a presentation by Mr. Shigenori Kotani (staff member of the production control department at Toyota Motor Corporation) at the conference of the Japan Operations Research Society, March 25, 1982, and his abstract (pp. 149-150) in the proceedings of this conference. This chapter is also based on follow-up discussions with Mr. Masuyama, Mr. Terada, and Mr. Kotani of Toyota Motor Corporation. The numerical examples here (except Figure 16.5) are made by the author.

Goal One
Concerning Goal One, it is important to note that a product might have a longer operation time than the predetermined cycle time. This is due to the fact that the line balancing on the mixed-model line is made under the condition that the operation time of each process, which was weighted by each quantity of mixed models, should not exceed the cycle time. This condition (constraint) will be described as the following formula:

$$\max_{l}\left\{\frac{\sum_{i=1}^{\alpha} Q_i T_{il}}{\sum_{i=1}^{\alpha} Q_i}\right\} \le C,$$

Q_i = planned production quantity of the product A_i ($i= 1, \ldots ,\alpha$)
T_{il} = operation time per unit of product A_i on the process l total operation time per day

C = cycle time = $\dfrac{\text{total operation time per day}}{\sum_{i=1}^{a} Q_i}$.

As a result, if products with relatively longer operation times are successively introduced into the line, the products will cause a delay in completing the product and may cause line stoppage. Therefore, a heuristic program can be developed for the assembly line model-mix sequencing problem to minimize risk of stopping the conveyor (for example, see Okamura and Yamashina [1979]).

Although this first goal is also considered in Toyota's sequencing program, it is incorporated in the solution algorithm which mainly considers the second goal. As a result, Toyota considers most important the second goal of the sequence schedule: keeping a constant speed in consuming each part.

Goal Two and the Sequencing Model
In the Kanban system used at Toyota, preceding processes supplying the various parts or materials to the line are given greatest attention. Under this "pulling" system, the variation in production quantities or conveyance times at preceding processes must be minimized. Also, their respective work-in-process inventories must be minimized. To do so, the quantity used per hour (i.e., consumption speed) for each part in the mixed-model line must be kept as constant as possible. Toyota's sequencing method is designed to reach this second goal. To understand this sequencing method, it is important to define several notations and values:

Q = Total production quantity of all products A_i ($i=1, \ldots, \alpha$)

$$= \sum_{i=1}^{\alpha} Q_i \, , \, (Q_i = \text{production quantity of each product } A_i)$$

N_j = Total necessary quantity of the part a_j to be consumed for producing all products A_i ($i=1, \ldots, \alpha$; $j=1, \ldots, \beta$)

X_{jk} = Total necessary quantity of the part a_j to be utilized for producing the products of determined sequence from first to Kth.

With these notations in mind the following two values can be developed:

N_j/Q = Average necessary quantity of the part a_j per unit of a product.

$\dfrac{K \cdot N_j}{Q}$ = Average necessary quantity of the part a_j for producing K units of products.

In order to keep the consumption speed of a part a_j constant, the amount of X_{jk} must be as close as possible to the value of $\dfrac{K \cdot N_j}{Q}$. This is the basic concept underlying Toyota's sequencing algorithm and is depicted in Figure 16.1.

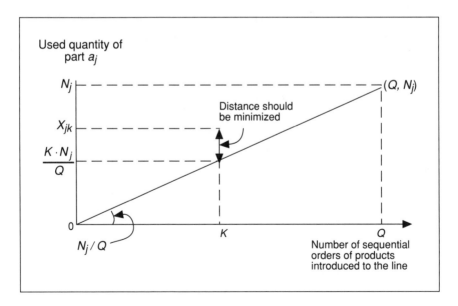

Figure 16.1. Relationship between X_{jk} and $K \cdot N_j/Q$.

It can now be further defined that:

A point $G_k = (K \cdot N_1/Q, K \cdot N_2/Q, ..., K \cdot N_\beta/Q)$,

A point $P_k = (X_{1k}, X_{2k}, ..., X_{\beta k})$.

In order for a sequence schedule to assure the constant speed of consuming each part, the point P_k must be as close as possible to the point G_k. Therefore, if the degree is measured for the point P_k approaching the point G_k by using the distance D_k:

$$D_k = \|G_k - P_k\| = \sqrt{\sum_{j=1}^{\beta} \left(\frac{K \cdot N_j}{Q} - X_{jk} \right)^2}$$

then, the distance D_k must be minimized. The algorithm developed on this idea by Toyota is called the *goal chasing method* (Figure 16.2).

Denote:

$b_{ij} =$ Necessary quantity of the part a_j $(j = 1,..., \beta)$ for producing one unit of the product A_i $(i = 1,..., \alpha)$.

Other notations are already defined.
Then,

Step 1   Set $K = 1$, $X_{j,k-1} = 0$, $(j = 1,..., \beta)$, $S_{k-1} = \{1, 2, ..., \alpha\}$.

Step 2   Set as Kth order in the sequence schedule the product A_{i^*} which minimizes the distance D_k. The minimum distance will be found by the following formula:

$$D_{ki^*} = \min_i \{D_{ki}\}, i \in S_{k-1},$$

$$\text{where } D_{ki} = \sqrt{\sum_{j=1}^{\beta} \left(\frac{K \cdot N_j}{Q} - X_{j,k-1} - b_{ij} \right)^2}.$$

Step 3   If all units of a product A_{i^*} were ordered and included in the sequence schedule, then

Set $S_k = S_{k-1} - \{i^*\}$.

If some units of a product A_{i^*} are still remaining as being not ordered, then set $S_k = S_{k-1}$.

Step 4   If $S_k = \emptyset$ (empty set), the algorithm will end.

If $S_k \neq 0$, then compute $X_{jk} = X_{j,k-1} + b_{i^*j}$ $(j = 1, ..., \beta)$ and go back to Step 2 by setting $K = K + 1$.

Figure 16.2. Goal-chasing method I.

Goal Chasing Method: A Numerical Example

To fully understand Toyota's goal chasing method, it is best to review an example. Suppose the production quantities $Q_i (i = 1, 2, 3)$ of each product $A_1, A_2,$ and $A_3,$ and the required unit $b_{ij} (i = 1, 2, 3; j = 1, 2, 3, 4)$ of each part $a_1, a_2, a_3,$ and a_4 for producing these products are as shown in Table 16.1:

Table 16.1. Production quantities Q_i and parts condition b_{ij}.

Product A_i	A_1	A_2	A_3	
Planned Production Quantity Q_i	2	3	5	
Products A_i / Parts a_j	a_1	a_2	a_3	a_4
A_1	1	0	1	1
A_2	1	1	0	1
A_3	0	1	1	0

Then, the total necessary quantity (N_j) of the part $a_j (j = 1, 2, 3, 4)$ for producing all products A_i $(i = 1, 2, 3)$ can be computed as follows:

$$[N_j] = [Q_i] [b_{ij}]$$

$$= [2, 3, 5] \begin{bmatrix} 1 & 0 & 1 & 1 \\ 1 & 1 & 0 & 1 \\ 0 & 1 & 1 & 0 \end{bmatrix} = [5, 8, 7, 5]$$

Further, the total production quantity of all products A_i $(i = 1, 2, 3)$ will be:

$$\sum_{i=1}^{3} Q_i = 2 + 3 + 5 = 10$$

Therefore,

$$[N_j/Q] = [5/10, 8/10, 7/10, 5/10]$$
$$(j = 1, 2, 3, 4)$$

Next, applying the values of $[N_j/Q]$ and $[b_{ij}]$ to the formula in step 2 of the above algorithm, when $K = 1$, the distances D_{ki} can be computed as follows:

for $i=1$, $D_{1,1} =$

$$\sqrt{\left(\frac{1\times 5}{10}-0-1\right)^2+\left(\frac{1\times 8}{10}-0-0\right)^2+\left(\frac{1\times 7}{10}-0-1\right)^2+\left(\frac{1\times 5}{10}-0-1\right)^2}$$

$= 1.11.$

For $i=2$, $D_{1,2} =$

$$\sqrt{\left(\frac{1\times 5}{10}-0-1\right)^2+\left(\frac{1\times 8}{10}-0-1\right)^2+\left(\frac{1\times 7}{10}-0-0\right)^2+\left(\frac{1\times 5}{10}-0-1\right)^2}$$

$= 1.01.$

For $i=3$, $D_{1,3} =$

$$\sqrt{\left(\frac{1\times 5}{10}-0-0\right)^2+\left(\frac{1\times 8}{10}-0-1\right)^2+\left(\frac{1\times 7}{10}-0-1\right)^2+\left(\frac{1\times 5}{10}-0-0\right)^2}$$

$= 0.79.$

Thus, $D_{1,i^*} = \min\{1.11, 1.01, 0.79\} = 0.79$
$\therefore i^* = 3$

Therefore, the first order in the sequence schedule is the product A_3. Proceeding to Step 4 of the algorithm,

$X_{jk} = X_{j,k-1}+b_{3j}$:
$X_{1,1} = 0+0 = 0$ $X_{3,1} = 0+1 = 1$
$X_{2,1} = 0+1 = 1$ $X_{4,1} = 0+0 = 0$

Thus, the first line in Figure 16.3 was written based on the above computations.

K	D_{k1}	D_{k2}	D_{k3}	Sequence Schedule	X_{1k}	X_{2k}	X_{3k}	X_{4k}
1	1.11	1.01	0.79	A_3	0	1	1	0
2	0.85	0.57*	1.59	$A_3 A_2$	1	2	1	1
3	0.82*	1.44	0.93	$A_3 A_2 A_1$	2	2	2	2
4	1.87	1.64	0.28*	$A_3 A_2 A_1 A_3$	2	3	3	2
5	1.32	0.87*	0.87	$A_3 A_2 A_1 A_3 A_2$	3	4	3	3
6	1.64	1.87	0.28*	$A_3 A_2 A_1 A_3 A_2 A_3$	3	5	4	3
7	0.93	1.21	0.82*	$A_3 A_2 A_1 A_3 A_2 A_3 A_3$	3	6	5	3
8	0.57*	0.85	1.59	$A_3 A_2 A_1 A_3 A_2 A_3 A_3 A_1$	4	6	6	4
9	1.56	0.77*	1.01	$A_3 A_2 A_1 A_3 A_2 A_3 A_3 A_1 A_2$	5	7	6	5
10	—	—	0*	$A_3 A_2 A_1 A_3 A_2 A_3 A_3 A_1 A_2 A_3$	5	8	7	5

* Indicates smallest distance D_{kj}.

Figure 16.3. Sequence schedule.

Next, when $k=2$, then

for $i=1, D_{2,1} =$

$$\sqrt{\left(\frac{2\times5}{10}-0-1\right)^2+\left(\frac{2\times8}{10}-1-0\right)^2+\left(\frac{2\times7}{10}-1-1\right)^2+\left(\frac{2\times5}{10}-0-1\right)^2}$$
$$= 0.85.$$

For $i=2, D_{2,2}=$

$$\sqrt{\left(\frac{2\times5}{10}-0-1\right)^2+\left(\frac{2\times8}{10}-1-1\right)^2+\left(\frac{2\times7}{10}-1-0\right)^2+\left(\frac{2\times5}{10}-0-1\right)^2}$$
$$= 0.57.$$

For $i=3, D_{2,3}=$

$$\sqrt{\left(\frac{2\times5}{10}-0-0\right)^2+\left(\frac{2\times8}{10}-1-1\right)^2+\left(\frac{2\times7}{10}-1-1\right)^2+\left(\frac{2\times5}{10}-0-0\right)^2}$$
$$= 1.59.$$

Thus, $D_{2,i*} = \text{Min } \{0.85, 0.57, 1.59\}$
$$= 0.57$$
$$\therefore i* = 2.$$

Therefore, the second order in the sequence schedule is the product A_2. Also, X_{jk} will be computed as:

$$X_{jk} = X_{j,k-1} + b_{2,j}:$$
$$X_{1,2} = 0 + 1 = 1$$
$$X_{2,2} = 1 + 1 = 2$$
$$X_{3,2} = 1 + 0 = 1$$
$$X_{4,2} = 0 + 1 = 1$$

This procedure was used to develop the second line of Figure 16.3. The remaining lines in Figure 16.3 can also be written by following the same procedures. As a result, the complete sequence schedule of this example will be:

$$A_3, A_2, A_1, A_3, A_2, A_3, A_3, A_1, A_2, A_3.$$

Evaluation of the Goal Chasing Method

The values of $K \cdot N_j / Q$ and X_{jk} for each part a_j in the previous example are depicted as graphs in Figure 16.4. The figure shows that all parts a_1, a_2, a_3 and a_4 are attaining optimality.[1]

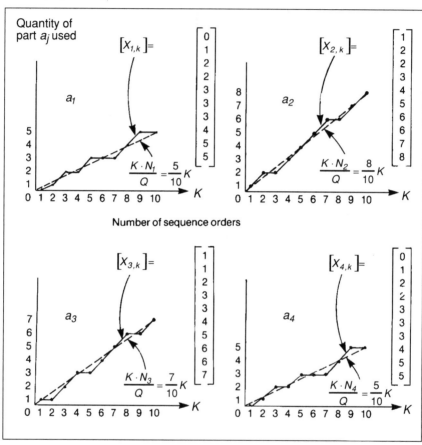

Figure 16.4. How X_{jk} approached to $K \cdot N_j / Q$.

---

1. The meaning of "optimality" in this section is as follows: Suppose $[[K \cdot N_j / Q]]$ denotes the integer which is closest to $K \cdot N_j / Q$.

Then, if $X_{jk} = [[K \, N_j / Q]]$ holds for the part a_j, the optimality is achieved in this part. Figure 16.4 shows all parts attaining optimality in this meaning.

To further evaluate this algorithm, the mean and the standard deviation of the values were computed:

$$\left| \frac{K \cdot N}{Q} - X_{jk} \right| \text{ for each part } a_j$$

Then, the following results were found:

• When the number of varieties in parts items and/or the number of varieties in product-models were increased, both the mean and the standard deviation were increased.

• When the production quantity itself was increased, both the mean and the standard deviation were decreased.

It is clear from these results that the more the tendency to produce multi-varieties in each small quantity is promoted, the less likely smoothing of production will be attained.

Another general approach for verifying the usefulness of this hueristic algorithm is expressed by the following procedure. Suppose the total production quantity $Q(= \Sigma Q_j)$ is large (1,000 units, etc.). Then, the sequence determined by this algorithm can be divided into 16 equal ranges, with each range corresponding to approximately one hour of production. The quantity of each part contained in each range will be computed, and its standard deviation will be computed. The actual distribution of these values shows that the variation (σ) per each hour is fairly small. (See Figure 16.5.) The coefficient of variation ($= \sigma / \bar{x}$) in each range is small and its variance is also small.

Range Kinds of front axles	1	2	3	4	5	6	7	8	9	10	11	12	13	14	15	16	$\bar{x}$	σ
a_1	9	7	7	9	8	7	8	8	8	8	7	8	9	7	7	8	7.8	.73
a_2	6	5	7	6	5	6	7	5	7	6	5	7	6	6	5	6	5.9	.75
a_3	5	6	5	5	6	6	4	6	4	6	6	5	4	6	5	6	5.3	.77
a_4	3	3	3	2	3	3	3	3	3	2	3	3	3	2	3	3	2.8	.33
a_5	2	2	2	2	3	2	2	2	2	3	2	1	3	2	2	2	2.1	.48
a_6	1	1	1	1	1	2	1	1	2	0	2	1	1	1	1	1	1.1	.48

Figure 16.5. Distribution of each kind of front axle used.

The Toyota Approach: A Simplified Algorithm

To decrease computational time, a simplified algorithm known as *goal chasing method II* (Figure 16.6) can be developed. This simplified algorithm is evolved from Step 2 of goal chasing method I (Figure 16.2) and is based on the following proposition:

Among a product A_b and the other product A_c,

if $D_{k,b} \le D_{k,c}$, then the relationship:

$$\sum_{j_b \in B_b} \left(\frac{K \cdot N_{jb}}{Q} - X_{jb,K-1} \right) \ge \sum_{j_c \in B_c} \left(\frac{K \cdot N_{jc}}{Q} - X_{jc,K-1} \right)$$

will hold and vice versa, and where B_b is a set of constituent parts a_{jb}, for the product A_b. This equivalence relationship can hold under the condition that the number of items of parts used for each product must be the same among different products and that the necessary quantity of each part used for one unit of each product must be the same among different products.[2]

$$E_{ki} = \max\{E_{ki}\}, i \in S_{k-1}$$

$$\text{where } E_{ki} = \sum_{j_{i \in B_i}} \left(\frac{K \cdot N_{ji}}{Q} - X_{ji,k-1} \right)$$

(B_i is a set of constituent parts a_{ji} for the Product A_i)

Figure 16.6. Goal-chasing method II.

Applications of the simplified algorithm. The goal of the simplified algorithm is to keep a constant speed in the utilization of each part on the mixed-model assembly line. However, another goal to escape successive proceedings of the products which have a larger load of assembly time has also been considered.

In general, the kind of product that has a larger load is different when a different process is considered for the product in question. Toyota's line balancing is designed so that the car model which has a larger assembly-time always has larger loads at every process in the line. To avoid introducing successively the same product requiring a longer operation time, all automobiles on the line are classified according to large (a_l), medium (a_m), or small (a_s) total assembly times. Each a_j $(j = 1, m,$ and s in this situation) must be introduced to the line so as to keep the speed constant on the line. This goal can be achieved by using the same simplified algorithm for keeping the speed constant of utilizing each part a_j on the line.

---

2. The process to prove this proposition is as follows:

Denote:

W = necessary quantity of each item of part for a unit of a product,

then,

$$D_{k,c}^2 - D_{k,b}^2$$

$$= \sum_{j_c \in B_c - B_b} \left\{ \left(\frac{K \cdot N_{jc}}{Q} - X_{jc,k-1} - W \right)^2 - \left(\frac{K \cdot N_{jc}}{Q} - X_{jc,k-1} \right)^2 \right\}$$

$$+ \sum_{j_b \in B_b - B_c} \left\{ \left(\frac{K \cdot N_{jb}}{Q} - X_{jb,k-1} \right)^2 - \left(\frac{K \cdot N_b}{Q} - X_{jb,k-1} - W \right)^2 \right\}$$

$$= -W \sum_{j_c \in B_c - B_b} \left(2 \frac{K \cdot N_{jc}}{Q} - 2 X_{jc,k-1} - W \right)$$

$$+ W \sum_{j_b \in B_b - B_c} \left(2 \frac{K \cdot N_{jb}}{Q} - 2 X_{jb,k-1} - W \right)$$

$$= -2W \sum_{j_c \in B_c - B_b} \left(\frac{K \cdot N_{jc}}{Q} - X_{jc,k-1} \right) + 2W \sum_{j_b \in B_b - B_c} \left(\frac{K \cdot N_{jb}}{Q} - X_{jb,k-1} \right)$$

(because $|B_c - B_b| = |B_b - B_c|$ due to the assumption.)

$$= -2W \sum_{j_c \in B_c - B_b} \left(\frac{K \cdot N_{jc}}{Q} - X_{jc,k-1} \right) + 2W \sum_{j_b \in B_b - B_c} \left(\frac{K \cdot N_{jb}}{Q} - X_{jb,k-1} \right)$$

$$+ 2W \sum_{S \in B_c \cap B_b} \left\{ \left(\frac{K \cdot N_s}{Q} - X_{s,k-1} \right) - \left(\frac{K \cdot N_s}{Q} - X_{s,k-1} \right) \right\}$$

$$= 2W \left\{ \sum_{j_b \in B_b - B_c} \left(\frac{K \cdot N_{jb}}{Q} - X_{jb,k-1} \right) + \sum_{S \in B_c \cap B_b} \left(\frac{K \cdot N_s}{Q} - X_{s,k-1} \right) \right\}$$

$$- 2W \left\{ \sum_{j_c \in B_c - B_b} \left(\frac{K \cdot N_{jc}}{Q} - X_{jc,k-1} \right) + \sum_{S \in B_c \cap B_b} \left(\frac{K \cdot N_s}{Q} - X_{s,k-1} \right) \right\}$$

$$= 2W \left\{ \sum_{j_b \in B_b} \left(\frac{K \cdot N_{jb}}{Q} - X_{jb,k-1} \right) - \sum_{J_c \in B_c} \left(\frac{K \cdot N_{jc}}{Q} - X_{jc,k-1} \right) \right\}$$

Thus, the equivalence relationship was proved.

It is difficult to apply the goal chasing method since the number of different parts used in an automobile is about 20,000. Therefore, the parts are represented only by their respective subassembly, where each subassembly has many outputs. For example, a car brand may have the following production data:

- Planned production quantity=about 500.
  (= number of sequence orders)
- Number of kinds of cars = about 180.
  (therefore, each kind has about three units)
- Number of subassemblies = about 20.

The main subassembly names are as follows:

1. body types	11. wheels
2. engines	12. doors
3. transmissions	13. user's countries
4. grades (series)	14. air conditioners
5. frames	15. seats
6. front axles	16. etc.
7. rear axles	17. "
8. colors	18. "
9. bumpers	19. "
10. steering assemblies	20. "

Note that each subassembly must obviously contain many different parts. To the number of subassemblies the difference in loads (assembly hour) of various cars must be added to handle it in the same way as real parts.

Using the above data, a sequence schedule was developed by using goal chasing method II. Then, the sequence was divided into 16 equal ranges (each range corresponded to about one hour of production time). Using front axles as an example, refer to Figure 16.5 to see how many units of each kind of front axle were included in each range. Obviously from the figure, it can be seen that the value of the standard deviation (σ) displays a small variation of speed of utilizing each part.

In practice, Toyota "weights" important subassemblies and in some cases, provides some additional constraints such as facility capacities, etc. The classified categories (a_l, a_m, a_s) of assembly time loads are also given some weight to solve the conflict between the line balancing goal and the part smoothing goal.

17
New Sequence Scheduling
Method for Smoothing

Toyota's quantitative method used for the sequence scheduling of models to a mixed-model assembly line (goal chasing method described in the previous chapter) has evolved to a new version. Since this new method has a function to include multiple goals, I will call it the goals-coordinating method in this book. Furthermore, various improvement techniques to decrease the differences in assembly hours among models in an assembly line will be introduced.

BASIC LOGIC OF SEQUENCE SCHEDULING

The two main logical components of the sequence scheduling method for smoothing in an assembly line are the *appearance ratio control* and the *continuation and interval controls*. Appearance ratio control, or control by an average appearance ratio, can be defined as setting a target of the average "appearance ratio" of various items or specs and smoothing their appearances on the assembly line. The sequence schedule for vehicles should be prepared in accordance with this average ratio. The appearance ratio is calculated using the following formula:

$$\text{Appearance ratio} = \frac{\text{Total number of vehicles of certain spec}}{\text{Total number of all vehicles}}$$

This is the goal chasing method explained in the previous chapter. It results in selecting, one by one, those models that minimize the total deviation between an objective value of consumption based on the average appearance ratio and an actual consumption value for specs and parts to be smoothed.

Appearance ratio control cannot solve all the problems posed in the sequence scheduling. In reality, the strain caused by a daily scheduling process is shifted to about ten percent of vehicles sequenced around the end of the day. This shift means that the distance from the line of the average use or average appearance of each part or spec will be longer. Stated differently, smoothing in sequence can hardly be realized in the final ten percent of cars produced in a day.

To solve this strain problem, a new logic—*continuation and interval controls*—is used to ensure that specified vehicles appear in certain intervals instead of successively. Continuation and interval control is divided into two phases:

1. *Continuation control* directs the continuation of vehicles of a certain spec so that they do not exceed a designated maximum number of units. For example, two cars with the same spec may be approved to flow successively, but the third car must be different from the spec of the first two cars.

2. *Interval control* keeps the interval of units between the two same vehicles of a certain spec within a designated minimum interval. Suppose a spec B car (e.g., a car with grade H) is introduced with an interval of not less than three cars. The rule states that even if the *appearance ratio control* (goal chasing method) selects the spec B car again as the third car, the second best spec C must be introduced instead of the spec B car.

In this manner, the appearance ratio control of the goal chasing method is used as the main logic of the sequencing method, while the logic of continuation and interval controls is used as a restricting condition to the main logic.

The sequence in which models are introduced is initially determined by applying the appearance ratio control to the first car in the sequence. Each selected car is then examined to determine whether it also satisfies the rules of the continuation and interval controls. If a car that does not meet the rules is encountered, another car with the optimum spec will be selected by applying the appearance ratio control to the remaining cars while ignoring the spec in question.

If the maximum number of cars having sun roofs in a sequence is two, the sequence of a vehicle will be as above. Out of the vehicles without a sun roof, the car which minimizes the amount of the total deviation in the following formula should be selected as the $K'th$ car.

$$\sum_{j=1}^{n} \left| \frac{\text{Total number of vehicles of the specified spec } i}{\text{Total number of vehicles}} \times K - \frac{\text{Accumulated number of spec } j}{\text{up to } (k-1)\text{th}} + \frac{\text{Number of spec } j \text{ of } K'th}{\text{additional vehicle}} \right|$$

$$(j = \text{spec number})$$

Parts 1 and 2 of Figure 17.1 show actual computer input data concerning the appearance ratio control and the continuation and interval controls.

End items	Contents of input data		Process		
	Appearance ratio control	Continuation & interval control	W	T	A
Panoramic roof + sun roof	O	min. interval of 2 vehicles ④	O	O	O
Sun roof	O	min. interval of 2 vehicles ①	O		
5-door van	O	min. interval of 4 vehicles ⑥	O	O	O
Type of engine	O				O
Transmission	O				O
2-tone color	O	min. interval of 2 vehicles ⑪		O	
Grade	O	min. interval of 4 vehicles (Q grade) ⑦	O		O
Wagon	O	max. continuation of 4 vehicles ⑬			O
Automatic curtain	O	min. interval of 4 vehicles ⑧			O
Power-steering	O	min. interval of 3 vehicles ⑩			O
All metallic color	O	min. continuation of 2 vehicles ⑫		O	
Van + space wagon	O	min. interval of 3 vehicles (van) ③	O		O
Interior color	O				
4WD + 2WD	O	min. interval of 2 vehicles (4WD) ② min. continuation of 2 vehicles (2WD) ⑤	O		O
Suspended roof	O	min. interval of 3 vehicles ⑨			O
2-tone & roof	O				

Figures inside circles are priorities (weights).
W = welding
T = trimming
A = assembly

Figure 17.1 (part 1). Conditions of computer data for the appearance ratio control and the continuation and interval controls.

Computer data conditions of model B			Nov. 1993		
End items	**Contents of input data**		**Process**		
	Appearance ratio control	**Continuation & interval controls**	**W**	**T**	**A**
1 Type of floor	○		○		
2 Single sun roof W sun roof	○		○		
3 Suspended roof and sun roof	○	min. interval of 2 vehicles (sun roof) ①			○
4 Grade	○	max. continuation of 5 vehicles (H grade) ③	○		○
5 Generator	○	min. interval of 2 vehicles ④	○		○
6 Air conditioner	○				○
7 Transmission	○				○
8 4 drives	○	min. interval of 2 vehicles ②			○
9 Turbo	○				○
10 All metallic color (3 coatings)	○	max. continuation of 2 vehicles ⑤		○	
11 Interior color	○				
12 2- tone color	○			○	
13 Different lock	○		○		

Figures inside circles are priorities (weights).
W = welding T = trimming A = assembly

Figure 17.1 (part 2). Conditions of computer data for the appearance ratio control and the continuation and interval controls.

Assisting Rules

The following three assisting rules are used to determine parameters of the previous two restricting rules (continuation and interval controls).

1. *Weighting control.* If it is desirable under the appearance ratio control to realize an objective value of the average appearance ratio for a certain spec in preference to other specs, a relatively bigger weight is given to such a ratio. Attention must be paid to the fact that the expected weight for smoothing a certain spec is different among different processes. For example, in an assembly line, smoothing of painting colors is unnecessary because color has no effect on the assembling of vehicles. However, in a painting line, the smoothing of colors is an important matter. Therefore, when the average appearance ratio of each item is controlled by the sequence schedule of an assembly line, weight values for each average appearance ratio of an individual spec must be considered carefully.

2. *Feasibility to implement.* Under the continuation and interval controls, the value of the maximum continuation or the minimum interval should be checked for feasibility and should be moderated in advance if necessary. The parameter should be modified automatically if the following conditions are not met in each case: plus one to the maximum continuation number or minus one from the minimum interval number.

For continuation control:

$$\text{Number of vehicles concerned} \times \frac{\text{Max. continued no. of vehicles of the same spec} + 1}{\text{Max. continued no. of vehicles of the same spec}} \leq \text{Total number of all vehicles}$$

For the interval control:

$$\text{Number of vehicles concerned} \times \left(\text{Min. interval between vehicles of the same spec} + 1 \right) \leq \text{Total number of all vehicles}$$

3. *The availability of appropriate models and the minimum appearance ratio.* If no more models are available that satisfy the rules of the continuation and interval controls, then some conditions of the continuation and interval controls should be relieved from the inferior conditions one by one. Stated differently, if the continuation and interval controls might give so strong an influence on the appearance ratio that no models could be acceptable, the overcharged influence would need to be adjusted.

When determining the $K'th$ vehicle, the continuation and interval control rules suggest an answer of non-sun roof but the formula below, which suggests the attachment of a sun roof to the $K'th$ vehicle, should be approved. Using a non-sun roof vehicle in the $K'th$ spot would be too big of a deviation from the objective value.

$$\left| \begin{array}{c} \text{Objective value of} \\ \text{the } K'th \text{ vehicle} \end{array} - \begin{array}{c} \text{Actual value of} \\ \text{the } (K-1)'th \text{ vehicle} \end{array} \right| \geq 2.0$$

Sequence Scheduling Using Artificial Intelligence

Recently at Toyota, the continuation and interval controls described in the previous sections were used at a painted body storage area between a painting process and an assembly process separately from the appearance ratio control by the goal chasing method (see Figure 17.2). A main-frame computer in the central office determines the sequence schedule of models with different specs for the body-welding process. This allows us to realize the smoothing goal of an appearance ratio by the goal chasing method.

Sequentially, each vehicle gets into the painting process, but here the predetermined introduction sequence is disturbed. One reason is that two-tone color cars are painted once, and then returned to the start of the painting process and painted again with another color. The second reason is that defective cars are picked out of the main painting line, remedied, and returned to the line again. Because of these disruptions, the sequence when all painting processes are

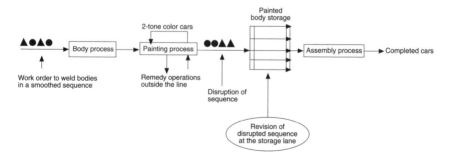

Figure 17.2. Introduction of various vehicles in a smoothed sequence.

complete will be different from the initial sequence. This altered sequence is likely to cause a line stop at an assembly process unless it is rearranged.

The threat of line stoppages caused by altered sequences mandates the installation of painted body storage, in which cars are transposed in their sequence and delivered to the assembly line. In other words, it is necessary to transpose the sequence of cars coming out of the painting process at the painted body storage for the assembly process to achieve a smoothed work load and not cause line stops.

The painted body storage has five conveyers, and the painted cars are organized to flow in accordance to each main spec. Formerly, a well-skilled operator working at the storage exit would decide what the satisfactory sequence of jobs was, move the conveyers, and introduce them into the assembly line one by one. In the past, when a skilled operator was absent, it was difficult for even two or three section leaders working together to deal with these tasks. Now artificial intelligence (AI) performs all of these operations in the following manner.

Initially, the vehicle coming out of the painting process must be identified. Information about the vehicle, such as the ID number, specifications, etc., is already stored in a remote ID (IC card or memory card that can be read and written on through electronic waves) attached to the body chassis during the middle of the

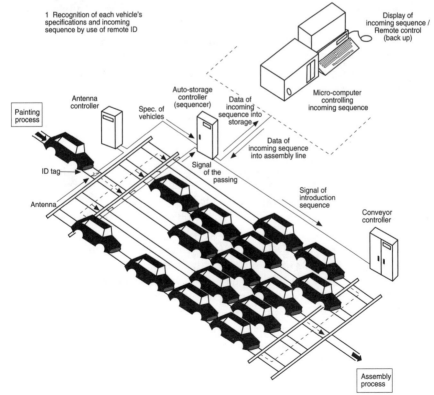

Figure 17.3. Smoothed sequence of vehicles by AI and FA system.

painting process. An antenna reads this information as each vehicle enters a storage lane (see Figure 17.3).

The spec of each car in storage and its flowing sequence are recognized and transmitted to a micro-computer in the control room. The AI processing calculates the smoothed sequence of vehicles and sends its signal to the storage at the work place, thereby moving conveyors automatically.

These sequence decisions require thought and judgment; therefore, automation in this area requires rules concerning various complex conditions and superior judgments. Also, it is the nature of the process to change: a change in production volume, changes of each spec's proportion, change of production conditions caused by improvement at an assembly process, etc. are common. For example, while the continuation control checks the minimum successive number of vehicles, this control rule is not as restrictive a constraint as the interval control that keeps the maximum interval. Which restricting rule will be applied to a particular spec of a vehicle may be altered suddenly in accordance with the change of production volume or change of a spec rate. If the alteration is managed by an ordinary computer program, it will need to be renewed each time a change occurs.

In the example above, the expert system supported by AI technology makes it possible to revise the existing program for the stated changes at the plant. In the past, the FA System Department changed it, and plants independently managed it.

Presently, AI is a technology used to make computers perform intelligent activities, i.e., assimilate human intelligent behaviors. Intelligent activities are mainly based on the abilities to understand natural language and to infer solutions to problems.

As AI research continues, the inferring system used to solve problems has been given more emphasis relative to natural language processing. The inferring system answers problems by using the professional knowledge of experts. This inferring system is called an *expert system.*

An expert system consists of a *knowledge base* and an *inferring engine* which includes procedures of reasoning. The inferring engine will be operated by referring to data (a set of rules) stored in the knowledge base. These rules are in the form of *if, then* statements. These rules should be written so that people can easily revise them at any time. Compared with the ordinary system, the expert system has an advantage in that the structure enables easy rewrite of the set of rules without the need to revise the inferring engine's program.

The operator's way of thinking and judgment in deciding the introduction sequence of cars consists of two parts A and B, as follows. Part A is an area of knowledge that the operator will use in selecting restrictions and priority. Part B is a vehicles introduction decision procedure.

Part A can be expressed with several patterns. Because contents of these patterns are dependent on the production condition, this knowledge will be subject to revision. On the contrary, Part B is independent of production conditions and is a neutral procedure that could be applied at any time. It is the procedure of inferring itself.

Five Patterns for Deciding the Sequence Schedule
The five patterns for selecting restrictions and priorities presented here are
conditions that the introduction sequence of vehicles must meet. By entering specs
or values into the blanks ([*****]) in A-1 to A-5, they become customized
patterns.

> A-1 = "If a spec of a car is [******]
> and if [max. continuation]
> (or [min. interval]) is not more (or less)
> than [******],
> then introduce the car."

For example, if the spec of a car is [*for domestic use*] and if [*max. continuation*] is not more than [*three*], then introduce it. Also, if spec of a car is [*4WD*] and if [*min. interval*] is not less than [*four*], then introduce it, etc.

> A-2 = "If number of cars being conveyed in the storage
> (i.e.- stored on the way to the entrance of an
> assembly line) is not less than [*****], then stop
> to introduce the second car in the [*****]'th lane."

This A-2 rule is based on the following circumstance. It is difficult to
introduce a car at the rear of the storage line to the assembly line. Therefore, a lane
is located apart from the storage line to move the front car in a storage lane and
return it to the rear. This enables the car in the rear to be introduced first to the
assembly line. However, because returning takes a long time, it should not be done
frequently. This is controlled by rule A-2.

> A-3 = "If spec of a car is [*****]
> and if a rate of inventory (in the storage) is
> not less than [*****] to [******] %,
> then suspend its introduction,
> and if it is [*****] to [*****]%,
> then introduce it,
> and if it is [*****] to [*****]%,
> then give it the highest priority for introduction."

Suppose a production rate of a certain spec model is 33%, that is, one car out
of three will meet this spec. By introducing the car with spec Z first and then
sequentially two cars with different specs, spec Z will flow evenly at a rate of 33%.
Pattern A-3 is the rule that was used in this case.

A-4 ="If spec of a car is [*****],
   then give the priority [*****] to it."

For example, if spec of a car is [*sun roof*], then give the priority [*1*] to it.

A-5 = "If spec of a car is [*****]
   and if [max. continuation] is less than [*****],
   then give the priority [*****] to it,
   but if [min. interval] is not less than [*****],
   then give the priority [*****] to it."

As examples for A-5, if the spec of a car is [*2WD*] and if [max. continuation] is less than [*two*], then give priority [*low(5)*] to it. Or if spec of a car is [*4WD*] and if [*min. interval*] is more than [*two*], then give the priority [*high(2)*] to it, etc.

It is necessary to let operators know the five patterns discussed above so that they can make decisions by them. An operator in the storage area only has to put in the number of the spec and the priority in a revisions case (A-4), for example. This appears on a personal computer terminal in a spreadsheet format through the use of a knowledge editor (see Figure 17.4). As seen on the display in the figure, all the operator has to do to complete the A-4 pattern is enter the digit number mark and priority.

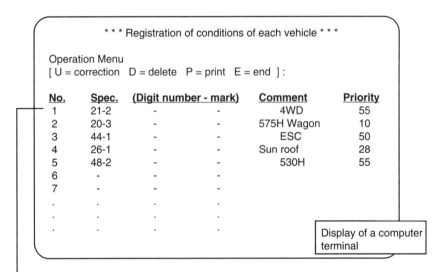

* * * Registration of conditions of each vehicle * * *

Operation Menu
[U = correction   D = delete   P = print   E = end] :

No.	Spec.	(Digit number - mark)		Comment	Priority
1	21-2	-	-	4WD	55
2	20-3	-	-	575H Wagon	10
3	44-1	-	-	ESC	50
4	26-1	-	-	Sun roof	28
5	48-2	-	-	530H	55
6	-	-	-		
7	-	-	-		
.	.	.	.		
.	.	.	.		
.	.	.	.		

Display of a computer terminal

Meaning of Knowledge of No. 1: If spec. of a car is [21 - 2 (4WD)], then give the prioroty [55] to it.

Figure 17.4. A knowledge editor in the form of a table.

DIMINISHING DIFFERENCES BETWEEN THE PRODUCT LEAD TIMES

In addition to the sequence scheduling solution are various other means of absorbing differences of lead time (length of process) and man hours.

Two measures for abolishing the lead time differences are:

- Prior work order—Since a two-tone color car circulates twice through a painting line, it should have priority introduced into the line.
- Buffer line—Cars that are out-of-order are diverted to a buffer line, placed in proper sequence, and returned to the regular line. (See Figure 17.5.)

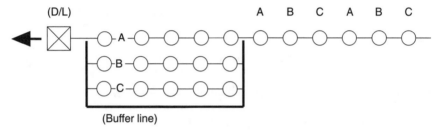

Figure 17.5. Buffer line.

Several means of absorbing differences in man hours are:

- Bypass process—For vehicles requiring long man hours, a bypass line is installed. These vehicles are removed from the regular line to the bypass line which has a slower tact time. Two types of bypass lines exist; the first one is installed close to the head of the assembly line and called "former bypass." The second type is located toward the end of the assembly line and called "letter bypass" (see Figure 17.6).

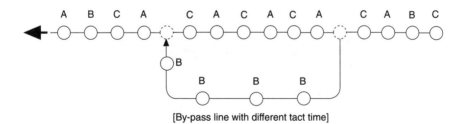

Figure 17.6. Installation of a by-pass line.

- Exceptional operations—Vehicles requiring exceptional operations are handled via a subassembly line which configures the specialized parts and then attaches them to the car while it is still in the regular assembly line. (See Figure 17.7.)

Main Line

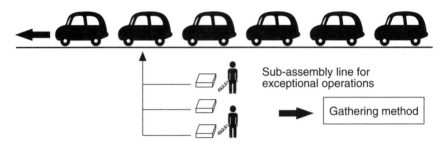

Figure 17.7. Exceptional operations.

- Inside bypass (two-range usage)—Suppose a car requiring 1.1 minute of labor time is introduced into a line that has a one-minute tact range. The operator will have cut into the range for the next car when he completes the operation. Again, if the same kind of a car comes successively, he has to start the second car's assembly 0.1 minute later, thus the operation still eats into his subsequent range even further than the previous cycle. Moreover, imagine a case where the third car is the same type again. The condition will worsen as he has to start its assembly around the middle of his range, and by the time he finishes he will have used up half of the subsequent range.

In such a case, if an another operator is not allocated to his subsequent range, he can manage such work by using two ranges on his own. Although continuation of such cars necessarily causes a line stop, if the fourth car needs just 0.7 minutes labor time, it becomes possible to complete the assembly within the first range (see Figure 17.8).

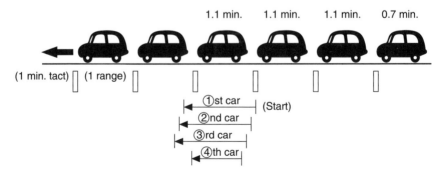

Figure 17.8. Inside bypass (two- range usage).

- Exclusive use line (two-range usage)—When a car is to be equipped with a sun roof, for example, a workstation is exclusively used for attaching the sun roof. The other cars just pass through the workstation. This is another type of the two-range usage (see Figure 17.9).

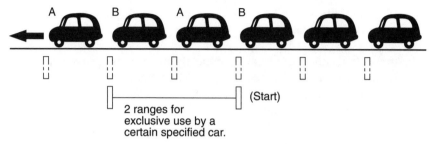

Figure 17.9. Exclusive use of work stations within a main line (two-range usage).

- Unreserved seat—Reserved seat system is an ordinary way for specified cars to be introduced one by one in a predetermined order; it is generally used for a mixed-model line. Assembly lines, waiting lines, painting lines, etc. have a certain number of positions for each vehicle within the line. To absorb variances in man hours, some positions within the line can remain empty.

- Baton touch zone—Figure 17.10 shows the concept of preparing broad spaces for respective preceding and subsequent processes and intersecting them with each other. By using this method, line balance can be kept constant even if a difference exists in man hours as calculated by the models. This is known as the baton touch zone method because it is similar to the zone used in a relay race for handing over a baton.

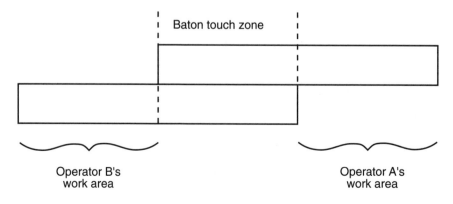

Figure 17.10. Baton touch zone method.

In conclusion, a countermeasure against an operational delay in an assembly line is needed to clearly signal a line stop to Andon. Some operational causes of delay are:

• incorrect assignment of work to a process
• operators not fully skilled
• operation itself contains waste

After investigating these factors sufficiently, the causes of line stoppage must be eliminated. No matter what the problem is—lead time and man hour variances, scheduling or operational delays, etc.—the causes should be identified and essential improvements should be implemented.

18

Determining the Number of Kanban Pertinent to the Alternative Withdrawal Systems

The Toyota Kanban system is a pulling system: a withdrawal system where a manufacturing process withdraws parts from a preceding process and then the preceding process begins to produce as many units as withdrawn. In a sense, the subsequent process orders the necessary parts from the preceding process in the right quantity at the right time. As a result, the Kanban system can be examined from the viewpoint of inventory control systems.

Two types of inventory control systems exist: the *constant order-quantity system* and the *constant order-cycle system.* Under the constant order quantity system, the predetermined fixed quantity will be ordered when the inventory level recedes to the reorder point (which is the expected usage during lead time). Although the order quantity is fixed, the reorder date is irregular. Under the constant order-cycle system, however, the reorder date is fixed and the quantity ordered depends on the usage since the previous order was placed and the outlook during the lead time. This outlook occurs after the order is placed but before it is received.

In the Kanban system, the total number of each part finally stored at the subsequent process and the number of Kanban delivered to the preceding process at each withdrawal point in time are determined by these two kinds of inventory models. At Toyota, two kinds of withdrawal systems correspond to these two different inventory systems: the *constant quantity, nonconstant cycle withdrawal system* and the *constant cycle, nonconstant quantity withdrawal system.*

Although basic similarities exist between the Kanban system and the inventory control systems, many significant differences are evident. For example, when using Kanban, there is no need to examine the inventory quantity continuously; however, this is required in the constant order quantity system. In the constant order-cycle system, the inventory quantity must be examined at each order time. At the same time, this amount must be subtracted from the standard quantity. With Kanban, the number of withdrawal Kanban detached at the subsequent process since the previous order is what must be ordered. Inventory calculations become very simple in Kanban systems.

With these points in mind, the Kanban can be defined as a medium of information for dispatching the right quantity of the right item at the right time.

Standard inventory control systems will not have the means of conveying such information although the contents of such information is provided as logic. The Kanban system is a complete information system to control inventory.

The Kanban system is an indispensable subsystem of Toyota's total production system. To implement the Kanban system, overall production system preparations must include scheduling a smoothed sequence of products at the final assembly line, designing a layout of machines, standardizing operations, and shortening the setup time, etc. Further, as explained in Chapter 2, the Kanban system is a very powerful means for improving each production process.

CONSTANT QUANTITY, NONCONSTANT CYCLE WITHDRAWAL SYSTEM

The processes within the Toyota Motor Corporation plants normally use the constant quantity withdrawal system, whereas the supplier Kanban exclusively uses the constant cycle withdrawal system. This is due to geographical distance. Within the Toyota plant, for example, the lead time is relatively short because of the short distance between processes and also the well improved processes. However, the total lead time for a supplier's products is relatively long because of the greater distance from the supplier, resulting in a longer conveyance time. The Kanban system has some similarity to the *two-bin* system, which is a type of constant order quantity inventory system, although it is not a derivative of this type of system.

The following formulas are used in the constant order-quantity inventory system:

The *order-quantity* at each order or lot size (Q) is determined by the EOQ model as follows:

$$(\text{A-1}) \quad Q = \sqrt{\frac{2AR}{ic}}$$

where A = ordering cost per lot
R = monthly estimated demand quantity
i = carrying cost per dollar of an item
c = unit cost

The *reorder point*, which is the quantity level that automatically triggers a new order, is determined as:

(B-1) Reorder Point = average usage during lead time + safety stock –
orders placed but not yet received

where the average usage during lead time = average usage per day lead time.

The lead time in this formula is simply the time interval between placing an order and receiving delivery. Also the last term in (B-1) is usually zero.

Kanban Number Under Constant Quantity Withdrawal System

The constant quantity system at Toyota will not use the EOQ model to determine the lot size. To reduce the production lead time, the lot size must be minimized and setup times per day must be increased. However, there is a constraint for resizing the lot size: the necessary time span for the external setup (Chapter 8). Although the internal setup time at Toyota has been reduced to less than ten minutes, the external setup still requires one half to one hour. Without this minimum time span, you cannot step to the next lot. As a result, the lot size—or the number of setups per day at Toyota—must be determined by the constraint of the time span of external setup. Some efforts to reduce the external setup time must be made. For example, using a crane to fix the die on the bolster takes much time, so some method must be devised to do away with the crane.

Thus, although the lot size at Toyota is different among various plants, the use of lot sizes of 2 or 2.5 shifts is very prevalent. Suppose the body line assembles 400 units per shift of a particular body style. Then a lot size of 2.5 shifts used for this body style means 1,000 units (= 2.5 x 400). If the SPH (stroke per hour) of the punch press is 500, it must run two hours for this lot size, and then the setup must be done. Since the lot size at Toyota is determined as shown here, it is not changed frequently. However, the reorder point is often changed because the daily average usage will change due to seasonal fluctuations.

There are three applications of Toyota's constant quantity withdrawal system. In the case where the lot size is fairly large, or the setup action is not sufficiently improved, the following formula is applied:

(A-2)   Total Number of Kanban

$$= \frac{\text{economic lot size} + (\text{daily demand} \times \text{safety coefficient})}{\text{container capacity}}$$

or

$$= \frac{\left[\dfrac{\text{monthly demand}}{\text{monthly number of setups}}\right] + \left[\dfrac{\text{daily}}{\text{demand}} \times \dfrac{\text{safety}}{\text{coefficient}}\right]}{\text{container capacity}}$$

In this instance, the signal Kanban is used in the die-casting, punch press and forging processes. The position of a triangular Kanban is then computed by the following formula:

(B-2)   Position of the Triangular Kanban

$$= \frac{\text{average daily demand} \times \text{lead time} \times (1 + \text{safety coefficient})}{\text{container capacity}}$$

Some companies in the Toyota group are also using the following formula:

(B-3)   Position of the Triangular Kanban

$$= \left[\!\!\left[\frac{\text{daily average demand}}{\text{container capacity}} \right]\!\!\right] + 1,$$

where[[ ]] means the minimum integer not less than the figure in it.

Where the setup methods are improved and the distance between the subsequent and preceding processes is short, the "constant quantity" will be equivalent to one pallet or one cart which corresponds to a sheet of Kanban. When the subsequent process withdrew one box of parts (fixed quantity), the preceding process must pick up the one empty box and immediately begin to produce the number of parts to be contained in this box. However, each withdrawal time cannot be known by the preceding process. The "whirligig beetle" explained in Chapter 2 is an example of this case.

In such cases, the maximum necessary inventory is equal to the reorder point. Therefore, the total number of Kanban which must correspond to the maximum inventory follows:

(A-3) Total Number of Kanban

$$= \frac{\text{average daily demand} \times \text{lead time} \times (1 + \text{safety coefficient})}{\text{container capacity}}$$

where the lead = processing time + waiting time + conveyance time + Kanban collecting time.

The ideal condition for Just-in-time production is that each process can produce only one piece, convey it one at a time, and also have only one piece in stock both between the equipment and the processes. This is known as one piece production and conveyance. This type is a synchronization or a total conveyor-line production system connecting all the external and internal processes with invisible conveyor lines.

Suppose, that, in the equation (A-3):

the safety coefficient   = 0,
the waiting time   = 0,
the Kanban collecting time = 0,
and, the container capacity = 1.

Then the Kanban system, which connects the two processes, is nothing but a conveyor line. In such a case, there is no need to use Kanban between two adjacent processes. If plural processes are connected very closely with each other, one sheet of Kanban is used commonly by these plural processes. This is the case of a *through* Kanban (also called *tunnel* Kanban), which is similar to the through ticket used between two adjacent railways.

CONSTANT CYCLE, NONCONSTANT QUANTITY WITHDRAWAL SYSTEM

In the constant order-cycle system for inventory control, the following formula is used to calculate the necessary quantity for the period of order cycle plus lead time. This necessary quantity is called the standard quantity:

(C-1)   Standard Quantity
         = daily demand $\times$ (order cycle + lead time) + safety stock,

where the order cycle is the time interval between one order time and the next order time, and the lead time is simply the time interval between placing an order and receiving delivery. The order cycle plus the lead time is often called the replenishment lead time.

Theoretically, the order cycle is determined by the formula:

$$\text{Order Cycle} = \frac{\text{economic lot size for expected demand}}{\text{daily average demand}}$$

However, the order cycle is often determined by an external constraint such as steps in the monthly production scheduling or a contract between the supplier and the paternal maker.

Next, the order quantity in this system is measured by the formula:

(D-1)   Order Quantity
         = (standard quantity – existing inventory)
           – (orders placed but not yet received),

where the last term (orders placed but not yet received) is sometimes equal to zero.

Kanban Number Under Constant Cycle Withdrawal System
In the case of Toyota's Kanban system using the constant cycle withdrawal approach, the following formula is used for computing the total number of Kanban:

(C-2)   Total Number of Kanban

$$= \frac{\text{daily demand} \times (\text{order cycle} + \text{lead time} + \text{safety period})}{\text{container capacity}}$$

where the lead time = processing time + waiting time
                    + conveyance time + Kanban collecting time

When analyzing this formula, it is important to note the following:

- The *order cycle* is the time interval (measured by days) between instructing a production order to the line and instructing the next production order. Also called a *Kanban cycle*.

- The *processing time* is the time interval (days) between placing a production order and completing its production. This time interval corresponds to the number of Kanban of the work-in-process being kept or processed within the line.

- The *Kanban collecting time* is the time interval (days) between picking up Kanbans from the post, which were detached at the subsequent process, and placing the production order to the preceding process. This is equivalent to the total number of Kanbans kept in (1) the withdrawal Kanban post, (2) the Kanban receiving post, and (3) the production ordering Kanban post in Figure 2.9 of Chapter 2.

- The *safety inventory period* corresponds to the stock kept at the store. This inventory responds to defective products, machine troubles, etc. To determine the level of safety inventory, the probabilities of occurrence of each trouble factor must be estimated respectively.

Next, by using the following formula, the order quantity under this Kanban system is determined in the following manner:

(D-2)   Order Quantity
        = (number of Kanban detached by the time of regular Kanban collection since the previous collection) × container capacity

Therefore, there is no need to compute the order quantity by using the formula (D-l). Under this type of Kanban system, the order quantity is automatically specified by the number of Kanban detached by the time of regular Kanban collection since the previous collection.

The equation (D-2) is validated by the following relationship:

(D-3)

$$
\begin{pmatrix}
\text{Number of Kanbans} \\
\text{detached by the regular} \\
\text{point in time since the} \\
\text{previous collection of Kanban}
\end{pmatrix}
+
\begin{pmatrix}
\text{Number of Kanban} \\
\text{still kept in the} \\
\text{preceding process}
\end{pmatrix}
$$

$$
=
\begin{pmatrix}
\text{Total number} \\
\text{of Kanbans}
\end{pmatrix}
-
\begin{pmatrix}
\text{existing number of Kanban} \\
\text{attached to the existing inventory} \\
\text{at the subsequent store,} \\
\text{at a regular point in time}
\end{pmatrix}
$$

This relationship is equivalent to the formula (D-l).

CHANGING THE CYCLE TIME OF STANDARD OPERATIONS ROUTINE INSTEAD OF THE NUMBER OF KANBAN

Even if the total number of each Kanban is calculated by computer using each pertinent formula (described before), the computed number should not be applied automatically without exercising the improvements recommended by the supervisor. In other words, the factors in the right-hand side of each formula should not be regarded as constant, given conditions. During the implementation phase to apply the computed number of Kanban, the final authority to change the number of Kanban is delegated to the supervisor of each shop.

The variables which determine the total number of Kanban in any formula follow:

1. Average daily demand
2. Lead time
3. Safety coefficient or safety stock
4. Container capacity

At first, the average daily demand is determined by the smoothed amount per day derived from a monthly demand quantity. When the monthly demand has changed, the total number of Kanban per day would also be changed. At Toyota plants, however, changing lead time is more important and more often made than revising the total number of Kanban. Such an idea is unique when compared with ordinary inventory systems. Toyota recognizes that an increase of inventory level is not only the worst phenomenon among various wastes, but it is also the ultimate origin of all kinds of wastes. Thus, the total number of each Kanban is kept rather constant at Toyota. When the average daily demand increases, the lead time should decrease. This means that the cycle time of a standard operations routine (Chapter 10) can be reduced by changing the allocations of workers in the line. For example, suppose it is expected that the average daily demand of next month will be two times the demand of the current month. Then, according to the formulas (A-2) and (A-3), the total number of Kanban will be doubled under ceteris paribus conditions. At Toyota, however, the cycle time is cut in half and the turnover (circulation speed) of Kanban is doubled, resulting in the total number of Kanban being unchanged. This approach can hardly be adopted under the constant cycle withdrawal system unless the regular withdrawal cycle is changed.

Under Toyota's approach, if a workshop is incapable of sufficient improvement, it will have overtime or line-stop because the number of Kanban is fixed. As a result, the Kanban system can quickly visualize the trouble. Such troubles will evoke immediate improvement actions. However, incapable shops might increase the safety stock or the total number of Kanban to adapt to demand increase. Therefore, the size of safety stock is an indicator of the shop's ability to improve.

In the case of a demand decrease, the cycle time of the standard operations routine will be increased. However, the probable idle time of workers must be avoided by reducing the number of workers from the line (Chapter 11). Moreover, in order to reduce inventory level, the container capacity should also be minimized. Since this is a minimum lot size, it must be determined by considering the process ability of each station to approach a one-piece production and conveyance scheme.

In order to grasp the up-to-date nature of Kanbans, it is important to understand the master files of Kanbans in Toyota's plant. When the supervisor of each process makes some improvements that change data and factors in the implementation phase, the new data will be introduced to the master file for adjustment each month.

THE INFLUENCE OF THE SUPERVISOR ON THE TOTAL NUMBER OF KANBAN

The actual number of Kanbans at each process within Toyota's factories is not determined automatically by the specific formula. The supervisor influences the number of Kanbans in the system. In fact, each supervisor is given very specific instructions: "You can have as many Kanban as you want. You should reduce the number of Kanban (i.e., inventory level) one sheet by one sheet down to your minimum possible limit as you are able to improve your process."

The goal of this system is that when the subsequent process withdraws its parts, the inventory level at the product store of the preceding process would be zero and the next replenishment would be made immediately. This goal is somewhat hard to achieve.

When it is found that the present number of Kanban is not suitable and causes trouble in the shop, the number of Kanban should be changed (increased) immediately. In a sense, this is a trial-and-error method; but this approach is very practical and useful for motivating the supervisor and workers to reduce the number of Kanban and improve their process.

While reducing the number of Kanban, the size of the safety inventory or the safety coefficient has some influence on the worker's attitude. If the safety stock level is too small, it will be regarded as too tight or too severe, and the workers will lose their motivation to attain its level. On the contrary, if the safety level is too big, it will be accepted as too loose or indulgent, and the worker will again lose his motivation. Therefore, the tightness of the number of Kanban is very important for worker motivation. The level which is somewhat tight but attainable would be the best level for achieving good performance.

CONSTANT WITHDRAWAL CYCLE SYSTEM FOR THE SUPPLIER KANBAN

Since the cooperative supplier companies are located somewhat distant from the paternal manufacturer, the total lead time, including conveyance time, is relatively long and therefore the constant quantity withdrawal system might cause a shortage of parts. As a result, only the *constant cycle, nonconstant quantity withdrawal system* is used for the supplier Kanban.

Moreover, the parent manufacturer is withdrawing many varieties of parts from various vendors at the same time. If the maker applied the constant quantity withdrawal system to these suppliers, the order time to each supplier would be varied, making it unfeasible to withdraw small quantities of parts frequently from various, distant vendors. As a result, the round tour, mixed-loading system explained in Chapter 2 has been used by subcontractors under the constant withdrawal cycle system. It can gather the various parts ordered to different suppliers at each regular point in time.

Also, the total number of each supplier Kanban is definitely computer calculated by a paternal maker. However, the number of Kanban to be delivered to the supplier at each regular cycle is still subject to the paternal maker's production situation.

Now, returning to the formula (C-1) of the constant order-cycle system, the total number of each supplier Kanban will be computed by the following formula:

(C-3) Total Number of Kanban

$$= \frac{\text{daily demand} \times \left(\begin{array}{c} \text{order cycle} \\ \text{to the} \\ \text{supplier} \end{array} + \begin{array}{c} \text{production lead time} \\ \text{of the supplier} \end{array} + \begin{array}{c} \text{safety} \\ \text{coefficient} \end{array} \right)}{\text{container capacity}}$$

The *order cycle* (or Kanban cycle) to the supplier is the time interval (measured by days) between placing one order with the supplier and placing the next order. In other words, the order cycle corresponds to the number of hours set by the paternal maker to bring the supplier Kanban to the supplier. The order cycle is calculated by using the following formula:

(C-3-1) Order Cycle to the Supplier

$$= \frac{\left[\left[\text{number of days spent for one}-\text{time conveyance}\right]\right]}{\text{number of times of conveyance per day}}$$

where [[ ]] means the minimum integer not less than the accurate figure in it. Therefore, even though a conveyance time may only be two hours, it must be counted as one day.

The *production lead time of the supplier* is the time interval between placing the production order by the supplier to his line and completing his production. This time interval is measured by the following formula:

(C-3-2) Production Lead Time of the Supplier
= order cycle to the supplier × conveyance interval,

where the conveyance interval can be understood through the following example. Suppose there are several Kanban conveyances per day from the paternal manufacturer to the vendor. Then, how many times of Kanban conveyances must be required by the vendor to be able to deliver the ordered quantity to the paternal maker after the maker has placed the order in question at a certain point in time? This times of Kanban conveyance is the conveyance interval in this formula. It is essentially based on the processing time of the supplier.

The order cycle and the conveyance interval is usually written on the supplier Kanban, such as the description of *"1.6.2"* at the bottom of a supplier delivered six times a day and the actual withdrawals of parts must be made two times later after the Kanban is brought at a certain point in a withdrawal time. Thus, using the equations (C-3-1) and (C-3-2), the following relationship can be developed:

(C-3-3)

$$
\begin{bmatrix} \text{order cycle} \\ \text{to the} \\ \text{supplier} \end{bmatrix} + \begin{bmatrix} \text{production} \\ \text{lead time of} \\ \text{the supplier} \end{bmatrix}
$$

$$
= \left[\begin{bmatrix} \text{number of days spent} \\ \text{for one} - \text{time} \\ \text{conveyance} \end{bmatrix} \right] \times \left(\frac{1 + \text{conveyance interval}}{\begin{array}{c} \text{number of conveyance} \\ \text{times per day} \end{array}} \right)
$$

As a result, the equation (C-3) can be transformed as:

(C-4)   Total Number of Kanban

$$
= \frac{\text{daily}}{\substack{\text{demand} \\ \text{container} \\ \text{capacity}}} \times \left\{ \left[\begin{bmatrix} \text{number of} \\ \text{days spent} \\ \text{for one} - \text{time} \\ \text{conveyance} \end{bmatrix} \right] \times \left(\frac{1 + \text{conveyance interval}}{\begin{array}{c} \text{number of conveyance} \\ \text{times per day} \end{array}} \right) + \text{safety coefficient} \right\}
$$

where the safety coefficient or the level of safety inventory is dependent on the supplier's ability to cope with the following disturbances:

1. Since the supplier Kanban is delivered on the constant withdrawal-cycle system, the quantity withdrawn must be varied at each withdrawal time. For example, the customer-maker (Toyota) may pull five pallets of parts at a certain point in time, but may withdraw seven pallets at another point in time. However, if the quantity withdrawn at each time is leveled because of the smoothed production by the customer-manufacturer, the constant cycle system is almost the same as the constant quantity system.

2. Even if the daily production level is averaged, the actual monthly production quantity based on the actual daily dispatchings from Toyota through Kanban may deviate from the predetermined monthly production plan sent from the customer-maker. This difference is usually ±10%. This also means the actual daily demand may deviate from the planned average daily quantity by + 10%.

3. The variance in the number of Kanban brought to the supplier may sometimes be due to the driver's error that he forgot some of the Kanbans. However, this can be avoided by the driver's care.

4. Machine breakdowns may occur.

5. Traffic accidents may occur on the road to the customer/client. This probability may increase in proportion to the length of the conveyance period or the value of the equation (C-3-3).

The supplier's ability to cope with the above disturbances will be summarized by the worker's ability to adapt to demand increases, the shop's ability to reduce the lead time by changing the cycle time, and the ability of equipment maintenance.

Let us take a numerical example for the formula (C-4):

Suppose,
the number of days spent for one-time conveyance = 1 day,
the number of times of conveyance per day = 6 times,
the conveyance interval = 2 times later after the original conveyance of Kanban,
the average daily demand = 100 units,
the container capacity = 5 units, and
the safety coefficient = 0.2.

Then,
the total number of Kanban

$$= \frac{100}{5} \times \left\{ \left[1 \times \left(\frac{1+2}{6} \right) \right] + 0.2 \right\}$$

$$= 20 \times (0.5 + 0.2) = 14$$

Finally, the withdrawal quantity to be made at a regular point in time is determined by the number of Kanban detached since the previous conveyance. That is, the equations (D-2) and (D-3) explained previously can also be used for the supplier Kanban.

19
Computer System
for Kanban System Support

Through lack of understanding, the Toyota production system is sometimes considered far removed from modern computerized information systems. Moreover, it is felt that Just-in-time (JIT) production can be realized only by the Kanban pull system. However, before applying Kanban, detailed schedules must be prepared in advance for each production process using monthly planning data. This scheduling is accomplished by a computerized information system.

Toyota production is supported by an electronic data processing (EDP) system. The example in this chapter is based primarily on the supply systems of Kyoho-Seisakusho Company, Ltd. and Aisin-Seiki Company, Ltd. However, since companies of the Toyota group are closely aligned with the Toyota Motor Corporation, similar systems are being developed among various companies.

The computerized information system reported herein consists of seven subsystems that may be classified roughly into three categories (Figure 19.1):

1. *Technology data base* subsystem, which maintains the data base for the planning and actual performance subsystems.
2. *Planning* subsystem, which provides plant managers with information for preparing production arrangements for the next month, such as determining the number of Kanban and the distribution of workers on the assembly line.
3. *Actual performance* subsystem, which supplies attention directing information to improve processes by comparing actual performance with planned data.

The subsystems will be examined in detail in the following sections. However, it should be recognized that another computerized planning system (i.e., the heuristic sequencing program) exists for mixed assembly lines at Toyota and its suppliers and is discussed in Chapter 16.

TECHNOLOGY DATA BASE SUBSYSTEM

The technology data base subsystem maintains the basic data for production controls. It includes a parts data base (bill of materials) to compute the various

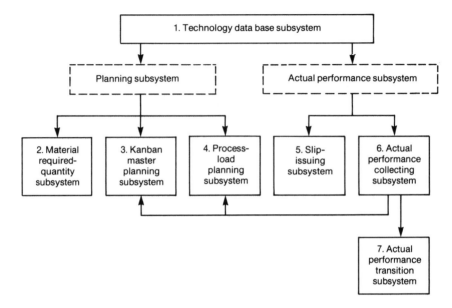

Figure 19.1. Framework of the information system supporting Kanban.

parts quantities required for each finished product and a collection of data to reflect the steps in producing a company's products from beginning to end.

Kyoho-Seisakusho Company, Ltd. uses a UNIS data base (UNIVAC Industrial System) with software developed by Japan UNIVAC Company, Ltd. for this subsystem. This UNIS was originally developed for MRP. In this meaning, the Kanban system is compatible with MRP.

Material Requirement Planning Subsystem
This subsystem receives a predetermined three-month production information tape as input data provided monthly by Toyota to its cooperative parts suppliers. The subsystem then computes the quantity of material required by each process. The outputs of this system are summarized as follows:

- Daily required quantities of each material to be used within the company or by its suppliers.
- Number of pallets to contain each material.
- Production schedule of each finished product to be supplied to each customer company.

In order to accomplish JIT production, daily required materials must be prepared in advance to be available at any necessary point in time. Also, in accordance with Rule 3 of the Kanban system: "defective units should never be conveyed to the subsequent process." The defective rate cannot be considered in computing the required material quantities. The Toyota production system consists not only of the Kanban information system, but also the production methods to improve the process when defective units are discovered.

KANBAN MASTER PLANNING SUBSYSTEM

The Kanban master planning subsystem computes the following data based on a daily leveled (average) production quantity:

- Number of each Kanban required for producing a lot.
- Increased or decreased number of each Kanban compared with the previous month.
- Position of a triangle Kanban (which corresponds to a reorder point and triggers production timing).
- Lot size.

This data will be printed out as a *Kanban master table,* as shown in Figure 19.2. The table is delivered to the manager of each process for preparation of the actual number of Kanban. Further, since the daily average production quantity changes basically once a month, the data must be recomputed monthly.

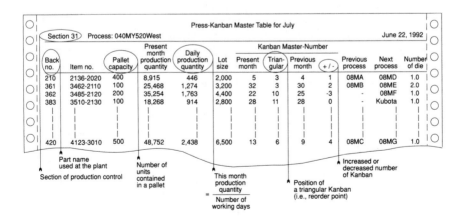

Figure 19.2. Kanban master table.

Three different kinds of Kanban master tables are used, depending on the following application:

• *Internally produced parts.* This table is printed out for each part/ item at each process. The table is delivered to the production control department for preparation of Kanban and reorganization of each process (i.e., reallocation of workers) in response to demand changes. The formulae used at some suppliers follow:

$$\text{Lot size} = \frac{\text{Monthly production quantity of particular product}}{\text{Monthly setup times for particular product}} \tag{1}$$

$$\text{Number of Kanban per lot} = \frac{\text{Lot size}}{\text{Pallet capacity}} \tag{2}$$

$$\text{Position of triangular Kanban} = \left[\left[\frac{\text{Daily average production quantity}}{\text{Pallet capacity}}\right]\right] + 1 \tag{3}$$

Detailed information is available for the above formulae in Chapter 19.

• *Externally produced parts.* This table is printed out for each supplier and each Kanban cycle so that each supplier will know the monthly change in his required production quantities. The formulae used to compute the number of supplier Kanban are different from the equations for internal Kanban because a constant cycle withdrawal system is applied to the supplier Kanban while a constant quantity withdrawal system is normally applied to internal Kanban. More detailed information and the Kanban cycle concept appear in Chapter 19.

• *Material usage.* This table is printed out for delivery to the material supplier. For example, if a punch press process is involved, the number of Kanban for a coil lot will be sent to the coil supplier.

Process-Load Planning Subsystem
Monthly production quantities fluctuate depending on the predetermined production plan published monthly by Toyota. Thus, each production line must be able to adapt to these monthly changes in production quantity by changing the capacity of each line, that is, by increasing or decreasing the work force at each line. Such changes can be attained through improvement activities or multi-function workers in a special layout of machines.

In order for each process to impact the work force capacity change, this subsystem computes the following data into a *process-load plan* based on the monthly predetermined production plan:

• Cycle time at each process.
• Processing time or loading time to be spent for a given lot at each process.
• Setup time and the times of setup at each process.

By comparing loading time to the existing capacity at each process, a series of production preparations such as work force planning, machinery layout, and overtime planning can be calculated. The process-load plan reflects data generated for the Kanban master plan and required material quantities. Thus, if the load at a process changes, the work force or number of Kanban changes accordingly. The following formula is used to compute loading time spent for a given production lot:

$$\text{Loading time} = \frac{\text{Order quantity} \times \text{Standard hour}}{\text{Standard quantity} \times \text{Process utilization rate}} + \text{Setup time} \qquad (4)$$

The standard quantity and the standard hour are usually predetermined at each process. For example, assume an order quantity (lot size) of 100 units, standard hour equal to one hour to produce ten units of standard quantity, and the setup time of two hours. Then, the loading time for this process is computed as:

$$\frac{100 \times 1}{10} + 2 = 12 \text{ hours}$$

In the case of a punchpress department, "strokes per hour" (SPH) is substituted for "standard quantity times process utilization rate," as noted here:

$$\text{Loading time} = \frac{\text{Order quantity} \div \text{Quantity produced by one pressing}}{\text{SPH}} + \text{Setup time} \qquad (5)$$

where SPH and setup time are computed based on data from the past three months as collected by the *Actual Performance* subsystem. Additionally, cycle time will be used to standardize the operations routine and to determine the standard quantity of in-process inventory.

Slip-Issuing Subsystem

Kanban may be regarded as a kind of money because when a process withdraws a part from the previous process, a withdrawal Kanban must be shown in the part making process. However, a Kanban specifies only what type of part is required, where the part must be transferred to and from, and the quantity of parts to be produced until what time. The *transfer price* is not defined by the Kanban, whereas the price and monetary information are necessary between a supplier and a user company. Therefore, in order to deal with accounts payable and accounts receivable in the accounting departments of both companies, some invoices must be issued. Such invoices are also used to confirm and inspect the total quantity of the item supplied by the vendor.

As described in Chapter 3, Toyota applies two different systems to withdraw parts from various suppliers, depending on the physical size of the part. The most prevalent system is the *later-replenishment* system that uses a supplier Kanban. The second system is the *sequenced withdrawal* system based on a sequence schedule for the mixed-parts assembly line (Figure 19.3). The following are steps involved in the sequenced withdrawal system:

1. Sequence schedule data on *magnetic tape* for transmissions to be produced at the Shiroyama plant of the Aisin Seiki Company, Ltd. is delivered by truck each morning to the EDP section of the Aisin Seiki Company from Toyota.

2. The EDP section duplicates the magnetic tape on a *magnetic disk* (floppy disk).

3. The magnetic disk is then delivered to the control center at the Shiroyama plant. (Note Figure 3.4 in Chapter 3.)

4. The data on the disk is input into a computer terminal (called System K) to print out the sequence schedule. At the same time, labels for each type of transmission are printed out, along with a set of *OCR cards* including a *delivery slip card* and a *receipt slip card*. (Note Figure 3.4 in Chapter 3.)

In another situation, the contents of the magnetic tape may be transmitted directly from the main office EDP to the computer terminal at the Shiroyama plant via an on-line system at Aisin Seiki.

If the later-replenishment system is applied, the supplier Kanban is bar coded for processing by a computer. At Toyota all supplier Kanbans are *bar coded* Kanbans and are also known as *OCR* Kanbans, as shown in Chapter 2, Figure 2.5. In this case, two types of bar coded Kanbans are used to issue vouchers:

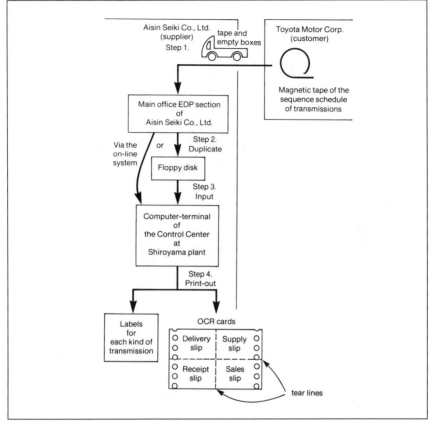

Figure 19.3. Sequenced withdrawal within the slip-issuing subsystem.

1. The Toyota OCR supplier Kanban is processed through a bar code reader at Toyota to print out the OCR cards. These cards are delivered to the supplier along with the supplier Kanban itself. At the supplier, the parts, Kanban, and cards are loaded together onto the truck and delivered to the Toyota process (Figure 19.4).

2. The Toyota OCR supplier Kanban is delivered directly to the supplier where it is processed through the supplier's bar code reader. The OCR cards are generated and matched with parts for delivery to the Toyota plant along with the supplier Kanban (Figure 19.5). At present, this situation is the most prevalent among Toyota suppliers.

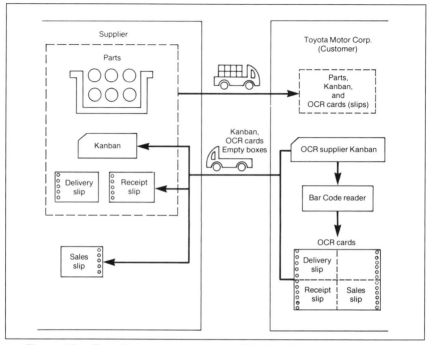

Figure 19.4. Type I later-replenishment within the slip-issuing subsystem.

There are four types of OCR cards: delivery slip, supply slip, receipt slip, and sales slip. The supplier delivers its parts with the delivery and receipt slips.

At the Toyota receiving location (i.e., purchasing department), both the delivery slip and the receipt slip will be sealed (signed). Toyota retains the delivery slip and returns the receipt slip to the supplier. The delivery slip is forwarded to the Toyota computer department where it is processed to output accounts payable data. This data, in turn, will be given to the accounting department for entry in the creditors ledger, the purchase book, and the accounts payable section of the general ledger.

The sales slip, on the other hand, is kept by the supplier where it is processed through the OCR to output accounts receivable data. The supplier enters this data in his customers' ledger, the sales book, and accounts receivable section of the general ledger. An example of the flow of these vouchers between Toyota and its suppliers appears in Figure 19.6.

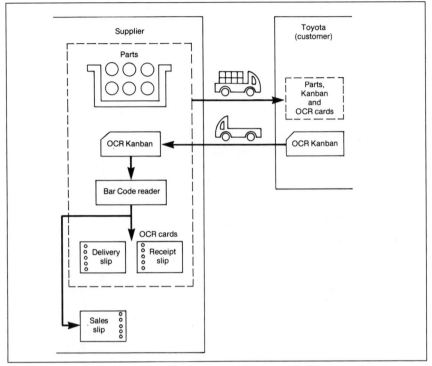

Figure 19.5. Type II later-replenishment within the slip-issuing subsystem.

When Aisin Seiki delivers its finished parts to another cooperative company (in this case, Hino Motors, Ltd.), it sends the delivery slip, the receipt slip and the supply slip along with the parts. Hino Motors retains the sealed delivery slip, returns the sealed receipt slip to Aisin Seiki, and sends the sealed supply slip to Toyota. Toyota processes this supply slip through OCR to output accounts payable data. The amount of this accounts payable data will be paid to Aisin Seiki by Toyota. The same amount will be paid later to Toyota by Hino Motors (Figure 19.7).

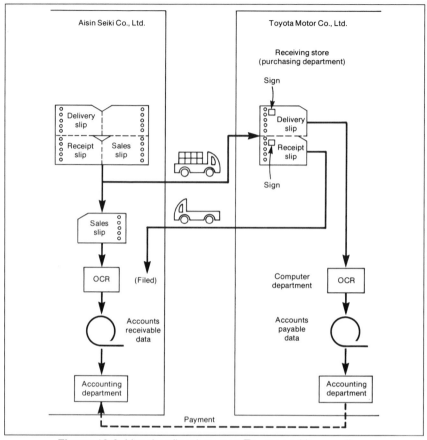

Figure 19.6. Voucher flow between Toyota and its suppliers.

ACTUAL PERFORMANCE COLLECTION AND TRANSITION SUBSYSTEMS

The *Actual Performance Collection* subsystem daily collects the actual performance data of each process and compiles it as monthly production information. The performance data includes production quantity, processing time, setup time, cycle time, machine idle time, stroke number, etc. Monthly production data is included in the monthly planning cycle. Comparing actual performance data to the planned figures produces variance figures. If these variances are unfavorable (i.e., processing too slow), some remedial action must be taken to minimize the variances. In other words, this subsystem highlights problem areas and helps to evoke improvement activities to optimize Toyota production methods. Additionally, actual performance data, such as stroke number and setup time, are fed back as basic data for computation of the loading or cycle time for the next period.

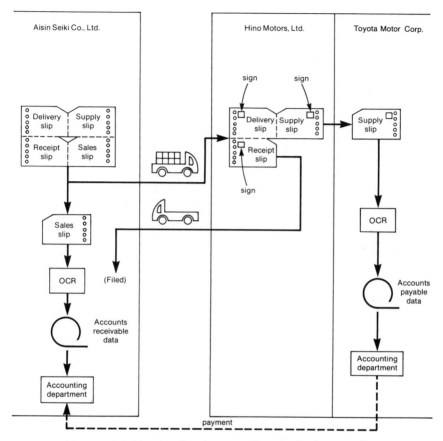

Figure 19.7. Voucher flow between Toyota, the first supplier, and the second supplier.

The *Actual Performance Transition* subsystem transforms the actual performance data into time-series data of the latest three months to show the progress of actual performance. This time-series information emphasizes the technical differences between processes and the capacity-utilization situations within each process, thus enabling promotion of company-wide improvements in engineering techniques.

20
Numerical Analysis
for Productivity Improvement

ANALYSIS METHOD FOR WORK PLACE IMPROVEMENTS

Let's consider an improvement method for realizing "Shojinka" (flexible work force), the practice of assigning one man day to each worker. One man day is the operation volume each worker should perform during one day's regular operating hours and is based on the proper output per hour and per worker. Since knowledge of the actual conditions existing in the work place is very important for this improvement, present performance analysis will be discussed first. The author is indebted to H. Kawaguchi [1990] of Toyota Gosei for this chapter.

Worker Capacity Concepts and Formulae Calculations
Worker capacity refers to the number of processes a worker can handle during the time necessary for producing one unit, calculated on the daily salable quantity. It is useful to clearly differentiate between *tact time* and *cycle time* for this calculation (these concepts were not completely differentiated in previous chapters).

$$\text{Tact time} = \frac{\text{Regular operating hours}}{\text{Salable quantity of products}}$$

Regular operating hours are calculated by subtracting rest time from scheduled work hours per day, excluding overtime. Generally, daily regular work hours total nine hours (8 a.m. to 5 p.m.) and labor hours amount to eight hours after subtracting a one-hour lunch break from regular work hours. Regular operating hours amount to 460 minutes per shift, or 27,600 seconds, after subtracting two ten-minute breaks (once in the morning and once in the afternoon).

As seen above, the tact time shows how many minutes or seconds are needed to produce one unit when considering the daily salable quantity. Letting a worker handle as many processes as possible during tact time increases productivity. In other words, when the daily salable quantity is relatively small, a decrease in the number of workers combined with expansion of one operator handling processes enables productivity to increase in spite of the decrease in output. Conversely, when demand is relatively great and tact time is short, the number of processes handled by one operator will decrease.

The tact time concept provides a framework for realizing multi-process handling, thereby allowing a rise in the actual operating rate of workers by more than 90 percent. At the same time, the actual operating rate of machines is decreased, but this does not matter.

Next, let us consider cycle time compared to tact time.

Cycle time = Total time necessary for performing manual operations for processes described by the standard operations routine sheet (including walking time).

During the planning stage, the cycle time is determined so that it does not exceed tact time, but in the actual work place the cycle time may be longer than the tact time. This is because variances in operation time are not considered when determining cycle time. In short, standard operations are developed according to the minimum operation time. Therefore, unless operations are carried out according to the standard operation routine, cycle time will become longer than tact time, making overtime necessary.

The following are methods for evaluating worker capacity.

$$\text{Rational load time of worker} = \text{Cycle time} \times \text{Salable quantity}$$

$$\frac{\text{Rational quota}}{\text{of worker *}} = \frac{\text{Cycle time} \times \text{Salable quantity}}{\text{Regular operating hours}}$$

* excludes setup time

or,

$$\frac{\text{Rational quota}}{\text{of worker *}} = \frac{\text{Cycle time} \times \text{Salable quantity} + \text{Setup time}}{\text{Regular operating hours}}$$

*including setup time

If a large variety of products is to be sold, Σ_i is added to the numerator of the formulae above where i = the product variety number for each term of the cycle time, the salable quantity, and the setup time. The *rational quota of worker* is also called *rational man days*. The *actual operating hours* and *actual quota of worker* (actual man days) is used for calculating the total quota of all multi-process workers within a line. They are measured with the formulae below and then compared to the *rational load time of workers* and the *rational quota of workers* above.

$$\text{Actual operating hours} = \text{Regular operating hours} + \text{Overtime}$$

$$\frac{\text{Actual quota}}{\text{of worker}} = \frac{\text{Regular operating hours} + \text{Overtime}}{\text{Regular operating hours}}$$

or,

$$\frac{\text{Actual quota}}{\text{of worker}} = \frac{\frac{\text{Allocated}}{\text{work force}} \times \frac{\text{Regular}}{\text{operating hours}} + \frac{\text{Accumulated}}{\text{overtime}}}{\text{Regular operating hours}}$$

The second equation above is used for calculating the total quota of all multi-process workers within a line.

Facility Capacity Concepts and Formulae Calculation
A facility capacity refers to the number of products an individual facility can process during the regular operating hours (also called processing ability). It is calculated as follows:

$$\frac{\text{Processing}}{\text{ability}} = \frac{\text{Regular operating hours}}{\frac{\text{Completion}}{\text{time per unit}} + \frac{\text{Setup time}}{\text{per unit}}}$$

or,

$$\frac{\text{Processing}}{\text{ability}} = \frac{\text{Regular operating hours - Total setup time}}{\text{Completion per unit}}$$

When the total setup time in the second formula is equal to the value of [Processing ability × Setup time per unit], then these two formulae are equivalent.

The processing ability of a multi-process handling line is determined by the minimum processing time of the various components. If a bottleneck occurs in the process, it will determine the process's maximum capacity.

For example, suppose a bottleneck process's regular operating time is 460 minutes (or 27,600 seconds) and completion time per unit of a product (walking and manual operations time + automatic conveyance time) is 63 seconds. Assume that a cutting tool can use 300 units in 120 seconds. Then,

$$\text{Facility's maximum capacity of the line} = 27{,}600 / [63 + (120/300)]$$
$$= 435.3 \text{ units}$$

The following formula provides the maximum introducible quota of workers to the multi-process handling line.

$$\frac{\text{Maximum introducible}}{\text{quota of workers}} = \frac{\text{Cycle time}}{\text{Completion per unit}}$$
$$\text{in the bottleneck process}$$

Provided the cycle time is 96 seconds and the completion time per unit in the bottleneck process is 63 seconds.

$$\text{Upper limit quota of 1 worker} = 96 / 63$$
$$= 1.52 \text{ quota of worker}$$

(considering the facility's maximum capacity)

A worker in the multi-process handling line in this example can handle a maximum quota of 1.52 units, even if the efficiency of the line does not increase as workers (over the 1.52 quota) are introduced to the line.

When the facility's maximum capacity is very high, adding more workers to respond to the increase of salable quantity will not result overtime; thus, accumulated operating hours will not be increased either. On the contrary, when maximum facility capacity is low, overtime will be essential in spite of additional workers; thus, the actual operating hours increase.

Workable Rate Concept and Formula Calculation

Generally, the *operating rate* of a machine refers to the proportion of the present production performance to the full production ability of the machine for a certain time. Therefore, it may be more or less than 100 percent.

The workable rate shows to what extent the machine is ready to fully operate every moment. The ideal percentage is 100; actual conditions are apt to fall below it. While the operating rate has possibilities of being more or less than 100% according to the salable quantity, the workable rate is always expected to be 100%.

$$\text{Workable rate} = \frac{\dfrac{\text{Actual}}{\text{operating hours}} - \text{Unworkable time}}{\text{Actual operating hours}} \times 100$$

$$= \frac{\text{Rational load time}}{\text{Actual operating time}} \times 100$$

Here, it must be noted that the workable rate can be calculated for both facility and worker. Therefore, the *rational load time* in the formula above may be replaced by *rational load time of worker* or *rational load time of facility*. Rational load time may be calculated with setup time and without setup time. The rational load time of a facility is shown below.

$$\text{Rational load time of facility} = \text{Completion time per unit} \times \begin{array}{c}\text{Salable quantity}\\\text{of products}\end{array}$$

A means to improve the workable rate will be described later.

PERFORMANCE ANALYSIS OF FACILITY AND WORKER

By conducting a *performance analysis of facility and worker,* the areas for improvement on a multi-process handling line and facility become obvious. Once discovered, the areas for improvement can also be prioritized.

Drawing a Performance Analysis Figure of Facility and Worker

Figure 20.1 shows a performance analysis for one worker in one facility. In practice, primary performance analysis figures are drawn for every worker in a multi-process handling line and lined up horizontally with every worker in actual sequence. For example, Figure 20.2 shows the layout of operators and equipment of an assembly line for a brake-hose. From that layout, a performance analysis figure for facility and worker in the assembly line can be drawn (see Figure 20.3).

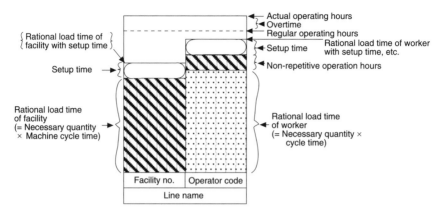

Figure 20.1. Performance analysis figure for facility and operator.

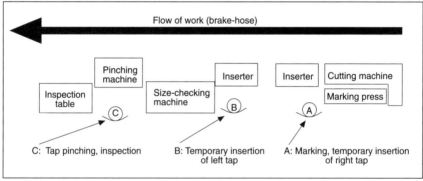

Figure 20.2. Layout of machines and operators in a brake-hose assembly line.

Utilizing the Performance Analysis of Facility and Worker

The performance analysis is useful to find and measure the following seven parts of an operation.

1. Bottleneck facility and worker. A bottleneck refers to the place where the rational load time of a worker or a facility added to the setup time and the non-repetitive operation hours (inspection time plus each unit's processing time) is greater than the regular operating hours. For example, see process *C,* pinching, in Figure 20.3.

2. Worker capacity. As mentioned previously, the rational quota of a worker is found by dividing the rational load time of a worker by regular operating hours, (either with setup time or without it). As seen in Figure 20.3, if the *actual* quota of a worker is heavier than the *rational* quota of a worker, it must be recognized as a problem because this indicates that standard operations are not being properly observed, thus overtime work is inevitable.

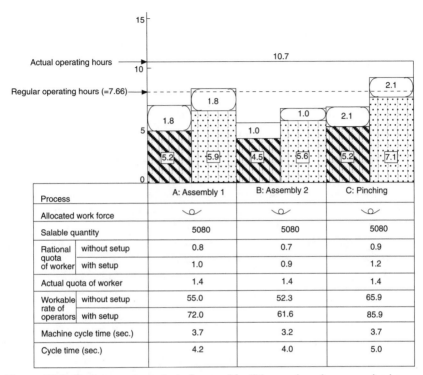

Figure 20.3. Performance analysis figure of facilities and workers on a brake-hose assembly line.

3. Facility capacity. If the rational load time of facility plus setup time is longer than regular operating hours, overtime work will be required, which means the facility's capacity is insufficient. The *operating rate of a facility* is found by dividing *machine cycle time* by tact time. The *machine cycle time* is the completion time per unit, including such motions as attachment and detachment of the work piece, starting, automatic conveyance, etc.

4. Workable rates of facility and worker. It has been mentioned already that workable rates are calculated in two ways; *with* setup time and *without* setup time. Raising a workable rate up to 100% is equivalent to reducing the actual operating hours of a worker or facility to its rational time; that is,

standard time = (rational load time of worker or facility + setup time)

To improve the workable rate, the bottleneck among facility and worker must first be identified. Then, the actual operating hours of the worker or facility in question should be reduced to their rational time. Investigating and eliminating the causes of unworkable time leads to shortening actual hours. Five probable causes of unworkable time are (see also Figure 20.4):

• excessive setup time
• machine breakdown
• defects
• variances in machine and overall cycle time
• parts shortages

Of these five items, the variances in machine cycle time cause the workable rate to be lower than 100%. When calculating a process's capacity and rational load time of a facility, the shortest time is applied as a rational value even though machine cycle times vary (except in the case of a completely automatic machine). Cycle time in terms of a worker is treated the same way.

Machine and worker cycle time should not be conveyed as "good" or "bad" but as "high" or "low" when informing workers.

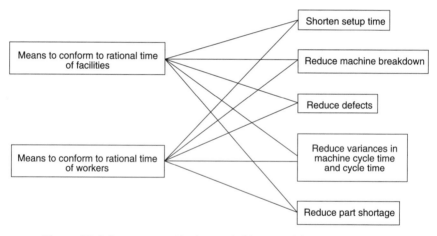

Figure 20.4. Improvement in the workable rate of facility and worker.

5. Balance of facility load. A performance analysis figure of a facility, as shown horizontally in the left side of Figure 20.3, will indicate this balance problem. That is, the rational load time of facility A, B, and C is 7.0 (5.2 + 1.8), 5.5 (4.5 + 1.0), and 7.3 (5.2 + 2.1), respectively. This means the balance of the facility load is not well attained among these three machines.

6. Balance of worker's allocated operations. The right side of each process in Figure 20.3 shows this balance problem. The rational load time of workers A, B, and C are

Worker A: 7.7 (5.9 + 1.8)
Worker B: 6.6 (5.6 + 1.0)
Worker C: 9.2 (7.1 + 2.1)

Therefore, the load is not balanced.

7. Priority of improvement activities. Which worker or facility should be improved first is made clear by numbers 5 and 6 above. According to Figure 20.3, the operation allotment is not well balanced among workers of this line because the rational load time of operator C at a tap-pinching process is too long compared with others. Thus, operations to be done by operator C will be divided into elemental tasks, which may be transferred to a subsequent process or assigned to two other operators in the same line. At the same time, the need to shorten the operator's cycle time becomes obvious.

EVALUATION OF OVERALL PRODUCTION PERFORMANCE AFTER IMPROVEMENT

Productivity, defined as output per worker per hour, is the most appropriate scale for evaluating the results of improvement activities. Here, it is a prerequisite condition that output per month or per week be the same as the salable quantity during the period. Therefore, if the salable quantity per month increases, total output per month should be increased; and if it decreases, the total output must be decreased.

Even though the number of workers increased or decreased in response to the salable quantity for the month in question, this productivity measure can present production efficiency independent from the salable quantity because it is always based on output per operator. The output per worker and hour is something like the instantaneous car velocity measured in kilometers per hour on an hourly basis when driving. Consider the multi-process brake hose assembly line operated by three operators as seen in Figure 20.2. If 5,081 hoses are to be assembled per day during daily regular operating hours (10.7 hours), then the output per worker in a given month is

Productivity = 5,081 hoses / 3 operators / 10.7 hours
= 158 hoses / (operator and hour)

Such a productivity criterion can also incorporate productivity improvement targets. If the target is to increase productivity by 20%, the target can be expressed numerically as

$$158 \times 1.20 = 190 \text{ hoses / (operator and hour)}$$

When productivity mandates are given, the following measures should be taken.

1. Improve the workable rate
2. Shorten cycle time
3. Shorten machine cycle time

Improvement of the workable rate is achieved by trimming down actual operating hours to a rational time (standard time), as seen by the direction of the arrows in Figure 20.5, number 1. If actual operating hours conform to the rational time, the workable rate is 100%. After attaining a 100% workable rate, cycle time and machine cycle time (illustrated as numbers 2 and 3 in Figure 20.5) are further reduced, thereby enabling a decrease in the rational time.

Improvement should be promoted by repeating steps 1, 2, and 3.

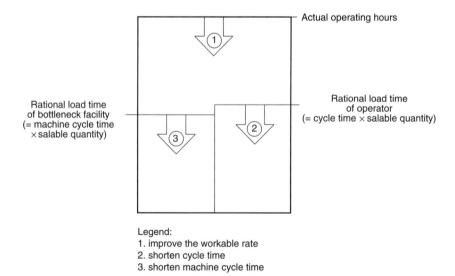

Legend:
1. improve the workable rate
2. shorten cycle time
3. shorten machine cycle time

Figure 20.5. Means for productivity improvement.

PART IV
IMPLEMENTATION

21
Review of Kanban System Principles

This chapter will attempt to explain the many miscellaneous practices of the Kanban system. The Toyota Kanban system is used to control processes so that every process will produce a single unit of product within a predetermined cycle time. Therefore, the ability to produce a *one-piece conveyance* (called "Ikko-Nagashi" in Japanese) is viewed as the ideal state of this system. From this fundamental viewpoint, the production of large lot sizes and the holding of large inventories between processes are redundant. In such a situation, the number of Kanbans required is also increased.

Although one-piece conveyance is the ideal state of this system, many processes have great difficulty in achieving such a goal. An example of this occurs in the pressing process of automobile manufacturing. In such lot production processes, even though a *triangular Kanban* or *signal Kanban* is used, a continuous improvement effort must be made to ensure that the lot size is minimized.

FUNCTIONS OF A KANBAN

The Kanban system can be used to perform the following functions:

• instruction
• self-control to prevent overproduction
• visual control
• improvement of process and manual operations
• reduction of managerial costs

The Kanban serves as an instruction instrument between production and conveyance. This role differentiates the Kanban from item tags. When a part needs to be withdrawn, or a conveyance order is issued, an address is written on a Kanban. This address informs the preceding process where to store the processed parts and informs the subsequent process where the required parts are located. It is very important that this address be precise (see 5S, Chapter 13).

Self-control is needed to prevent overproduction. Each process must be autonomously controlled to ensure that it only produces salable products, in salable quantities, at salable times in accordance with the cycle time. This autonomous control ensures that production will not take place at excessively high speeds. The Kanban system is also a self-control mechanism in that it makes it possible for each individual process to make minor supply adjustments to its monthly production schedule as may be warranted by monthly demand fluctuations.

In conveyance systems, the Kanban system functions as a tool that enables withdrawal by a subsequent process because the essence of the Kanban system lies in its pull function. It enables a preceding process to produce the exact amount that was withdrawn by the subsequent process. Such a pull system can be thought of as a decentralized control system.

Self-control to restrict overproduction can be achieved on a parts storage floor by separation lines without using Kanban cards. For example, suppose that the parts storage area is divided into two areas by painted lines, A and B. The rule in such a storage area is that when the inventory in area A is out of stock, enough parts have to be produced to replenish both areas A and B. Such a two-bin system can also be classified as a type of pull system.

The Kanban system serves as a tool for visual control as it not only gives numerical information, but also physical information in the form of a Kanban card. This enables each process' production level to be visually checked. For instance, if the production-ordering Kanbans are not stacked on the production-ordering post on time, the production of the subsequent process is delayed. Conversely, if Kanbans are stacked too early, the subsequent process can be seen to be ahead of its production schedule. (An example involving the production-ordering process at a machining line will be given later in this chapter.)

Also, if the stock level in storage does not decrease by a predetermined amount when the vendor delivers its next shipment, this signals that the factory's production is delayed. The number of supplier-Kanbans used is only revised monthly because the frequency of revisions is constrained by the manpower available to perform the required paperwork. (Ideally, the number of supplier-Kanbans used should be revised weekly or even daily.) The maximum and minimum quantities should also be revised every month.

Using the Kanban system to aid improvement of operations is very significant because improving productivity leads to financial improvements, thus improving the enterprise as a whole.

The Kanban system also serves to reduce management costs by helping reduce the number of planners to zero. Planners (forecasters) are not needed because the pulling nature of the Kanban system coupled with the flow of sales information from dealers serve as indicators for when and how much material is needed.

Additional Rules for Applying the Kanban System
The five application rules of the Kanban system, explained in Chapter 2, are listed below.

Rule 1. The subsequent process should withdraw the necessary products from the preceding process in the necessary quantities at the necessary point in time.

Rule 2. The preceding process should produce its products in quantities withdrawn by the subsequent process.

Rule 3. Defective products should never be conveyed to the subsequent process.

Rule 4. The number of Kanbans should be minimized.

Rule 5. Kanbans should be used to adapt to small fluctuations in the demand (fine-tuning of production by Kanban).

A sixth application rule of parts also exists for the Kanban system.

Rule 6: The actual quantity of parts contained in a box or packed in a load must be equal to the quantity written on the Kanban.

This rule may seem to be overstating the obvious, but when there is a difference between the actual quantity in a load and the quantity designated on the Kanban, production speed is adversely affected.

Suggestions for applying the Kanban system are as follows:

1. Since Toyota carries out monthly production planning, the number of total Kanbans issued can be allowed to vary each month. The Kanban system allows for daily minor adjustments as the sequence schedule for the final assembly line is planned according to the daily order from dealers.

2. The number of extra Kanbans issued according to their safety coefficient must be made as small as possible through continuous improvements.

3. The Kanban attached to the parts box must be detached and placed in the Kanban Receiving Post when the first part unit is used. These Kanbans have to be frequently collected and transferred to the preceding process. This transfer of Kanbans is usually done hourly.

4. A leveled production rate at the final process is crucial. Therefore, the quantity of parts withdrawn from each preceding process has to be equalized.

5. If overtime work is required to provide extra production, the scheduling staff should be informed in advance. Express Kanbans must also be issued in small quantities and promptly collected when the extra production run is completed.

Conveyance Characteristics

Although many different kinds of conveyance systems have been developed, they all work to simultaneously achieve two main goals: frequent and cost-effective conveyance. The Kanban system utilizes the conveyance principle by simultaneously conveying the product and information (Kanban) together. Hourly conveyance is the accepted frequency.

Most of the time, Toyota's plants produce and convey using the *constant order-quantity system* and use the *constant order-cycle system* as the alternative policy. However, for parts purchase, conveyance by the constant order-cycle system should be used.

If a supplier is located far away, conveyance should be based on the *constant cycle, inconsistent quantity system.* This constant cycle can be classified as a kind of Kanban cycle, and is usually drawn up as a relatively long-term contract between Toyota and its suppliers.

Toyota precisely schedules receiving times every thirty minutes because irregular receiving times will disrupt the receiving schedule. The supply schedule is always specified on the supplier Kanban. The Kanban cycle is not commonly specified since it is specified for each individual supplier based on their distance from Toyota.

Two conditions are required to introduce the supplier Kanban: a smoothed production system in Toyota plants and simultaneous process improvements at supplier plants. The following example shows how the Kanban system and less-than-smoothed production can cause problems for suppliers. Assume that a smoothed production was not performed by the Toyota plant and a two-shift production schedule was set for the assembly line. A worker who cannot work both day and night shifts does the required work for both shifts during the day. The job, which is to manufacture a required quantity of parts A and B, should have been done evenly in two shifts. Instead, all Kanbans for both parts are taken from their respective parts boxes, resulting in an Express Kanban being issued at the supplier. The only information the supplier has is that the parts were used and needed to be replaced. What the supplier is unaware of is that the need is not urgent. This phenomenon has to be remedied as soon as it is discovered.

It is very unusual for part makers to be compensated for pecuniary suffering caused by the Kanban system. Since each part maker usually supplies many kinds of parts used for various types of cars, a *decrease* in the withdrawal quantity of parts used for a certain model is usually compensated for by an *increase* in the withdrawal quantity of parts for another model. Thus, the total quantity of parts withdrawn stays constant. Also, if surplus workers exist in a supplier's assembly lines due to Toyota's faulty demand forecast, they may be transferred to Toyota's production lines.

Is it possible for suppliers to suffer due to an increased delivery frequency? In general, as the conveyance frequency increases, the cost of conveyance increases proportionately. However, this situation is based on the assumption that the efficiency of the conveyance method has been improved to an extreme point. If the round-tour system or the mixed-loading system is applied, transportation costs will not increase despite the increase in the frequency of conveyance. Under existing conditions at Toyota, it is possible to increase the frequency of conveyance while maintaining the current cost. That is, it is still possible to eliminate slack in the conveyance method and increase its frequency without changing conveyance costs. Under these conditions, it is not appropriate to formulate conveyance costs as a function of frequency as is done in inventory models used in the field of operations research.

One of the merits of the Kanban system is that it enables observation of the work place at short intervals of time and is thus able to realize frequent improvements. For example, if products are conveyed in one-hour intervals by the Kanban system, control of the proceedings in one-hour intervals is possible; if products are transported every ten minutes, the proceedings can be controlled every ten minutes. In the latter case, since the process speed is checked every ten minutes, its activities will be made clearer and machining or assembling speed can be checked.

By adopting a system in which the preceding process produces the same quantity of parts as is withdrawn by the subsequent process, waste (in this case overproduction) becomes clearly visible. For example, operator waiting time at a conveyor line becomes obvious by comparing actual cycle time with the required tact time. In lines that do not contain conveyors, if conveyance from a subsequent process is made at ten-minute intervals and if the activities of the preceding process are observed at the same ten-minute interval, the amount of waiting time experienced by the preceding process will also become visible. If the waiting time is transformed into actual physical products, the existence of this idle time will be masked. But, as long as the Kanban system's principles are followed, the masking of idle time by its conversion into physical products will be avoided.

For accounting and monthly maintenance of the number of Kanbans used, Toyota has implemented computer and bar code technology. However, in-process Kanbans are not bar coded because a monthly payment is not required for the units to be conveyed within Toyota's plant. Also, grasp of the actual production quantity by bar coding is unnecessary as it is already monitored by *production control boards* (a type of Andon), hourly for every process. In assembly lines, etc., assembling is designated by the issue of magnetic card instructions or IC cards, while actual control of the proceedings is maintained by the reading of these ID cards at the end of several processes. Activity control in processes other than these is maintained by Kanbans.

CONTROLLING PRODUCTION-ORDERING KANBANS

The function of a production-ordering Kanban on a gear-grinding line for small trucks will be examined in this section. At the starting point of this machining line, the production Kanban posts are equipped for every part to be processed. White, green, and yellow sheets are placed in the Kanban for each part. This makes it possible to see how many stocked Kanbans are in this Kanban post at the beginning of the process. When the Kanbans are stocked in the white or green frames, production of these parts need not be started yet; but the moment the Kanban is put into a yellow frame, production should begin. Consequently, the total number of Kanbans stocked up to the yellow frame is directly equivalent to the number of Kanbans in the lot size minus a reorder point. An example of the production Kanban post in Daihatsu's plant is shown in Figure 21.1.

In general, an acceptable number of Kanbans stocked in the *production-ordering post* is determined by the daily average figure determined from the monthly production quantity. Although this number generally depends on the turnover time, it usually ranges between one to three Kanbans.

The progress made on each process can be detected by the Kanban system. For example, if the Kanbans are not smoothly stocked on time in a *production-ordering post,* production is delayed in a subsequent process. Vice versa, if Kanbans are stocked earlier than scheduled, the subsequent process is proceeding too fast. Just by looking at the *production Kanban post,* operators can visually understand the rate of production at a subsequent process.

Triangular Kanban and Material Requisition Kanban on a Press line

Next, the structure of a press plant will be examined to understand how a Kanban circulates there. Basically, in a press plant there are two kinds of lines: a cutting line for coils and a press line. The purchased coils are stocked in a storage area located just before a coil-cutting line. Another storage area (called a sheet-store) containing the cut coil (steel-sheets) is situated after the coil-cutting line. Ideally, the quantity of stocked coil should be just enough for one-shift's use; however, there are times when a roll of coil is too big to be finished in one shift. In this case, the same roll is used in two or three shifts. In addition, enough inventory for one-shift is also kept at the storage area for the cut steel sheet. Several press lines exist. Behind each is a storage area for processed sheet metal where various pressed parts are placed in pallets. A triangular Kanban and a material requisition Kanban are hung from these pallets.

When the pallets have been used down to the material requisition Kanban, the Kanban is removed. Similarly, when pallets have been used down to the point of a Triangular Kanban (reorder point), it is also detached. The triangular Kanban will be hung on a Kanban post (or a Kanban hangar) on the way to the press line. Triangular Kanbans are then collected from the Kanban post two times a day—at precisely 9 a.m. and 4 p.m.—and hung on a production-ordering post (called a

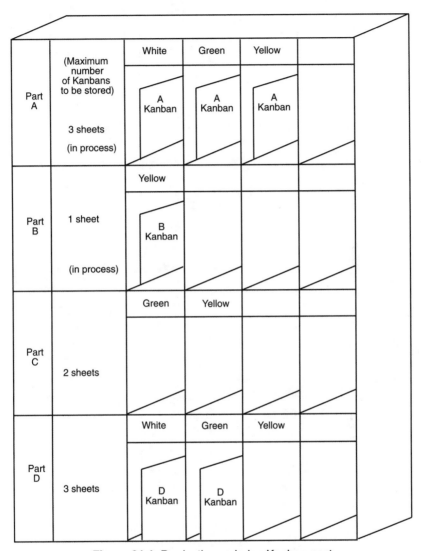

Figure 21.1. Production-ordering Kanban post.

stamping-order control board) at the start of the press line. The production-ordering post is used to signal the start for the pressing process at the press line.

Triangular Kanbans are not carried directly to the production-ordering post from pallet storage because a press line is very long and it is more efficient to let these pile up and be transferred in groups. Triangular Kanbans are first stocked in the Kanban hangar and conveyed together to the production-ordering post twice daily. Figure 21.2 shows how material requisitions and triangular Kanbans circulate within the press plant.

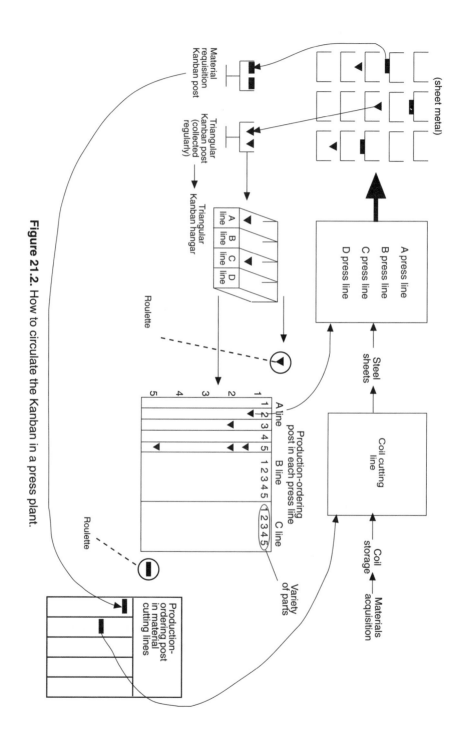

Figure 21.2. How to circulate the Kanban in a press plant.

The Roulette System

A roulette is used for processing press parts that have relatively small consumption quantities. These are parts that have usage quantities smaller than the pallet size. Ideally, the pallet size should be reduced and the amount contained per pallet should be decreased. However, if the pallet size is not reduced, the roulette is utilized. The instructions for the use of a roulette appear in Figure 21.3.

For example, suppose a pallet contains 60 pieces of a particular part and the actual consumption of the part per shift is only ten. This means that enough parts for 6 shifts are being stored on one pallet. Thus, the necessary quantity for one shift is only one-sixth of the entire pallet. This can be expressed as

$$\text{standard pallet quantity} = 1/6 = 0.17$$

Rounding off 0.17 to 0.2, the standard pallet quantity comes to one-fifth of the box. Therefore a triangular Kanban is put in area five of the roulette. For this type of part, production should not be started immediately even when the triangular Kanban is put in its hangar because the parts stored in the pallet are enough for five shifts.

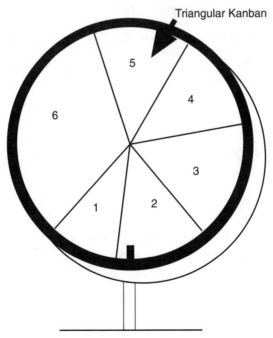

Figure 21.3. The roulette is rotated clockwise one block for each shift. In this example, when block 5 gets to the place now occupied by block 2, a triangular Kanban is put into the production ordering post.

The Hired Taxi System

A parts-supplying method based on the *hired taxi system* is used at Daihatsu Motors sheet metal process. It gets its name from the unhired taxis in Japan that drive around town irregularly looking for customers, while a hired taxi waits for passengers at base points.

In the sheet metal process, operators push a button beside the welding line just before they run out of parts. This activates a lamp above the respective part card on the *parts-calling lamp board* (also called *hire control board*). Once this lamp is illuminated, a carrier takes down the part card from the board and brings the required part to the welding line from its position noted on the card. (See Figures 21.4 and 3.10.)

For orderly part replenishment, a chute keeps various cards in the same sequence in which they were requested. Cards are put in the chute in the order in which their lamps were illuminated and a new card is put in place of the one just taken out. If five lamps are switched on simultaneously, all affected cards are put into the chute simultaneously. If a chute becomes filled with cards, a buzzer will sound to warn that sheet metal line operations are proceeding at a high rate and that the part replenishment rate should be increased.

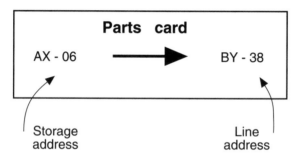

Figure 21.4. Parts card for hired taxi system.

CONTROL OF TOOLS AND JIGS THROUGH THE KANBAN SYSTEM

Machining tools, such as various cutting bites or drills, have to be replaced regularly because of constant use. The specific quantity of parts that can be manufactured before the tools have to be replaced can be determined and planned in advance.

To control tool replenishment using the Kanban system, tool boxes containing replenishment tools for every type of tool are kept beside the machining line. Every morning, a tool setter in charge of checking the tools replenishes the boxes with new tools. A daily record is kept of the number of tools that have been consumed and replenished. A tool-order Kanban (a type of triangular Kanban) is also used to order the tools needed.

According to Figure 21.5, a tool with item code T-3905 is to be ordered when six pieces remain according to the tool ledger. Tool-order Kanbans have magnetic strips on the back, which can be read by a card reader and electronically transmit the required order quantities to suppliers instantly.

The reorder point is examined monthly by reviewing consumption quantities over the previous two-month period. Reorder points are revised as warranted.

Tool-order Kanban	
Item name code	T-3905
Reorder point	6 units
Lot-size (order-quantity)	10 units

Figure 21.5. Tool-order Kanban.

SEQUENCED WITHDRAWAL AND THE LATER-REPLENISHMENT SYSTEM WITHDRAWAL

Sequence Schedule Sheet Sample

Typically, automobile assembly lines are characterized as mixed-model assembly lines where different car models are manufactured. As an example, we shall examine a motorbike assembly line at Kawasaki Heavy Industries.

In this assembly line, different types of motorbikes are assembled on the line in a mixed order. The same type of motorbike is manufactured successively in lots of five units instead of the ideal lot size of one. All parts required for the production of five motorbikes are ordered as one lot.

This plant has four main assembly lines and assembles 50 models. The length of assembly time required for each model is different. If assembly times for two sequential models differ greatly, they are simply produced nonsequentially, and a few models from the former five motorbikes are inserted into the production mix to take up slack time. Figure 21.6 shows the actual production sequence for the F-3 assembly line.

F3 Line Production Instruction Sheet				
Date		Kawasaki Heavy Ind. (motorcycle) Manufacturing Department		
Sequence	**Model**	**Spec.**	**Color**	**Lot size**
16-001	ZX 400D	C 101	BLK	5
16-002	ZX 400F	A 101	BLK	5
16-003	ZX 600C	A 402	RED	5
16-004	ZX 400D	C 101	BLK	5
16-005	ZX 600C	A 201	RED	5
16-006	KZ 750P	E 405	RED	5
16-007	ZX 400D	C 101	BLK	5
16-008	ZX 400F	A 101	BLK	5
16-009	ZLT 00A	A 303	BLU	5
16-010	ZX 400D	C 101	BLK	5
16-011	ZX 600C	A 201	RED	5
16-012	ZX 600c	A 402	RED	5
16-013	ZX 400D	C 101	BLK	5
16-014	KX 600A	C 402	BLK	5
16-015	ZX 400D	C 101	BLK	5
16-016	ZX 600C	A 402	WHT	5
16-017	ZX 400F	A 101	BLK	5
16-018	ZX 400D	C 101	BLK	5
16-019	ZX 550A	D 405	BLK	5
16-020	ZX 600C	A 201	RED	5
16-021	KZ 400D	C 101	BLK	5
16-022	ZX 600A	D 401	BLU	5
16-023	ZX 600A	C 402	BLK	5

Figure 21.6. Sequence instruction sheet for F3 assembly line.

Sequenced Withdrawal of Engines
Final assembly is achieved in the following manner at Toyota's Takaoka factory. Trucks bring 12 engines at a time to the plant in regular intervals of ten to fifteen minutes. This process insures almost zero inventory. The engines are unloaded and fitted with transaccelerators, transmissions, etc. before being put in line for assembly with the car body. This sequenced withdrawal system is based on the *constant-quantity and inconstant-cycle* principle.

The engine factory has produced engines according to a production schedule corresponding to car body production because the final assembly begins only two hours after the car body is painted. If the assembly plant issues the production order to the engine factory after the painting process, the required engines cannot be supplied in time. If this happens, a small inventory of additional engines is usually stored so adjustments can be made.

The production sequence in the final assembly line is: accelerator pedal, heater, ceiling, instrument panel, quarter glass, rear glass, wiring, gas tank, engine, and tires. Cars are suspended on the chassis assembly line for attachment of suspension systems, brakes, and exhaust systems. After the door handles and wipers have been attached, assembly work is complete and detection and adjustments are performed on each car.

Engine Withdrawal by the Later-Replenishment System
Withdrawal is sometimes made by the *later-replenishment system,* a pull system using Kanbans based on the *constant-cycle and inconstant-quantity* principle. Using this method, the ideal withdrawal lot size is between one and three units.

The type of withdrawal system used depends on two factors: 1) the time the withdrawal sequence is determined and 2) the conveyance lead time. Conveyance lead time is dependent on the distance between the engine factory and the final assembly line. For example, for two- or three-toned auto bodies, repainting is sometimes necessary for defective jobs, and the final withdrawal sequence cannot be confirmed until the painting process is completely finished. Auto bodies are put into the final assembly line two hours after being painted. Therefore, the sequenced withdrawal method is useful in this case only if the engine factory is located within a two-hour delivery area.

A specific engine line will supply engines to several subsequent car assembly lines, each of which also receives engines from several other engine lines. Toyota produces engines in-house in 16 lines with 32 subsequent processes. In terms of engine line combinations and subsequent processes, there are 36 sequenced withdrawal courses and 68 Kanban withdrawal courses for a total of 104 courses. (See Figure 21.7 next page.)

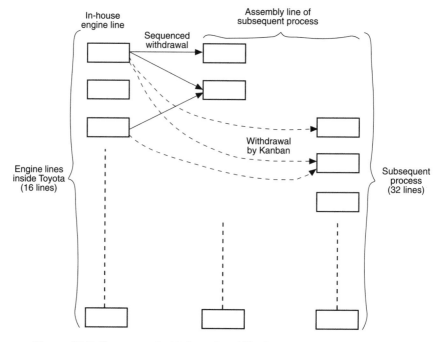

Figure 21.7. Sequenced withdrawal and Kanban withdrawal for engines.

22

Prerequisites to Implementing the Toyota Production System

What has been described thus far are the basic methods and concepts of the Just-in-time (JIT) production system used at Toyota. However, there is more to successfully implementing JIT than studying the system itself. The steps for introducing a JIT process will be discussed in this chapter.

Introductory Steps to the Toyota Production System

Step 1: Upper management plays a key role. Radical changes in top management's consciousness is often triggered by a business crisis caused by environmental or economic changes. Management must saturate every worker with this consciousness and increase profits by motivating workers to decrease costs by thinking of a new business innovation.

   When introducing JIT, it is important that upper management (not middle or line management) launch the effort to the line laborers. Doing so effectively conveys that upper management is in complete support of the change and, in fact, mandates change.

   Upper management must provide resources necessary to improve the manufacturing facility. For example, installation of an order entry communication network, a scheduling system, and a supplier delivery system are necessary investments. Management must also realize and recognize that line stops will increase, initially.

Step 2: Establish a project team. A project team comprised of plant, department, and section managers should be established and trained in JIT production. A project leader, usually the department manager, is appointed. The project team has three main objectives:

1. to organize seminars and training about JIT concepts and techniques
2. to prepare an implementation schedule and set goals to be achieved within the schedule
3. to organize a JIT practice team for sectional and sub-sectional managers

Step 3: Introduce a pilot project. Recognizing that the introduction of a JIT production system calls for revolutionary changes, it is advisable to start small. One manufacturing line should be chosen as a pilot project. Once JIT implementation is successful on that line, other lines can be included until JIT is realized plant-wide.

Step 4: Establish quality control circles. To keep employees involved in continuous improvement activities, each should participate in a quality control circle. This allows each employee to take ownership and accountability for their work and to demonstrate positive individual attributes.

Application Order of JIT Techniques

Implementation of Toyota production system techniques must be done in the same order as continuous improvement steps are taken. A basic approach is to improve in the direction "from means to goals," corresponding to Figure 22.1, that shows

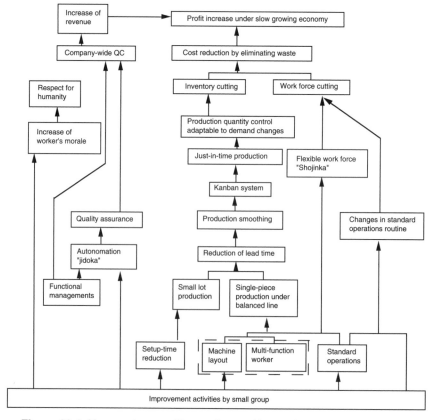

Figure 22.1. How costs, quantity, quality, and humanity are improved by the Toyota production system.

the systemized relationship between goals and means in the Toyota production system. The direction will be from the lowest box to the highest box in the figure. It is as follows:

1. Introduction of 5S—foundation of improvement
   The foundation for improvements at the workplace is the 5S concept: Seiri (arrangement), Seiton (tidiness), Seiso (cleaning), Seiketsu (cleanliness), and Shitsuke (training). Late delivery and defective goods often happen when the 5S has not been realized. In such places, worker morale is often low in general.

2. Introduction of one-piece production to realize line balancing
   Once the 5S concept has prevailed in a plant, the following fundamental prerequisites for JIT should be implemented:
   a. layout machinery in the process sequence
   b. connect adjacent processes
   c. construct U-shaped lines
   d. deploy multi-process holding by multi-functioned workers
   e. change from sitting labor to standing labor

3. Implementation of small lot size production and improvement of the setup method

4. Introduction of the standard operation
   a. base assembly line layout on cycle time
   b. create a standard operations sheet

5. Smoothed production by assembling products in response to sale velocity

6. Autonomation ("Jidoka")

7. Introduction of Kanban cards

In brief, the introductory steps consist of making a schedule, setting a goal, providing educational activities, and moving from a down-stream process to an up-stream process. Then, it continues with the 5S concept and proceeds to the changing of machinery layout, standard operations, and finally production smoothing.

Introduction of JIT at Toyo Aluminum—A Case Study

In this section, a JIT method adopted by Toyo Aluminum Corporation, an aluminum sheet plant, will be discussed as an example. Below is an overview of how they began.

1. A JIT project promotion committee and a practice team were established.
2. The team set a goal to reduce lead time by 50 percent. They then set four sub-goals to help realize the final objective.
3. The 5S improvement concept was promoted through quality control circles.
4. A training program on 5S, JIT, TQC, and TPM encompassing every organizational level was developed.

The challenging task of introducing the JIT production system at this plant has been promoted through the GO GO campaign and was followed by the Jump 60 campaign. The GO GO campaign was designed in 1986 to commemorate the 55th anniversary of the company founding. Its purpose was to reduce five main items by 50 percent during a two and one-half year period from June 1985–December 1987. The overview of this plan is depicted in Figure 22.2.

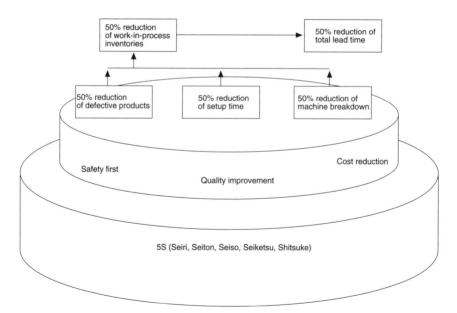

Figure 22.2. Target of GO GO campaign.

The final target was to reduce total lead time by 50 percent. The first step of their strategy to achieve this goal was to decrease the quantity of work-in-process (WIP) by half and continue improving until the goal was reached. To decrease WIP by 50 percent, three other items would have to be decreased: defective products, setup time, and machinery breakdowns. The reduction in these three items was supported by the 5S concept. Figure 22.3 shows the organization to promote the GO GO campaign.

The committee overseeing the campaign consisted of the divisional managers and five to six operation teams made up of section managers. Under these teams, training groups of shift foremen were directed to study industrial engineering foundations or the KJ method (card system for creating ideas by group members) full time for eight weeks. Additionally, an efficiency improvement team was created to advance the campaign, but actual promotion activities were carried out through the QC circles.

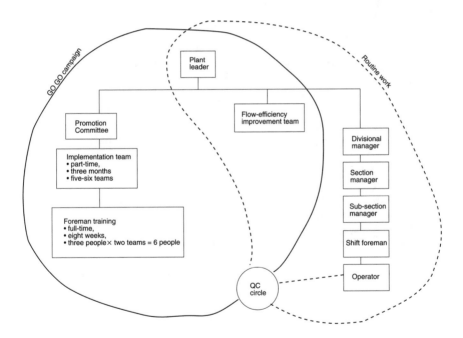

Figure 22.3. Structure of GO GO campaign.

The objective of the Jump 60 campaign was to increase productivity and decrease costs by the time the company reached its 60th anniversary in 1991. Most of the goals set in this project were achieved by 1990, even though it was originally scheduled to take three years (1989-1991) to reach the goals.

The goal of 34,000t at the top of Figure 22.4 shows that it was aimed to increase the present production capacity of 31,000t by ten percent per year without additional capital investment or worker transfers. A sub-goal was to diminish the amount of scrap material in order to shorten the total production lead time. Another sub-goal was to reduce manufacturing costs by ten percent.

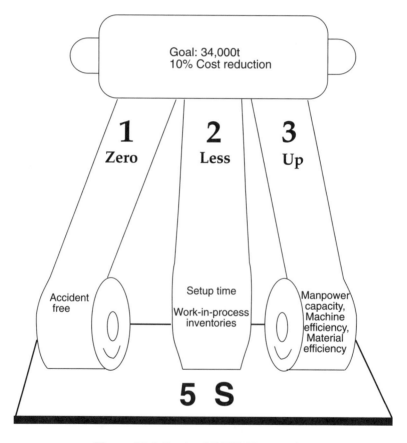

Figure 22.4. Goals of JUMP 60 campaign.

The three sub-goals for these reductions are 1 Zero, 2 Less, and 3 Up. *1 Zero* means the plant was accident free. Between the time the campaign was started until the author's visit on October 4, 1989, this company had attained 2,440 consecutive accident-free days and was awarded the Labor Minister Prize. One of its purposes was to renew this accident-free record.

2 Less means reduction of setup time and WIP inventories. The company has already reached the sub-goal of a 30-minute setup with certain targeted machines, for both the external and internal actions; this project's target was to extend this result horizontally to all machines. As for the targeted machines, the next objective will be to experiment with a new method to realize single setup—setup in less than ten minutes.

A WIP inventory reduction goal was set to decrease inventories by 300t to 1,200t. To meet this goal, smoothed production must be promoted, a Kanban system must be applied, and efficiency in small lot production must be attained.

3 Up in the Jump 60 campaign is composed of three components: manpower capacity, machine efficiency, and material efficiency. Manpower capacity is managed by reducing the work force by using multi-functional workers. This requires an investment in skill development and training. Seminars on JIT, QCT, TPM, and 5S should be offered company-wide. Department and section managers should be allowed to benchmark other organization's methods for solving setup problems, machine breakdowns, and prevention of defects. Improving the efficiency of machines requires eliminating factors disturbing the operating rate (operation at high speeds) and the workable rate (up time of machines). Advancement of material efficiency is checked by continuous quality improvement and by measuring the rate of good products.

In the end, the following formula depicts the total efficiency of facilities:

workable rate × speed operating rate × good product rate

23
Applying the
Toyota Production System Overseas

Japan's share of the automobile market increases each year. In the American market, Japanese subcompact cars have become more accepted than American cars by consumers. This is because of the superiority in terms of quality and price of Japanese cars. Recently, there has been a strong interest in transferring the Japanese production control system abroad shown among both foreign and Japanese companies. Is such a transfer possible? Environmental conditions among the companies are so different that the possibility of a transfer seems impossible. On the contrary, the Japanese system is already being transferred. American motor companies have been trying to achieve quality improvement and cost reduction through applying the Japanese production system to their manufacturing processes. Japanese companies have been asked to voluntarily restrict automobile exports in order to deal with the trade imbalance. In the meantime, producing units in the U.S. is becoming very profitable due to the appreciation of the yen.

Toyota, Nissan, Honda, Matsuda, and Mitsubishi have all started individual or joint ventures in the United States. Japanese parts makers have also entered into the American market either singly or by means of a joint venture and are bringing with them the Japanese production system.

Will the international transfer of the Japanese production system by both countries' car makers be feasible? In other words, does the Japanese system have international applicability?

CONDITIONS FOR INTERNATIONALIZING THE JAPANESE PRODUCTION SYSTEM

First of all, let us examine the social background by which the Japanese companies have attained such a strong competitive edge and define prerequisite conditions for international transfer. It was process innovation by improvement as well as product innovation by research and development that gave the Japanese motor industries the international competitive edge. Japanese auto makers got their start after the second world war utilizing American and European development technology. However, in the automobile industry where development technology had been standardized, the superiority of Japanese management allowed Japan to gain control of its competition.

The innovative Japanese process control technology was originally created by Toyota and has spread to other Japanese companies. It is referred to as the Toyota production system, or the Just-in-time (JIT) production system. The foundation of the JIT production system is backed by social and institutional conditions peculiar to Japan. Here, the social conventions and the institutions supporting the Japanese production system can be called the social production system.

Two essential factors composing the social production system are: (1) maker-supplier relationships and (2) management-labor relationships. While the educational system has great influence on people's values, only the former external and industrial conventions will be analyzed here.

The international transfer of the Japanese production system is possible if and only if the social environment of the country is altered to adapt to the new system. In the business field, a *contingency theory* has been advocated by P.R. Lawrence, J.W. Lorsch, and others, which says that the formal organizational structure is a dependent variable to be defined by the environmental variables of technology, scale, and uncertainty. It has been theorized that an organization spontaneously establishes for itself the most effective organizational structure for the environment in which it exists. According to such a theory, the most efficient production systems for the U.S. and Japan are different because of differences in their respective environmental conditions.

Another school of thought proposes that a proficient management system can exist and be applied in any country. For example, a long-practiced lifetime system is not peculiar to Japan, but can also be seen in American companies such as Kodak and Xerox.

My own theory is slightly different. In contingency theory, the environment is viewed as a given factor and is also regarded as a non-operational, uncontrollable exogenous variable. But management does not always view the whole of environmental conditions surrounding companies as given factors. Environmental conditions are controllable in the long run and can be thought of as decision (endogenous) variables. Even the cultural aspect is changeable in the long run. For example, Buddhism was introduced into Japan (where only Shintoism had existed) and was absorbed spontaneously by the Japanese. It has since become very popular. Of course, there are some cultured or religious environments that may be difficult to change initially.

The fact that American companies are regarded as possessions of the shareholders while Japanese companies are possessions of the employees is also difficult to change. The environmental conditions necessary for the smooth transfer of the Japanese JIT production system are the maker-supplier relationship and the management-labor relationship. These environmental conditions must be changed as a prerequisite to the introduction of the Japanese control system. Unlike Lorsch and Lawrence, I propose that the environmental conditions do not necessarily shape the organizational structure. Key environmental factors such as the maker-supplier relationship and the management-labor relationship can be changed to accommodate the introduction of a production control system. In order for the transfer of the Japanese system to work, these environmental conditions must be implemented.

ADVANTAGES OF THE JAPANESE MAKER-SUPPLIER RELATIONSHIP

As described previously, international industrial competition largely relies on the superiority of the global social production system. When comparing the Japanese maker-supplier relationship with that of America's, two remarkable differences in the relationship between paternal companies and their contractors are revealed.

First, a hierarchical subcontract organization form the primary step to each succeeding step in Japan. This hierarchical structure has not been constructed in American companies. In the U.S., the use of external suppliers has prevailed, but suppliers to subcontractors have not been sufficiently utilized. Chrysler has business relations with 3,000 to 4,000 suppliers and General Motors (GM) deals directly with more than 10,000 suppliers. In comparison, Japanese car makers withdraw directly from 100 to 300 primary subcontracted companies. Each level's paternal company in the hierarchical subcontract organization deals with as few as ten subcontractors in accordance with their management ability.

The second difference is that Japanese subcontracted companies get orders from one particular paternal company under a long-term contract arrangement. Nearly 38 percent of all Japanese subcontractors make 75 percent of their total sales to one paternal company. In total, 63 percent of the subcontracted companies rely on their primary paternal company for more than 50 percent of their total sales.

Considering the two features above, it is not surprising that the Japanese subcontract structure rests on the very close relationship between paternal companies and their subcontractors. This close relationship enables the easy transfer of information thus reducing transactions costs. Both the paternal companies and subcontractors reap the benefits of the subcontractor's growth in profits because of the production experience accumulated in long-term relationships. The criterion for being selected as a subcontractor is the ability to provide high quality, low cost, and short delivery time.

Regarding special technology, medium and small enterprises have already been taken over by big companies, and a divisional system among varying technologies has been formed. This has created strong, competitive power for Japanese companies in international assembly-machining type industries. To be more specific, many subcontractors are providing their paternal companies with in-house programmed processes, new technology developed in-house, dies made in-house, exclusive use machinery developed and manufactured in-house, and original technologies.

In JIT systems, it is possible for Japanese subcontracted companies to react to hourly delivery schedules by using the Kanban. The JIT method can be attained through the close relationship over a long period of time between a paternal company and a few subcontractors. The stable quality in the relationship is supported by high technology, and the shortening of production lead time is supported on the subcontractors side. (See Figure 23.1.)

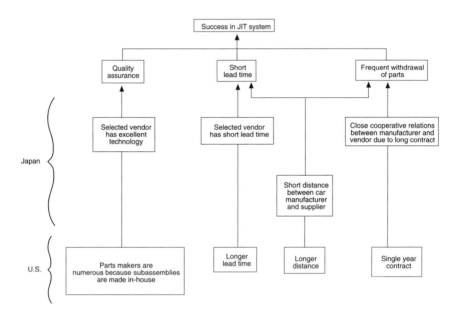

Figure 23.1. Comparison of transactions between manufacturer and supplier.

REORGANIZATION OF EXTERNAL PARTS MAKERS IN THE UNITED STATES

Comparing the characteristics of parts makers in American and Japanese motor industries will highlight differences between the two. In Japan, the close cooperative relationships between parts makers and finished car manufacturers have enabled the JIT system to succeed. In contrast, it is believed that there are many problems in applying the JIT system in the U.S. due to the independence of American parts makers. However, this is a shallow viewpoint because Japanese parts makers as a group resemble the parts manufacturing divisions of American motor companies. In the U.S., the parts manufacturing department within a company has the close (dependent) characteristics seen in Japan.

In Japan, most of the stock of primary parts makers is owned by the motor company. By contrast, this equity ownership does not exist between an American motor company and its parts supplier. The in-house manufacturing rate at American motor companies is so high that numerous terminal parts for subassembly are purchased from the external parts makers. As a result, the numbers of parts to be purchased and the number of parts makers being dealt with is very large. Since the relationship with parts makers is not very reliable in terms of price and quality, the motor companies must maintain relationships with many parts makers.

In order to be competitive, the in-house manufacturing rate in American motor companies will have to decrease as will the number of parts makers that companies deal with. In regard to these points, let us examine General Motor's (GM) present method of dealing with external parts makers.

A GM assembly plant used to receive major parts in a predetermined quantity according to a calculation based on the average necessary quantity per day, but that quantity had not always matched the actual consumption rate of the plant. Once GM changed this plant to the JIT system and instructed its suppliers to deliver the necessary quantity of parts each day, this quantity matched the actual quantity consumed in the assembly plant.

The American car market has become very competitive since it was opened to Japanese parts makers. Other Japanese parts makers have followed Honda and Nissan in expanding their business to America. The establishment of a joint venture by Toyota and GM in California will also urge the extension of Japanese auto makers. Although the primary role of such Japanese companies is to produce parts for Japanese car plants, they gradually and certainly will be strong rivals for domestic American parts makers.

As for GM, it has been revealed that their ordering policy has been revised. For example, GM is the biggest customer for the steel industry. In steel transaction negotiations in 1984, GM selected steel plants on the basis of price, production quantity, and distance to GM stamping plants. Although GM did not abandon all twelve former suppliers at that time, they decided to centralize the orders to several subcontractors.

It is assumed that GM's purpose was to develop close relationships with its suppliers through annual contracts and a shared weekly production forecast in order to hold the inventory down to a minimum. This idea was borrowed from Japanese methods in which suppliers transport materials just-in-time corresponding to a production schedule of the motor companies. Additionally, GM is trying to select the suppliers that will further reduce the number of subcontractors. In July 1983, GM announced that it would decrease the number of the steel suppliers, explaining that if the number of suppliers were reduced, those adopted by GM would be able to operate more economically, thereby leading to decreased steel costs.

Another reason that GM attempted to prolong contract periods with suppliers resulted when the motor industry was recovering from a recession in 1981 to 1983. Any rise in price demanded by parts makers would not be accepted; however, some of the parts makers were offered Japanese-like, multi-year contracts, which were considered to be an incentive for those suppliers to invest in automating factories and improving facilities. The advanced productivity made possible by such an investment would give bonuses in the long run to both parts makers and motor companies. For example, a three-year contract came out of the 1983 negotiations between tire manufacturers and motor companies. Although it involved a decrease in prices of about one percent, the subcontractor could depend on that business for three years instead of one.

SOLUTION OF GEOGRAPHICAL PROBLEMS INVOLVING EXTERNAL TRANSACTIONS

Another problem in applying the Kanban to part delivery in the U.S. is the long distance between suppliers and finished car makers in such a vast land. Most parts are conveyed by train or large trailer in the U.S. In the case of rail transport, it takes about ten to twelve days from California to Detroit, and by trailer, the same distance takes about seven or eight days. On the average, one to three days are needed. A quantity of parts corresponding to this number of days is regarded as a moving inventory.

When arriving at a plant, the rear part of a trailer bearing a load is detached, and it is kept in a station for the exclusive use of trailers. Then, the plant holds the parts for three to five days waiting for processing. Consequently, hundreds of large containers are left in the yard until a delivery dock foreman instructs them to unload the parts. Because of the long conveyance distance, distribution costs necessarily increase, and thus the frequency of conveyance decreases. It is normal to deliver units by a large trailer from one to three times a week.

The author suggested in May, 1981 that American automobile companies "should look for a means of adopting subcontractors located closer geographically" (Monden 1981). Thereafter, GM adopted a system that closely resembles this in Buick City in Flint, Michigan. Buick is one of the five biggest divisions in GM, along with Cadillac, Chevrolet, Oldsmobile, and Pontiac. General Motors gathered its parts makers around this main plant, Buick City, and asked them to produce and deliver parts by the Kanban system. This industrial area was started in 1985 along the same lines as the Mikawa district in Aichi, where Toyota realized the Kanban system by centralizing its parts makers nearby.

According to the plan, 83 percent of the parts were to be produced within a 100-mile radius of Buick City, and 100 percent were to be produced within a 300-mile radius . This meant that all parts could be delivered within eight hours and inventory could be reduced from eight days worth to four hours worth in regard to main parts, and from twenty days to only five days in regard to engine parts. However, it is regrettable that the Buick City became very depressed as the documentary film, "Roger and Me," showed because of the recession due to decreased sales.

The next adjustment between Japanese motor companies and parts makers is often carried out through associations established by each motor company. Toyota has three types of associations for parts makers within each district. (Each of these associations consists of 137 firms, 63 firms, and 25 firms, respectively.) Furthermore, big parts makers have their own organizations. In the U.S., these types of associations did not exist at all until recently. In January 1983, the Japan GM Association was organized. This association is made up of almost 100 companies including Japanese parts makers such as TDK, NEC, National, Hitachi, Funuk, machinery makers, and robot makers for industry.

General Motors has expanded its use of the JIT system in the following way. A large assembly plant was built in Orion, Michigan, by the assembly division of GM. In this plant, in order to realize the JIT system, parts are delivered by trucks, not trains, to a parts arrival point. Also, at the Hamtramic plant in Detroit, 48 truck starting points are located near workshops using the materials. This is in contrast to the previous system GM used in which large containers were controlled at a huge stations and unloaded at only one receiving dock before finally being transported to a storage facility. In Buick City, receiving docks are located in 100m intervals. As parts arrive, they are immediately taken to the assembly line.

As previously mentioned, in Japan usually only one or two parts makers are used for purchasing particular parts, whereas in the U.S. many parts makers are used. Geographic location can sometimes make it difficult for parts makers to react to production demand. Additional complications, such as a blizzard in the Midwest may force plants in the South to stop their operations, hindering the delivery of parts. Or, a strike at a plastic plant in California may force electronics companies in New York to stop their operations.

EXTERNAL TRANSACTIONS OF NUMMI

How are external transactions being performed at New United Motor Manufacturing, Inc. (NUMMI), a joint venture between Toyota and GM? This is an interesting subject because the Toyota production system has been applied to this company for the first time in the history of American automobile manufacturing.

The parts required at NUMMI are not only produced in America but are also produced in and transported from Japan. For example, about 1,500 types of parts for the subcompact car Nova are sent from Japan, and most of them are manufactured at Toyota and its subcontracted companies.

New United Motor Manufacturing, Inc. has business relations with 75 suppliers in North America, and 700 kinds of parts for the Nova are purchased from those companies. Fifty-five out of 75 suppliers are located in the Midwest, six are in the Southeast, three are in Mexico, and eleven are in California. These parts suppliers are regarded as members of the NUMMI team, so naturally mutual trust and respect between NUMMI and the suppliers are cultivated and maintained. Since this sort of friendly automotive relationship, while typical in Japan, is fairly rare in the United States, special consideration was taken in evaluating and selecting the suppliers. General selection criteria, such as quality, price, location, etc., were important, but the supplier's cooperative attitude was the most significant factor. The suppliers were examined to see if they could willingly accept the constraints of a new production system.

Team members from its production control, quality, manufacturing, and purchasing departments at NUMMI are dispatched to supplier's facilities. These team members provide training, support for problem solving, and assistance in practicing Kaizen. In general, they work to strengthen the relationship between NUMMI and the parts makers. Periodic parts-maker conferences are held in which common problems are discussed, and information concerning future events is provided.

Suppliers in North America are given a weekly forecast of requirements. This forecast contains seven weeks of part number level shipping requirements. This preliminary schedule is used only for planning purposes; it does not signify a commitment by NUMMI (resembling the three-months forecast in Japan). The forecast is either delivered by air mail or transmitted electronically to parts makers. While the preliminary schedule is updated weekly for seven weeks, the final requirement quantity is issued once to parts makers, two days before the shipment date. The parts makers are telephoned, or instructed through other electronic communications as to what the final requirement schedule regarding the specific day's shipment will be. This final requirement schedule is the commitment to the parts makers. As most parts are shipped every day, the final requirement schedule is communicated daily.

This final requirement schedule is based on the actual consumed quantity of parts in NUMMI's production process. The actual usage is calculated by counting the Kanban cards for materials or parts used in a day's production. To this calculated quantity, miscellaneous usage and expected future schedule adjustments (overtime, holidays, etc.) are considered. The changes in the methods of transactions described up to now are summarized in Figure 23.2.

---

1. Number of part makers reduced.
2. Contract period extended.
3. In-house manufacturing rate of parts decreased.
4. Proximity of part maker to manufacturer considered (i.e., Buick city).
5. Local association of part makers established.
6. Joint effort between Japan and U.S. car manufacturer established.
7. Team members from NUMMI dispatched to part makers.

Figure 23.2. Changes of transaction convention in U.S.

INDUSTRIAL RELATIONS INNOVATIONS

According to Prof. Kuniyoshi Urabe (1984), transferring the JIT system to the United States is not impossible, but it is obvious that the differences in industrial relations between America and Japan will become large obstacles. A discussion of the obstacles follows.

Prerequisites of Flexible Labor Systems

Under the JIT system, it is a prerequisite that worker transfer within a plant, exclusive of worker transfer between plants be performed without restriction. In this manner, a flexible labor system is realized. Specific institutional features, i.e., educational training, wage system, and labor-management relations, which are inherent in Japanese companies, serve as the basis and enable a flexible work force. Japanese companies provide the necessary training for employees to become multi-functional workers who can handle various jobs.

The Japanese wage system has traditionally been based on seniority. The wage system depends on a person's attributes. In other words, attributes such as academic career and years of work experience are evaluated in deciding each person's salary, not the content of the work itself. Although the Japanese wage system has been changing to a job-class wage system having a competitive aspect and to a qualification-ordered wage system, wages are mainly decided by considering attributes. Because of the attribute-ordered wage system in Japan, the transfer of workers to different jobs in response to the needs of the company does not pose a problem.

In contrast, American companies apply the job-class wage system in which one is paid on the basis of the job itself. Under the JIT system, if a worker is transferred to another type of job in the U.S., problems will occur because the transfer might involve a change of job and thus of wage classification. If a worker is transferred to a lower-ranked job classification, it will mean a cut in wages and a major labor-management dispute.

The Japanese wage system is a fixed daily or monthly wage system. In the U.S., most laborers are paid according to an hourly or weekly wage system, and an incentive wage system is the most common. The incentive wage system is one in which a worker can achieve additional wages if certain predetermined standards of operations are achieved. Although this standard of operations is based on a time and motion study, it becomes under American industrial relations subject to collective bargaining with the union. After the transfer of a worker, a standard of operations of the new job must be discussed between members of the union and the company. Some labor unions have a clause in the labor agreement keeping the tradition of craft unions in which worker transfers among different kinds of jobs falling under different union jurisdictions are prohibited. Since automobile assemblers and machinists who make parts are different occupations which require different skills, the transfer of workers between these jobs is prohibited. Even if the worker transfer between different jobs is allowed, if seniority rule is one of the articles of the labor contract, the transfer to a requested workplace is granted to workers by reason of seniority at the present job.

Prerequisites of Work Place Improvements

Under Japanese industrial relations, matters within a manufacturing process, such as reduction in the work force, improvement of methods and standards of operations, and automation of machinery are not a part of the collective bargaining process, although they can become a topic of dispute between labor and management. In Japan, only basic labor conditions, i.e., salary, extra income based on company profits, and labor hours are brought up as subjects of collective bargaining, and sometimes as issues to go to strike over.

American industrial relations are fundamentally hostile. If a reduction in work force is desired, management and labor must reach an agreement through collective bargaining or it will not be possible to implement such a change. The union might resist a reduction in work force. Even matters within the manufacturing process itself which have great influence over the advancement of quality and productivity, such as the improvement of operation methods and the automation of machinery, have become subject to the collective bargaining process because they affect labor conditions in the work place.

The features of American industrial relations described above have been changing recently in an attempt to introduce the Japanese production system. A discussion of these attempts follows. (See Figure 23.3.)

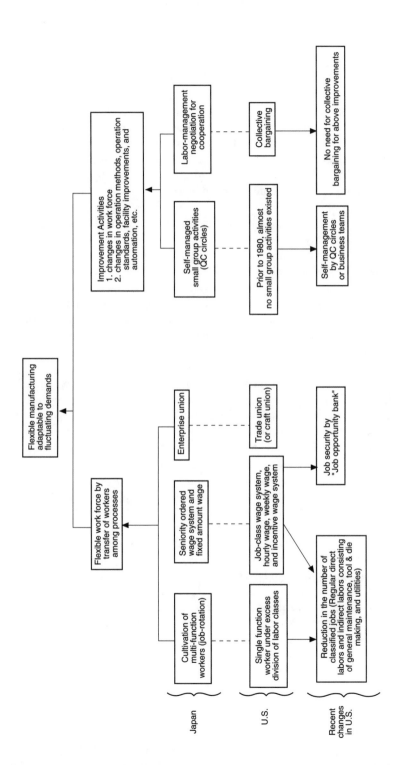

Figure 23.3. Labor–management relationship.

Features of New Labor Contracts

New United Motor Manufacturing, Inc. has concluded a labor contract with the United Automobile Workers Union (UAW), aimed at eliminating all obstacles to the introduction of the Toyota production system. According to Mr. Simpson, a production management chief at NUMMI, NUMMI has been operating with two-shift production since early 1986. Eighty-five to 90 percent of the 2500 employees are paid on an hourly basis and are represented by the UAW. The balance consists of unrepresented salaried personnel.

The new labor contract includes three points:

1. While there are 31 job classifications in the UAW, NUMMI has only two classifications for hourly employees.
   a) Division 1—regular direct labor
   b) Division 2—indirect labor

These are skilled positions further divided into three classifications: general maintenance, tool and die maintenance, and utilities. As a result of simplifying the job classifications, worker transfer has become easier within each division, and the goal of having a multifunctional work force has been achieved.

2. The workers are organized into teams similar to Japanese quality control circles. Each team consists of five to ten members, including an hourly-paid team leader. This team leader is similar to a coach for a sports team. Three to five teams are collectively supervised by a group leader, the first level salaried supervisor, and report directly to him. He reports to either a manager or an assistant manager.

It should be noted that each team operates autonomously, taking full responsibility for manufacturing, quality, cost, safety, and other work goals. In short, the team sets its goals and works together to attain them. The team leader is a working member who has the capability and knowledge to deal with every operation proficiently as well as to motivate the team. He trains and looks after other team members, maintains safety and training records, and assists the group leader with the management and functioning of the team.

All team leaders and group leaders (more than 300 total) were sent to Japan and given actual training at a Toyota assembly plant so that they could understand the Toyota production system and Japanese management techniques in general. Toyota also dispatched 200 people to NUMMI as instructors. These Toyota instructors worked at NUMMI for three to four weeks. Also, Toyota assigned twenty-four management personnel to supervise each manager to assure the coordinated application of the Toyota production system.

3. Altering production systems and standards, which formerly required negotiations between management and labor unions, is easily executed, thereby making the flexible manufacturing system feasible. All changes in machinery, materials, labor utilization, and even the details of the production system are possible without union negotiations.

It is said that the corporate culture or business climate is being changed to a system of mixed Japanese and American culture. It may be called an atmosphere of mutual reliance and respect. For example, the NUMMI plant has open office areas and one cafeteria. A first-come-first-served parking system, warm-up exercises in the morning, and uniforms have been introduced. Sports facilities, team meeting rooms, and locker rooms have been installed throughout the plant.

In the author's view, it is correct to present the full Japanese system in order to have the right foundation for the Toyota production system. For the Toyota production system to take firm root, not only are formal orientation and training programs needed, but also daily team meetings in which the initiated Toyota concepts are emphasized, i.e., "Jidoka" (autonomous automation), "Kaizen" (improvement), "Bakayoke" (foolproof), "Muda" (waste), "Five Whys", "Heijunka" (smoothing), "Kanban" (Kanban system), "Andon", etc. It is gratifying that the Japanese manufacturing management words are prevailing in the U.S.

In 1984, a job *opportunity bank* system was introduced in a new labor contract between GM and the UAW . This job opportunity bank accepts members of the union who are likely to lose their jobs due to new technology, process changes, productivity improvement, or integration of parts manufacturing, and offers them opportunities for retraining for a job with an equivalent wage (provided the workers have more than one-year seniority).

A joint UAW–GM *employment assurance committee* constructed by management and labor at every level, district, and area establishes and organizes job opportunity banks as necessary. The company provides ten billion dollars for its operation.

According to Prof. Haruo Shimada, introduction of this system has provided a win–win situation. Management has gained one method for management control of a flexible labor force and laborers enjoy the benefit of job security. In other words, by establishing this system, management obtained, with the order of parts, a business relationship with foreign enterprises and innovation of industrial technology.

The labor conditions described above, which did not previously exist in the American car manufacturing plants, will allow for the flexibility needed to completely introduce the Toyota production system. United States car manufacturers now have access to new production technology and have developed a strategic alliance with respectable foreign businesses.

CONCLUSION

The transfer of Japanese production control techniques and Japanese management systems to other nations has and is occurring as evidenced by the joint venture between Toyota and GM. This transfer of technology and management principles can take on several forms:

1. The Japanese management system can be adapted to include American or European concepts like reducing the work week, promoting women to management positions, etc.
2. The Japanese management system could be implemented exactly as it operates in Japan.
3. A new management system could be created that would combine the technology of both countries. I.e., the Japanese Kanban system has been connected to the American MRP concept; also, robotics and a computer network system developed in the U.S. have been applied to the Japanese system.
4. A new cultural environment, conducive to implementing the Toyota production system, could be initiated in the other country. Once achieved, the Japanese management system would be applied and adjusted to the new environment.

It is the author's opinion that one of the four scenarios described above will emerge as the most beneficial approach and that for JIT production systems to be implemented successfully the last approach would be the most appropriate.

Although basic differences in company concepts, culture, historical perspective, and regional affairs cannot be bridged overnight, creating new procedures, rules, thought processes, etc., to apply the Japanese system is feasible. Regardless of how the transformation is accomplished, it should not be forced on the other country. On the contrary, the approach should be mutually agreed upon and planned by both countries. We can find this cooperative attitude in action at the NUMMI plant.

Appendix 1
JIT Delivery System Can Ease Traffic Congestion and the Labor Shortage

JIT WILL CONTRIBUTE TO RATIONALIZATION OF PHYSICAL DISTRIBUTION

In recent years, there has been growing criticism of the Just-in-time (JIT), known as the Kanban system, accusing it of being the ultimate cause of physical distribution problems. It is argued that JIT has caused (1) increased physical distribution costs (transportation costs), (2) a shortage of drivers, (3) traffic congestion, and (4) exhaust gases that pollute the environment.

No doubt, when the JIT system is examined in terms of individual parts, it is in essence a system involving the transporting of small lots—small volumes—of goods on each trip, and frequent deliveries carrying the average volume of goods each time. But it is illogical to say that this distribution system is the ultimate cause of the problems listed above.

For example, a glass manufacturer that delivers automobile glass to automakers in accordance with the Kanban system is expected to deliver glass to the factory 20 times every day. If that total volume of glass is considered to equal 40 truck loads, and all the deliveries are done once in the morning, 40 trucks must leave at the same time every morning.

If every parts maker delivered parts in such large lots, the roads leading to the auto maker's factory would be terribly congested. Forty truck drivers would be required at the same time, further aggravating the labor shortage. And because drivers would be on stand-by except when they were actually driving, this method would, in terms of society as a whole, constitute a terrible waste of human resources.

Now let us consider the small lot frequent delivery system. To begin with, because transportation costs are charged based on a contract which states that "payment of a certain amount is made for each shipment by each truck on each route," physical distribution costs remain the same whether 40 trucks are dispatched simultaneously or whether two trucks are dispatched together at 20 different times.

Editor's note: This appendix is the author's response to criticism in both Japanese and American literature and press of the JIT system.

349

The multiple delivery approach means that each driver is involved in many trips each day, so that the turn-around rate per person increases, alleviating the labor shortage. Also, frequent deliveries of standardized small lots relieve traffic congestion the same way as a staggered work hour system. The same volume of exhaust gas is emitted by 40 trucks dispatched at the same time as by two trucks dispatched 20 times. If traffic congestion is avoided through small lot deliveries, specific products are delivered more quickly than they are when delivered in large lots, and the volume of physical distribution in a single day can be increased.

The ideals of the JIT system are satisfied if the physical distribution volume required in a single month is ordered during the month based on equalized daily requirements, not ordered during a designated week or on a designated day each month. This also serves to alleviate the labor shortage and traffic congestion.

GENUINE JIT SYSTEM HAS PREREQUISITE CONDITIONS

What then is the correct JIT physical distribution? The system in use at Toyota was basically developed as a JIT production control system (Toyota production system). Therefore, the application of their system's concepts to the physical distribution for establishing a real JIT delivery system will be considered here.

The first condition is smoothing (leveling). At Toyota, smoothed production means calculating the approximate average daily sales volume for each month based on anticipated monthly sales, and producing (with the greatest possible accuracy) the average daily sales volume every day throughout the month. Accordingly, parts makers are to deliver almost the small average volume of parts each day. This smoothing concept is achieved by having frequent small lot deliveries even during each day. But "just in service," a term used by large volume retailers, cannot mean to provide consumers with equalized sales even though retailers ask wholesalers and part makers to provide a frequent small-volume delivery service. It is therefore difficult to equalize physical distribution in obtaining supplies.

The second condition is that it must not be non-stock production. On the average, inventories are maintained at half the volume indicated by the number of Kanban cards, which is revised monthly. (One Kanban card is the equivalent of one container of parts.) Leveled physical distribution at Toyota is possible because its dealers retain buffer inventories.

The third condition is that trucks must always be fully loaded. Trucks used to deliver parts must always achieve 100 percent loading efficiency. If this condition is not met—if each truck carries a different volume and partially empty trucks are frequently dispatched to deliver small lots—the systems cannot properly be called JIT physical distribution. It is far different from real JIT physical distribution; it is nothing more than high-handedness on the part of the party ordering the goods.

Certainly at Toyota too, the necessary quantity of each part item is getting smaller because of the tendency of an increased variety of cars with each small quantity. But, using the mixed loading method of various small lot items, Toyota has achieved full loading efficiency for each truck. From such an efficient mixed loading method, they developed their own standardized polyethylene containers of various sizes.

The final condition is that there must be leeway in the scheduled times that trucks arrive at their destinations. What happens if truckers are ordered to arrive according to a designated schedule which does not allow them any flexibility? Trucking company managers dispatch their trucks early so that they will not arrive at their destinations late, which forces truckers to wait on the highway to use up their excess time, or to drive aimlessly around their destination killing time until they can complete their deliveries.

EXTERNAL ENVIRONMENT FOR PHYSICAL DISTRIBUTION SHOULD BE RATIONALIZED

Criticism of JIT physical distribution occurs because of confusion surrounding the meaning of JIT physical distribution. Converting incorrect or fake JIT distribution methods into genuine JIT distribution will help to alleviate some of the problem.

There are other factors besides the proliferation of fake JIT physical distribution systems behind the problems which have plagued physical distribution in recent years. Many are primarily the results of an increase in the overall volume of goods handled by the system (the weight multiplied by the distance) which has accompanied the expansion of the Japanese economy, and the increasing demand for convenience among Japanese consumers. The expansion of social capital in the form of a road network able to satisfy the increased scale of physical distribution has also lagged behind. It is necessary to increasingly build up the nation's road stock by improving intersections and by building loop expressways and bypasses. Other measures that would help include the completion of highway traffic information systems and traffic control systems.

It is also vital that the external environment surrounding physical distribution be rationalized by, for example, promoting a reduction in the number of different products transported, establishing joint delivery systems among parts makers, and establishing joint delivery centers so that the convenience store industry and manufacturers can deliver goods to each of their stores.

Reprinted with permission of Nikkei. Originally published in the Japanese language in *Nikon Keizai Shibun,* August 7, 1991.

Appendix 2
Goals Coordination Method

This appendix will describe an experiment with an assembly line using the Just-in-time (JIT) system. The experiment will attempt to prepare a satisfactory sequence schedule for a mixed model assembly line using the goals coordination method.

The primary problems with the line are production smoothing and prevention of line stops posed by differences in the assembly times among attached parts. To solve these problems, a computer program was designed for the goal chasing method on the basis of the procedure described in Chapter 16. To shorten calculation time, goal chasing method II was applied. Then, the combined logic of the continuation and interval control and *weight control* was incorporated into the problem. A complete flowchart of this decision model is depicted in Figure A2.1.

EXPERIMENT OUTLINE

In this experiment, realistic conditions were simulated by compiling actual product data to determine the sequence scheduling on the assembly line. First, the bill of materials was prepared for each car according to the information in dealer catalogs about engines, bodies, and options. Next, each model's production quantity was determined using actual monthly sales data obtained from several magazines and from interviews with dealers. Dealers were asked which model sold and in what proportion. Then, the goal chasing method was applied to this data. Toyota's model Mark II was chosen because it is representative of Japanese cars and nearly twenty thousand are produced every month.

Since the number of component parts used for one automobile is almost twenty thousand, it would have been difficult and time consuming to make the calculations of the goals coordination method for all of the components. Therefore, only parts classified in catalogs as components or specs for the Mark II were listed. (Calculations for the sequence schedule at Toyota are actually conducted in this manner by using only sub-assembly parts, such as end items.) Listing such end items evenly from every portion of an automobile was considered carefully,

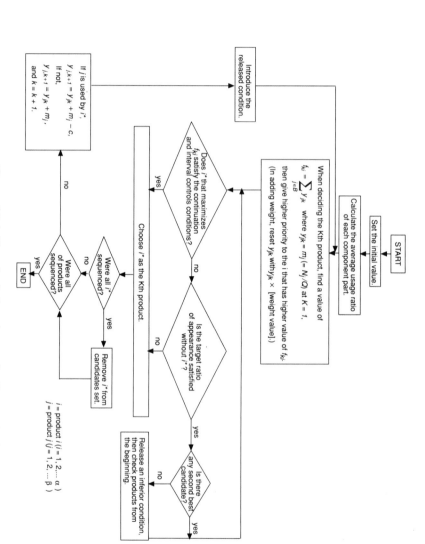

Figure A2.1. Flowchart of goals coordination method.

and 18 kinds of end items were selected. These end items included body, grade, engines, etc. Supposing each item has a few different varieties, 48 varieties of parts were prepared, resulting in 344 varieties of cars. (If body color and interior color are added as items, the total number of car varieties increases to more than ten times the number of current varieties. Therefore, those items were not included in this experiment.)

It was assumed that every day 400 cars having the parts listed on the bill of materials would be manufactured in a mixed-model assembly line. The total required quantities of the 48 parts, which can be completed by applying daily production volume to the bill of materials, are shown in Figure A2.2. It is further assumed that each part's appearance ratio must be regulated under the constraints of the continuation and interval controls as seen in Figure A2.3.

Part number	1	8	15	22	29	36	43
Required quantity	17	114	201	17	179	24	335
Part number	2	9	16	23	30	37	44
Required quantity	302	65	24	1	363	66	58
Part number	3	10	17	24	31	38	45
Required quantity	7	119	95	83	37	25	7
Part number	4	11	18	25	32	39	46
Required quantity	70	363	10	23	221	57	221
Part number	5	12	19	26	33	40	47
Required quantity	4	179	92	103	142	318	131
Part number	6	13	20	27	34	41	48
Required quantity	129	352	146	191	37	225	48
Part number	7	14	21	28	35	42	
Required quantity	92	48	15	221	370	175	

Figure A2.2. Required quantity of each part.

Priority	Part number	Control condition	Quality of controlled cars
1	37	Not less than 5-car interval	66 units
2	6	Not less than 2-car interval	129 units
3	2	Up to 5 successive cars	302 units
4	15	Up to 2 successive cars	201 units
5	41	Up to 3 successive cars	225 units

Figure A2.3. Each part's control condition and the quantity of cars to be controlled.

Experiment 1: Appearance Ratio Control by the Goal Chasing Method
In the first experiment, the goal chasing method without constraints and weighting will be tested. Only the appearance ratio of each part is considered. The component parts will be withdrawn from processes as they are needed, but not necessarily as they are consumed. To facilitate fluctuations in withdrawal of component parts, safety inventories are stored at the preceding process. However, since a sequence schedule that requires big safety inventories may cause overproduction and excessive inventories (secondary and tertiary wastes), these inventories must be kept at a minimum. Stated a different way, fluctuation in withdrawal quantity must be controlled through the sequence schedule so that even a small quantity of safety inventories can respond to the fluctuation.

To check the withdrawal quantity fluctuation in this experiment, the quantity consumed of each component part was examined for the first 25 cars introduced to the line. Figure A2.4 is a result of this experiment.

It is supposed that the final assembly line withdraws parts regularly because each hour, 25 units of cars will be assembled. The number of units is derived by dividing 400 cars, which is the total production volume of a day, by 16 operating hours (two shifts).

Referring to the output figures in Figure A2.4, the variance in the number of times each part appears can be regarded as very small; this means that the withdrawal quantity from a preceding process is almost constant. Next, to evaluate the degree of variance, the width of deviations concept (range) was used. This is the difference between the largest and the smallest number of appearance. Concerning part 2, the largest number is 20 while the smallest is 18, thus the width of deviations is 2 (= 20 − 18). For the distribution of this width, see Figure A2.5.

Appearance results in each hour																Average	Variance
Part 1	1	1	1	1	1	1	2	0	1	2	1	1	1	1	1	1	1.06	0.18
Part 2	19	19	18	19	19	18	20	19	19	19	18	20	18	20	18	19	18.88	0.48
Part 3	0	1	0	1	0	1	0	1	0	0	1	0	1	0	0	1	0.44	0.25
Part 4	5	3	6	4	4	5	3	5	4	4	5	4	5	4	5	4	4.38	0.61
Part 5	0	1	0	0	1	0	0	0	1	0	0	0	0	0	1	0	0.25	0.19
Part 6	8	8	8	8	8	9	8	8	7	9	8	8	8	8	8	8	8.06	0.18
Part 7	6	6	5	6	6	5	6	6	6	5	6	6	6	5	6	6	5.75	0.19
Part 8	7	7	7	7	7	7	7	7	8	7	7	7	7	8	7	7	7.12	0.11
Part 9	4	4	5	4	4	4	4	4	4	4	4	4	4	4	4	4	4.06	0.06
Part 10	7	8	7	7	7	9	8	6	7	8	8	7	8	7	7	8	7.44	0.50
Part 11	23	23	22	23	22	23	23	23	22	23	23	22	23	23	22	23	22.69	0.21
Part 12	11	11	12	11	10	12	11	11	12	10	13	10	12	10	11	12	11.19	0.78
Part 13	22	22	22	22	22	22	22	23	21	22	22	22	22	22	22	22	22.00	0.12
Part 14	3	3	3	3	3	3	2	4	3	3	3	3	3	3	3	3	3.00	0.12
Part 15	13	12	13	12	12	13	13	12	13	12	13	13	12	12	13	13	12.56	0.25
Part 16	1	2	1	2	1	2	2	1	1	2	2	1	2	1	1	2	1.50	0.25
Part 17	6	6	6	5	6	7	6	5	6	6	6	6	6	6	6	6	5.94	0.18
Part 18	1	0	1	1	1	0	0	2	0	1	0	1	0	1	1	0	0.62	0.36
Part 19	6	6	5	6	6	5	6	6	6	5	6	6	6	5	6	6	5.75	0.19
Part 20	9	10	9	9	9	9	9	9	10	9	9	8	9	10	9	9	9.12	0.23
Part 21	1	0	2	1	1	1	0	1	1	1	0	2	1	1	1	1	0.94	0.31
Part 22	1	1	1	1	1	1	2	0	1	1	2	1	1	1	1	1	1.06	0.18
Part 23	0	0	0	0	0	0	0	1	0	0	0	0	0	0	0	0	0.06	0.06
Part 24	6	5	5	5	5	6	6	5	5	5	5	5	5	6	5	5	5.19	0.15
Part 25	1	1	2	2	1	2	1	1	2	1	2	2	1	1	1	2	1.44	0.25
Part 26	6	7	6	6	7	6	7	6	7	7	5	6	8	6	7	6	6.44	0.50
Part 27	12	12	12	12	12	12	12	12	11	12	13	12	11	12	12	12	11.94	0.18
Part 28	14	14	13	14	14	14	14	14	13	14	14	14	14	13	14	14	13.81	0.15
Part 29	11	11	12	11	11	11	11	11	12	11	11	11	11	12	11	11	11.19	0.15
Part 30	23	23	22	23	22	23	23	23	22	23	23	22	23	23	22	23	22.69	0.21
Part 31	2	2	3	2	3	2	2	2	3	2	2	3	2	2	3	2	2.31	0.21
Part 32	14	14	13	14	14	14	14	14	13	14	14	14	14	13	14	14	13.81	0.15
Part 33	9	9	9	9	8	9	9	9	9	9	9	8	9	10	8	9	8.88	0.23
Part 34	2	2	3	2	3	2	2	2	3	2	2	3	2	2	3	2	2.31	0.21
Part 35	23	23	23	23	24	22	24	23	23	23	24	23	23	23	23	23	23.12	0.23
Part 36	1	2	2	1	1	3	0	2	2	1	1	2	1	2	2	1	1.50	0.50
Part 37	4	4	4	4	4	5	4	4	4	4	4	4	5	4	4	4	4.12	0.11
Part 38	2	1	2	1	2	2	1	1	2	1	2	2	2	1	2	1	1.56	0.25
Part 39	3	4	4	3	4	3	4	4	3	4	3	4	3	4	3	4	3..56	0.25
Part 40	20	20	19	21	19	20	20	20	20	20	20	19	20	20	20	20	19.88	0.23
Part 41	14	14	14	14	14	14	14	15	14	13	15	14	14	14	13	15	14.06	0.31
Part 42	11	11	11	11	11	11	11	10	11	12	10	11	11	11	12	10	10.94	0.31
Part 43	21	21	20	21	21	21	21	21	21	21	21	21	21	21	21	21	20.94	0.06
Part 44	3	4	4	4	4	3	4	3	4	4	3	4	3	4	3	4	3.62	0.23
Part 45	1	0	1	0	0	1	0	1	0	0	1	0	1	0	1	0	0.44	0.25
Part 46	14	14	13	14	14	14	14	14	13	14	14	14	14	13	14	14	13.81	0.15
Part 47	8	8	9	8	8	8	9	7	9	8	8	8	8	9	8	8	8.19	0.28
Part 48	3	3	3	3	3	3	2	4	3	3	3	3	3	3	3	3	3.00	0.12

Figure A2.4. Results of experiment without any constraint and weighting.

(Largest appeared number) - (Least appeared number)	Number of part varieties
0	0
1	25
2	18
3	5

Figure A2.5. Width of deviation (range).

Note that Figure A2.5 is used to determine whether or not the appearance ratio goal was attained.

Here, a part whose width of deviation is zero can be regarded as having no deviation. If the total required quantity per day of a certain part is a multiple of 16 and equals the amount required each hour, then its width of deviation results in zero. On the other hand, if the total amount required of a part per day is not a multiple of 16, then each hour's withdrawal quantity will never be leveled equally and the minimum width of deviation for this part will be one.

Further analysis of Figure A2.4 reveals that the most frequent width of deviation in withdrawal quantity of parts from a preceding process is one. Therefore, production smoothing was accomplished to a very satisfactory degree and the goal chasing method realized the goal of a constant appearance ratio of each component part.

Experiment 2: Continuation and Interval Controls

Figure A2.6 shows the state of appearance of those component parts subject to the rules of continuation of interval controls. The symbol * means that this part is used by a selected car at this order position, while a period symbol (.) means it is not. For instance, the fifth car is the first one that uses part 37.

According to this figure, the parts to be restricted obviously did not meet the conditions of continuation and interval controls mentioned in Figure A2.3. For example, part 37 was used successively once, although according to Figure A2.3 it should be used with not less than a five-car interval. Part 37 was also used once by a two-car interval, four times by a three-car interval, and fourteen times by a four-car interval. Note that Figure A2.6 is used to check if the conditions of continuation and interval controls are satisfactory.

The goal chasing method was applied under the constraint of continuation and interval controls. The results of this experiment are shown in Figure A2.7.

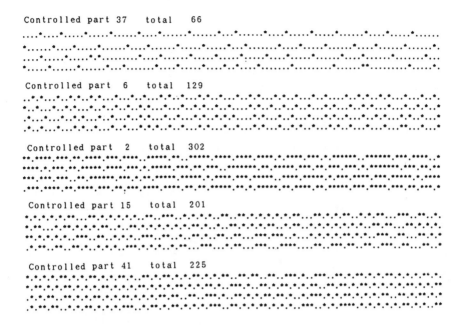

Figure A2.6. Appearance results under no additional constraints.

As in the first experiment, these results can be examined by using the value of [largest appeared number of cars] - [least appeared number of cars] (see Figure A2.8). Upon examination, it would be reasonable to say that in this experiment, the width of deviation in quantity of appearances is still small enough and at a satisfactory value.

Experiment 3: Appearance Ratio Check and Weight Control

The parts under continuation and interval controls completely satisfied the constraints in Figure A2.9, although parts 37 and 6 did not meet the interval conditions at the end of their sequences. In order for parts 37 and 6 to completely satisfy these conditions, their appearance was restricted by using the weighting approach: the values Y_{jk} for parts 37 and 6 were multiplied by 1.5 and 1.3, respectively.

Control conditions:

Rank 1 ====>	Part 37	Continuation = 0	Interval = 5
Rank 2 ====>	Part 6	Continuation = 0	Interval = 2
Rank 3 ====>	Part 2	Continuation = 5	Interval = 0
Rank 4 ====>	Part 15	Continuation = 2	Interval = 0
Rank 5 ====>	Part 41	Continuation = 3	Interval = 0

Appearance results in each hour																	Average	Variance
Part 1	1	1	1	1	1	1	1	1	2	0	1	2	0	1	1	2	1.06	0.31
Part 2	19	19	19	19	18	19	19	19	19	19	18	19	20	18	19	19	18.88	0.23
Part 3	0	1	0	1	0	0	1	1	0	1	0	0	1	1	0	0	0.44	0.25
Part 4	5	3	5	4	5	5	4	4	4	5	5	4	4	4	5	4	4.38	0.36
Part 5	0	1	0	0	1	0	0	0	0	0	1	0	0	1	0	0	0.25	0.19
Part 6	8	8	8	7	9	8	8	8	8	8	8	8	8	8	8	9	8.06	0.18
Part 7	6	6	6	6	5	6	6	5	6	6	6	6	5	6	7	4	5.75	0.44
Part 8	7	7	6	8	7	7	7	7	8	7	7	7	8	7	6	8	7.12	0.36
Part 9	4	4	5	4	4	4	4	4	4	4	4	4	4	4	4	4	4.06	0.06
Part 10	7	8	7	7	8	7	8	7	8	7	7	8	7	8	7	8	7.44	0.25
Part 11	23	23	22	23	22	23	23	23	22	23	22	23	23	23	23	22	22.69	0.21
Part 12	12	11	11	10	12	11	11	11	12	11	11	11	11	11	12	11	11.19	0.28
Part 13	22	22	22	22	22	22	22	22	22	22	22	22	22	22	22	22	22.00	0.00
Part 14	3	3	3	3	3	3	3	3	3	3	3	3	3	3	3	3	3.00	0.00
Part 15	13	13	12	12	13	12	13	13	12	13	12	13	13	12	12	13	12.56	0.25
Part 16	1	2	1	2	1	1	2	2	2	1	1	2	1	2	1	2	1.50	0.25
Part 17	6	6	6	5	7	6	6	5	6	6	6	6	6	6	6	6	5.94	0.18
Part 18	1	0	1	0	1	1	0	1	0	1	1	0	1	0	1	1	0.62	0.36
Part 19	6	6	6	6	5	6	6	5	6	6	6	6	5	6	7	4	5.75	0.44
Part 20	9	10	8	10	9	9	9	10	8	9	9	9	10	10	8	9	9.12	0.48
Part 21	1	0	2	1	1	1	0	1	1	1	1	1	1	1	1	1	0.94	0.18
Part 22	1	1	1	1	1	1	1	1	2	1	1	1	1	0	1	2	1.06	0.18
Part 23	0	0	0	0	0	0	1	0	0	0	0	0	0	0	0	0	0.06	0.06
Part 24	5	5	6	5	5	5	5	6	5	5	5	5	5	5	6	5	5.19	0.15
Part 25	1	1	3	1	1	2	1	1	2	1	2	1	1	1	1	2	1.44	0.37
Part 26	6	7	5	8	6	6	7	6	6	7	6	7	7	7	5	7	6.44	0.62
Part 27	13	12	11	11	13	12	12	12	12	12	12	11	12	12	13	11	11.94	0.43
Part 28	14	14	14	13	14	14	14	13	14	14	14	14	13	14	15	13	13.81	0.28
Part 29	11	11	11	12	11	11	11	12	11	11	11	11	12	11	10	12	11.19	0.28
Part 30	23	23	22	23	22	23	23	23	22	23	22	23	23	23	23	22	22.69	0.21
Part 31	2	2	3	2	3	2	2	2	3	2	3	2	2	2	2	3	2.31	0.21
Part 32	14	14	14	13	14	14	14	13	14	14	14	14	13	14	15	13	13.81	0.28
Part 33	9	9	8	10	8	9	9	10	8	9	8	9	10	9	8	9	8.88	0.48
Part 34	2	2	3	2	3	2	2	3	2	3	2	2	2	2	1	3	2.31	0.21
Part 35	23	23	23	23	24	23	23	23	23	23	23	23	24	23	23	23	23.12	0.11
Part 36	1	2	2	1	1	2	1	2	1	2	1	2	1	2	1	2	1.50	0.25
Part 37	4	4	4	4	4	4	4	5	3	4	4	4	4	5	4	5	4.12	0.23
Part 38	1	2	2	1	2	2	1	2	1	2	1	2	1	2	2	1	1.56	0.25
Part 39	4	3	4	3	4	3	4	3	4	3	4	4	3	3	4	4	3.56	0.25
Part 40	20	20	19	21	19	20	20	20	20	20	20	19	21	20	19	20	19.88	0.36
Part 41	14	14	14	14	14	14	15	14	13	15	13	15	14	14	15	13	14.06	0.43
Part 42	11	11	11	11	11	11	10	11	12	10	12	10	11	11	10	12	10.94	0.43
Part 43	21	21	20	21	21	21	21	21	21	21	21	21	21	21	21	21	20.94	0.06
Part 44	3	4	4	4	4	3	4	3	3	4	4	3	4	3	4	4	3.62	0.23
Part 45	1	0	1	0	0	0	1	0	1	1	0	0	1	0	1	0	0.44	0.25
Part 46	14	14	14	13	14	14	14	13	14	14	14	14	13	14	15	13	13.81	0.28
Part 47	8	8	8	9	8	8	8	9	8	8	8	8	9	8	7	9	8.19	0.28
Part 48	3	3	3	3	3	3	3	3	3	3	3	3	3	3	3	3	3.00	0.00

Figure A2.7. Results under continuation and interval control.

(Largest appeared number) - (Least appeared number)	Number of part varieties
0	3
1	21
2	23
3	1

Figure A2.8. Width of deviation.

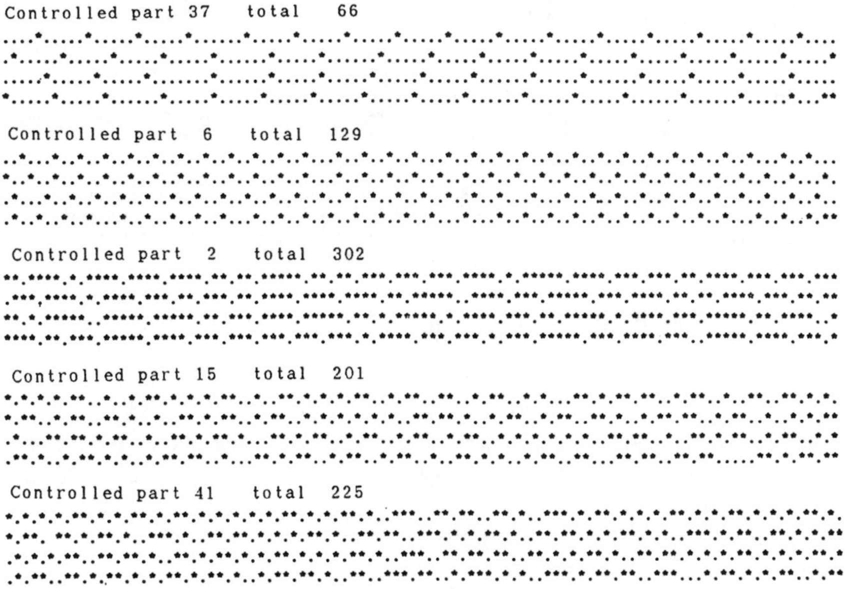

```
Controlled part 37   total   66
....•.....•.....•..•.....•.....•.....•.....•.....•.....•.....•.....•.....•.....•....
.•.....•.....•.....•.....•.....•.....•.....•.....•.....•.....•.....•.....•.....•.....•
....•.....•.....•.....•.....•.....•.....•.....•.....•.....•.....•.....•.....•.....•
•.....•.....•.....•.....•.....•.....•.....•.....•.....•.....•.....•.....•.....•..••

Controlled part  6   total   129
..•...•..•.•..•.•..•.•..•.•..•.•..•.•...•.•..•.•..•.•..•.•..•.•..•.•..•.•...•.•..
•.•..•.•..•.•..•.•..•.•..•.•..•.•..•.•..•.•..•.•..•.•..•.•..•.•..•.•..•.•..•.•.
.•.•..•.•..•.•..•.•..•.•..•.•..•.•..•.•..•.•..•.•..•.•..•.•..•.•..•.•..•.•.
.•.•..•.•..•.•..•.•..•.•..•.•..•.•..•.•..•.•..•.•..•.•..•.•..•.•..•.•..•.•..••

Controlled part  2   total   302
••.•••••.•.••••.••••.••••.••.••.•••••.••.••.•••.•••.•••.••••.•.•••••.••••.•••.•••.••.•••.•••
.•••.••••.•.••••.•••.••.•••.••.••••.••••.••••.••.•••••..•••.•••.•••••.•••.••••.••.••.•••••.•••.••.••
••.•.••••••..••••.••••.••.•••.•••.•••.••.•.••••••.•.••••.•••.••.•••••••.•.••••.•••.••••••.••.••••..•
••••.••.•••.•••••.••••.•••.•••.••.•.••••.•••.••.•.•••.•••••.•••.••••.••..••••.•••••.•••.•

Controlled part 15   total   201
•.•.•.••...•.•.•••..•.•••..•.•.•.••.•.•.•••..•.••..•.•.••.•.•.••...••.•.•.••.•.
•.••...•.••..••.•.•.••.•••..•.••..•.•.•.•.•.••...•.••..•.•••..••...•.•.••...•.
.•....••.••.••...•.••.••...•.•••.•.•.•.•••.•.••...••.•.•.•.•.•...••.•.•.•.••...
.••.•..••.•.•..••.••...•..•.••.••.•.•.••.••...••.•...••.••...•.••....••.•.••.••

Controlled part 41   total   225
•.•.•.••.•.•.••.•.•.•.•.•.•.••.•.•.••.•..••••..••.••..••.•.••••.•.•.•.•.•.••.•.
•.••...••.•.•••.•...••.•••.•.••.•.••...•••...•.•.••.••...•••.•.•.•.•..•.•.•.•.•
.•.•.•.••...••.••.•.•.•.•.•.•.•.••.•..•••...••.••.••...•.•.•.•.•.••.•.•.••.•.•.•
.•.••...••.•.•••.•.••.•.••.•..•.••.••.•..••.•••.••...•.•.•.•.•.•••.•.•.••...•.••.•.••
```

Figure A2.9. Appearance results under additional constraints.

Figure A2.10 shows that every part has now satisfied the continuation and interval control conditions. However, as shown in Figure A2.11, the deviation in withdrawal quantity under the weight control became somewhat bigger than the deviation under non-weighted control. Even so, the deviation was small enough so that only a small safety inventory was needed to adapt to the fluctuation. That is, this weight control satisfies the condition of the constant appearance ratio.

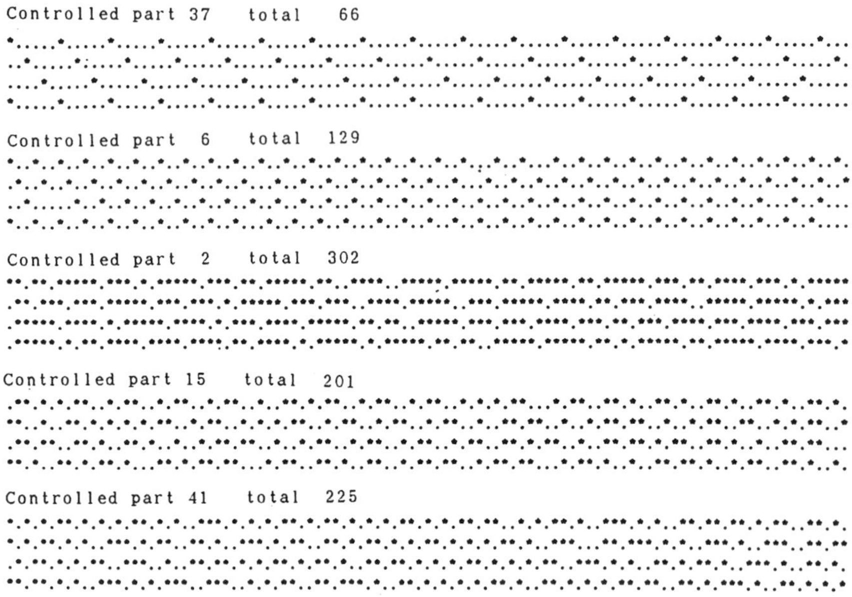

Figure A2.10. Appearance results under weight [1.5, 1.3].

To strictly control part appearances, the weight values 1.5 and 1.3 (determined arbitrarily) were applied to parts 37 and 6 in the example above. What effect will changing the values of weight have? To answer this, two different sets of weighted values, (5, 4) and (1.1, 1.05), will be applied to parts 37 and 6. The width of deviations in the withdrawal quantity in these two cases can be seen in Figures A2.12 and A2.13, respectively.

Compared to the weight (1.5, 1.3), both of these parts increased their frequency in the range where width of deviation was bigger. The results of interval control of these parts can be seen in Figures A2.14 and A2.15. According to these figures, although each part appeared to meet the respective conditions of interval controls, the weights (5, 4) had more of an affect than the weights (1.1, 1.05). In this way, the results of continuation and interval controls are influenced by the values of weight.

(Largest appeared number) - (Least appeared number)	Number of part varieties
0	0
1	24
2	21
3	3

Figure A2.11. Width of deviation.

(Largest appeared number) - (Least appeared number)	Number of part varieties
0	0
1	14
2	27
3	7

Figure A2.12. Width of deviation under weight [5, 4].

(Largest appeared number) - (Least appeared number)	Number of part varieties
0	0
1	11
2	35
3	2

Figure A2.13. Width of deviation under weight [1.1, 1.05].

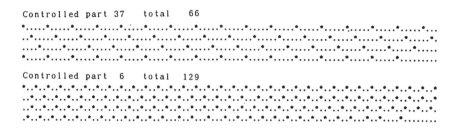

Figure A2.14. Appearance results under weight [5, 4].

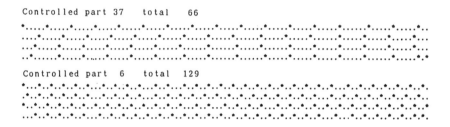

Figure A2.15. Appearance results under weight [1.1, 1.05].

Other sets of weights were tested, and weight values 1.3 and 1.2 were found to work properly under the continuation and interval controls. The variance in withdrawal quantity was also at a lower, more acceptable level. The width of deviation and the results of constraint controls in this case are shown in Figures A2.16 and A2.17, respectively.

CONCLUSION

The goal chasing method is a technique of sequence scheduling that is intended to make the actual appearance ratio of component parts constant. Although it is possible to consider the assembly hour difference of various component parts by the goal chasing method (see Chapter 17), this problem can be considered using continuation and interval controls. Doing so in this experiment resulted in confirmation that the continuation and interval control of each component part is more likely if the width of deviation in withdrawal quantity is kept at a low level. However, when examining the results carefully, unsatisfactory results were seen in terms of continuation and interval control at the ending pattern of the sequence in a day. Weight control was introduced as a corrective measure to the goal chasing method, thereby enabling a more accurate continuation and interval control.

(Largest appeared number) - (Least appeared number)	Number of part varieties
0	0
1	24
2	24
3	0

Figure A2.16. Width of deviation under weight [1.3, 1.2].

```
Controlled part 37    total    66
•.....•.....•.....•.....•.....•.....•.....•..:.•.....•.....•....,•.....•.....•.....•.....•.....•.....•....•...
..•.....•.....•.....•.....•.....•.....•.....•.....•.....•.....•.....•.....•.....•.....•.....•.....•.....•.....•.
....•.....•.....•.....•.....•.....•.....•.....•.....•.....•.....•.....•.....•.....•.....•.....•.....•.....•.....
•.....•.....•.....•.....•.....•.....•.....•.....•.....•.....•.....•.....•.....•.....•.....•.....•.....•.....•...

Controlled part  6    total   129
•.•..•..•..•..•..•..•..•.•..•..•..•..•..•.•..•..•..•..•..•.•..•..•..•..•..•.•..•..•..•..•.•.
.•..•..•..•...•..•..•..•..•..•..•..•..•..•..•..•..•..•..•..•..•..•..•..•..•..•..•..•..•..•..•
..•.•..•.•..•..•..•..•..•.•..•..•..•..•..•..•..•..•..•..•..•..•..•..•..•..•..•..•..•..•..•..•..•
..•..•..•..•..•..•..•..•..•..•..•..•..•..•..•..•..•..•..•..•..•..•..•..•..•..•..•..•..•..•..•.•
```

Figure A2.17. Appearance results under weight [1.3, 1.2].

Regarding the values of weight, too heavy a weight led to an excessively strict control while too light a weight made the controls too loose. Thus, both types of weights caused larger widths of deviation in withdrawal quantity. Since the appearance results and the deviation in withdrawal quantity both change depending on the values of weight, the best or most satisfactory values of weight must be the ones that make the deviation as small as possible.

This experiment, which decided the values of weight and determined the sequence schedule that makes the deviation in withdrawn quantity as small as possible, was effective because the calculation time taken in one sequencing operation of the experiment (for 400 car units) was only about three or four minutes. Further research for developing a systematic method for deciding the values of weight is needed.

Appendix 3
Quantitative Analysis of Stocks in a JIT Multistage Production System Using the Constant Order Cycle Withdrawal Method

INTRODUCTION

In the Just-in-time (JIT) system a certain amount of inventory is held at each stage. The number of Kanban is determined by estimating this amount of inventory. If overestimated, the benefit of inventory reduction via JIT is lost. On the other hand, if the number of Kanban is underestimated, the subsequent process cannot fulfill the purpose of JIT production. Therefore, setting the inventory level is the most important decision option in the JIT system. In the multistage production system, variables affecting required inventory in any stage (process) are demand and lead time for output. Given the fluctuation in demand for the output of the first stage and fluctuation in lead time in each stage, the amount of stock required for the purpose of JIT production will be quantitatively investigated in this appendix. Certain production prerequisites affect the amount of stock will also be analyzed.

HYPOTHETICAL PRODUCTION SYSTEM

For this study, a hypothetical JIT production system will be used, which consists of a single model multistage production system (Figure 1). The most completed processing is at stage one. Two stockpoints are considered before (store I_i) and after (store B_i) each stage. Kanbans determine the order for producing parts in each stage and for transporting parts from one stage to another. The method of constant cycle withdrawal is used. The flow of Kanbans and materials are shown in Figure 1 by dashed and solid lines respectively. Cycle time is the time interval between two orders. It is also called Kanban cycle and is regarded as a review period. All time concepts are measured in terms of the multiple of review period.

It is assumed that Kanban transportation time, which is the time interval between the moment Kanbans are collected and the moment production begins, is zero. Notice that production lead time is shown in Figure A3.1 by (_ _ _ _ _ _) line.

Appendix 3 is authored by Y. Monden, Institute of Socio-Economic Planning, University of Tsukuba, Japan, and M. Aghdassi, School of Engineering, Tarbiat Modarres University, Tehran, Iran.

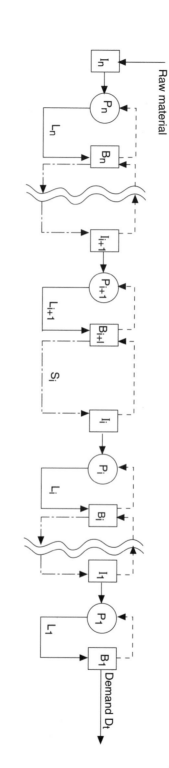

Figure A3.1. Hypothetical production system.

Mathematical Model of the Hypothetical Production System
The following notations are used in a mathematical model.

t :　review period
L_i :　production lead time of process i in a multiple of the review period
S_i :　transportation lead time between store B_{i+1} and store I_i in a multiple of the
　　review period
$I_{i,t}$:　inventory level of store I_i at the end of $t'th$ period
$B_{i,t}$:　inventory level of store B_i at the end of $t'th$ period
$I_{i,o}$:　initial inventory of store I_i
$B_{i,o}$:　initial inventory of store B_i
$q_{i,t}$:　production quantity of process P_i where production starts at the beginning of
　　the $t'th$ period

The assumption is made that enough inventory exists in each store so that
shortages never occur. Considering this assumption, the equation for the on-hand
inventory in each store is determined. Figure A3. 2 shows the status of stores B_i,
I_i and B_{i+1} at the $t'th$ period. For example, Figure A3.2(b) indicates that during the
$t'th$ period the quantity $q_{i,t}$ is withdrawn from store I_i and the quantity q_{t-s_i-1}
which was ordered at the beginning of period $t-S_i$ is received at the beginning of
the $t'th$ period. Thus, inventory on hand at the beginning of $t'th$ period is,

$$I_{i,t} = I_{i,t-1} + q_{i,t-S_i-1} - q_{i,t} \qquad (1)$$

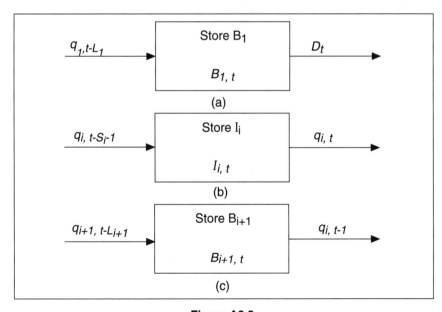

Figure A3.2.

By the same discussion, the on-hand inventory level for store B_1 and B_i are,

$$B_{1,t} = B_{1,t-1} + q_{1,t-L_1} - D_t \tag{2}$$

$$B_{i+1,t} = B_{i+1,t-1} + q_{i+1,t-L_{i+1}} - q_{i,t-1} \tag{3}$$

The order quantity for store B_1 will be rounded up by the pallet size, so we have,

$$q_{1,t} = D_t + d_t \quad \text{or} \quad q_{1,t-L_1} = D_{t-L_1} + d_{t-L_1} \tag{4}$$

where, d_t is a fractional part of $q_{1,t}$ when D_t is rounded up by pallet size M. It is a random variable ($0 \le d_t \le M\text{-}1$) with mean $\overline{d}$ and σ_d^2.

The consumption quantity of a subsequent process during the $t'th$ period is the order quantity received by the preceding process at the beginning of the $t+1'th$ period (i.e., information lead time between two processes is one period). Thus we have,

$$q_{i,t-1} = q_{i+1,t} \tag{5}$$

Substituting equation (4) into (2) and (5) into (3), we obtain,

$$B_{1,t} = B_{1,t-1} + D_{t-L_i} + d_{t-L_i} - D_t \tag{6}$$

$$B_{i+1,t} = B_{i+1,t-1} + q_{i+1,t-L_{i+1}} - q_{i+1,t} \tag{7}$$

Solving equation (1), (6), and (7) we have,

$$B_{1,t} = B_{1,o} - \sum_{j=t-L_1+1}^{t} D_j - \sum_{j=1}^{t-L_1} d_j \tag{8}$$

$$B_{i+1,t} = B_{i+1,o} - \sum_{j=t-L_{i+1}+1}^{t} q_{i+1,j} \tag{9}$$

$$I_{i,t} = I_{i,o} - \sum_{j=t-S_i}^{t} q_j \tag{10}$$

Equations (5), (8), (9), and (10) show the production quantity and the level of on-hand inventory for each stage.

Now let us investigate the fluctuation pattern of inventory in store B_i and then determine the largest amount of minimum required inventory in that store. Equation (9) can be rewritten for the inventory level of store B_i as follows:

$$B_{i,t} = B_{i,o} \sum_{j=t-L_i}^{t} q_{i,j} \tag{11}$$

It is easy to show that $q_{i,j}$ (for all i, j), when pallet size (M) is small, are random variables with the same distribution function as the demand (D). Therefore, regarding equation (11), B_i is also normally distributed with the following mean and variance.

$$\overline{B}_i = \left(B_{i,o} - L_i \overline{q} \right) \quad \text{and} \quad \sigma_{B_i} = \sqrt{L_i} \sigma_{L_i} \tag{12}$$

Enough parts must be in the store of the preceding process so that the subsequent process can withdraw its necessary parts. Therefore, the following condition should be satisfied.

$$B_{i,t} \geq 0 \tag{13}$$

If we consider a certain confidence probability, α, for the above condition, we have,

$$\text{Prob } (B_{i,t} \geq 0) = \alpha \tag{14}$$

As equation (12) shows, the mean of $B_{i,t}$ depends on the initial inventory (i.e., $B_{i,0}$). Therefore, we can determine that $B_{i,0}$ satisfied the condition in equation (14). However, this approach only gives an approximate solution to the problem of minimum required inventory because the logic corresponding to equation (12) will hold when no backorders occur. If, for example, backorders occur with 5% probability we can trust this equation with 95% probability rather than 100%. Later in this appendix, a simulation approach will be used to determine the required inventory in a backorder situation.

Suppose the distribution function of $B_{i,t}$ is f_B (b), then the problem is to determine B_i satisfying the following condition.

$$\int_0^\infty f_B(b)db = \alpha$$

it follows that,

$$\int_{\frac{-\overline{B}_i}{\sigma_{B_i}}}^\infty f_z(z)dz = \alpha$$

where, f_z (z) is a standard normal density function.

Thus, we can find Z for a given value of α where,

$$\frac{-\overline{B}_i}{\sigma_{B_i}} = Z \tag{15}$$

Substituting $\overline{B}_i$ and δ_{Bi} from equation (12) into (15), we have,

$$B_{i,o} = L_i\overline{q} - Z\sqrt{L_i\sigma_q} \tag{16}$$

Using equation (16), the initial inventory in store B_i. In this equation, Z can be found for a given value of α (keeping in mind that Z has a negative value), L_i is the production lead time of process i, $\overline{q}$ and σ_q are the mean and the standard deviation of production quantity.

Safety Stock, Reducing Lead Time and Production Smoothing
Equation (16) will now be interpreted to quantitatively investigate safety stock, reducing the lead time and production smoothing. The second part of equation (16) is safety stock needed for responding to fluctuations in demand. But the policy of a JIT system is not to respond to all fluctuations by keeping such amounts of stock. Flexibility in the work force changes loading levels by using overtime or improving labor efficiency. However, changed loading levels correspond to ±10% in demand fluctuations.

Equation (16) also shows the importance of shortening the lead time to eliminate unnecessary inventory which is the ultimate goal of a JIT system.

The significance of production smoothing (leveling) for the purpose of the JIT production is also shown by equation (16). If we suppose D_t is the withdrawal quantity of the final assembly line, this equation shows that if fluctuation consumption (i.e., σ_q) is small, inventory reduction can be better attained.

Analysis of the JIT System When Uncertainty in Demand and Lead Time Exist

This section investigates the required stock, safety stock, and machine maintenance when demand and lead time uncertainty exist. Uncertainty in demand may exist due to various factors such as worker deficiency, machine trouble, defective products, etc.

A manufacturing environment with a certain lead time is considered a condition for employing the JIT system. Therefore, analyzing the effects of fluctuating lead time on the performance of the JIT system has many benefits. If we suppose that lead time is a random variable and fluctuates independently of demand, then equations (10) and (11) can be rewritten as follows,

$$B_{i,t} = B_{i,o} - \sum_{j \in T_{it}(\omega)} q_{i,j} \tag{17}$$

$$I_{i,t} = I_{i,o} - \sum_{j \in X_{it}(\omega)} q_{i,j} \tag{18}$$

where,

$$T_{it}(\omega) = \left\{ j \,\middle|\, t - L_{it}(\omega) + 1 \le j \le t \right\}$$

$$X_{it}(\omega) = \left\{ j \,\middle|\, t - S_{it}(\omega) \le j \le t \right\}$$

L_{it} and S_{it} = production lead time in process i and transportation time between store B_{I+1} and store I_p respectively. They are random variables with means L_i and S_i and variances $\sigma_{L_i}^2$ and $\sigma_{S_i}^2$, respectively.

Taking mean and variance, from equation (17) and (18), the following are obtained:

$$\overline{B}_i = B_{i,o} - \overline{L}_i \overline{q} \tag{19}$$

$$\sigma_{B_i}^2 = \overline{L}_i \sigma_q^2 + \overline{q}^2 \sigma_{L_i}^2 \tag{20}$$

$$\overline{I}_i = I_{i,o} - \left(\overline{S}_i + 1\right)\overline{q} \tag{21}$$

$$\sigma_{I_i}^2 = \left(\overline{S}_i + 1\right)\sigma_q^2 + \overline{q}^2 \sigma_{S_i}^2 \tag{22}$$

The above equations show the mean and variance of the on-hand inventory. Now the minimum required inventory is determined by substituting these equations into equation (15). Thus,

$$B_{i,0} = \overline{L}_i \overline{q} - Z\sqrt{\overline{L}_i \sigma_q^2 + \overline{q}^2 \sigma_{L_i}^2} \tag{23}$$

The second part of equation (23) shows that safety stock responds to demand and lead time fluctuations. This part is denoted by $B_{\gamma_1 \gamma_2}$ thus,

$$B_{\gamma_1 \gamma_2} = -Z\sqrt{\overline{L}_i \sigma_q^2 + \overline{q}^2 \sigma_{L_i}^2}$$

If we assume the production quantity (i.e., demand) is deterministic (i.e., $\sigma_q^2 = 0$), the safety stock respond to uncertainty in the lead time,

$$B_{\gamma_2} = -Z\overline{q}\,\sigma_{L_i} \tag{24}$$

Machine Maintenance Ability and Corresponding Safety Stock in JIT Systems

The possibility of trouble should be minimized. But as long as this possibility exists, the safety stock should be maintained. If trouble occurs, production lead time increases. On the other hand, the probability of trouble occurrence reflects machine maintenance ability. Thus, the problem of distributing lead time might be considered equivalent to dealing with machine maintenance problems.

Many patterns of fluctuation exist in the lead time. If we assume that minor troubles have no effect on lead time, serious troubles in the machine or in the entire line can be investigated by the following simple, but important pattern.

$$P_L(1) = Prob(L = 1) = \begin{cases} \lambda & 1 = L_2 \\ 1 - \lambda & 1 = L_1 \\ 0 & otherwise \end{cases} \quad (25)$$

where, $\lambda, L_1,$ and L_2 are, respectively, probability of trouble occurrence, production lead time when there is no trouble, and production lead time when some troubles occur.

If we determine the variance of lead time (i.e., $\lambda(1-\lambda)(L_2 - L_1)^2$) and substitute it into equation (24), we have,

$$B_{\lambda_2} = -Z\overline{q}(L_2 - L_1)\sqrt{\lambda(1-\lambda)} \quad (26)$$

The above equation shows the impact of maintenance ability on the safety stock. This is also depicted in Figure A3.3 when $L_1 = 1, L_2 = 2, Z = -2.33$ (i.e., 99%), and $\overline{q} = 100$.

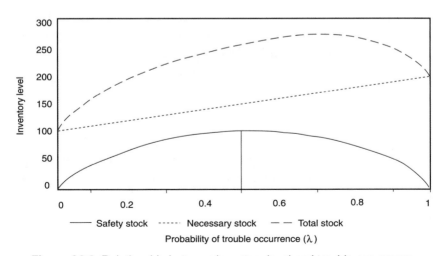

Figure A3.3. Relationship between inventory level and trouble occurrence.

Figure A3.3 indicates that if maintenance ability decrease (i.e., λ increases), safety stock increases. But there is an upper limit for the safety stock responding to any level of maintenance ability.

ANALYSIS OF THE HYPOTHETICAL SYSTEM USING THE SIMULATION APPROACH

In the previous section, required stock was determined using an analytical approach which gave an approximate solution because backorders were not assumed to occur. However, under more realistic assumptions, backorders will be assumed to occur, and then the problem of required stock will be analyzed using a simulation model.

Now let us add the following notations to those that were previously defined.

$\hat{O}_{i,t}=$ The quantity of the order received by the process P_i at the beginning of the $t'th$ period.

$O_{i,t}=$ The amount of actual order whose production should start at the beginning of period t in the quantity of the order received by the process Pi at the beginning of the $t'th$ period.

$\hat{R}_{i,t}=$ The quantity of orders received by the store B_i at the beginning of the $t'th$ period.

$R_{i,t}=$ The amount of actual orders whose transportation should start at period t from the store B_i. This is not necessarily equal to the quantity of the order received by the store B_i at the beginning of the $t'th$ period.

$W_{i,t}=$ The actual withdrawal quantity from store B_j whose withdrawal starts at the beginning of $t'th$ period.

The received order quantity and the production quantity at period t are not necessarily equal because of the possibility of a shortage. Thus, when available stock is less than the order received, the order will have to be filled in the future, but the quantity of the parts order released to the preceding stage will not reflect the stock shortage.

Simulation Model
First, the basic relationship among order quantities, production quantities, and withdrawal quantities will be determined in each stage. Then, the behavior of the system can be analyzed using those basic relationships in a simulation model.

The order quantity in each stage is the summation of the order received at period t and the backorder (if any) from the previous period. The production quantity is equal to the minimum number between order quantity and available stock. Thus,

$$O_{i,t} = \left(O_{i,t-1} - q_{i,t-1}\right) + \hat{O}_{i,t} \tag{32}$$

$$q_{i,t} = Min\left\{O_{i,t}, I_{i,t-1} + W_{i+1,t-S_i}\right\} \tag{33}$$

Store B_{i+1} (see Figure A3.1) can also be regarded as a kind of operating process whose operation is to supply parts to store I_i. Therefore, by the same reasoning as above we have,

$$R_{i+1,t} + \left(R_{i+1,t-1} - W_{i+1,t-1}\right) + \hat{R}_{i+1,t} \tag{34}$$

$$W_{i+1,t} = Min\left\{R_{i+1,t}, B_{i+1,t-1} + q_{i+1,t-L_{i+1}}\right\} \tag{35}$$

It is also obvious that,

$$\hat{R}_{i+1,t} = \hat{O}_{1,t-1} \tag{36}$$

In the simulation developed below, the system's functional relationships are explained by equation (32) through (36).

SLAM II simulation software is used as a modeling tool. SLAM II allows the modeler to select alternative modeling orientations; however, the process orientation, which in SLAM employs a network structure comprised of specialized symbols called nodes and branches, is used in this case. These symbols are model elements in a process, such as queue, server, and decision points. The modeling task consists of combining these symbols into a network model which pictorially represents a system of interest. The entities in the system flow through the network model and the network is transcribed by the modeler into an equivalent statement model for input into the SLAM processor.

The network model of the system and its equivalent statement model (computer program), the analysis of validation of the model (including staring and stooping conditions), length of simulation, and the number of replications are available from the authors. The input data including demand distribution for store B_1, initial inventory without safety stock (safety stock is added separately for each experiment), and replenishment lead time are shown in Table A3.1. The simulation model was tested under various operating conditions and was found to replicate the production system operation example. A detailed event trace was used to verify the model.

Table A3.1. Simulation parameters.

Demand for store $B_1 = N \sim (100, 10)$
Initial inventory in store B_1 (i = 1, ..., 5) = 200 units
Initial inventory in store I_i (i = 1, ..., 4)   = 300 units
Initial inventory in store I_5 = 2×10^{10}
Production lead time at process
P_i (i = 1, ..., 5)   = 2 periods
Transportation lead time between
stores B_{i+1} and I_i (i = 1, ..., 4)   = 2 periods

Results of the Simulation Experiments

The objective was to evaluate the required stock needed for JIT production. The first experiment examined the validity of the model by comparing the simulation experiment results with the analytical results discussed in the previous section. If the input data of the simulation model is set so that it satisfies the assumption of the analytical approach, the same results should be obtained. Thus, in the first simulation experiment, the initial inventory (summation of safety stock and initial stock shown in Table A3.1) for each store should be enough to respond to demand fluctuation without any shortages occurring (i.e., 233 units for each store B_i (i=1,...4) and 340 units for each store I_i (i= 1,...4), respectively). Mean and variance of inventory are computed based on 1,000 observations. Table A3.2 shows that expected results were obtained successfully. For example, if in using equation (12), the mean and variance of on-hand inventory in store B_i are

$$\overline{B}_i = B_{i,o} - L_i \overline{q} = 233 - 2 \cdot 100 = 33$$

$$\sigma_{Bi} = \sqrt{L_i} \sigma_q = 2 \cdot 10 = 14.14$$

then the same result is attained by the simulation experiment shown in Table A3.2 which confirms the validity of the analytical formula and supports the proposition that the model replicated the production system example.

The second experiment, will attempt to show that the analytical approach used to determine minimum required stock level is valid even though the assumption associated with that approach is not always satisfied. In developing equation (16), which gives minimum required inventory, the assumption was made that each store had a sufficient inventory. This assumption simplified the problem of determining required inventory by determining a separate inventory level for each stage. But if the assumption is not considered, the wider aspects of the multistage production system must be considered in determining the minimum required stock for each store. This experiment will attempt to show, however, that

Table A3.2. Mean and standard deviation of the on-hand inventory.

Store	Computed from equation (12)		Obtained by the simulation model	
	Mean	Standard deviation	Mean	Standard deviation
B_1	33	14.4	33.46	13.93
B_2	"	"	33.43	13.94
B_3	"	"	33.41	13.98
B_4	"	"	33.42	13.98
B_5	"	"	33.50	13.99
I_1	40	17.3	40.67	17.14
I_2	"	"	40.64	17.18
I_3	"	"	40.63	17.19
I_4	"	"	40.65	17.18

the minimum required stock derived in the previous section under the simplified assumption is a good estimate for actual minimum required stock.

Data input to this experimental simulation is shown in Table A3.1, but the initial stock is changed for different simulation runs. This helps to determine the confidence probability that production interruption for each value of initial stock, i.e., minimum required stock, will not occur.

The result of this experiment shows that, if the high confidence probability is chosen, then the level of required stock derived by equation (16) is almost the same as that determined by the simulation experiment (Figure A3.4). Therefore, equation (16) is also valid for the multistage inventory system when the policy for required stock is based on a high confidence probability (i.e., more than 80% in this case) that a shortage will not occur.

Figure A3.4 shows that the amount of required inventory derived by the simulation model for store B_5 is almost equal to that derived by equation (16) for all values of confidence probability. However, as store B_1 is approached, the simulation approach showed an evident difference in the required inventory,

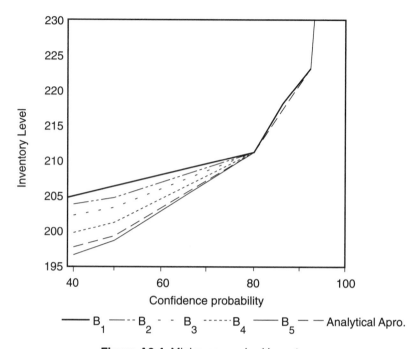

Figure A3.4. Minimum required inventory.

especially for the lower confidence probability. But for the high confidence probability (i.e., 80%), the level of required stock for all stores is likely to be equal. Initial inventory in store I_5 is almost infinite, and therefore, store B_5 is not likely to have a shortage.

Thus, as a conclusion to these experiments, we can offer the following proposition:

> In a JIT multi-stage production system, estimation of the number of Kanban is significant. If the interruption ratio in the production of each stage is kept within 20 percent, the number of Kanban for each stage including that stage's actual demand fluctuation and the production lead time can be estimated.

Appendix 4
Quantitative Analysis of Lot Size in a JIT Production System Using Constant Order Quantity Withdrawal Method

INTRODUCTION

In a Just-in-time (JIT) production system, assembly lines (including subassemblies) are usually loaded by multi-model products or components and run by sequence schedule information to smooth production. Production smoothing is the most important condition for production by Kanban and for minimizing slack time in manpower, equipment, and work-in-process (WIP). Under the Kanban production rule, if the subsequent process withdraws parts in different quantities and at different times, the preceding process should prepare as much inventory, equipment, and manpower as is needed to adapt to the variance of quantities demanded. Therefore, an attempt must be made to minimize the fluctuation in the final assembly line. Loading the assembly line by the smoothed method regarding variety and quantity helps to minimize variance in quantities withdrawn from the preceding process.

The objectives of the study in this appendix are (1) to determine the required level of WIP stock between an assembly line and its preceding process under the condition stated above (i.e., production smoothing), and (2) to analyze the effects of requirements on WIP stock levels.

HYPOTHETICAL PRODUCTION SYSTEM

We consider a JIT production system that uses a *constant order quantity* approach. The predetermined fixed quantity in this system would be ordered when the inventory level recedes to the reorder point. A signal Kanban (triangle Kanban) is used for ordering and it should be tagged to the reorder point. When the pallets of goods are picked up from the store, the signal Kanban should be moved to the reorder instruction post. When it is moved to the dispatching post, operation will

---

Appendix 4 is authored by Y. Monden, Institute of Socio-Economic Planning, University of Tsukuba, Japan, and M. Aghdassi, School of Engineering, Tarbiat Modarres University, Tehran, Iran.

begin. Figure A4.1 shows the hypothetical two-stage production system[1] in which the following procedures are carried out.

1. Multi-model bodies of cars are assembled in the body line.

2. Production begins according to the sequence schedule for different models received at the beginning of each day.

3. The body line uses different parts for different models that are produced by the press line and stored in store *B* in different lots. Each lot has several pallets. Lot size refers to the number of pallets in each lot. A withdrawal Kanban is attached to each pallet, and a signal Kanban is attached to one of the pallets in each lot at the reorder point for reordering.

4. When the body line begins and uses parts from the pallet in store *I*, a worker detaches a withdrawal Kanban, picks up parts from store *B*, and carries it to store *I*. If the worker picks up a pallet with a signal Kanban, an order for that part is made by putting the signal Kanban in the production ordering Kanban post.

5. The press line takes the Kanban from the post and produces the quantity ordered by it. The press line then attaches a withdrawal Kanban to each pallet and a signal Kanban to the related pallet and puts them in store *B*.

MODELING THE HYPOTHETICAL JIT SYSTEM

A model is needed that can quantitatively analyze the impact of the system's parameters (such as production smoothing) on the measurement of the system's effectiveness (i.e., stock level). These system parameters relate to the press and body line.

The production scheduling department uses the daily demand information for seven different models and the goal chasing method[2] to prepare and introduce a sequence schedule to the assembly line. Production in the assembly line takes place according to the sequence schedule by consuming parts for ten different models produced by the preceding stage (i.e., press line).

The system can be analyzed in two steps: in the first step the information for the parts consumed is generated from the demand for multiple products so that a computer program for the goal chasing method under the uncertainty in the

1. In this analysis, we assumed the body line is a subsequent process and the press line is its preceding process. However, similar analysis can be done for other preceding processes such as casting, forging, etc.
2. A method used by some Japanese manufacturers to determine sequence schedule for a mixed-model assembly line.

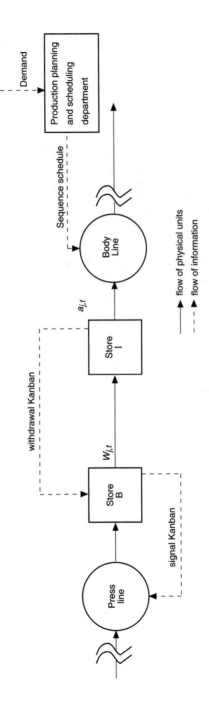

Figure A4.1. Functional operations of the hypothetical production system.

demand can be developed. In the second step, the information generated in the first step is input in the analytical model of the system with a queue logic to quantitatively analyze the average level of WIP stock. Further, the waiting time equation obtained by analyzing the queue system can then be used to develop an optimization problem to find minimum lot sizes.

First Step for Modeling the System

Mixed-model assembly lines are often used in manufacturing. The goal chasing method is one of the sequencing approaches used to prepare schedules for the mixed-model assembly line to keep the per hour consumption quantity of assembly parts as constant as possible.

The goal chasing method makes the consumption speed as constant as possible. However, depending on demand for the final product and the bill of materials, the consumption speed of parts has a small variance during the production time. In the JIT system the goal chasing method is used when demand for the finished products has only a small fluctuation.

Now the question arises: what is the ability of the goal chasing method to absorb the fluctuations in demand so that they will not increase the fluctuation in the number of parts consumed? The number of parts consumed may fluctuate even under a certain demand. To answer this question, the goal chasing method will be simulated under stochastic demand. In this example, the system has seven product models. The mean of demand, the coefficient of variation for the different simulation runs, and the quantity of each part required for each product (i.e., bill of materials) are shown in Table A4.1. In all simulated runs, the mean of demand is kept constant, while the coefficient of variation is changed. Ten units of the final products can then be assumed to be produced in one hour. Under these assumptions, the variance can be computed and consequently the coefficient of variation for hourly consumption quantity of parts can be computed as the output of each simulated run.

Figure A4.2 shows the relationship between the consumption quantity coefficient variation for each part and the demand variation coefficient. This figure leads to the following proposition:

Proposition 1

The coefficient of the variation for parts consumption quantity is almost constant (i.e., very slowly increases) when the coefficient of the variation for the demand increases from 0% to 30%. In other words, when the coefficient of variation of demand increases from 0% to 30% (a 30% increase), the coefficient of variation for parts consumption (for example, for parts a_2) increases from 6.2% to 11.5% (i.e., a 5.3% increase). *Therefore we can conclude that the goal chasing method has a good ability to keep consumption speed (i.e., quantity per hour) of the parts as constant as possible, even when there is uncertainty in the demand.*

Table A4.1. Simulation input.

1) Number of the product's model = 7
2) Number of the part's model = 10
3) Bill of material is shown in the following matrix.

<table>
<tr><td colspan="2"></td><td colspan="10" align="center">Number of required parts</td></tr>
<tr><td colspan="2">parts</td><td>a_1</td><td>a_2</td><td>a_3</td><td>a_4</td><td>a_5</td><td>a_6</td><td>a_7</td><td>a_8</td><td>a_9</td><td>a_{10}</td></tr>
<tr><td rowspan="7">p
r
o
d
u
c
t
s</td><td>A_1</td><td>0</td><td>1</td><td>1</td><td>0</td><td>1</td><td>1</td><td>0</td><td>1</td><td>0</td><td>1</td></tr>
<tr><td>A_2</td><td>1</td><td>0</td><td>1</td><td>1</td><td>0</td><td>1</td><td>1</td><td>0</td><td>1</td><td>0</td></tr>
<tr><td>A_3</td><td>0</td><td>1</td><td>1</td><td>0</td><td>1</td><td>0</td><td>1</td><td>1</td><td>1</td><td>0</td></tr>
<tr><td>A_4</td><td>1</td><td>1</td><td>0</td><td>1</td><td>1</td><td>1</td><td>0</td><td>1</td><td>0</td><td>1</td></tr>
<tr><td>A_5</td><td>1</td><td>0</td><td>0</td><td>1</td><td>1</td><td>0</td><td>1</td><td>0</td><td>1</td><td>1</td></tr>
<tr><td>A_6</td><td>0</td><td>1</td><td>1</td><td>0</td><td>1</td><td>1</td><td>0</td><td>1</td><td>1</td><td>0</td></tr>
<tr><td>A_7</td><td>1</td><td>1</td><td>0</td><td>1</td><td>0</td><td>0</td><td>1</td><td>1</td><td>0</td><td>1</td></tr>
</table>

4) Number of simulation runs = 7
5) Simulation time for each run = 150 days
6) The mean of the demands for all runs is the
   same but the coefficient of the variation for
   each run is different. They are shown below.

Means of the demand for each model of product
a_i (i = 1, ..., 7) are 8, 12, 10, 11, 13, 9, and 7 respectively.
The coefficients of variation for the first through
seventh run are 0%, 5%, 10%, 15%, 20%, 25%, and 30%
respectively.

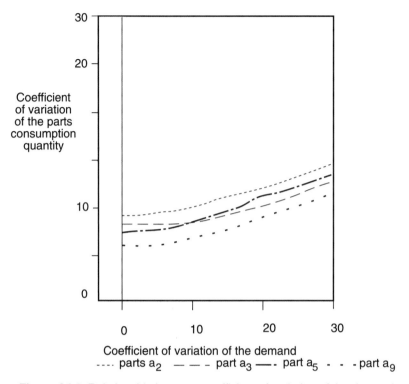

Figure A4.2. Relationship between coefficient of variation of the demand and coefficient of variation of the parts consumption quantity.

Second Step: Analysis of WIP Stock

The production system operation can be formulated using a queue logic. Then using the information obtained in the first step, the level of WIP stock required between an assembly line and its corresponding process (i.e., press line) can be determined.

The following notations will be used in this example:

D_i: Demand for the product of a model i. It has a triangle distribution function with mean of $\overline{D}_i$ and variance of σ_D^2.

$a_{j,t}$: Hourly consumption quantity of the part j in the body line during time t (i.e., one time implies one hour). It is a random variable with mean $\overline{a}_j$ and variance $\sigma_{a_j}^2$.

$W_{j,t}$: The quantity of the part j transported from store B to store I during time t. It is a random variable with mean $\overline{W}_j$ and variance $\sigma_{W_j}^2$.

M: Pallet or container size.

λ_j: Average number of orders received by the press line during an hour for part j.

λ: Average number of orders of any kind of parts received by the press line during an hour (arrival rate into the system).

S_j: Setup time for a lot of the parts j in the press line.

t_j: Per unit processing time for parts j in the press line.

q_j: Ordering lot size of part j.

T_j: Total production time (excluding waiting time) for each lot of parts j.

$\overline{T}$: Mean of the total production time of any lot.

σ_T^2: Variance of the total production time of any lot.

$\overline{V}$: Average waiting time for a lot of any kind of parts.

σ_v^2: Variance of the waiting time for a lot of any kind of parts.

L_j: Total lead time (including waiting time) for each lot of part j. It is a random variable with mean $\overline{L}_j$ and variance $\sigma_{L_j}^2$.

Assume that the per hour transportation quantity of the part j from store B to store I is

$$W_{j,t} = \left(\left[\frac{\overline{a}_{j,t} - Z_{j,t-1}}{M} \right] + 1 \right) M$$

where, $Z_{j,t-1}$ is the quantity in the partially used pallet of part j in the t-1'th period (hour), and $[x]$ is the largest integer number less than or equal to x.

The above equation can be rewritten as follows:

$$
W_{j,t} = \begin{cases} \left(\left[\dfrac{\overline{a}_{j,t}}{M} \right] + 1 \right) M & \text{if } mod\left(a_{j,t}, M\right) \geq Z_{j,t-1} \\[3ex] \left[\dfrac{\overline{a}_{j,t}}{M} \right] M & \text{if } mod\left(\overline{a}_{j,t}, M\right) < Z_{j,t-1} \end{cases} \tag{1}
$$

In general, for a random variable X which is normally distributed and a small constant M ($M < 20\% E(X)$), we can approximately conclude that the mode (X, M) is uniformly distributed between 0 and $M-1$ (Aghdassi 1988). Thus, we have,

$$
Pro\left\{ mod\left(\overline{a}_{j,t}, M\right) \leq Z_{j,t-1} \right\} = Pro\left\{ mod\left(\overline{a}_{j,t}, M\right) \leq Z_{j,t-1} \right\} = 0.5 \tag{2}
$$

Using equations (1) and (2), the mean of the per hour quantity of part j transported from store B to store I is

$$
\overline{W}_j = E\left\{ \left[\dfrac{\overline{a}_{j,t}}{M} \right] M \right\} + \dfrac{M}{2} \tag{3}
$$

On the other hand,

$$
\overline{a}_{j,t} = \left[\dfrac{\overline{a}_{j,t}}{M} \right] M + mod\left(\overline{a}_{j,t}, M\right) \tag{4}
$$

Taking the mean from the above equation, we obtain

$$
\overline{a}_j = E\left\{ \left[\dfrac{\overline{a}_{j,t}}{M} \right] M \right\} + \dfrac{M}{2} \tag{5}
$$

From equations (3) and (5), we can conclude that

$$\overline{W}_j = \overline{a}_j \tag{6}$$

$$\lambda_j = \frac{\overline{a}_1}{q_j} \tag{7}$$

$$\lambda = \sum_{j=1}^{m} \lambda_j \tag{8}$$

On the other hand, in the first step, we showed that a_j (j=1, 2, ...) can be determined by information from the demand. Therefore, we can conclude that they are independent, and thus, we can assume that receiving an order from the press line is an event which randomly occurs with the rate of λ. In other words, the number of arrivals (orders) into the system can be estimated by the Poisson distribution function with the parameter of λ. Therefore, the interarrival time has an exponential distribution function with the parameter of $1/\lambda$.

The stochastic pattern of the production time (summation of the setup and processing time) will now be discussed. The production time for an order (or service time for an arrival) corresponding to part j is

$$T_j = S_j + q_j t_j \tag{9}$$

As the order corresponding to part j occurs with the rate of λ_j, the mean and variance of production time for all models of parts are

$$\overline{T} = \frac{1}{\mu} = \sum_{j=1}^{m} \frac{\lambda_j}{\lambda} T_j \tag{10}$$

$$\sigma_T^2 = \sum_{j=1}^{m} \frac{\lambda_j}{\lambda} \left(T_j - \overline{T}\right)^2 \tag{11}$$

where, μ refers to the service rate or machine processing rate.

Considering the above discussion, the queue system of our problem is, $M/G/1$. Using the well-known Pollaczek-Khintchine formula in the queuing theory (Gross and Harris 1985), the mean and variance of the waiting time to receive service (i.e., production) can be determined by the following equations:

$$\overline{V} = \frac{\lambda \beta_2}{2(1-\rho)} \tag{12}$$

$$\sigma_v^2 = \frac{\lambda}{12(1-\rho)^2}\left[3\lambda\beta_2^2 + 4(1-\rho)\beta_3\right] \tag{13}$$

where, $\rho = \lambda\overline{T} = \dfrac{\lambda}{\mu}$

and β_n is the n moment of the service time or

$$\beta_n = \sum_{j=1}^{m}\frac{\lambda_j}{\lambda}T_j$$

The lead time in the press line for producing one lot of part j can be estimated by the following equation:

$$L_j = T_j + V_j \tag{14}$$

Taking mean and variance from the above equation, we have

$$E\left(L_j\right) = T_j + E\left(V_j\right)$$
$$= T_j + E(V) \tag{15}$$

$$Var\left(L_j\right) = Var\left(V_j\right)$$
$$= Var(V) \tag{16}$$

The reorder point and the average inventory level are determined by the following formulas respectively (Tersine 1982):

$$RP_j = \bar{a}_j\left(\bar{L}_j + \alpha\sigma_{Lj}\right) + \alpha\sigma_{aj}\sqrt{\bar{L}_j + \alpha\sigma_{Lj}} \tag{17}$$

$$\bar{I}_j = \tfrac{1}{2}q_j + \alpha\bar{j}\sigma_{Lj} + \alpha\sigma_{aj}\sqrt{\bar{L}_j + \alpha\sigma_{Lj}} \tag{18}$$

To determine the mean and variance of waiting time when the production time of any lots of different parts are identical (i.e., setup time, lot size, and unit processing time for different model parts are equal), equations (12) and (13) can be simplified as follows:

$$\bar{V} = \frac{A\left[t^2q^2 + tSq + S^2\right]}{2\left[(1 - At)q - AS\right]} \tag{19}$$

$$\bar{\sigma}_v^2 = \frac{A(S + tq)^3\left[4q - A(S + tq)\right]}{12\left[q - A(S + tq)\right]^2} \tag{20}$$

where, $A = \sum_{j=1}^{m} a_j$

$T = tq + S$

q, s, and t are the lot size, setup time, and unit processing time for all lots of different model parts, respectively.

Quantitative Analysis of the Lot Size

In the JIT constant order quantity system, the lot size is the maximum inventory level kept in stockpoints between work centers, and the number of Kanbans is actually decided by the level of this stock. The purpose of this section is to make a quantitative analysis of the minimum lot size such that each work center can perform its operations without interruption.

In the JIT system, the economic order quantity (EOQ) model is not used to determine the lot size. To reduce production lead time, the lot size must be minimized. If the setup time is shortened, the lot size can be reduced, and the number of setups per day will be increased.

The need for a company to develop a short setup time was first recognized in Japanese companies when they realized that by shortening the setup time, they could minimize the lot size and therefore reduce the stock of finished and intermediate products. However, the framework of the idea in a JIT system lies on the reduction of the stock level (i.e., lot size), and it is quite different from the logic corresponding to the EOQ model which justifies the inventory by ordering and inventory costs. The factors which justify keeping a little inventory in the JIT system can be time and uncertainty. Regarding these factors and using the result obtained in the previous section for the mean and variance of the lead time, the optimization model can be developed to determine minimum lot size and analyze the effect of the corresponding parameters on it.

It is obvious that if setup time is reduced to $1/n$ of the initial time, lot size can be reduced to $1/n$ of the initial size without changing the total production time. Now the question arises: is it possible to reduce the lot size without any setup time reduction and without increasing total operation time? It is clear that when setup time is constant, the reduction of lot size increases the number of setups, and therefore, the total operation time increases. But if the waiting time can be assumed as an increasing function of the lot size, then it may be possible to reduce the lot size without increasing the total production time. Lot size reduction increases the number of setups on the one hand, and reduces the waiting time on the other hand. As a result, there is a possibility for reducing the lot size without increasing the total operation time. To investigate this possibility, an optimization problem will be developed to find the minimum level of the lot size.

Min q
s. t.

$$\frac{A}{q}\left(S+\overline{V}+tq\right)\leq 1 \tag{21}$$

$$\rho \leq 1 \tag{22}$$

Constraint (21) indicates that production speed in the press line should respond to the consumption speed in the body line. Constraint (22) shows that the order arrival rate should be less than or equal to order producing rates.

Substituting equation (19) into (21) and considering that $\rho = \lambda T$, we obtain,

Min q
s. t.
$$f(q)=(4At-A^2t^2-2)q^2 + 2AS(2-At)q - A^2 S^2 \leq 0 \tag{23}$$

$$q \geq \frac{AS}{1-At} \tag{24}$$

To solve the above problem, first solve the inequality constraint (23). By solving $f(q)=0$ we have

$$q_1 = \frac{S}{\left(2+\sqrt{2}\right)t'-t} \quad \text{and} \quad q_2 = \frac{S}{\left(2+\sqrt{2}\right)t'-t} \tag{25}$$

On the other hand, if we assume $t' = 1/A$ as an average time for consuming one part in the subsequent stage, and define q_3 as a righthand side of the inequality, we obtain

$$q_3 = \frac{S}{t'-t} \tag{26}$$

The values of q_1, q_2, and q_3 for the different values of t (i.e., $0<t<t'$) are depicted in Figure A4.3. As the figure indicates, we have

$$0 \le t < \left(2-\sqrt{2}\right)t' \Rightarrow q_2 < q_3 < q_1 \tag{27}$$

$$t' \ge t > \left(2-\sqrt{2}\right)t' \Rightarrow q_1 < q_2 < q_3 \tag{28}$$

The space of the feasible solution of our optimization problem is shown in Figure 4. Keeping in mind that the area of convexity or concavity of the function $f(q)$ is found by taking the second derivation of the function as follows.

$$\frac{d^2 f(q)}{dq^2} = 4At - A^2t^2 - 2 = 2-(2-At)^2 \tag{29}$$

Therefore, we have,

$$\frac{d^2 f(q)}{dq^2} \begin{cases} > 0 \Leftrightarrow \textit{function is convex} & \textit{if } t > \left(2-\sqrt{2}\right)t' \\ \le 0 \Leftrightarrow \textit{function is concave} & \textit{if } t \le \left(2-\sqrt{2}\right)t' \end{cases} \tag{30}$$

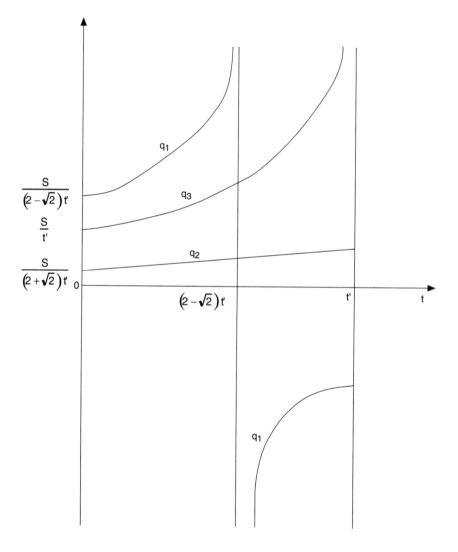

Figure A4. 3. Relationship between t, q_1, q_2, and q_3.

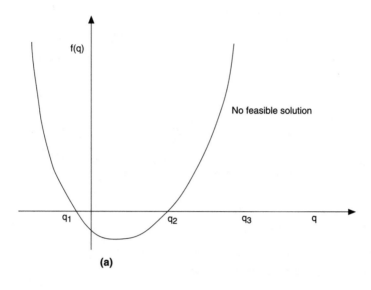

(a)

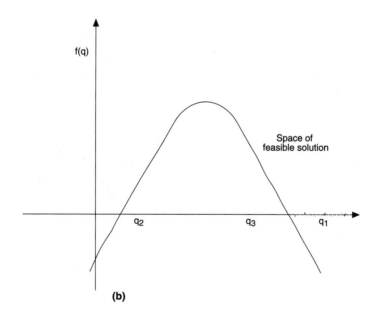

(b)

Figure A4.4. Space of feasible solution.

The obtained feasible solution should satisfy both constraints (23) and (24). Therefore under the condition in (28) (i.e., Figure A4.4a), there are no feasible solutions. However, when $t \le \left(2 - \sqrt{2}\right)t'$ (i.e., condition (27) which is depicted in Figure A4.4b), the feasible solution belongs to the space shown by the following inequality.

$$q \ge \frac{S}{\left(2 - \sqrt{2}\right)t' - t} \tag{31}$$

Therefore, the optimum solution (i.e., minimum lot size) is,

$$q^* = \frac{S}{\left(2 - \sqrt{2}\right)t' - t} \tag{32}$$

Inequality (28) can be rewritten as follows:

$$\frac{t'}{t} < 1 + \frac{\sqrt{2}}{2}$$

Therefore, the quantitative analysis of the optimum lot size for the constant order quantity JIT system (i.e., the upper bound inventory which determines the number of Kanbans) leads to the following propositions and conclusion.

Proposition 2

In the constant order quantity JIT production system, if the time span for consuming one unit of parts in the subsequent process is less than or equal to $(1 + \sqrt{2}/2)$ multiplied by the time span for producing one unit of parts in the preceding stage, then regardless of the lot size, the preceding stage cannot finish its operation during the total operation time of the subsequent stage.

Proposition 3

In the constant order quantity JIT production system, if the time span for consuming one unit of parts in the subsequent process is greater than $(1 + \sqrt{2}/2)$ multiplied by the time span for producing one unit of parts in the preceding stage, then the minimum lot size which allows the preceding stage to finish its operation during the total operation time of the subsequent stage is determined by the quotient of the setup time in the preceding stage divided by the difference between consumption time of $(2 - \sqrt{2})$ units and the unit producing time in the subsequent and preceding stages, respectively.

The proof for the above two propositions has already been shown by analyzing the space of the feasible and optimum solution for the lot size (see Figure A4.3).

From proposition 3 the following conclusion can be derived.

Conclusion

The reduction of the lot size under the constraint that total operation time does not increase, can be achieved not only by reducing the setup time, but also by reducing the unit producing time in the preceding stage.

Production Smoothing and WIP Level

One of the purposes of a mixed-model assembly line production is to keep the flow of material as constant as possible. Using the goal chasing method to introduce the sequence schedule into the mixed-model assembly line minimizes fluctuations in part consumption. This is called production smoothing. Through production smoothing, a production line is no longer committed to the manufacture of a single type of product in a vast lot size. Instead, a single line can produce many varieties each day in response to varying customer demands.

The equation for average WIP obtained in the previous section will be interpreted from the viewpoint of production smoothing in this section. As equation (18) shows, the level of average WIP stock is the increasing function of the standard deviation of parts consumption quantity a_j (Figure A4.5). Therefore, a smaller variance of the parts consumption quantity will cause a smaller stock level. On the other hand, we showed that production smoothing realized by the goal chasing method (notice that production smoothing may be realized by other approaches) leads to the smallest variance in the parts consumption quantity. Therefore, we can conclude that production smoothing will reduce the average WIP stock. Furthermore, it has already been concluded that such a production smoothing can be realized even under uncertainty in demand (see Figure A4.6). Therefore, the following proposition can be derived.

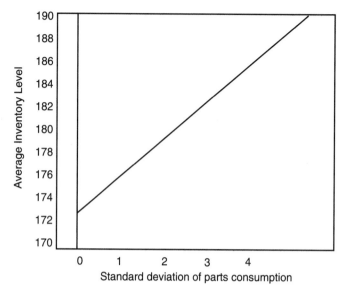

Figure A4.5. Average stock level and standard deviation of the parts consumption.

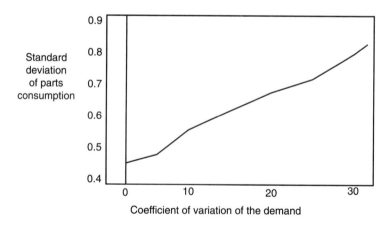

Figure A4.6. Relationship between standard deviation of the demand and parts consumption quantity under production smoothing.

Proposition 4

In a JIT system, even when the demand variability increases, production smoothing realized by the goal chasing method will not cause the inventory to increase rapidly (see Figure A4.7 which is derived from Figures A4.5 and A4.6), where we assume the conditions that safety stock level (α) and the mean and variance of the lead time ($\overline{L}_j$ and $\sigma^2_{L_j}$) are all in low values. However, these prerequisite conditions are all satisfied by implementing the JIT techniques.

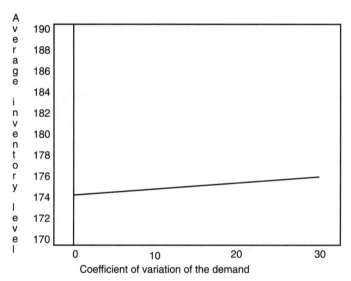

Figure A4.7. Relationship between the standard deviation of the demand and the average stock level under production smoothing.

REFERENCES

Aghdassi, M. 1988. *A Quantitative Analysis of Just-in-time Production.* Ph.D. Thesis, Institute of Socio-Economic Planning, University Tsukuba, Japan.

Gross, D. and Harris, C. M. 1985. *Fundamentals of Queuing Theory.* John Wiley & Son: New York.

Tersine, J. R. 1982. *Principle of Inventory and Materials Management.* North Holland: New York.

Epilogue

The Toyota production system is a technology of comprehensive production management the Japanese invented a hundred years after opening up to the modern world. More than likely, another gigantic advance in production methods will not appear for some time to come.

Mr. Taiichi Ohno, former vice-president of Toyota Motor Corp., who wrote the foreword to this book, is the inventor and promoter of the Toyota production system at Toyota. In developing the system, he has developed various unique ideas, implemented them, and corrected them. While machining department manager of the Honsha plant in 1949-50 up to vice-president in 1975 of Toyota, he gradually spread his original methods throughout the company, finally applying these methods to all the companies of the Toyota group.

Also, for the development and promotion of the Toyota system, the support of top executives, the strenuous efforts of Ohno's competent subordinates, and the various ideas of all Toyota's workers must be recognized. In a sense, Mr. Ohno has built and promoted the system as an excellent conductor for gathering together all the ideas developed by these people.

It was just after the first oil shock in late 1973 that the Toyota production system attracted the attention of Japanese industries. Facing unprecedented cost-push inflation, most of Japanese companies had run into the red, except Toyota, which had shown a huge profit. In order for these companies to overcome the oil shock, it became clear that the company constitution had to be made slim and tough. From this viewpoint it would not be too much to say that Japanese companies have conquered the depression of oil shock by introducing the Toyota production system partially or totally.

From this Japanese experience, the author firmly believes the Toyota production system can play a great role in the task for improving the constitutions of American and European companies as well as companies worldwide—especially those of the automotive industry. Thus, the author's chief purpose of publishing this book is to offer some support to the companies in the U.S. and elsewhere that are making efforts to improve productivity, thereby promoting friendship between Japan and many countries

The basic idea of Toyota production system is to maintain a continuous flow of products in factories in order to flexibly adapt to demand changes. The realization of such production flow is called Just-in-time production at Toyota, which means producing only necessary items in a necessary quantity at a necessary time. As a result, the excess inventories and the excess work force will be naturally diminished, thereby achieving the purposes of increased productivity and cost reduction.

In 1980, the turnover ratio of inventory assets (= annual sales/average inventories) at Toyota Motor Company was 87; in other words, the inventory period (= average inventories/average monthly sales) was merely 0.138 months or 4 days. This means the Toyota Motor Company had inventories (including materials) for only four days of sales. Also, the inventory turnover ratio at Toyota Motor Sales Company was 40, while its inventory period was merely 9 days.

Moreover, the safety margin (= break-even point sales/sales plus other income) of Toyota Motor Corp. in 1980 was only 64%, which means Toyota can earn a profit even if the present sales might reduce to 64%. Such a remarkably low break-even point was created by decreasing the work force. It must be added that Toyota has consistently achieved these figures over the past several years, and in some cases even bettered them.

The basic principle of JIT production is universally rational; that is, the Toyota production system has been developed by steadily pursuing the orthodox way of production management. Therefore, the author believes people in any country who evaluate the reasonableness can understand this system without any trouble. However, the problem for the author in writing the book was to find the reasonable framework of Toyota production methods.

As Mr. Taiichi Ohno mentioned in the foreword of this book, the Toyota production system "has a strong feature of emphasizing practical effects, and actual practice and implementation over theoretical analysis." The existing books on Toyota manufacturing methods have all been written by the practitioners of the system; they all contain proficient descriptions of individual topics of Toyota's methods, and my book is partially indebted to these books. However, as I see it, they do not incorporate the methods into a whole and present them in a theoretical, systematic manner. Certainly Toyota's unique manufacturing methods are linked by an underlying system; and certainly the benefits of these methods can be demonstrated; but it is very hard to explain the methods systematically and theoretically.

Mr. Ohno also said in his foreword, "We are very interested in how Professor Monden has *theorized* our practice from his academic standpoint and how he has explained it to the foreign people." Therefore, the central mission of this book is to develop a "theory" to the "practices" of Toyota manufacturing methods.

What is a theory or theorization? It is a process of building an ideal model of the real, empirical object by using the following procedures:

- Abstracting from the empirical world the important factors which seem most relevant to the research objective.
- Connecting the selected factors in a logical way.

Our research objective is to build a practically applicable model; that is, this model must be able to be utilized for each company to prepare and implement the actual system of production management. Further, since the Toyota production system is a kind of typical system which transforms various input factors to its outputs, this transformation mechanism, or the structure of goals-means relationships, must be described as a "theory" in this book.

Since this process of theorization seemed to me a very creative task, I approached it not as a mere commentator but as a "novelist," with the cooperation of many people of the Toyota group. Many times I visited not only the Toyota Motor Company, but also several companies of the Toyota group, observed their plants, and interviewed the managers of plants and staffs of production control-departments. Moreover, the experiences I had in 1981 in visiting the plants of the General Motors Corporation and the Ford Motor Company were very useful when considering the uniqueness of the Japanese production systems.

As a result of these efforts, the simplest model of the Toyota production system was constructed as shown in Chapter 1, Figure 1.1. Although this model excludes detailed relations, it describes the broad outline of relationships among various subsystems of the total system. The internal structure of each subsystem and its relations to various other subsystems are explained in detail in each chapter. Furthermore, the theoretical analysis of determining the number of Kanban (described in Appendix 1) is my original work. In this appendix I have proved the reasonableness of the "rules of thumb" of calculating the total number of Kanban by applying two alternative inventory control models; i.e. constant order-quantity system and constant order-cycle system.

However, the model of the Toyota production system is merely my model and will not necessarily coincide with the real manufacturing methods existing at Toyota. There are two reasons: first, there are many variations of Toyota production methods even among various Toyota plants as well as among many cooperative companies of the Toyota group. Second, the Toyota production system itself is continually evolving, perfecting itself day by day in response to competition. As suggested in this book, the present and future development of the Toyota production system would be to adapt the system to the rapidly rising movement of factory automation such as FMS, robotics, and CAD/CAM. Any errors which this edition might contain will hopefully be corrected with the aid of reader feedback.

Moreover, in this book I have also taken into account criticism of the Toyota system; I have especially considered criticisms made by the Japanese communist party and the Fair Trade Commission to check if some flaw in the system might— exist. Also, the "contingency theoretic" approach was partially applied in various chapters concerning the topics such as the problem of geographical distance between suppliers and the paternal maker, the types of industries, the difference in industrial relations and wage payment methods, and the problem of financial ability to invest in multipurpose machines and autonomous defect-control systems. However, such critical considerations and the contingency approach are not the main subject of this edition. Such approaches will be taken more in the following editions. Also, there still remains several more topics to be discussed for this system. Such topics will also be included in the following editions.

Next, let us consider the productivity problem between different countries. The competitive power of Japanese automobiles lies in their low cost and high quality, which have been accepted by American consumers. This has caused the serious economic and political problems between two countries. The present situation between both countries resembles closely the evening before World War II. Now is the time both Japan and the U.S. should keep cool and not give themselves over to their emotions.

At this very time I would like to contend to American friends that the present success of the Japanese has been acquired by steady efforts of "self-help." One of the main purposes of this book is to offer evidence that the Japanese have been making efforts earnestly and independently to increase productivity and improve quality. This evidence may be merely a sample, but considering the heavy weight of the auto industry in Japan and U.S., it has an important meaning.

If Americans intentionally avoid recognizing the true problems behind the present situations of their industries and go to a policy of protectionism, it will not give any advantage to them in the long run because it cannot revive the vital power of the industries. Import restrictions would enable U.S. industries to perpetuate inefficient production methods and raise prices, thereby inflicting a loss on American consumers. Protectionism in the United States would also decrease the influence of U.S. foreign and defense policy because of counter-reactions around the world.

On the contrary, by observing the free trade system (and by accepting foreign challenges as good incentives), U.S. industries could improve their productivity and promote more innovation in new technologies. American people who respect freedom, friendship, and decorum will not resort to criticizing another nation to defend themselves. Expecting the rebirth of U.S. vitality, the author has written this book to support and encourage the movements of productivity improvement in the U.S. and many other countries.

Studying this book will be the first step to introduce the Toyota production system to each company. For this purpose, this book should be read not only by industrial engineers but by people in all levels of the company. The application of such a comprehensive production system as Toyota's will. Involve the entire revolution of the present system, which requires the understanding and strategic decisions of top executives. Also, the Toyota production system rests on a foundation of improvement activities by individual workers in the plant, so the book is hopefully read as a text for QC circle meetings, etc. At Toyota, the introductory manual of the Toyota manufacturing methods is given to all workers for their complete understanding of the methods.

Moreover, this book has advantages to Japanese companies, too. Without the prosperity of the U.S. and many other countries, Japan will not have a place to sell its products. If we Japanese could be of any help to reviving the world economy, our own survival itself could also be assured. In order for Japanese companies (including the automotive industry) to survive in the long run in this world market, we will have to cooperate with foreign companies so that Japanese companies can jointly produce products in foreign countries with foreign companies. Also, Japanese companies must go to foreign countries independently to manufacture products with foreign workers and managers. Therefore, the production system described in this book must also be used by the partner companies and foreign people. To advance Japanese technologies further in the future, we should recognize that "no human condition is ever permanent and we should not be overjoyed in good fortune."

In conclusion, even though different in race and nation, we are all children of mother earth. By encouraging each other to polish up each other's skills, people in all countries can survive and prosper at the same time.

Yasuhiro Monden
Tsukuba, Japan

Bibliography and References

English Language Literature

AIAG and APICS. 1981. *Proceedings of the Production and Inventory Control Conference, Fall 1981.* Sponsored by Detroit chapter of APICS and Automotive Industry Action Group.

American Machinist. 1981. Kanbans are discovered. February: 222.

American Production and Inventory Control Society. 1980. Pittsburgh Chapter, *Proceedings* from "Productivity: The Japanese formula." October.

Ashburn, A. 1977. Toyota's famous Ohno system. *American Machinist.* July: 120-123.

Bodek, N., ed. 1980. Kanban—the coming revolution? *Productivity* 1(7): 1-2.

_____. 1981. *Productivity: Three Practical Approaches.* Proceedings of the Productivity Seminar held by Productivity, Inc., February 23. Cambridge, MA: Productivity Press.

Buffa, E.S. 1984. *Meeting the Competitive Challenge: Manufacturing Strategy for U.S. Companies.* Homewood, IL: Irwin.

Burck, C.G. 1983. Will success spoil General Motors? *Fortune.* August: 22.

Butt, D. 1981. Just-in-time in Lincoln, Nebraska: Why and how. In: Bodek, N. ed. *Productivity: Three Practical Approaches.* Cambridge, MA: Productivity Press.

Cho, F. and Makise, K. 1980. Toyota's kanban, the ultimate in efficiency and effectiveness. American Production and Inventory Control Society.

Drucker, P.F. 1971. What we can learn from Japanese management? *Harvard Business Review.* March-April.

_____. 1981. Behind Japan's success. *Harvard Business Review.* January-February.

Ellis, E.B. 1981. U.S. production, Japanese style: Kawasaki motorcycle plant in Nebraska. *The Christian Science Monitor.* March 6: 1.

Feigenbaum, A.V. 1961. *Total Quality Control.* New York: McGraw-Hill.

Fortune. 1981. How the Japanese manage in the U.S. June 15: 97-103.

Fujimoto, K. 1980. Serving the big manufacturers: how to cope with short lead time and changing delivery schedules. American Production and Inventory Control Society.

Hall, R.W. and Vollman, T.W. 1978. Planning your material requirement. *Harvard Business Review.* September-October.

Hall, R.W. 1981. *Driving the Productivity Machine: Production Planning and Control in Japan.* Falls Church, VA: American Production and Inventory Control Society.

Harsh, J. 1981. U.S. executives eager to import ringi, ukezara. *The Christian Science Monitor.* March 6:1.

Japan Management Association. 1980. *Proceedings of the International Conference on Productivity and Quality Improvement—Study of Actual Cases.* Tokyo: October.

Kimura, O. and Terada, H. 1981. Design and analysis of pull system—a method of multi-stage production control. *International Journal of Production Research.* 19(3): 241—253.

Konz, S. 1979. Quality circles: Japanese success story. *Industrial Engineering.* October: 24-27.

Kraft, J. 1981. Japan's sick of being punished for excellence. *Chicago Sun-Times.* May 6.

Lawrence, P.R. and Lorsch, J.W. 1967. *Organization and Environment: Managing Differentiation and Integration.* Boston: Harvard University Press.

Monden, Y. 1981a. What makes the Toyota production system really tick? *Industrial Engineering.* January: 36-46.

_____. 1981b. Adaptable kanban system helps Toyota maintain just-in-time production. *Industrial Engineering.* May: 28-46.

_____. 1981c. Smoothed production lets Toyota adapt to demand changes and reduce inventory. *Industrial Engineering.* August: 41-51.

_____. 1981d. How Toyota shortened supply lot production time, waiting time and conveyance time. *Industrial Engineering.* September: 22-30.

_____. 1992a. *Cost Management of the New Manufacturing Age: Innovations in the Japanese Automotive Industry.* Cambridge, MA: Productivity Press.

_____. 1992b. Just-in-Time production system. In: Salvendy, G. ed. *Handbook of Industrial Engineering, Second Edition.* New York: John Wiley & Sons. pp. 2116-2130.

_____. 1993. *Toyota Management System.* Cambridge, MA: Productivity Press.

Monden, Y., ed. 1985. *Applying Just-In-Time: The American/Japanese Experience,* Norcross, GA: Industrial Engineering & Management Press.

Monden, Y. and Hamada, K. 1991. Target costing and kaizen costing of Japanese automobile companies. *Journal of Management Accounting Research,* Vol. 3, Fall: 163-164.

Monden, Y. and Sakurai, M., eds. 1989. *Japanese Management Accounting.* Cambridge, MA: Productivity Press.

Monden, Y., Shibakawa, R., Takayanagi, S., and Nagao, T., eds. 1986. *Innovations in Management: The Japanese Corporation.* Norcross, GA: Industrial Engineering & Management Press.

Mori, M. and Harmon, R.L. 1980. Combining the best of the west with the best of the east—MRP and kanban working in harmony. American Production and Inventory Control Society.

Muramatsu, R. and Miyazaki, H. 1976. A new approach to production systems through developing human factors in Japan. *International Journal of Production Research.* 14(2): 311-326.

Muramatsu, R., Miyazaki, H., and Tanaka, Y. 1980. An approach to the design of production systems giving a high quality of working life and production efficiency. *International Journal of Production Research.* 18(2): 131-141.

_____. 1981. Example of increasing productivity and product quality through satisfying the worker's desires and developing the worker's motivation. *AIIE 1981 Spring Annual Conference Proceedings.* Norcross, GA: Industrial Engineering and Management Press. pp. 652-660.

Okamura, K. and Yamashina, H. 1979. A heuristic algorithm for the assembly line model-mix sequencing problem to minimize the risk of stopping the conveyor. *International Journal of Production Research.* 17(3): 233-247.

Patchin, R. 1981. Quality control circles. In: Bodek, N., ed. *Productivity: Three Practical Approaches.* Cambridge, MA: Productivity Press.

Riggs, J.L. and Seo, K.K., 1979. Wa: personal factor of Japanese productivity. *Industrial Engineering.* April: 32-35.

Roos, D., Wamak, I.P., and Jones, D. 1990. *The Machine that Changed the World.* New York: Macmillan Publishing Company.

Runcie, J.F. 1980. By days I make the cars. *Harvard Business Review.* May-June.

Shingo, S. 1981. *Study of Toyota Production System from Industrial Engineering Viewpoint.* Japan Management Association.

Stewart. 1981. Productivity measurement. In: Bodek, N., ed. *Productivity: Three Practical Approaches.* Cambridge, MA: Productivity Press.

Sugimori, Y., Kusunoli, K., Cho, F., and Uchikawa, S. 1977. Toyota production system and kanban system, materialization of just-in-time and respect-for-humanity system. *International Journal of Production Research.* 15(6): 553-564.

Thompson, P.R. 1985. The NUMMI production system. In: *1985 Conference Proceedings.* Falls Church, VA: American Production & Inventory Control Society. p. 400.

Toyota Motor Co., Ltd. 1981a. *Outline of Toyota.*

_____. 1981b. *Toyota Motor Co., Ltd. Annual Report 1981.*

Vogel, E.F. 1979. *Japan as Number One: Lessons for America.* Boston: Harvard University Press.

Vollum, R.B. 1987. Production activity control. In: White, J. A. (ed.) *Production Handbook, Fourth Ed.* New York: John Wiley & Sons. pp. 3-194.

Waterbury, R. 1981a. How does just-in-time work in Lincoln, Nebraska? *Assembly Engineering.* April: 52-56.

_____. 1981b. Kanban cuts waste, saves $ with minimum effort. *Assembly Engineering.* April: 52-56.

Yamada, T., Kitajima, S., and Imaeda, K. 1980. Development of a new production management system for the co-elevation of humanity and productivity. *International Journal of Production Research.* 18(4): 427-439.

Japanese Literature

Akao, Y. 1980. Functional management and departmental management. *Hinshitsukanri.* 31(5): 14-18.

_____. 1978. *Toyota, Its True Nature.* Seki Bun Sha.

Aoki, S. 1981. Functional management as top management—concepts at Toyota Motor Co., Ltd. and its actual execution. *Hinshitsukanri.* 32(2): 92-98; 32(3): 66-71; 32(4): 65-69.

Aona, F. 1982. *Toyota's Strategy.* Diamond.

Arita, S. 1978. A consideration of the effect of smoothed production on the reduction of work-in-process inventory. *Kojokanri.* 24(13): 109-115.

Ban, S. and Kimura, O. 1986. Toyota's manufacturing departments: complete implementation of basic principles and incorporation of flexibility. *JMA Production Management.* October.

Endo, K. 1978. Toyota system—image and true nature. *Kojokanri.* 24(13): 141-145.

Fujita, A. 1978. Merits and faults of Toyota production system. *Kojokanri.* 24(13): 120-124.

Fukunaga, M. 1986. Control system for corresponding to multi-model production. *IE Review.* 27(1).

Fukuoka, Y. 1990. The new ALC system at Toyota. In: Fujitsu Co. ed. *Proceedings of Fujitsu CIM Symposium in Osaka.* pp. 44-71.

Fukushima, S. 1978. Toyota's parts-integration from product-planning stage. *IE.* March: 58-63.

Furukawa, Y. 1981. System theory of quality control. *Operations Research.* August: 443-450.

Harazaki, I. 1981. Multi-functioned worker role in many varieties, short-run production. *Kojokanri.* 27(2): 86-87.

Hasegawa, M. Tanaka, T., and Sugie, K. 1981. In-process quality control for each job position realized zero delivery claim at Akashi Kikai Co. Ltd. *Kojokanri.* 27(1): 15-24.

Hashimoto, F. 1981. Assignments to realize the unmanned plant from software viewpoints. *Kojokanri.* 27(4): 6-36.

Hatano, T. 1982. Vendor's on-line delivery system correspond to the line balanced production. *IE.* January: 30-34.

Hattori, M. 1981. Production system adaptable to changes—an example of Nippon-Denso's mixed-model high-speed automatic assembly line. *IE.* January: 22-27.

Hirano, H., ed. 1984. *Handbook of Factory Rationalization.* Nikkankogyo Shinbun-Sha.

Hitomi, K. 1978. A consideration of the Toyota production system. *Kojokanri.* 26(13): 116-119.

_____. 1979. GT system for many varieties, short-run production. *Kojokanri.* 25(18): 111-119.

_____. 1987. *Text Book of Production for Many Variety with Short Run.* Nikkankogyo Shinbun-Sha.

Honda, J. 1988. *5S Animation: Seiri, Seiton, Seiketsu, Seiso, and Shitsuke.* Nikkankogyo Shinbun-Sha.

Honjo, J. 1988. *Toyota's Marketing Power: Secret of Its Strength.* Nisshin-Houdo.

Iijima, A. 1981. Implementation of company-wide quality control at Toyota Auto Body Co., Ltd. *Hinshitsukanri.* 32(1): 20-26.

Ikari, Y. 1981. *Comparative Study, Japan's Automotive Industry—Production Technology of Nine Advanced Companies.* Nippon Noritsu Kyokai.

_____. 1983. *Development No. 179—The Road to Carolla.* Bungei-Shunjie.

_____. 1985. *Toyota vs. Nissan: The Front of New Car Development.* Diamond.

Ikeda, M. 1980. *Informal History of Toyota—Sakicht, Risaburo, Kiichiro, Ishida, and Kamiya.* Sancho Co., Ltd.

Ishikawa, K. 1981. *Japan's Quality Control.* Nikka Giren.

Ishikawa, K. and Isogai, S. 1981. Introduction and promotion of TQC: functional management. *Hinshitsukanri.* 32(11): 88-96.

Ishitsubo, T. 1978. Reduction of the die-change time for the washer outside-frame. *Kojokanri.* 24(7): 40-44.

Itami, H. 1982. *Beyond Japanese Management.* Toyokeizai Sinpo Sha.

Ito, T. 1979. Complete change in thinking lets Arai Seisakusho, Ltd. promote production smoothing. *Kojokanri.* 25(8): 157-163.

Iwai, M. 1981. How the no. 1 improvement proposers are making their ideas. *President.* December: 146-166.

Japan Management Association and Monden, Y. 1986. *New Edition: Toyota's Factory Management.* Japan Management Association.

Kanpo. 1982. Questions by Ms. Michiko Tanaka to the Ministers of State. *Proceedings of the House of Representatives,* no. 4. October 7: 62-66.

Kato, J. 1982. Introduction of robotics to the manufacturing floor—Japanese industrial relations will not break. *Nihon Keizai Shinbun.* May 3.

Kato, N. 1984. Mixed production of agricultural four wheel tractor. *Kojokanri.* 30(11).

Kato, T. 1981 and 1982. Revolutionary management of punchpress process—from the introduction of Kanban system to the scheduling by microcomputer (1-14). *Press Gijutsu.* 19(1-2, 4-13); 20(1-3).

_____. 1981. New production management for the punchpress process. *IE.* December: 77-80.

Kawaguchi, H. 1980. Visual control at Toyoda Gosei's cutting operation process. *Kojokanri.* 26(13): 26-33.

_____. Basic promotion method of Toyota production system. 1990. In: Chubu Industrial Engineering Association, ed. *Seminar Text of Toyota Production System Practice.* November: 11-20.

Kawashima, Y. 1980. Overseas strategy of honda, a pioneer company which extended to America. *Kojokanri.* 26(7): 40-47.

Kestler. A. 1983. Translated by Tanaka, M. and Yashioka, Y. *Holonic Revolution.* Kosakusha.

Kikuchi, H. 1978. Recent problems concerning the subcontract transactions. *Kosei-Torihiki.* November: 11-18.

Kobayashi, I. 1978. Remarkable reduction time and workforce by applying the single-setup at machining and pressing operations. *Kojokanri.* 24(7): 45-52.

Kohno, T. 1987. *Strategy for the New Product Development.* Diamond.

Kojima, A. 1980. Productivity arguments in the United States (1 and 2). *Nihon Kezai Shinbun.* June 10-1.

Kojokanri. 1978a. Standard operations and process improvements at Toyoda Gosei Co., Ltd. 24(13): 70-82.

_____. 1978b. Multi-process holdings at the casting processes of Aisin Seiki Co., Ltd. 24(13): 83-88.

_____. 1980. A case of the auto-parts maker who realized small lot, short-cycle delivery via MRI. 26(12): 61-67.

_____. 1981a. Production revolution at reviving Toyo Kogyo Co., Ltd. 27(6): 17-37.

_____. 1981b. Practices of the small lot, mixed-model production system—seven cases. 27(7): 17-64.

Kotani, S. 1982. On the sequencing problem of the mixed model line. *Japan Operations Research Society Spring Conference Proceedings.* pp. 149-150.

Koura, K. 1981. Quality and economy. *Operations Research.* August: 437-442.

Kubo, N. 1979. Production control at Yammer Diesel Co., Ltd. synchronizes with the master schedule. *Kojokanri.* 25(8): 149-156.

Kumagai, T. 1978. Characteristics of Toyota production system. *Kojokanri.* 24(13): 152-157.

Kuroyanagi, M. 1980. Visual control or Aisan Kogyo's machining line. *Kojokanri.* 26(13): 15-25.

Kusaba, et. al. 1981. Report of the 11th overseas quality control observation team. (2) *Hinshitsukanri.* 32(10): 58-64.

Maeda, S. 1982. FMS without failure—a case of Tokyo Shibaura Electric Co., Ltd. *Nippon Keizai Shinbun.* August 9.

Makido, T. 1979. Recent tendency of cost management practices in Japan. *Kigyo Kaike.* March: 126-132.

Masuyama, A. 1983. Idea and practice of Toyota's FMS. In: Ohno, T. and Monden, Y. eds. *New Development of Toyota Production System.* Japan Management Association. pp. 13-27.

Matsumae, H. 1978. Toyota production system and VE. *Kojokanri.* 24(13): 149-152.

Matsuura, M. 1979. *Secret of Toyota's Sales Power.* Sangyo Noritsu Tanki Daigaku Publishing Division.

Matsuura, T., Ojima, T., and Ohmori, K. 1978. Single-setup at punch press and resin-molding lines. *Kojokanri.* 24(7): 53-58.

Minato, T. 1984. Japan's subcontracting system is noticed in overseas. *Nihon-Keizai Shinbun.* August 14.

Monden, Y. 1978. Integrated system of cost management. *Sangyo Kanri.* December: 21-26.

_____. 1987. *Just In Time: Toyota Production System Going Across the Ocean.* Japan Productivity Center.

_____. 1989a. *Cases of JIT Product on System of Automobile Industry.* Japan Management Association.

_____. 1989b. *Foundation of Transfer Pricing and Profit Allocation.* Dobunkan.

_____. 1991a. *Toyota Management System.* Japan Management Association.

_____. 1991b. *Cost Management of Automobile Companies.* Dobunkan.

_____. 1991c. *New Toyota System.* Kodansha.

Monden, Y. and Ohno, T. 1983. *New Development of Toyota Production System.* Japan Management Association.

Mori, K. 1978. The negative and the positive of Toyota production system for my standpoint. *Kojokanri.* 4(13): 145-148.

Mori, M. and Yui, N. 1982a. Comparison of production systems of Japan—U.S. auto makers—productivity improvement strategy and system of U.S. automobile industry. *Kojokanri.* 28(8): 17-65.

_____. 1982b. Comparison of production systems between Japan and U.S. auto-makers. *Kojokanri.* 28(8).

Morimatsu, T. 1988. Setup improvements. In: Japan Management Association, *Seminar Text of Toyota Production System: Its Systematic Examination and Practical Application.* October 26-28.

Morita, T. 1979a. TQC and Toyota production system applied together to the production control of Akashi Kikai Co., Ltd. *Kojokanri.* 25(8): 174-181.

Muramatsu, R. 1978. Basic concepts and structure of Toyota production system. *Kojokanri.* 24(13): 162-165.

_____. 1979b. *Foundation of Production Control, A New Edition.* Kunimoto Shobo.

Nagata, T. 1985. Let's promote medical control of facilities by applying 5S. In: Kojokanri Editorial Dept. ed. *5S Technique, Kojokanri.* 31(11): Special issue, October.

Nakai, S. 1978. Toyota's unique vitality and practicing ability developed its own system. *Kojokanri.* 24(13): 158-161.

Nakamori, K. 1986. Cost management at the design department (1 and 2). *IE.* November: 65-70; December: 58-64.

Nakane, M. 1981. Mixed-model production system at the body assembling line. *Kojokanri.* 27(7): 59-64.

Nakata, I. 1978. Complete master of the basic concepts of Toyota system. *Kojokanri.* 24(13): 128-130.

Nakata, Y. and Monden. Y. 1985. Marketing strategy of automobile companies—theoretical analysis of Toyota's case. *Keieikoudo.* 4(11): 92-116.

Nikkan Kogyo Shinbun Sha. 1980a. Kojokanri editorial division, ed. *Honda's Small Group Activities.* Nikkan Shobo.

Nikkan Kogyo Shinbun Sha. 1980b. *Business Group for Support of Toyota.*

Nikko Research Center, ed. 1979. *Toyota in the 1980s—Its Growth Strategy Invested by Analysts.* Nihon Keizai Shinbun Sha.

Nippon Keizai Shinbun. 1981. Office rationalization by applying kanban. November 7.

_____. 1982a. Experimentation of life-time employment system—tentative agreement between Ford and UAW. February 15.

_____. 1982b. Teach me the kanban system—request by U.S. Bendix Company to Jidosha Kiki Co., Ltd. March 2.

_____. 1982c. Shock by the alliance of giant automotive companies. (1 and 2) March 9-10.

_____. 1982d. Cooperative movement in U.S. industrial relations is for real? June 7.

_____. 1982e. (News Colloq.) Acceleration to the effective management of new Toyota. Mr. Toyoda, President of Toyota Motor Corporation. July 5.

_____. 1982f. CAD/CAM system of Toyota—body development process. August 5.

Nishibori, E. 1985. Morale must come out from the bottom of heart. In: Kojokanri Editorial Dept. ed. *5S Technique, Kojokanri.* 31(11): 92-116.

Nissan Motor Company. 1981. *Annual Report (Financial Security Report). 1991 March.* Ministry of Finance, July.

Noboru, Y. and Monden, Y. 1983. Total cost management in Japanese auto industry. *Kigyo Kaikei.* February: 104-112.

_____. 1988. Cost management of an automobile company: Daihatsu Motor. In: Okamoto, K., Miyamoto, M., and Sakurai, M., eds. *High Tech Accounting.* Doyukan.

Ochiai, T. 1991. Automobile sequence scheduling for the assembly line by use of AI. Handout presented at the seminar of Japan Industrial Management Association, February 9.

Ohno, T. 1990. Multi-process holding is an effective method for preventing over-production. *Kojokanri.* 36(9).

Ohno, T. and Monden, Y. eds. 1983. *New Development of Toyota Production System.* Japan Management Association.

_____. 1978a. Companies gap will be determined by the productivity gap when the quantity decreases. *IE.* March: 4-9.

_____. 1978b. *Toyota Production System—Beyond Management of Large Scale Production.* Diamond Publishing Co., Ltd.

Ohshima, K. 1984. *Japan-U.S. Automobile Conflict—Investigation for the Strategy of Coexistence.* Nihon-Keizai-Shinbun-Sha.

Okada, Y. and Sasaki, T. 1986. Practice of production information management at Matsuda. *JMA Production Management.* July.

Okamura, M. 1979. Toyota's energy conservation prevailing throughout the shop floor. *IE.* September: 18-24.

Okano, M. and Yamamoto, K. 1986. New technology of assembly, machining, and inspection systems. In: Watanabe, S. and Akiyama, Y. eds. *Production System and New Automation Technology.* Nikkan-Kogyo Shinbun-sha. pp. 167-190.

Ryokaku, T. 1990. How the new model will be developed—case study of Celica. *Motor Fan.* Vol. 33, January.

Saito, S. 1978. *Secret of Toyota Kanban System.* Kou Shobo.

Sakakibara, K. Organizational structure and technology. *Business Review.* 27(1): 26-37.

Sekine, K. 1978a. Steps toward single-setup: Procedures and practices for reducing the setup time in half. *Kojokanri.* 24(7): 59-64.

_____. 1978b. Toyota kanban system, the practical manual. *Kojokanri.* 24(13): 2-52.

_____. 1981. *Practical Toyota Kanban System—How to Make a Profit by Eliminating Waste.* Nikkan Shobo.

Senju, S., Kawase, T., Sakuma. A., Nakamura, Z., and Yata, H. 1987. *Motion Study: Determinate Edition.* JIS.

Shibata, Y. and Hasegawa, N. 1981. Software package for support of kanban, new production control system at Kyoho Seisaku Co., Ltd. *Kojokanri.* 27(4): 17-25.

Shimada, H. 1981. U.S. industry is enthusiastic about its restoration efforts for improving the quality of labor. *Nihon Keizai Shinbun.* October 26.

_____. 1984. Changing labor union of America: new labor contract in automobile industry. *Nihon-Keiai-Shinbun.* December 11.

Shingo, S., et al. 1978a. Single-setup will change the business constitution. *Kojokanri.* 24(7): 1978a, 20-24.

Shingo, S. 1978b. Revolution of setup time development to the single-setup. *Kojokanri.* 24(7): 20-24.

_____. 1980. *Study of Toyota Production System from Industrial Engineering Viewpoint—Development to the Non-Stock Production.* Nikkan Kogyo Shinbun Sha.

Shinozawa, S. 1987. *Toyota's Chief-Engineer System of Automobile Development.* Kodansha.

Shioka, K. 1978. Toyota production system and work. *Kojokanri.* 24(13): 124-127.

Shishido, T. and Nikko Research Center, ed. 1980. *Japanese Companies in USA—Investigation in the Possibility of Japanese-Style Management.* Toyokeizai Shinpo Sha.

Shomura, O. 1981. Contemporary auto workers and their job discontent—an examination of the international comparative study by William H. Form. *Rokkodai Ronshu.* 28(2): 90-106.

Shukan Toyokeizai. 1982. Toyota kanban system greets the new stage. In: *The Toyota in 1990.* (Extra issue) July 1: 21-25.

Soukura, T. 1987. Setup-time reduction of tandem-press. In: *Setup-Time Improvement Manual. Kojokanri.* August. Special issue. pp. 82-93.

Sugiyama, T. 1985. Floor improvement should begin by 5S application. In: Kojokanri Editorial Dep. ed. *5S Technique, Kojokanri.* Special issue. 31(11): 38-67.

Suitsu, K. 1978. What we learn from the Toyota production system. *Kojokanri.* 24(13): 89-101.

_____. 1979. Eight articles of basic knowledge for introducing the Toyota production system. *Kojokanri.* 25(8): 202-220.

Suzuki, Y. 1980. Multi-functioned worker and job-rotation can make flexible workshop. *IE.* May: 22-28.

Tagiri, I. 1981. 'The Vitalities' are making lively activities around Mr. H.—a case of Toyota's QC circle. *Kojokanri.* 27(13): 139-144.

Takahashi, M., Kondo, J., and Tsuihiji, T. 1981. Fuji Heavy Industries, Ltd.—the present condition and purpose of the automation at its body welding plant. *Kojokanri.* 27(4): 37-45.

Takahashi, M. and Kondo, J. 1981. Microcomputer aided lamprey type, model discriminating system for supporting the flexibility of mixed-model production. *IE.* February: 28-30.

Takahashi, H. and Kubota, H. 1990. Assembly line control (ALC) system. In: Tokyo Management Association, *Seminar Text of Toyota Production System.* December 12: 1-16.

Takahashi, Y., Mixed production of tractor plant. *Kojokanri.* 35(1).

Takano, I. 1978. *Complete Information of the Toyota Group.* Nippon Jitsugyo Publishing Co.

Takao, T. 1990. Toyota's kaizen budget: original feature of Japanese style budgeting. *Kigyokaikei.* 42(3).

Takeuchi, T. 1986. *Automobile Saks.* Nihon-Keizai-Shinbun-Sha.

Tanaka, H. 1978. *Employment Conventions in Japan and U.S.* Nihon Seisansei Honbu (Japan Productivity Center).

Terayama, S. 1989. Can Toyota overcome a large company sickness of demerit-mark system? *Nikkei-Business.* October 9.

Tohno, H. 1978. Toyota system lets today's production follow yesterday's sales. *Kojokanri.* 24(13): 134-136.

Tokyo Shibaura Electric Co., Ltd., ed. 1977. *Promotion of Management by Objective.* Aoba Shuppan.

Tonouch Kogyo PCS Group. 1980. Computer-aided dispatching for the mixed body-models at an assembly painting maker. *Kojokanri.* 26(12): 68-72.

Toyota Motor Corporation. 1987. *Unlimited Creation: 50 Year History of Toyota.* Toyota Motor Corp.

——————. 1987. *Unlimited Creation: 50 Year History of Toyota Materials.* Toyota Motor Corp.

——————. 1991. *Annual Report (Financial Security Report): June 1991.* Ministry of Finance.

Toyota Motor Co., Ltd. 1964. Suggestion Committee office, ed. *Manual of Suggestion System.*

——————. 1966. QC Promoting office. Promotion of quality control at Toyota Motor Co., Ltd. *Hinshitsukanri.* 17(1): 14-17.

——————. 1973. *Toyota Production System for Cost Reduction.* (unpublished) 1st and 2nd editions. (1975).

Urabe, K. 1984. *Japanese Style Management Can Evolve.* Chuo-Keizaisha.

Wada, R. 1979. Machining automation in the flexible manufacturing system. *Kojokanri.* 25(8): 29-41.

Washida, A. 1978. A commitment on the Toyota manufacturing methods. *Kojokanri.* 24(13): 131-134.

Yamada, Y. 1979. Points of community and difference between MRP and Toyota production system. *Kojokanri.* 25(8): 96-110.

Yasuda, Y. 1989. *Suggestion Activities of Toyota.* Japan Management Association.

Yonezawa, N. 1983. Subcontractors under their reorganization in industry. *Nihon-Keizai-Shinbun.* May 24.

Yoshikawa, A. and Minato, A. 1980. Total optimization by integrating the design and manufacturing technologies. *IE.* April: 20-22.

Yoshimura, M., Miyamoto, T., and Hori, E. 1982. Optimal sequencing algorithm for the assembly line of the medium variety-medium quantity models. In: Japan Operations Research Society, ed. *Proceedings of Abstracts of 1982 Spring Research Conference.* pp. 147-148.

Yoshiya, R. 1979. Management revolution by means of MRP. *Diamond Harvard Business.* March-April: 85-90.

Yoshiya, R. and Nakane, J. 1977. *MRP System—New Production Control in the Computer Age.* Nikkan Kogyo Shinbuh Sha.

——————. 1978. Toyota production system viewed from the standpoint of the MRP system researchers. *Kojokanri.* 24(13): 102-108.

Index

Action step method, 230-231. *See also* Foolproof systems

Actual performance collection subsystem, 300. *See also* Computer support

Actual performance transition subsystem, 301. *See also* Computer support

Aisin Seiki Company, Ltd., 38; 42; 52; 55; 291

Altogether method, 230. *See also* Foolproof systems

Andon, 12; 30; 152; 154; 232. *See also* Visible control system; Visual control

Anti-Monopoly Law, 48-49

Artificial intelligence (AI), 270-275

Assembly Line Control (ALC), 91; 98-103

Autonomation, 5; 12; 224-236
See also Jidoka

Average daily number, 8

Bakayoke, 12
See also Foolproof systems

Bird-cage layout, 162

Cart or truck,
as Kanban, 32

Caterpillar Tractor Company, 173

Centralized control system, 89. *See also* Computer control system

Chrysler Corporation, 337

Cock System, 49

Commendation systems, 195-197. *See also* Quality control circle

Common Kanban, 30-31

Compensation, 50

Computer-aided design (CAD), 102; 117

Computer-aided manufacturing (CAM), 102; 117

Computer control system, 89-103

Computer-integrated manufacturing (CIM), 102

Computer support, 291-301. *See also* *specific entries*

Constant cycle, inconstant quantity withdrawal system, 25; 44; 283; 285; 287-290; 367-380

Constant cycle, round-tour mixed-loading system, 25-26

Constant quantity, inconstant cycle withdrawal system, 25; 44; 280-283; 381-400

Contact method, 229. *See also* Foolproof systems

Contingency theory, 336

Continuation control, 266. *See also* Sequence scheduling

Control chart, 113

Cost management, 240-245

Cycle time, 8; 27; 145; 303-304

Daihatsu Industry, 131

Daihatsu Motor Company, Ltd., 55; 151

Daily information. *See* Information

Daily alteration, 77

Decentralized control system, 89-99. *See also* Computer control system

Delivery times, 18

Demand fluctuation, 65-66. *See also* Production smoothing

Deming, W.E., 222

Double cycle time, 151

419

Double transfers, 177-178. *See also* Improvement activities

Electric Kanban. *See* Full-work system
Emergency Kanban, 30
Expert system, 275. *See also* Artificial intelligence
Express Kanban, 29
External setup, 10; 122; 132. *See also* Setup time reduction

Facility capacity, 305-306
Fair Trade Commission, 46; 48-50
Fatigue rank, 170. *See also* Job rotation
Feigenbaum, 237
Fine-tuned production, 28-29
First-In, First-Out (FIFO), 208
5S, 199-219
Flexible machinery, 70-71
Flexible manufacturing system (FMS), 71; 119
Flexible work force, 5. *See also* Shojinka
Foolproof systems, 12; 229-232
Ford, Henry, 163
Ford system, 1; 107
Fukuda, Takeo, 47-48
Full-work system, 34; 114
Functional management, 239-251

General Motors, 337; 339-340
General-purpose machines, 9
GO GO campaign, 330-331
Goal chasing method, 256-264
Goals coordination method, 353-380
Group consciousness, 175
Hierarchical decentralized control system. *See* Decentralized control system

Hirano, Hiroyuko, 199
Hired taxi system, 55; 322

Improvement activities, 13; 177-197
  manual operations, 177-179
  work force reduction, 179-183
  machinery, 183-185
  job, 185-186
  and Kanban, 190-192

In-process Kanban. *See* Production-ordering Kanban
Indicator plates, 205-207
Information, 38
Information system, 75-87
Inspectors, 221-222
Internal setup, 10; 122; 132. *See also* Setup time reduction
Interval control, 266. *See also* Sequence scheduling
Inventory control systems, 279
Invisible conveyor belt, 12
Ishikawa, Kaoru, 237
Isolated island layout, 162-163

Japan GM Association, 341
Japan Sheet Glass Company, Ltd., 59
Japanese Communist Party, 46-47
Jidoka, 5; 184; 224-225. *See also* Autonomation
Job characteristic, 170. *See also* Job rotation
Job-order Kanban, 30
Job rotation, 166-172
Jump 60 campaign, 330-332
Junjo-Biki. *See* Sequenced withdrawal system
Just-in-time (JIT), 5-6; 15-16
  criticism of, 349
  delivery system, 349-351
  quantitative analysis of stocks, 367-380
  quantitative analysis of lot size, 381-400
Just-on-time, 44

Kaizen. *See* 5S
Kaizen costing, 240-241. *See also* Cost management
Kanban collecting time, 284
Kanban system, 6-7; 15-35
  using, 21-24
  rules, 24-29
  overall planning, 25
  adaptability of, 27-29
  other types, 29-35
  problems and countermeasures with suppliers, 46-53
  adaptation to emergency, 60-62
  vs. MRP, 71-73

determining number of, 279-290
influence of supervisor, 286-287
computer support, 291-301
master planning subsystem, 293-294
review of principles, 313-326
functions, 313-315
production-ordering Kanban control,
   318-320
tool and jig control, 322-323
Kanto Auto Works, Inc., 90-91
Kawasaki Motors U.S.A., 51
Kikuchi, Hyogo, 49
Kinohbetsu Kanri. *See* Total quality control
Kyoho-Seisakusho Company, Ltd., 291-292

Label, 33; 45
Labor grade, 173-174
Labor union, 53
Last-In, Last-Out (LIFO), 208
Later replenishment system, 38-42; 78;
   323-326. *See also* Withdrawal methods
Layout design, 161-166. *See also specific*
   entries
Lead time reduction, 10-11; 105-120
advantages, 105-106
components, 106
five principles for factory automation,
   116-119
Leveled daily production, 24. *See also*
   Production smoothing
Line balancing, 145
Linear layouts, 163-164
Local area network (LAN), 98
   See also Assembly Line Control;
   Computer control system

Machine sequencing, 155
Mass-assembly line, 1
Master production schedule, 75. *See also*
   Order entry information system
Master schedule, 71
Material handling index of liveliness, 209
Material Requirement Planning (MRP), 71-
   73; 76; 292-293
Material-requisition Kanban. *See* Signal
   Kanban
Mizusumashi. *See* Whirligig

Model production quantity smoothing, 67-
   72. *See also* Production smoothing
Monthly information. *See* Information
Muda, 199-200
Multi-function worker, 10; 109-111; 166-
   175
Multi-process holding, 10
Music, 140
Mutual relief movement, 114

New United Motor Manufacturing, Inc.,
   342-343; 346-348
Nissan production planning system, 84-87
NUMMI. *See* New United Motor Manufacturing, Inc.

Ohno, Taiichi, 53; 121
One-piece production, 10
One-touch (shot) setup, 121; 155. *See also*
   Setup time reduction
Order cycle, 284
Order entry information system, 75-79. *See*
   also Information system
Ordering point system, 24
Overtime, 175

Pan Yamaha Manufacturing Control
   (PYMAC), 73
Parts requirement forecast, 76; 79-81. *See*
   also Order entry information system
Performance analysis, 307-311. *See also*
   Productivity improvement
Point photography, 218
Pokayoke, 12. *See also* Foolproof systems
Process-load planning subsystem, 294-295.
   See also Computer support
Processing time, 284
Product lead time differences, 275-278
Production Kanban. *See* Production-
   ordering Kanban
Production-ordering Kanban, 6; 16; 22-24.
   See also Kanban system
Production ordering post, 40
Production performance evaluation, 311-
   312. *See also* Productivity improvement
Production sequence, 8
Production smoothing, 8-9; 24; 63-73
Productivity improvement, 303-312

Pull system, 5
Pure waste, 177. *See also* Improvement
  activities
Push system, 5; 11; 114
PYMAC. *See* Pan Yamaha Manufacturing
  Control

Quality assurance, 240
Quality control (QC) circle, 13; 121; 177;
  193-197
Quorum system, 184

Red labels, 202-205
Red post, 30. *See also* Express Kanban
Reorder point, 19; 23; 280
Reserved seat, 33
Respect for humanity, 185-186; 225
Rewards, 190
Robotics, 236
Roulette system, 321

Safety inventory period, 284
Scientific management, 1
Seiketsu, 201; 214-217. *See also* 5S
Seiri, 200; 202. *See also* 5S; Red label;
  Visual control
Seiso, 201; 214-217. *See also* 5S
Seiton, 201; 205-214. *See also* 5S; Indicator
  plate; Visual control
Self-control, 216
Sequence schedule, 37-62; 68-71; 265-278
Sequenced production schedule, 78-79
Sequenced withdrawal system, 42-46. *See
  also* Withdrawal methods
Sequencing method, for mixed-model
  assembly line, 253-264
Setup time reduction, 9-10; 121-129
  procedures, 131-143
Shewhart, W.A., 222
Shimada, Haruo, 347
Shingo, Shigeo, 121
Shipping costs, 17
Shitsuke, 201; 214-217. *See also* 5S
Shojinka, 5; 159-160. *See also* Flexible
  work force
Shoninka, 175; 184
Shoryokuka, 184
Signal Kanban, 19. *See also* Kanban
  systems

Single setup, 121. *See also* Setup time
  reduction
Single-function worker, 173
Single-unit production and conveyance,
  107-113. *See also* Lead time reduction
Slack. *See* Muda
Slip-issuing subsystem, 296. *See also*
  Computer support
Small-lot production, 111-113; 121
Soikufu, 5
Standard operations, 11-12; 145-158
  determining components, 145-148
  determining routine, 149-151
  training and follow-up, 158
  changing cycle time, 285-286
Standard operations sheets, 11; 149-151;
  157. *See also* Standard operations
Statistical quality control (SQC), 222-224
Statistical sampling, 223
Stopping the line, 227-231
Store space, 44
Subcontractor Kanban. *See* Supplier
  Kanban
Subcontractor's Law, 48
Suggestion system, 186-190. *See also*
  Quality control circle
Sumimoto Denko, 18
Supplier Kanban, 17; 37-62. *See also*
  Kanban systems
Synchronization, 64; 221

Tact system, 154-155
Tact time, 303-304
Tanaka, Michiko, 47
Target cost, 242
Taylor system, 1; 47
Te-i-in-se-i. *See* Quorum system
Technology data base subsystem, 291-293
Three-truck system, 39
Through (tunnel) Kanban, 30
Time bucket, 71
Time phasing, 71
Top management, 24
Total quality control (TQC), 237-238; 239-
  251
Total quantity production smoothing, 63-
  66. *See also* Production smoothing
Toyo Aluminum Corporation, 330

Toyota production system, 1-14
  primary purpose, 1-6
  criticism of, 46-48
  implementation, 327-333
  case study, 330-333
  overseas application, 335-348
  industrial relations innovations, 343-348
  criticism of JIT, 349
  JIT delivery system, 349-351
  quantitative analysis of stocks in JIT,
    367-380
  quantitative analysis of lot size in JIT,
    381-400
Toyota Network System (TNS), 82-84
Triangular Kanban. *See* Signal Kanban

U-turn layout, 161
Unit cycle time, 8
Unit order table, 43

Value added, 179. *See also* Improvement
  activities
Value-added network (VAN), 43
Vendor, 17; 37
Visible control system, 12. *See also* Andon
Visual control, 202-207; 232-236

Wage, 173-174
Waiting time, 114-115; 179-183. *See also*
  Improvement activities
Waste, 2-3; 64
Whirligig, 25; 282
Withdrawal Kanban, 6; 16. *See also*
  Kanban system
Withdrawal methods, 38-46
Withdrawal systems, 25
Workable rate concept, 306-307
Worker capacity, 303-306

Yo-i-don system, 151

Zero defect (ZD) group, 121. *See also*
  Quality control circle